SWIFT™ FOR PROGRAMMERS
DEITEL® DEVELOPER SERIES

For information about buying this title in bulk quantities, or for special sales opportunities (which may include electronic versions; custom cover designs; and content particular to your business, training goals, marketing focus, or branding interests), please contact our corporate sales department at corpsales@pearsoned.com or (800) 382-3419.

For government sales inquiries, please contact governmentsales@pearsoned.com.

For questions about sales outside the U.S., please contact international@pearsoned.com.

Visit us on the web: informit.com/ph

Library of Congress Cataloging-in-Publication Data

On file

© 2015 Pearson Education, Inc.

ISBN-13: 978-0-13402136-2
ISBN-10: 0-13-402136-3

Text printed in the United States at Edwards Brothers Malloy in Ann Arbor, Michigan.
First printing, January 2015

SWIFT™ FOR PROGRAMMERS
DEITEL® DEVELOPER SERIES

Paul Deitel • Harvey Deitel
Deitel & Associates, Inc.

Upper Saddle River, NJ • Boston • Indianapolis • San Francisco
New York • Toronto • Montreal • London • Munich • Paris • Madrid
Capetown • Sydney • Tokyo • Singapore • Mexico City

Deitel® Series Page

Deitel® Developer Series

Android for Programmers: An App-Driven
    Approach, 2/E, Volume 1
C for Programmers with an Introduction to C11
C++11 for Programmers
C# 2012 for Programmers
iOS® 8 for Programmers: An App-Driven Approach
    with Swift™, Volume 1
Java™ for Programmers, 3/E
JavaScript for Programmers
Swift™ for Programmers

How To Program Series

Android How to Program, 2/E
C++ How to Program, 9/E
C How to Program, 7/E
Java™ How to Program, Early Objects Version, 10/E
Java™ How to Program, Late Objects Version, 10/E
Internet & World Wide Web How to Program, 5/E
Visual Basic® 2012 How to Program, 6/E
Visual C#® 2012 How to Program, 5/E

Simply Series

Simply C++: An App-Driven Tutorial Approach
Simply Java™ Programming: An App-Driven
    Tutorial Approach
(continued in next column)

(continued from previous column)
Simply C#: An App-Driven Tutorial Approach
Simply Visual Basic® 2010: An App-Driven
    Approach, 4/E

CourseSmart Web Books

www.deitel.com/books/CourseSmart/

C++ How to Program, 8/E and 9/E
Simply C++: An App-Driven Tutorial Approach
Java™ How to Program, 9/E and 10/E
Simply Visual Basic® 2010: An App-Driven
    Approach, 4/E
Visual Basic® 2012 How to Program, 6/E
Visual Basic® 2010 How to Program, 5/E
Visual C#® 2012 How to Program, 5/E
Visual C#® 2010 How to Program, 4/E

LiveLessons Video Learning Products

www.deitel.com/books/LiveLessons/

Android App Development Fundamentals, 2/e
C++ Fundamentals
Java™ Fundamentals, 2/e
C# 2012 Fundamentals
C# 2010 Fundamentals
iOS® 8 App Development Fundamentals, 3/e
JavaScript Fundamentals
Swift™ Fundamentals

To receive updates on Deitel publications, Resource Centers, training courses, partner offers and more,
please join the Deitel communities on

- Facebook®—facebook.com/DeitelFan
- Twitter®—@deitel
- Google+™—google.com/+DeitelFan
- YouTube™—youtube.com/DeitelTV
- LinkedIn®—linkedin.com/company/deitel-&-associates

and register for the free *Deitel® Buzz Online* e-mail newsletter at:

    www.deitel.com/newsletter/subscribe.html

To communicate with the authors, send e-mail to:

    deitel@deitel.com

For information on *Dive-Into® Series* on-site seminars offered by Deitel & Associates, Inc. worldwide,
write to us at deitel@deitel.com or visit:

    www.deitel.com/training/

For continuing updates on Pearson/Deitel publications visit:

    www.deitel.com
    www.pearsonhighered.com/deitel/

Visit the Deitel Resource Centers that will help you master programming languages, software development, Android and iOS app development, and Internet- and web-related topics:

    www.deitel.com/ResourceCenters.html

In Loving Memory of Aunt Rochelle Deitel:

The most positive person we ever knew.
You brought joy to our lives.

Harvey, Barbara, Paul and Abbey

Trademarks

Contents

3 Introduction to Classes, Objects, Methods and Functions   33

4 Control Statements; Assignment, Increment and Logical Operators   48

5   Functions and Methods: A Deeper Look; enums and Tuples   70

8 Classes: A Deeper Look and Extensions 157

9 Structures, Enumerations and Nested Types 194

10   Inheritance, Polymorphism and Protocols   214

13 iOS 8 App Development: Welcome App 288

14 iOS 8 App Development: Tip Calculator App 319

Preface

Welcome to Apple's new Swift programming language and *Swift for Programmers*! This book presents leading-edge computing technologies for software developers. It's designed primarily for three audiences of developers who already know object-oriented programming and are considering using Swift:

- Objective-C programmers who are developing *new* iOS and/or OS X apps and who want to quickly begin using Swift in their apps.

- Objective-C programmers who are enhancing *existing* iOS and/or OS X apps and who want to quickly begin using Swift in their apps.

- Java, C++ and C# programmers who are new to iOS and OS X development and who want to start developing iOS and/or OS X apps in Swift.

Chapters 1 through 12 focus on Swift programming, then Chapters 13 and 14 briefly introduce iOS 8 app development. The iOS 8 chapters are condensed versions of Chapters 2 and 3 of our book, *iOS® 8 for Programmers: An App-Driven Approach with Swift™*, in which we focus on building many complete iPhone® and iPad® apps.[1]

We emphasize software engineering best practices. At the heart of the book is the Deitel signature "live-code approach." Rather than using only code snippets, we present most concepts in the context of complete working Swift programs that run on OS X® and— in the last two chapters—iOS® 8. Each complete code example is accompanied by one or more live sample executions. In the few cases where we use code snippets, we always extract them from compiled, correctly executing, live-code examples. All of the book's source code is available at

```
http://www.deitel.com/books/SwiftFP
```

Some complete live-code programs might appear to be code snippets—this is because Swift eliminates various items that are common in many C-based languages, such as the need for a main method. For example, the following is actually a complete Swift program:

```
println("Welcome to Swift Programming!")
```

Swift Programming Language

Swift was a surprise announcement at Apple's WWDC (Worldwide Developer Conference) in June 2014. Because the language is so new, it's likely to evolve quickly over the next few years. Here's some key aspects of Swift:

---

1. Swift is a young language that's evolving rapidly. We plan to post bonus content covering important new features as they emerge. See http://www.deitel.com/books/SwiftFP for details.

- *Apple's Language of the Future*—Apple is the most valuable technology company in the world, and they've declared that Swift is their language of the future for app and systems programming.

- *Popular Language Features*—Swift is a contemporary language with simpler syntax than Objective-C. Because Swift is new, its designers were able to include popular features like those in Objective-C, Java, C#, Ruby, Python and many others. These features (which are listed in Fig. 1.1) include type inference, tuples, closures (lambdas), generics, operator overloading, functions with multiple return values, optionals, String interpolation, switch statement enhancements and more. We've found it easier and faster to develop iOS and OS X apps in Swift than in Objective-C.

- *Performance*—Swift was designed for better performance than Objective-C. Apple has observed that Swift code is about 1.5 times faster than Objective-C code on today's multi-core systems.

- *Error Prevention*—Swift eliminates many common programming errors, making your code more robust and secure. Some of these error prevention features (which are listed in Fig. 1.2) include automatic memory management, no pointers, required braces around every control statement's body, assignment operators that do not return values, requiring initialization of all variables and constants before they're used, array bounds checking, automatic checking for overflow of integer calculations, and more.

- *Interoperability with Objective-C*—You can combine Swift and Objective-C in the same app. This enables you to enhance existing Objective-C apps without having to rewrite all the code. Your apps will easily be able to interact with the Cocoa/Cocoa Touch frameworks, which are largely written in Objective-C.

- *Playgrounds*—A playground is an Xcode window in which you can enter Swift code that compiles and executes as you type it. This allows you to see and hear your code's results as you write it, to quickly find and fix errors, and to experiment with features of Swift and the Cocoa/Cocoa Touch frameworks.

Software Used in *Swift for Programmers*

To execute our Swift examples and write your own Swift code, you must install Xcode 6, which is available free from the Mac App Store. When you open Xcode for the first time, it will download and install additional features required for development. For the latest information about Xcode, visit

```
https://developer.apple.com/xcode
```

Swift Fundamentals: Parts I, II and III LiveLessons Video Training

Our *Swift Fundamentals: Parts I, II and III* LiveLessons video training product shows you what you need to know to start building robust, powerful software with Swift. It includes approximately 20 hours of expert training synchronized with *Swift for Programmers*. For additional information about Deitel LiveLessons video products, visit

```
http://www.deitel.com/livelessons
```

or contact us at deitel@deitel.com.

You also can access our books and LiveLessons videos on Safari Books Online

```
http://www.safaribooksonline.com
```

if you have an appropriate subscription. A limited free-trial is available. Safari is popular with large companies, colleges, libraries and individuals who would like access to video training and electronic versions of print publications.

Explosive Growth of the iPhone and iPad Is Creating Opportunity for Developers

iPhone and iPad device sales have been growing exponentially, creating significant opportunities for iOS app developers. The first-generation iPhone, released in June 2007, sold 6.1 million units in its initial five quarters of availability.[2] The iPhone 5s and the iPhone 5c, released simultaneously in September 2013, sold over nine million combined in the first three days of availability.[3] The most recent iPhone 6 and iPhone 6 Plus, announced in September 2014, pre-sold four million combined in just one day—double the number of iPhone 5 pre-sales in its first day of pre-order availability.[4] Apple sold 10 million iPhone 6 and iPhone 6 Plus units combined in their first weekend of availability.[5]

Sales of the iPad are equally impressive. The first generation iPad, launched in April 2010, sold 3 million units in its first 80 days of availability[6] and over 40 million worldwide by September 2011.[7] The iPad mini with Retina display (the second-generation iPad mini) and the iPad Air (the fifth-generation iPad) were released in November 2013. In just the first quarter of 2014, Apple sold a record 26 million iPads.[8]

There are over 1.3 million apps in the App Store[9] and over 75 billion iOS apps have been downloaded.[10] The potential for iOS app developers is enormous. It's likely that most new iOS and OS X development soon will be done in Swift, so there are great opportunities for Swift programmers.

Our Research Sources

Due to Swift's similarities with many of today's popular programming languages, we were able to repurpose and customize examples from many of our other programming textbooks and professional books. Because Swift is new, we performed most of our research using the Apple resources listed on the next page.

2. http://www.apple.com/pr/library/2009/07/21results.html.
3. https://www.apple.com/pr/library/2013/09/23First-Weekend-iPhone-Sales-Top-Nine-Million-Sets-New-Record.html.
4. http://techcrunch.com/2014/09/15/apple-sells-4m-iphone-6-and-6-plus-pre-orders-in-opening-24-hours/.
5. http://www.apple.com/pr/library/2014/09/22First-Weekend-iPhone-Sales-Top-10-Million-Set-New-Record.html.
6. http://www.ipadinsider.com/tag/ipad-sales-figures/.
7. http://www.statista.com/statistics/180656/sales-of-tablets-and-ipads-in-the-us-until-2012/.
8. http://www.theverge.com/2014/1/27/5350106/apple-q1-2014-earnings.
9. http://mashable.com/2014/09/09/apple-1-3-million-apps-app-store/.
10. http://techcrunch.com/2014/06/02/itunes-app-store-now-has-1-2-million-apps-has-seen-75-billion-downloads-to-date/.

- *The Swift Programming Language*—available in the iBooks store and at:

    ```
    https://developer.apple.com/library/ios/documentation/Swift/
        Conceptual/Swift_Programming_Language/
    ```

- *Using Swift with Cocoa and Objective-C*—available in the iBooks store and at:

    ```
    https://developer.apple.com/library/ios/documentation/Swift/
        Conceptual/BuildingCocoaApps
    ```

- The *Swift Standard Library Reference*:

    ```
    https://developer.apple.com/library/ios/documentation/General/
        Reference/SwiftStandardLibraryReference
    ```

- The Swift Blog:

    ```
    https://developer.apple.com/swift/blog/
    ```

- World Wide Developers Conference (WWDC) 2014 videos:

    ```
    https://developer.apple.com/videos/wwdc/2014/
    ```

Teaching Approach

Swift for Programmers contains numerous complete working code examples. We stress program clarity and concentrate on building well-engineered, high-performance software.

Syntax Shading. For readability, we syntax shade all the Swift code, similar to the syntax coloring in the Xcode 6 integrated-development environment. Our conventions are:

```
comments appear like this
keywords appear like this
constants and literal values appear like this
all other code appears in black
```

Code Highlighting. We place colored rectangles around key code segments.

Using Fonts for Emphasis. We place key terms and the index's page reference for each term's defining occurrence in bold colored text for easier reference. We emphasize on-screen components in the **bold Helvetica** font (e.g., the **File** menu) and emphasize Swift program text in the Lucida font (for example, println()).

Objectives/Outline. Each chapter begins with a list of objectives and a chapter outline.

Illustrations/Figures. Abundant tables, programs and program outputs are included.

Programming Tips. We include programming tips to help you focus on important aspects of program development. These tips and practices represent the best we've gleaned from a combined eight decades of programming experience.

Good Programming Practice 19.1

The Good Programming Practices *call attention to techniques that will help you produce programs that are clearer, more understandable and more maintainable.*

Common Programming Error 19.1

Pointing out these Common Programming Errors *reduces the likelihood that you'll make them.*

Error-Prevention Tip 19.1

These tips contain suggestions for exposing bugs and removing them from your programs; many describe aspects of Swift that prevent bugs from getting into programs in the first place.

Performance Tip 19.1

These tips highlight opportunities for making your programs run faster or minimizing the amount of memory they occupy.

Software Engineering Observation 19.1

The Software Engineering Observations *highlight design patterns and architectural issues that affect the construction of software systems, especially large-scale systems.*

Index. We've included an extensive index. Each key term's defining occurrence is highlighted with a **bold colored** page number.

Academic Bundle iOS® 8 for Programmers and Swift™ for Programmers

The *Academic Bundle iOS® 8 for Programmers and Swift™ for Programmers* is designed for professionals, students and instructors interested in learning or teaching iOS 8 app development with a broader and deeper treatment of Swift. You can conveniently order the Academic Bundle from pearsonhighered.com with one ISBN: 0-13-408775-5. The Academic Bundle includes:

- *Swift™ for Programmers* (print book)
- *iOS® 8 for Programmers: An App Driven Approach with Swift™, Volume 1, 3/e* (print book)
- Access Code Card for Academic Package to accompany *Swift™ for Programmers*
- Access Code Card for Academic Package to accompany *iOS® 8 for Programmers: An App Driven Approach with Swift™, Volume 1, 3/e*

The two Access Code Cards for the Academic Packages (when used together) give you access to the companion websites, which include self-review questions (with answers), short-answer questions, programming exercises, programming projects and selected videos chosen to get you up to speed quickly with Xcode 6, visual programming and basic Swift-based, iOS 8 programming.

Ordering the Books and Supplements Separately

The print books and Access Code Cards may be purchased separately from pearsonhighered.com using the following ISBNs (email deitel@deitel.com if you have questions):

- *Swift™ for Programmers* (print book): ISBN 0-13-402136-3
- Standalone access code card for Academic Package to accompany *Swift™ for Programmers*: ISBN 0-13-405818-6
- *iOS® 8 for Programmers: An App Driven Approach with Swift™, Volume 1, 3/e* (print book): ISBN 0-13-396526-0
- Standalone access code card for Academic Package to accompany *iOS® 8 for Programmers: An App Driven Approach with Swift™, Volume 1, 3/e*: ISBN 0-13-405825-9

Instructor Supplements
Instructor supplements are available online at Pearson's Instructor Resource Center (IRC). The supplements include:

- Solutions Manual with selected solutions to the short-answer exercises.
- Test Item File of multiple-choice examination questions (with answers).
- PowerPoint® slides with the book's source code and tables.

Please do not write to us requesting access to the Pearson Instructor's Resource Center. Certified instructors who adopt the book for their courses can obtain password access from their regular Pearson sales representatives (www.pearson.com/replocator). Solutions are *not* provided for "project" exercises.

Acknowledgments

Deitel Team
We'd like to thank Abbey Deitel and Barbara Deitel of Deitel & Associates, Inc. for long hours devoted to this project. Abbey co-authored Chapter 1 and this Preface, and she and Barbara painstakingly researched the world of Swift. Our Art Director, Jessica Deitel (age 10) chose the cover color.

Pearson Education Team
We're fortunate to have worked on this project with the dedicated publishing professionals at Prentice Hall/Pearson. We appreciate the extraordinary efforts and 20-year mentorship of our friend and professional colleague Mark L. Taub, Editor-in-Chief of Pearson Technology Group. Kim Boedigheimer recruited distinguished members of the iOS, OS X and emerging Swift communities to review the manuscript and she managed the review process. We selected the cover art and Chuti Prasertsith designed the cover. John Fuller managed the book's production.

Reviewers
We wish to acknowledge the efforts of our reviewers. They scrutinized the text and the programs and provided countless suggestions for improving the presentation.

- Scott Bossack, Lead iOS Developer, Thrillist Media Group
- René Cacheaux, iOS Architect, Mutual Mobile
- Ash Furrow, iOS Developer, Artsy
- Rob McGovern, Independent Contractor
- Abizer Nasir, Freelance iOS and OS X Developer, Jungle Candy Software Ltd.
- Rik Watson, Technical Team Lead for HP Enterprise Services (Applications Services)
- Jack Watson-Hamblin, Programming Writer and Teacher, MotionInMotion (https://motioninmotion.tv/)

A Special Thank You to Reviewer Charles Brown
When Swift was announced in June 2014, within days our publisher, Prentice Hall/Pearson, agreed to publish our Swift book, which at the time was just an idea. One key prob-

lem—where would we find Swift reviewers when the language was so new? We asked for help from our 75,000 social media and newsletter followers. Charles E. Brown, Independent Contractor affiliated with Apple and Adobe, was the first to respond and became the core member of our review team. He mentored us throughout the project, providing insights, encouragement, answers to our technical questions and appropriate cautions.

Keeping in Touch with the Authors

As you read the book, if you have questions, comments or suggestions, send an e-mail to us at

```
deitel@deitel.com
```

and we'll respond promptly. For updates on this book, visit

```
http://www.deitel.com/books/SwiftFP
```

subscribe to the *Deitel*® *Buzz Online* newsletter at

```
http://www.deitel.com/newsletter/subscribe.html
```

and join the Deitel social networking communities on

- Facebook® (`http://facebook.com/DeitelFan`)
- Twitter® (`@deitel`)
- Google+™ (`http://google.com/+DeitelFan`)
- YouTube® (`http://youtube.com/DeitelTV`)
- LinkedIn® (`http://linkedin.com/company/deitel-&-associates`)

Well, there you have it! As you read the book, we'd appreciate your comments, criticisms, corrections and suggestions for improvement. Please address all correspondence to:

```
deitel@deitel.com
```

We'll respond promptly. We hope you enjoy working with *Swift for Programmers* as much as we enjoyed writing it!

Paul and Harvey Deitel

About the Authors

Paul Deitel, CEO and Chief Technical Officer of Deitel & Associates, Inc., is a graduate of MIT, where he studied Information Technology. He holds the Java Certified Programmer and Java Certified Developer designations, and is an Oracle Java Champion. Paul was also named as a Microsoft® Most Valuable Professional (MVP) for C# in 2012–2014. Through Deitel & Associates, Inc., he has delivered hundreds of programming courses worldwide to clients, including Cisco, IBM, Siemens, Sun Microsystems (now Oracle), Dell, Fidelity, NASA at the Kennedy Space Center, the National Severe Storm Laboratory, White Sands Missile Range, Rogue Wave Software, Boeing, SunGard, Nortel Networks, Puma, iRobot, Invensys and many more. He and his co-author, Dr. Harvey M. Deitel, are the world's best-selling programming-language textbook/professional book/video authors.

Dr. Harvey Deitel, Chairman and Chief Strategy Officer of Deitel & Associates, Inc., has over 50 years of experience in the computer field. Dr. Deitel earned B.S. and M.S. degrees in Electrical Engineering from MIT and a Ph.D. in Mathematics from Boston University. He has extensive college teaching experience, including earning tenure and serving as the Chairman of the Computer Science Department at Boston College before founding Deitel & Associates, Inc., in 1991 with his son, Paul. The Deitels' publications have earned international recognition, with translations published in Japanese, German, Russian, Spanish, French, Polish, Italian, Simplified Chinese, Traditional Chinese, Korean, Portuguese, Greek, Urdu and Turkish. Dr. Deitel has delivered hundreds of programming courses to corporate, academic, government and military clients.

About Deitel® & Associates, Inc.

Deitel & Associates, Inc., founded by Paul Deitel and Harvey Deitel, is an internationally recognized authoring and corporate training organization, specializing in mobile app development, computer programming languages, object technology and Internet and web software technology. The company's training clients include many of the world's largest companies, government agencies, branches of the military and academic institutions. The company offers instructor-led training courses delivered at client sites worldwide on major programming languages and platforms, including Swift and iOS app development, Java™, Android app development, C++, C, Visual C#®, Visual Basic®, Python®, object technology, Internet and web programming and a growing list of additional programming and software development courses.

Through its 39-year publishing partnership with Pearson/Prentice Hall, Deitel & Associates, Inc., publishes leading-edge programming textbooks and professional books in print and a wide range of e-book formats, and *LiveLessons* video courses. Deitel & Associates, Inc. and the authors can be reached at:

```
deitel@deitel.com
```

To learn more about Deitel's *Dive-Into*® *Series* Corporate Training curriculum, visit:

```
http://www.deitel.com/training
```

To request a proposal for worldwide on-site, instructor-led training at your organization, e-mail deitel@deitel.com.

Individuals wishing to purchase Deitel books and *LiveLessons* video training can do so through www.deitel.com. Bulk orders by corporations, the government, the military and academic institutions should be placed directly with Pearson. For more information, visit

```
http://www.informit.com/store/sales.aspx
```

Before You Begin

This section contains information you should review before using this book. Updates to the information presented here will be posted at:

```
http://www.deitel.com/books/SwiftFP
```

Conventions

Font and Naming

We use fonts to distinguish between on-screen components (such as menu names and menu items) and Swift code or commands. Our convention is to emphasize on-screen components in a sans-serif bold Helvetica font (for example, **File** menu) and to emphasize Swift code and commands in a sans-serif Lucida font (for example, `println()`). When building user interfaces (UIs) using Xcode's Interface Builder, we also use the bold Helvetica font to refer to property names for UI components (such as a **Label**'s **Text** property).

Conventions for Referencing Menu Items in a Menu

We use the **>** character to indicate selecting a menu item from a menu. The notation **File > Open...** indicates that you should select the **Open...** menu item from the **File** menu.

Software Used in this Book

To execute our Swift examples and write your own Swift code, you must install Xcode 6. You can install the currently released Xcode version for free from the Mac App Store. When you open Xcode for the first time, it will download and install additional features required for development. For the latest information about Xcode, visit

```
https://developer.apple.com/xcode
```

A Note Regarding the Xcode 6 Toolbar Icons

We developed this book's examples with Xcode 6 on OS X Yosemite. If you're running OS X Mavericks, some Xcode toolbar icons we show in the text may differ on your screen.

Becoming a Registered Apple Developer

Registered developers have access to the online iOS and OS X documentation and other resources. Apple also now makes Xcode pre-release versions (such as the next point release or major version) available to all registered Apple developers. To register, visit:

```
https://developer.apple.com/register
```

To download the next pre-release Xcode version, visit:

```
https://developer.apple.com/xcode/downloads
```

Once you download a prerelease DMG (disk image) file, double click it to launch the installer, then follow the on-screen instructions.

Fee-Based iOS Developer Programs

In Chapters 13–14, you'll build two iOS apps and test them on your Mac using the iOS simulator that's bundled with Xcode. If you'd like to run iOS apps on actual iOS devices, you must be a member of one of the following iOS developer programs.

iOS Developer Program

The fee-based iOS Developer Program allows you to load your iOS apps onto iOS devices for testing and to submit your apps to the App Store. If you intend to distribute iOS apps, you'll need to join the fee-based program. You can sign up at

```
https://developer.apple.com/programs
```

iOS Developer Enterprise Program

Organizations may register for the iOS Developer Enterprise Program at

```
https://developer.apple.com/programs/ios/enterprise
```

which enables developers to deploy proprietary iOS apps to employees within their organization.

iOS Developer University Program

Colleges and universities interested in offering iOS app-development courses can apply to the iOS Developer University Program at

```
https://developer.apple.com/programs/ios/university
```

Qualifying schools receive free access to all the developer tools and resources. Students can share their apps with each other and test them on iOS devices.

Adding Your Paid iOS Developer Program Account to Xcode

Xcode can interact with your paid iOS and OS X Developer Program accounts on your behalf so that you can install apps onto your iOS devices for testing. If you have a paid iOS Developer Program account, you can add it to Xcode. To do so:

1. Select **Xcode > Preferences…**.
2. In the **Accounts** tab, click the **+** button in the lower left corner and select **Add Apple ID…**.
3. Enter your Apple ID and password, then click **Add**.

Obtaining the Code Examples

The *Swift for Programmers* examples are available for download as a ZIP file from

```
http://www.deitel.com/books/SwiftFP
```

under the heading **Download Code Examples and Other Premium Content**. When you click the link to the ZIP file, it will be placed by default in your user account's Downloads folder. We assume that the examples are located in the SwiftFPExamples folder in your user account's Documents folder. You can use Finder to move the ZIP file there, then double click the file to extract its contents.

Xcode Playgrounds and Projects for the Code Examples

Playgrounds are a new interactive coding capability in Xcode 6. They execute Swift code as you write it. They're particularly useful for learning and experimenting with Swift or the Cocoa and Cocoa Touch frameworks that are used to build iOS and OS X apps. Projects, on the other hand, are used to manage all the files for each app that you create.

For each example, we provide one of the following:

- an Xcode playground file with the .playground extension

- an Xcode project for an OS X **Command Line Tool** app that produces text output (such projects don't require you to develop a GUI or to run apps in the iOS simulator)

- an Xcode project for an iOS 8 app that runs in the iOS simulator bundled with Xcode.

An Xcode project is stored in a folder with the project's name. In that folder is a file with a .xcodeproj extension. You can double click a .playground or .xcodeproj file to open it in Xcode. Throughout this book, we use playgrounds for single-source-file examples and projects for multi-source-file examples.

Use Playgrounds for Learning

We recommend that as you learn Swift, you enter each example's code into an Xcode 6 playground so that you can immediately see the code in action as you write it. Sometimes you might need to restart the IDE if a playground stops working correctly. If you enter any of our multi-source-file examples into a playground, you must define any functions and types *before* they're used.

Viewing Output in a Playground

In a playground, the results of any output statements are visible only if the **Assistant Editor** is displayed. To open it in a playground, select **Assistant Editor > Show Assistant Editor** from Xcode's **View** menu. The **Assistant Editor** will appear at the playground window's right side.

Playground and Project Naming Conventions

Each project or playground is named based on its figure number(s) or the concept being presented. The comment in the first line of a source code file contains information to help you identifiy which playground or project to open from the chapter's examples folder:

- the project's or playground's base name—e.g., fig02-01 and fig03-01-11 correspond to fig02-01.playground and fig03-01-11.xcodeproj, respectively.

- the project's or playground's complete name—e.g., CompoundInterest.playground or Inheritance.xcodeproj.

Configuring Xcode to Display Line Numbers

Many programmers find it helpful to display line numbers in the code editor. To do so:

1. Open Xcode and select **Preferences...** from the **Xcode** menu.

2. Select the **Text Editing** tab, then ensure that the **Editing** subtab is selected.

3. Check the **Line Numbers** checkbox.

You're now ready to begin learning Swift with *Swift for Programmers*. We hope you enjoy the book! If you have any questions, please email us at deitel@deitel.com.

Introduction to Swift and Xcode 6

Objectives

In this chapter we discuss:

- The iOS® and OS X® operating systems.

- Swift—Apple's programming language of the future for developing iOS and OS X apps.

- Key software for iOS and OS X app development, including the Xcode® integrated development environment and the Cocoa® and Cocoa Touch® frameworks.

- Basics of Xcode 6 and Playgrounds.

1.1 Introduction

Welcome to Swift—Apple's new programming language for developing iOS and OS X applications (apps). If you're a programmer in a C-based, object-oriented language, such as Objective-C, Java, C# or C++, *Swift for Programmers* will get you started quickly with Swift programming. It's designed primarily for three audiences:

- Objective-C programmers who are developing new iOS and OS X apps and who want to quickly begin using Swift in their apps.

- Objective-C programmers who are enhancing existing iOS and OS X apps and who want to quickly begin using Swift in their apps.

- Java, C++ and C# programmers who are new to iOS and OS X development and who want to start developing iOS and OS X apps in Swift.

Please read the Before You Begin section for important information about this book, the software required for Swift programming and how to become a registered Apple developer. For regular updates and to download the book's code examples, visit

```
http://www.deitel.com/books/SwiftFP
```

This book provides a broad, syntactic and semantic introduction to the Swift programming language. If you're interested in developing iOS 8 apps using Swift, you might want to check out our related book, *iOS 8 for Programmers: An App-Driven Approach with Swift*. The book includes many completely coded, working iOS 8 apps—new features are discussed in the context of complete working iPhone or iPad apps. There are many good books on OS X app development in Objective-C. We expect Swift-based OS X app-development books to appear soon.

1.2 Apple's OS X® and iOS® Operating Systems: A Brief History

Apple was founded in 1976 by Steve Jobs and Steve Wozniak and quickly became the leader in personal computing. In 1979, Jobs and several Apple employees visited Xerox PARC (Palo Alto Research Center) to learn about Xerox's desktop computer that featured a graphical user interface with a mouse. That trip inspired the Apple Lisa computer (designed for business customers) and, more notably, the Apple Macintosh personal computer. Steve Jobs left Apple in 1985 and founded NeXT Inc. to develop computers primarily for use in colleges.

Apple bought NeXT in 1997 and Steve Jobs briefly served as an advisor to Apple's CEO before taking over that position. Apple's **Mac OS X** (now simply called OS X) is a descendant of the NeXTSTEP operating system developed by NeXT. Apple's mobile operating system, **iOS**, is derived from OS X and is used in the iPhone, iPod Touch, iPad and Apple TV. OS X and iOS are proprietary operating systems controlled by Apple and available only on Apple's devices. They do use some open-source libraries—for information, visit:

```
http://opensource.apple.com
```

The newest versions of OS X and iOS—**OS X Yosemite** and **iOS 8**—were announced at WWDC in June 2014 and were released to the public in the fall of 2014. Apple now makes each operating system available for free to anyone with a device that meets the operating system's requirements. Apple also provides the Xcode IDE for free. For details, visit:

```
https://developer.apple.com/xcode/downloads/
```

The OS X Yosemite documentation is available to all developers registered for the Mac Dev Center at

```
http://developer.apple.com/mac
```

The iOS documentation is available to all developers registered for the iOS Dev Center at

```
http://developer.apple.com/ios
```

The OS X 10.10 Yosemite and iOS 8 software is free for users with Mac and iOS devices that meet the minimum system requirements.

1.3 Objective-C

The C programming language was developed in the early 1970s by Dennis Ritchie at Bell Laboratories. It initially became widely known as the UNIX operating system's development language. The **Objective-C** programming language, created by Brad Cox and Tom Love at StepStone in the early 1980s, added object-oriented programming capabilities to C. In 1988, NeXT licensed Objective-C from StepStone and developed an Objective-C compiler and libraries which were used to build the NeXTSTEP operating system's user interface. NeXT also developed **Interface Builder** for creating graphical user interfaces with drag-and-drop. Objective-C became enormously popular due to its use in developing iPhone and iPad apps.

1.4 Swift: Apple's Programming Language of the Future

The Swift programming language was arguably the most significant announcement at Apple's WWDC in 2014. Swift has been under development by Apple's Developer Tools team since 2010. Very few people—including Apple insiders—were aware of the project.[1] Although apps can still be developed in Objective-C, Apple says that Swift is its applications programming and systems programming language of the future.

1.4.1 Key Features of Many Popular Languages

Swift is a contemporary language with simpler syntax than Objective-C. Because Swift is a new language, its designers were able to include popular programming-language features from languages such as Objective-C, Java, C#, Ruby, Python and others. Figure 1.1 lists some of Swift's key features that are not in Objective-C.

Swift feature	Description
Type inference	Though Swift is a strongly typed language, in many cases you do not need to specify a variable's or constant's type—Swift can infer the type based on the variable's or constant's initializer value.
switch statement enhancements	Unlike switch statements in other C-based languages, which can test only constant integral expressions and sometimes Strings, Swift's switch statement can test values of any type. Also, its cases are much more flexible than those in other languages—you can have cases for individual values, sets of values and ranges of values. You can also specify boolean criteria that must be true for a match to occur.
Tuples	Swift provides tuples—collections of values that can be of the same or different types. The language provides syntax for composing (creating) and decomposing (extracting values from) a tuple.
Closures (lambdas)	Swift supports functional-programming techniques via closures (anonymous functions that some languages call lambdas). Closures can be manipulated as data—they can be assigned to variables, passed to functions as arguments and returned from functions. Several of the Swift Standard Library's global functions receive closures as arguments—for example, there's a version of the sort function that receives a closure for comparing two objects to determine their sort order.
Optionals	Optionals enable you to define variables and constants that might not have a value. The language provides mechanisms for determining whether an optional has a value and, if so, obtaining that value. Optionals work for any Swift type, whereas the corresponding concept in Objective-C—a pointer that points to an object or is nil—works only for reference types.

Fig. 1.1 | Some key features in Swift that are not in Objective-C. (Part 1 of 2.)

---

1. http://nondot.org/sabre/.

Swift feature	Description
Dictionary type	Swift's Dictionary type provides built-in support for manipulating data in key–value pairs.
Array, String and Dictionary value types	Swift types Array, String and Dictionary are value types (not reference types as you might expect) that are implemented as structs. Objects of value types are *copied* when you assign them to variables or constants, pass them to functions or return them from functions. The Swift compiler optimizes value-type copy operations, performing them only when necessary.
Array bounds checking	A *runtime* error occurs if you access an element outside an Array's bounds.
Class-like struct and enum value types	Swift's struct and enum types have many class-like features, making them more robust than their Objective-C counterparts. Objects of struct and enum types are value types.
Functions with multiple return values (via tuples)	Functions can specify multiple values of possibly different types as tuples.
Generics	Rather than writing separate code to perform identical tasks on different types (e.g., summing an Array of integers vs. summing an Array of floating-point values), generics enable you to write the code once and use placeholders to represent the type(s) of data to manipulate. The placeholders are replaced with actual types when you call a generic function or create an object of a generic type. Swift's Array and Dictionary types are generic types, and many of its global functions are generic methods. When you use generic functions and types, compile-time type checking is performed to ensure that you use the functions and types correctly. For example, if you create an Array of integers, then attempt to place a String into that Array, you'll receive a compilation error.
Operator overloading	You can define functions that overload existing operators to work with new types, and you can also define entirely new operators.
Overflow checking in integer calculations	By default, all integer calculations check for arithmetic overflow and result in a runtime error if overflow occurs.
String interpolation	String interpolation enables you to build Strings by inserting variable, constant and expression values into placeholders directly in String literals.
Nested types	You can define types nested in other type definitions—commonly used to define enums or utility classes and structs that are hidden in the scope of another type.
Nested functions	You can define a function nested in another function definition—such a nested function is callable in the scope of its enclosing function and can be returned from that function for use in other scopes.

Fig. 1.1 | Some key features in Swift that are not in Objective-C. (Part 2 of 2.)

1.4.2 Performance

Swift was designed for better performance than Objective-C on today's multi-core systems. At the WWDC 2014 main keynote address, Apple observed that Swift code was about 1.5 times faster than Objective-C code.

Although `Array`, `String` and `Dictionary` are value types whose variables are normally copied when passed or assigned, the Swift compiler optimizes value-type copy operations by performing them only when necessary.

1.4.3 Error Prevention

Swift was also designed to eliminate many common programming errors, making your code more robust and secure. Swift's language features that eliminate common programming errors are listed in Fig. 1.2—many of these (such as not returning a value from the assignment operator) could not have been added to Objective-C, because doing so would have broken backward compatibility with legacy code.

Swift features that eliminate common programming errors

- Curly braces (`{}`) are required around every control statement's body. This eliminates the "dangling-else" problem in `if...else` statements. For all control statements this helps ensure that you do not accidentally forget the braces around multi-statement bodies—you could, of course, still place some of the statements incorrectly outside the braces.
- Unlike Objective-C, C and C++, Swift does not include pointers.
- The assignment operator (`=`) does not return a value. A compilation error occurs if `=` is used in a condition rather than the equal-to operator (`==`).
- Semicolons are optional unless you need to separate multiple statements on the same line.
- Parentheses around conditions in control statements are optional, making the code a bit easier to read.
- Variables and constants must be initialized before they're used—either in their definitions or via initializer methods in type definitions.
- Integer calculations are checked for overflow by default—a runtime error occurs if a calculation results in overflow.
- Swift does not allow implicit conversions between numeric types.
- Array indices (subscripts) are bounds checked at execution time—a runtime error occurs if you access an element outside an `Array`'s bounds.
- Automatic memory management eliminates most memory leaks—it's still possible to maintain references to objects that are no longer used and thus prevent their memory from being reclaimed by the runtime. Swift also has weak references for cases in which circular references between objects would prevent those objects' memory from being reclaimed.

Fig. 1.2 | Swift features that eliminate common programming errors.

1.4.4 Swift Standard Library

The Swift Standard Library contains Swift's built-in types (`String`, `Array`, `Dictionary` and the integer and floating-point numeric types), protocols (`Equatable`, `Comparable` and `Printable`) and global functions (e.g., printing and sorting). We discuss these as we use them throughout the book. For complete details on these types, protocols and global functions, see Apple's *Swift Standard Library Reference* document at:

```
https://developer.apple.com/library/ios/documentation/General/Ref-
erence/SwiftStandardLibraryReference
```

1.4.5 Swift Apps and the Cocoa® and Cocoa Touch® Frameworks

Swift, like Objective-C, has access to OS X's Cocoa frameworks and iOS's Cocoa Touch frameworks. These powerful libraries of prebuilt components help you create apps that meet Apple's requirements for the look-and-feel of iOS and OS X apps. Some Cocoa and Cocoa Touch frameworks are discussed in this book and many more in our related book *iOS 8 for Programmers: An App-Driven Approach with Swift*. The frameworks are written mainly in Objective-C (some are written in C), though Apple has indicated that new frameworks will be developed in Swift.

Cocoa evolved from projects at NeXT. OpenStep was developed as an object-oriented programming API for developing an operating system. After Apple acquired NeXT, OpenStep evolved into Rhapsody, and many of the base libraries became the Yellow Box API. Rhapsody and Yellow Box eventually evolved into the Mac's OS X operating system and Cocoa, respectively. Cocoa Touch is the version of Cocoa for iOS devices—these are resource constrained (compared to desktop computers, mobile devices typically have smaller memory, slower processing speeds and limited battery power) and offer different functionality than desktop computers. Three key OS X and iOS frameworks are Foundation, AppKit and UIKit.

Foundation Framework

The **Foundation** framework—in both Cocoa and Cocoa Touch—includes class NSObject for defining object behavior. Foundation also has classes for basic types, storing data, working with text and strings, filesystem access, calculating differences in dates and times, inter-app notifications and much more.

AppKit Framework

Cocoa's **AppKit** framework is for developing the GUIs of OS X apps. AppKit provides controls, windows, menus, buttons, panels, text fields, dialogs, event-handling capabilities, gesture support and more. It also supports content sharing between services (e.g., e-mail), iCloud integration, printing, accessibility (for users with disabilities), push notifications, graphics and more.

UIKit Framework

Cocoa Touch's UIKit framework is similar to AppKit, but optimized for developing iOS app GUIs for mobile devices. UIKit includes multi-touch interface controls that are appropriate for mobile apps, event handling for motion-based events, event handling for sensors (e.g., proximity, motion, accelerometer, ambient light, gyroscope) and more.

Other Cocoa and Cocoa Touch Frameworks

Figures 1.3 and 1.4 list the Cocoa and Cocoa Touch frameworks, respectively. To learn more about the Cocoa and Cocoa Touch frameworks, see the *Mac Developer Library Reference* (http://developer.apple.com/mac) and the *iOS Developer Library Reference* (http://developer.apple.com/ios).

List of Cocoa frameworks

Cocoa Layer	CoreMIDI	*Core Services Layer*	OpenDirectory	Exception-Handling
AppKit	CoreMIDIServer	Accounts	PublicationSub-scription	IOSurface
FinderSync	DVDPlayback	AddressBook	QuickLook	LocalAuthentica-tion
GameKit	DiscRecording	Application-Services	ScriptingBridge	OpenCL
MapKit	DiscRecordingUI	Automator	Security	SystemConfigura-tion
Notification-Center	GLKit	Carbon	SecurityFounda-tion	
PreferencePanes	GameController	CloudKit	ServiceManage-ment	
ScreenSaver	IMServicePlugIn	Collaboration	Social	*Kernel & Driver Layer*
Security-Interface	InstantMessage	CoreData	StoreKit	CoreWLAN
	iTunesLibrary	CoreFoundation	WebKit	FWAUserLib
Media Layer	MediaAccess-ibility	CoreLocation		ForceFeedback
AVFoundation	MediaLibrary	CoreMedia		IOBluetooth
AVKit	OpenAL	CoreServices	*Core OS Layer*	IOBluetoothUI
AudioToolbox	OpenGL	EventKit	AGL	IOKit
AudioUnit	QTKit	Foundation	Accelerate	ImageCapture-Core
AudioVideo-Bridging	Quartz	InputMethodKit	CoreBluetooth	Kernel
CoreAudio	QuartzCore	JavaScriptCore	DirectoryService	System
CoreAudioKit	QuickTime	LatentSemantic-Mapping	DiskArbitration	
	SceneKit			
	SpriteKit			

Fig. I.3 | List of Cocoa frameworks.

List of Cocoa Touch frameworks

Cocoa Touch Layer	AssetsLibrary	OpenAL	CoreLocation	Social
AddressBookUI	AudioToolbox	OpenGLES	CoreMedia	StoreKit
EventKitUI	AudioUnit	Photos	CoreMotion	SystemConfig-uration
GameKit	CoreAudio	QuartzCore	CoreTelephony	UIAutomation
MapKit	CoreGraphics	SceneKit	EventKit	WebKit
MessageUI	CoreImage	SpriteKit	Foundation	
Notification-Center	CoreMIDI		HealthKit	
PhotosUI	CoreText	*Core Services Layer*	HomeKit	*Core OS Layer*
Twitter	CoreVideo	Accounts	JavaScriptCore	Accelerate
UIKit	GLKit	AdSupport	MobileCore-Services	CoreBluetooth
iAd	GameController	AddressBook	Multipeer-Connectivity	ExternalAccessory
	ImageIO	CFNetwork	NewsstandKit	LocalAuthen-tication
Media Layer	MediaAccess-ibility	CloudKit	PassKit	Security
AVFoundation	MediaPlayer	CoreData	QuickLook	System
	Metal	CoreFoundation		

Fig. I.4 | List of Cocoa Touch frameworks.

1.4.6 Swift and Objective-C Interoperability

You can combine Swift and Objective-C in the same app, so you can use Swift to code portions of existing apps without rewriting all your Objective-C code. Most of the Cocoa and Cocoa Touch APIs are still written in Objective-C, so Swift programmers typically create apps that interact with existing Objective-C code, as we'll do in some of this book's examples.

Apple's document *Using Swift with Cocoa and Objective-C* at

```
https://developer.apple.com/library/ios/documentation/Swift/Concep-
tual/BuildingCocoaApps
```

(and available in the iBooks store) discusses:

- Setting up a Swift app project that can use the Cocoa or Cocoa Touch frameworks.
- Swift and Objective-C interoperability—e.g., interacting with the Objective-C APIs, creating Swift classes for use from Objective-C code and more.
- Projects that contain Swift and Objective-C files.
- Tips for migrating your legacy Objective-C code to Swift.

1.4.7 Other Apple Swift Resources

In addition to the documents mentioned in Sections 1.4.4– and 1.4.6, Apple provides other resources to help you learn Swift:

- Apple's Swift Blog is located at:

```
https://developer.apple.com/swift/blog/
```

- The sample code for Apple's WWDC 2014 Swift demos is located at:

```
https://developer.apple.com/wwdc/resources/sample-code/
```

- Apple's book *The Swift Programming Language* introduces Swift and contains a brief tour of the language, the language guide (covering Swift's key features in more depth) and the language reference (presenting Swift's grammar and the details of each language feature). This is available in the iBooks store and at:

```
https://developer.apple.com/library/ios/documentation/Swift/
Conceptual/Swift_Programming_Language/
```

- The WWDC 2014 videos are available at:

```
https://developer.apple.com/videos/wwdc/2014/
```

1.5 Can I Use Swift Exclusively?

As we mentioned in Section 1.1, this book is intended for the following audiences:

- Objective-C programmers who are developing new iOS and OS X apps.
- Objective-C programmers who are enhancing existing iOS and OS X apps.
- Java, C++ and C# programmers who are new to iOS and OS X development.

One of your biggest questions is probably, "Can I program my iOS and OS X apps purely in Swift?" Let's consider the issues by audience.

1.5.1 Objective-C Programmers Who Are Developing New iOS and OS X Apps

Apple encourages Objective-C programmers to use Swift for new app development. When Swift is released, you'll be able to create entire apps in Swift, though for years to come you'll still use Cocoa and Cocoa Touch frameworks, which are largely written in Objective-C. If your new app must interact with C++ libraries, you'll need to do so from Objective-C or C code that you can invoke from Swift.[2]

1.5.2 Objective-C Programmers Who Are Enhancing Existing iOS and OS X Apps

Apple also encourages Objective-C programmers to use Swift to enhance *existing* apps. Even if you write your enhancements using only Swift, they'll still interact extensively (and seamlessly) with your existing apps' Objective-C code and the Cocoa and Cocoa Touch frameworks. Rather than converting your existing apps to Swift, you can preserve the investments you've made in them by reusing your debugged, tested and performance-tuned Objective-C code. Be sure to read Apple's document *Using Swift with Cocoa and Objective-C* (discussed in Section 1.4.6) for details on Swift and Objective-C interoperability issues.

1.5.3 Java, C++ and C# Programmers Who Are New to iOS and OS X App Development

Apple also encourages Java, C++ and C# programmers who don't know Objective-C to use Swift for new app development. Apple believes that for these programmers Swift lowers the barriers to entry to iOS and OS X app development. Its similarities to these other popular programming languages make it more familiar and easier to learn than Objective-C. You'll still need to use Cocoa and Cocoa Touch frameworks written in Objective-C, but Apple provides Swift interfaces for these existing frameworks.

1.5.4 Significant Language Changes Expected

Because Swift is so new, it is likely to evolve rapidly. Apple has stated that Swift will be *binary compatible* with future Swift versions and with Objective-C. However, future Swift versions might not be *source-code compatible* with older versions. Apple plans to provide code converters to help you update your existing Swift source code with new language features.

1.5.5 A Mixture of Swift and Objective-C

We believe most existing iOS and OS X app developers will use Swift and Objective-C, rather than converting all of their legacy code to Swift. In this book, we write all of our application code in Swift, using existing Cocoa and Cocoa Touch frameworks when necessary.

1.6 Xcode 6 Integrated Development Environment

To program in Swift you'll need the Xcode 6 integrated development environment (IDE), which includes support for the Swift, Objective-C, C++ and C languages. Xcode's editor

---

2. https://developer.apple.com/library/ios/documentation/Swift/Conceptual/
    BuildingCocoaApps.

supports syntax coloring, auto-indenting, auto-complete and more. See the Before You Begin section of the book the details of configuring your Mac to work with this book's examples. Figure 1.5 lists several key new Xcode 6 features,[3] plus some other important features from recent releases. We'll frequently refer to Xcode 6 simply as Xcode.

Feature	Description
Key New Features in Xcode 6	
Playgrounds	A Playground is an Xcode window in which you can enter Swift code that executes as you type it, allowing you to fix errors immediately and see your code's results (text outputs, graphics, animations and more). You no longer have to build and run the code to debug it, saving you time as you develop your apps. Playgrounds also provide interesting features such as timelines that enable you to see how an algorithm executes over time—for example, using a slider you can view the results of each iteration of a loop or each frame of an animation.
Read-Eval-Print-Loop (REPL)	Read-Eval-Print-Loop (REPL) is a debugging tool for interacting with a running app. Like a playground, you can also use it to write statements that execute immediately, but REPL does not have a playground's capabilities for writing large amounts of code or rendering complex results (e.g., graphics and animations), though you can use it to run Swift files. REPL can be used directly in Xcode 6 or in OS X's Terminal app.
Interface Builder, Storyboarding and Auto Layout adaptive design	Xcode's Interface Builder enables you to create your apps' GUIs using drag-and-drop GUI design techniques. Typically, you create GUIs in Storyboards that graphically map the paths a user can take through your app, including each screen and the transitions between screens. By default, new OS X and iOS storyboards use Interface Builder's **Auto Layout** capabilities, which enable you to create responsive GUIs that update based on device orientation changes, screen-size changes and the user's locale. Prior to Xcode 6, you'd provide multiple storyboards to support various device sizes (e.g., iPhone and iPad) and orientations (portrait and landscape). Xcode 6 adds Auto Layout **adaptive design,** which enables you to use one storyboard to design your app's GUI for all supported device sizes and orientations.
iOS 8 Simulator	The iOS 8 Simulator enables you to test your iOS 8 apps on your Mac. It provides support for various iPhone and iPad devices. It also includes new resizable iPhone and iPad "devices" that enable you to test your Auto Layout adaptive designs by resizing the simulator window.
Live rendering in Interface Builder	As you design your GUI (including custom GUI components) and write code that manipulates it, Interface Builder renders the resulting GUI so you can see what it will look like when the app runs.

Fig. 1.5 | Key features in Xcode 6 and other recent releases. (Part 1 of 2.)

---

3. https://developer.apple.com/library/ios/documentation/DeveloperTools/Conceptual/ WhatsNewXcode/Articles/xcode_6_0.html.

Feature	Description
View debugger	The view debugger allows you to find and fix problems with your app's user interface. When you use the view debugger to pause an app, the view debugger displays the app's user interface in a 3D rendering so that you can quickly see where an error has occurred. You can then go to the corresponding code to fix the problem.
Game design features	Xcode now has support for 2D and 3D game design as well as a particle editor that can be used to create complex animations (e.g., fire, smoke, moving water and fireworks).
Other Xcode Features	
LLVM Compiler	LLVM (Low Level Virtual Machine; llvm.org) is a fast, open-source compiler for Swift, Objective-C and several other languages that's fully integrated into Xcode.
Fix-it	Fix-it feature flags code errors and suggests corrections as you type—you don't need to build the app first. Playgrounds also use this feature.
LLDB Debugger	Includes a fast, efficient multicore debugging engine.
Interface Builder	Interface Builder is a visual GUI design tool. GUI components can be dragged and dropped into place to form simple GUIs without any coding. Interface Builder files use the .xib extension—earlier versions used .nib, short for NeXT Interface Builder. For this reason, .xib files are often referred to as "nib files." To open Interface Builder, select the .nib (or .xib) file in the project. The utilities on the right include controls, UI objects, etc. Simply drag-and-drop controls onto the user interface for your app.
Assistant editor	When you work in Xcode's editor with two panes, the Assistant editor anticipates other files that you might need to look at. For example, if you're working on a GUI in Interface Builder, the Assistant editor displays the corresponding code file, or if a new Swift class you're defining inherits from a superclass, the Assistant editor displays the superclass.
Location Simulation	You can select from a list of locations in the simulator to run location-based apps that use the Core Location framework, which enables an app to determine a device's location and heading (i.e., the direction in which the device is moving).
Version Editor	If you use source-code control (such as GIT), Xcode's Version Editor can show you multiple versions of your source code side by side so you can easily compare them, view a log of past events and more.
Instruments	The Instruments tool helps you test your app, monitor memory allocation, track graphics performance with OpenGL ES, track the interaction of system processes, locate and remove performance bottlenecks, and more.
XCTest	XCTest is a unit-testing tool. Unit tests help ensure that software components in an app function as expected. You can use XCTest to automate testing of your app's features, view the test results, determine whether any problems occurred and fix those problems. For more on unit testing, visit http://bit.ly/TestingWithXcode.

Fig. 1.5 | Key features in Xcode 6 and other recent releases. (Part 2 of 2.)

1.7 Creating Swift Apps with Xcode 6

The examples in *Swift for Programmers* were developed using Xcode 6.1.1. We assume that you're familiar with OS X and that you've already set up Xcode, as discussed in the book's Before You Begin section. Now we provide an overview of Xcode and show you how to create files for writing your own Swift code. We'll introduce additional Xcode features throughout the book.

Launching Xcode

To launch Xcode, open a Finder window, select **Applications** and double click the Xcode icon ( ). If this is your first time running Xcode, the **Welcome to Xcode** window will appear (Fig. 1.6).

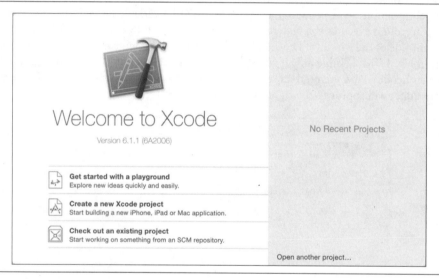

Fig. 1.6 | **Welcome to Xcode** window.

The left side of the dialog contains links for:

- Getting started with a playground.

- Creating a new project.

- Checking out existing projects—connecting to *source-code management (SCM) repositories*, which are often used to manage the interactions among many developers on a single project.

The right side of the dialog shows the list of recently opened projects and playgrounds; you can also open these via the **File** menu. This list will be empty until you create your first projects or playgrounds.

Close the **Welcome to Xcode** window for now—you can access it any time by selecting **Window > Welcome to Xcode**. We use the **>** character to indicate selecting a menu item from a menu. For example, the notation **File > Open...** indicates that you should select the **Open...** menu item from the **File** menu.

Creating a Playground

As we mentioned in Fig. 1.5, Xcode 6 Playgrounds execute your Swift code as you type it, allowing you to experiment with Swift and Cocoa/Cocoa Touch features, and to fix errors as they occur.

To create a playground:

1. Select **File > New Playground…**.

2. Name your playground file.

3. Select either **iOS** or **OS X** as the **Platform** and click **Next**. (Unless we specify otherwise, the choice of **Platform** does not matter for this book's examples.)

4. Specify where to save the playground, then click **Create**.

Figure 1.7 shows a sample playground with the default name `MyPlayground.playground`. It contains sample Swift code that assigns a `String` to a variable named `str`, by default. The playground executes this statement and shows you `str`'s value in the gray sidebar at the right side of the window. The results of any output statements in your code (there are none in Fig. 1.7) are visible only if you show the **Assistant Editor** in the playground. To do so, open Xcode's **View** menu, then select **Assistant Editor > Show Assistant Editor**. The **Assistant Editor** will appear to the right of the gray sidebar.

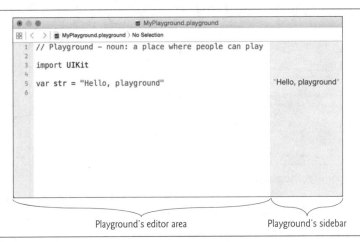

Playground's editor area   Playground's sidebar

Fig. 1.7 | Sample Xcode playground

Creating a Project

A **project** is a group of related files, such as the Swift code files and any accompanying media files (e.g., images, video, audio) that compose an app. Most of the Xcode projects we created for this book's examples are **OS X Command Line Tool** projects. To create one:

1. Select **File > New > Project…**.

2. In the **OS X** subcategory **Application**, select **Command Line Tool** and click **Next**.

3. Provide a name for your project in the **Product Name** field.

4. Optionally change the **Organization Name** and **Organization Identifier** values. The **Organization Name** is typically the developer's company or institution name. The

Organization Identifier is combined with the **Product Name** to form a *bundle identifier* that uniquely identifies the product in various project settings and in the iOS or Mac App Store. Typically, the **Organization Identifier** is a *company's domain name in reverse*—for this book's examples, we used the **Organization Identifier** com.deitel.

5. Ensure that the selected **Language** is **Swift** and click **Next**.

6. Specify where you want to store your project, then click **Create**.

Figure 1.8 shows the window that appears after you create the project. In this case, we selected the file main.swift from the project's files—main.swift is the starting point of a Swift program and contains some sample Swift code that displays the string "Hello, World!". To build and run the project so you can see its output, simply click the run (▶) button at the left side of Xcode's toolbar. This builds and runs the program, opens Xcode's **Debug** area (at the bottom of the **Editor** area) and shows the program's output in the right half of the **Debug** area (Fig. 1.9).

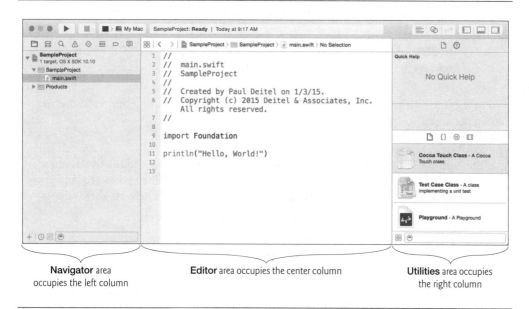

Navigator area occupies the left column   **Editor** area occupies the center column   **Utilities** area occupies the right column

Fig. 1.8 | Sample Xcode Swift project with main.swift selected.

Result of running the project

Fig. 1.9 | Debug area showing the output of the Swift program in Fig. 1.8.

Workspace Window

A new project's window (Fig. 1.8) is known as a **workspace window**, which is divided into four main areas below the toolbar: the **Navigator** area, **Editor** area, **Utilities** area and the **Debug** area (which is not initially displayed—we'll explain how to display it shortly).

Navigator Area

At the top of the **Navigator** area are icons for the *navigators* that can be displayed there:

- **Project** (☐)—Shows all the files and folders in your project.
- **Symbol** (⛁)—Allows you to browse your project by classes and their contents (methods, properties, etc.).
- **Find** (🔍)—Allows you to search for text throughout your project's files and frameworks.
- **Issue** (⚠)—Shows you warnings and errors in your project by file or by type.
- **Test** (⊘)—Enables you to manage your unit tests (for more about unit testing with Xcode, visit `http://bit.ly/TestingWithXcode`).
- **Debug** (▤)—During debugging, allows you to examine your app's threads and method-call stacks.
- **Breakpoint** (▷)—Enables you to manage your debugging breakpoints by file.
- **Report** (▤)—Allows you to browse log files created each time you build and run your app.

You choose which navigator to display by clicking the corresponding button above the **Navigator** area of the window.

Editor Area

To the right of the **Navigator** area is the **Editor** area for editing source code and designing GUIs. This area is always displayed in your workspace window. When you select a file in the project navigator, its contents are displayed in the **Editor** area. There are three editors:

- The **Standard** editor (☰) shows the selected file's contents.
- The **Assistant** editor (◎) shows the selected file's contents on the left and related file contents on the right—for example, if you're editing a class that extends another class, the **Assistant** editor will also show you the superclass.
- The **Version** editor (⇄) allows you to compare different versions of the same file (e.g., old and new versions).

Utilities Area and Inspectors

At the right side of the workspace window is the **Utilities** area, which displays **inspectors** that allow you to view and edit information about items displayed in the **Editor** area. The set of inspectors you can choose from depends on what you're doing in Xcode 6. By default, the top half of the **Utilities** area shows either the **File** inspector (☐) or the **Quick Help** inspector (⑦). The **File inspector** shows information about the currently selected file in the project. The **Quick Help** inspector provides context-sensitive help—documentation that's based on the currently selected item in a GUI or the cursor position in the source code. For example, clicking on a method name shows a description of the method, its parameters and its return value.

Debug Area

When displayed, the **Debug** area appears at the bottom of the editor area and provides controls for stepping through code, inspecting variable contents and more. We discuss how to hide and show the **Navigator** area, **Utilities** area and **Debug** area momentarily.

Xcode Toolbar

The Xcode toolbar contains options for executing your app (Fig. 1.10(a)), a display area (Fig. 1.10(b)) that shows the progress of tasks executing in Xcode (e.g., project build status) and buttons (Fig. 1.10(c)) for hiding and showing areas in the workspace window. Figure 1.11 overviews the toolbar.

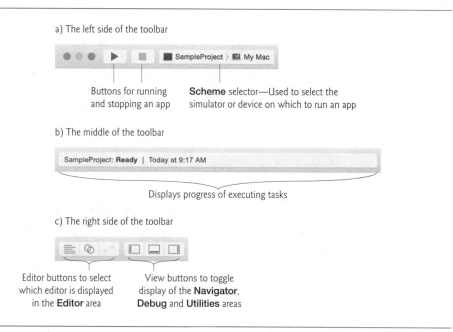

a) The left side of the toolbar

Buttons for running and stopping an app

Scheme selector—Used to select the simulator or device on which to run an app

b) The middle of the toolbar

Displays progress of executing tasks

c) The right side of the toolbar

Editor buttons to select which editor is displayed in the **Editor** area

View buttons to toggle display of the **Navigator**, **Debug** and **Utilities** areas

Fig. 1.10 | Xcode 6 toolbar.

Control	Description
▶	Builds then runs the project on the currently selected simulator or device as specified in the **Scheme** selector (Fig. 1.10(a)). Clicking and holding on this button displays **Run**, **Test**, **Profile** and **Analyze** options. The **Test** option allows you to run unit tests on your app. The **Profile** option collects information about your running code to help you locate performance issues, memory leaks and more. The **Analyze** option checks your source code for potential logic errors.
■	Terminates the running app.

Fig. 1.11 | Xcode 6 toolbar elements. (Part 1 of 2.)

Control	Description
Scheme selector	Specifies the simulator or device on which the app will run when the **Run** button is clicked.
Editor buttons	Click one of these buttons (Fig. 1.10(c)) to specify which editor is displayed in the **Editor** area.
View buttons	Click these toggle buttons (Fig. 1.10(c)) to specify whether the **Navigator**, **Debug** and **Utilities** areas of the workspace window are displayed.

Fig. 1.11 | Xcode 6 toolbar elements. (Part 2 of 2.)

Project Navigator

The **Project** navigator (left side of Fig. 1.8) provides access to all of a project's components. It consists of a series of groups (folders) and files. The most used group is the **project structure group**, which Xcode names the same as the project. This group contains your project's source files, media files and supporting files. The **Products** group contains the .app files for your project. The .app files execute when you test your apps and are also used to distribute your apps via the iOS and Mac app stores.

Keyboard Shortcuts

Xcode provides many keyboard shortcuts for useful commands. Figure 1.12 shows some of the most useful ones. For more, visit http://bit.ly/XcodeShortcuts.

Shortcut	Function	Shortcut	Function
shift + ⌘ + *N*	Create new project.	⌘ + *B*	Build project.
⌘ + *N*	Create new file in current project.	⌘ + *R*	Build and run project.
⌘ + *S*	Save current file.	*shift* + ⌘ + *K*	Clean project.

Fig. 1.12 | Common Xcode keyboard shortcuts.

1.8 Web Resources

Deitel Resource Centers

Check out our Swift Resource Center at http://www.deitel.com/swift. It includes links to documentation, tutorials, videos, articles, sample code, blogs, forums and more. We'll update it as new and updated resources become available. We'll also be putting up related resource centers which we'll announce via our online communities.

Deitel Social Networking Communities

Join the Deitel social networking communities on:

- Facebook® (http://www.deitel.com/deitelfan)
- Twitter® (@deitel)
- Google+™ (http://google.com/+DeitelFan)

- YouTube® (http://youtube.com/DeitelTV)
- LinkedIn® (http://linkedin.com/company/deitel-&-associates)

As you read the book, if you have a question, send an e-mail to us at deitel@deitel.com and we'll respond promptly. We'd also appreciate your comments, criticisms and suggestions for improving the book.

2

Introduction to Swift Programming

Objectives

In this chapter you'll:

- Write simple Swift applications.
- Use output statements.
- Learn about boolean and numeric types.
- Use arithmetic operators.
- Learn the precedence of arithmetic operators.
- Make decisions with the `if` conditional statement.
- Use comparative operators.

2.1 Introduction

This chapter introduces Swift programming. We begin with examples that display text on the screen. We then present a program that introduces constant and variable declarations in which we calculate the sum of two integers and display the result. We present Swift's arithmetic operators, and its boolean and numeric types. The chapter's last example demonstrates decision making with the `if` statement and the comparative operators.

2.2 A First Swift Program: Printing a Line of Text

We now present our first program and discuss how to run it. First we consider a simple application that displays a line of text. Figure 2.1 shows the program followed by a box containing its output. The line numbers in the program listing are not part of the program—we include them for ease of referencing the code. Line 2 displays the text `Welcome to Swift Programming!`.

```
1   // fig02-01: Text-printing program
2   println("Welcome to Swift Programming!")
```

```
Welcome to Swift Programming!
```

Fig. 2.1 | Text-printing program.

Swift Code Files

Unlike many C-based programming languages, Swift does not have a `main` function or method. Rather, in an Xcode project, the file that contains the entry point for a Swift app must be named `main.swift`—code files end with the `.swift` filename extension. Any globally scoped statements in `main.swift`—that is, statements that are not written inside function, method or type definitions—serve as the app's entry point.

When you enter code in an Xcode playground, it compiles and executes as you complete each statement. We discuss this in more detail at the end of this section. We recommend that as you learn Swift, you enter each single-source-file example's code into an Xcode playground so that you can immediately see the code in action as you write it. If you have not done so, read the Before You Begin section for information on downloading the book's examples and Xcode, and ensuring that your system is configured properly. In addition, be sure to read the Xcode overview in Section 1.6.

Commenting Your Programs

The compiler *ignores* comments. Our convention is to begin every program with a comment that includes the figure number (e.g., fig02-01 corresponds to Fig. 2.1) and purpose of the program. The first line comment helps you locate the corresponding Xcode playground (or Xcode project for multi-source-file examples) in the chapter's examples folder.

The comment in line 1 begins with //, indicating that it's a **single-line comment**—it terminates at the end of the line on which the // appears. A single-line comment also can begin in the middle of a line, possibly after some code, and continue until the end of that line.

Swift also has **multiline comments**, which can be spread over several lines as in

```
/* This is a multiline comment. It
   can be split over multiple lines */
```

These begin and end with the delimiters, /* and */. The compiler ignores all text between the delimiters. In this book, we use // comments.

Unlike most C-based languages, Swift's multiline comments may be *nested*, allowing you to easily comment-out large blocks of code (e.g., for debugging purposes) that contain multiline comments.

Performing Output with Function println

Line 2 displays the characters contained between the double quotation marks (the quotation marks themselves are not displayed). Together, the quotation marks and the characters between them are a **String literal**. String literals have the Swift type **String**. White-space characters in String literals are not ignored by the compiler. String literals *cannot* span multiple lines of code, but you may concatenate multiple Strings into a longer String by using the + operator. As you type code in the source-code editor, Xcode displays context-sensitive, *code-completion suggestions* that help you write code quickly and correctly.

Function println displays (or prints) a line of text to the **standard output**. This is one of the Swift Standard Library's **free (global) functions**. Where the standard output appears depends on the type of program and where you execute it:

- If you execute a println in a playground, the result displays in playground's **Assistant Editor** window.

- If you execute any app from an Xcode project, the output appears in the **Debug** area at the bottom of the Xcode window.

- If the statement is part of a **Command Line Tool** application, when you execute the application in a **Terminal** window, the output appears in that window.

- If you execute an OS X app outside of Xcode, the result is sent to a log file that you can view in the **Console** app.

- If you execute an iOS app on a device, the result is sent to a log file that you can view in Xcode's **Devices** window. When your device is connected to the computer, select **Window > Devices**, select your device in the **Devices** window, then click **View Device Logs**.

The String literal in the parentheses is println's argument. Function println's output is followed by a line break, which indicates that the next character output will be displayed at the beginning of the next line in the standard output.

Semicolons Are Not Required in Swift

The entire line 2, including `println` and the argument `"Welcome to Swift Program-` `ming!"` in the parentheses, is called a **statement**. A program typically contains one or more statements that perform its task. Unlike other C-based programming languages, Swift statements are not required to end with a semicolon (;), though you can use them if you like. If you place more than one statement on the same line, they must be separated by semicolons.

Executing the Application

This example is provided as a playground, so it executes immediately when you load it. If you enter the code into a playground, the application executes as you complete each statement (in this case, the program contains just one statement). The results of any output statements are visible only if you show the **Assistant Editor** in the playground. To do so, open Xcode's **View** menu, then select **Assistant Editor > Show Assistant Editor**, or click the **Assistant Editor** button (⌥) on the Xcode toolbar. By default the toolbar is not displayed in a playground window. To display it, select **View > Show Toolbar**.

Compilation and Syntax Errors

As you write code in a playground or in a `.swift` file that's part of an Xcode project, the compiler continuously compiles your code. Any compilation errors are indicated by a red stop-sign-shaped symbol (●) displayed to the left of the lines of code in which the errors occur. You can click the symbols to view the error messages that apply to your code.

2.3 Modifying Your First Program

Let's modify the example in Fig. 2.1 to print text on one line by using multiple statements and print text on several lines by using a single statement.

Displaying a Single Line of Text with Multiple Statements

Figure 2.2 uses two statements to produce the output shown in Fig. 2.1. [*Note:* From this point forward, we highlight the new and key features in each code listing, as we've done in lines 2–3.] Line 2 uses the free function **print** to display a `String`. Each `print` or `println` statement resumes displaying characters from where the last `print` or `println` statement stopped displaying characters. Unlike `println`, after displaying its argument, `print` does *not* issue a line break—the next character the program displays will appear *immediately after* the last character that `print` displays. So, line 3 positions the first character in its argument (the letter "S") immediately after the last character that line 2 displays (the *space character* before the `String`'s closing double-quote character).

```
1   // fig02-02: Printing a line of text with multiple statements
2   print("Welcome to ")
3   println("Swift Programming!")
```

```
Welcome to Swift Programming!
```

Fig. 2.2 | Printing a line of text with multiple statements.

Displaying Multiple Lines of Text with a Single Statement
A single statement can display multiple lines by using line-feed characters, which indicate to the print and println functions when to position the output cursor at the beginning of the next line in the standard output. Blank lines, spaces, tabs and line-feed characters are whitespace. Line 2 of Fig. 2.3 outputs four lines of text, using three line feeds to determine when to begin each new line.

```
1    // fig02-03: Printing multiple lines of text with a single statement
2    println("Welcome\nto\nSwift\nProgramming!")
```

```
Welcome
to
Swift
Programming!
```

Fig. 2.3 | Printing multiple lines of text with a single statement.

Special Characters
Normally, the characters in a String are displayed *exactly* as they appear in the double quotes. However, the paired characters \ and n, repeated three times in the statement, do *not* appear on the screen. The backslash (\) is an escape character, which has special meaning in a String literal—\n, for example, represents the line-feed special character. When a line-feed character appears in a String being output, the line-feed character causes the screen's output cursor to move to the beginning of the next line in the standard output. Figure 2.4 lists Swift's special characters.

Special character	Description
\n	Line feed (often called newline in other languages). Position the screen cursor at the beginning of the next line.
\t	Horizontal tab. Move the screen cursor to the next tab stop.
\\	Backslash. Used to print a backslash character.
\r	Carriage return. Position the screen cursor at the beginning of the *current* line—do *not* advance to the next line. Any characters output after the carriage return *overwrite* the characters previously output on that line.
\"	Double quote. Used to insert a double-quote character.
\'	Single quote. Used to insert a single-quote character.
\0	Null character.
\u{n}	A Unicode character—n is between one and eight hexadecimal digits.

Fig. 2.4 | Swift special characters in String literals.

2.4 **Composing Larger** Strings **with** String **Interpolation**

Swift provides **String interpolation** to allow you to insert values into String literals. Figure 2.5 uses this capability to output a constant's value as part of a String.

```
1   // fig02-05: Inserting content into a String literal with interpolation
2   let name = "Paul"
3   println("Welcome to Swift Programming, \(name)!")
```

```
Welcome to Swift Programming, Paul!
```

Fig. 2.5 | Inserting content into a String literal with String interpolation.

Declaring Constants and Variables

Line 2 uses the **let** keyword create a *constant* called name that is initialized with the String literal "Paul". A constant cannot be modified after it's initialized. You use the **var** keyword to declare *variables* that can be modified.

Type Inference and Type Annotations

Swift uses **type inference** to determine a constant's or variable's type from its initializer value. Recall that String literals have the type String, so in line 2, the type of name is String because the constant is initialized with a String literal. You may also use a **type annotation** to explicitly specify a constant's or variable's type. For example

```
var number1: Int
```

declares that the variable number1 has type Int, which represents a whole-number integer value. Every variable must be assigned a value before it can be used in your code. You may also provide an initializer in the preceding statement, as in

```
var number1: Int = 4
```

Figure 2.6 shows Swift's numeric and boolean types—each begins with a capital letter. For the integer types, each type's minimum and maximum values can be determined with its **min** and **max** properties—for example, Int.min and Int.max for type Int.

Type	Description
Integer types	
Int	Default signed integer type—4 or 8 bytes depending on the platform.
Int8	8-bit (1-byte) signed integer. Values in the range −128 to 127.
Int16	16-bit (2-byte) signed integer. Values in the range −32,768 to 32767.
Int32	32-bit (4-byte) signed integer. Values in the range −2,147,483,648 to 2,147,483,647.
Int64	64-bit (8-byte) signed integer. Values in the range −9,223,372,036,854,775,808 to 9,223,372,036,854,775,807.

Fig. 2.6 | Swift numeric and boolean types. (Part 1 of 2.)

Type	Description
UInt8	8-bit (1-byte) unsigned integer. Values in the range 0 to 255.
UInt16	16-bit (2-byte) unsigned integer. Values in the range 0 to 65,535.
UInt32	32-bit (4-byte) unsigned integer. Values in the range 0 to 4,294,967,295.
UInt64	64-bit (8-byte) unsigned integer. Values in the range 0 to 18,446,744,073,709,551,615.
Floating-point types (conforms to IEEE 754)	
Float	4-byte floating-point value.
	Negative range: $-3.4028234663852886e+38$ to $-1.40129846432481707e-45$
	Positive range: $1.40129846432481707e-45$ to $3.4028234663852886e+38$
Double	8-byte floating-point value.
	Negative range: $-1.7976931348623157e+308$ to $-4.94065645841246544e-324$
	Positive range: $4.94065645841246544e-324$ to $1.7976931348623157e+308$
Boolean type	
Bool	true or false values.

Fig. 2.6 | Swift numeric and boolean types. (Part 2 of 2.)

String Interpolation

In line 3, the expression \(name) uses String interpolation to insert the name constant's value (Paul) before the ! in the String literal. To perform String interpolation insert a backslash (\) followed by a set of parentheses containing the constant, variable, expression or literal value that you'd like to insert at that position in the String literal.

Identifier Naming

Identifiers for constants and variables typically begin with a lowercase first letter and may contain letters, numbers and most other Unicode characters—this includes even special characters like emojis (e.g., 😃), which you can access in the **Characters** dialog (press ⌘ + *control* + *space* to view the dialog). Identifiers may not begin with a digit, and the following characters are not allowed in identifiers:

- Whitespace.
- Math symbols.
- Arrows.
- Private use (or invalid) Unicode characters—that is, characters defined by third parties for their own use that are not considered to be part of the Unicode standard.
- Line- and box-drawing characters.

Normally, an identifier that does not begin with a capital letter is not a type name. Swift is *case sensitive*—uppercase and lowercase letters are distinct—so value and Value are different (but both valid) identifiers.

Good Programming Practice 2.1

By convention, variable-name identifiers begin with a lowercase letter, and every word in the name after the first word begins with a capital letter. For example, variable-name identifier firstNumber *starts its second word,* Number, *with a capital* N. *This naming convention is known as camel case, because the uppercase letters stand out like a camel's humps.*

2.5 Another Application: Adding Integers

Our next application (Fig. 2.7) computes and displays the sum of two integers.

```
1   // fig02-07: Addition program that displays the sum of two integers
2   let number1 = 45 // keyword let declares a constant
3   let number2 = 72
4   let sum = number1 + number2
5
6   println("number1 = \(number1)")
7   println("number2 = \(number2)")
8   println("Sum = \(sum)")
```

```
number1 = 45
number2 = 72
Sum = 117
```

Fig. 2.7 | Addition program that displays the sum of two integers.

Declaring Constants to Store Integers
Lines 2–4 declare the constants number1, number2 and sum, each holding data of type Int (integer). The compiler infers the types of number1 and number2 to Int based on the literal values 45 and 72, respectively, that are used to initialize the constants. Whole-number values are treated as type Int. The type of sum is determined by the type of its initializing expression—in this case, the sum of two Ints results in an Int, so sum is an Int.

Software Engineering Observation 2.1

Use constants rather than variables when you know a value will not change after it's initialized. Compilers can perform optimizations on constants that cannot be performed on variables. Constants also eliminate accidental modifications of data that should remain constant.

Other Numeric Data Types
Some other data types are Float and Double, for holding real numbers, and Bool for holding true/false values. Real numbers contain decimal points, such as in 3.4, 0.0 and –11.19. Floating-point literals are treated as type Double (an eight-byte floating point number). Type Float represents a four-byte floating-point number. In addition, there are signed integer types (Int8, Int16, Int32 and Int64 for positive and negative integer values) and unsigned integer types (UInt8, UInt16, UInt32 and UInt64 for nonnegative

integer values). These are used to specify integer values that must be represented in a specific number of bytes or that must be unsigned.

Good Programming Practice 2.2

The Swift documentation states that you generally should use the Int type for all integers in your code, even if they're nonnegative: "Using the default integer type in everyday situations means that integer constants and variables are immediately interoperable in your code and will match the inferred type for integer literal values."

Using Constants in a Calculation

Line 4 calculates the sum of number1 and number2, then assigns the result to the constant sum by using the assignment operator, =. Portions of statements that contain calculations are called **expressions**. An expression is any portion of a statement that has a value associated with it. The value of the expression number1 + number2 is the sum of the numbers.

Displaying the Results

After the calculation has been performed, lines 6–8 use function println to display the values of number1, number2 and sum by inserting their values into String literals via String interpolation. Rather than declaring the constant sum, we could have performed the calculation and displayed its result as follows

```
println("Sum = \(number1 + number2)")
```

2.6 Arithmetic

The **arithmetic operators** are summarized in Fig. 2.8. The asterisk (*) indicates multiplication, and the percent sign (%) is the remainder operator, which we'll discuss shortly. The arithmetic operators in Fig. 2.8 are binary operators.

Operation	Operator	Algebraic expression	Swift expression
Addition	+	$f + 7$	f + 7
Subtraction	–	$p - c$	p - c
Multiplication	*	bm	b * m
Division	/	x / y or $\frac{x}{y}$ or $x \div y$	x / y
Remainder	%	$r \bmod s$	r % s

Fig. 2.8 | Arithmetic operators.

Integer division yields an integer quotient. For example, the expression 7 / 4 evaluates to 1, and the expression 17 / 5 evaluates to 3. Any fractional part in integer division is simply *truncated*—no *rounding* occurs. The remainder operator, %, yields the remainder after division—the expression x % y yields the remainder after x is divided by y. Thus, 7 % 4 yields 3, and 17 % 4.5 yields 3.5. If the left operand of % is negative, the result will also be negative. This operator is most commonly used with integers but it can also be used with floating-point types. One interesting application of the remainder operator is determining whether the left operand is a multiple of the right operand—in this case, the remainder is 0.

2.6.1 Automatic Arithmetic Overflow Checking

The arithmetic operators in Fig. 2.8 check for *overflow*—a condition that occurs when the result of a calculation becomes greater than the highest value or less than the lowest value that a particular type can represent. Overflow can lead to unexpected results, so by default a calculation that overflows results in a runtime error that terminates execution. Swift also provides **overflow operator** versions of each operator in Fig. 2.8—&+, &-, &*, &/ and &%— that allow overflow to occur, so you can "opt in" to overflow.

2.6.2 Operator Precedence

The operators in arithmetic expressions are applied in a precise sequence determined by the **rules of operator precedence**, which are generally the same as those in algebra:

1. Multiplication, division and remainder operations are applied first. If an expression contains several such operations, they're applied from left to right. Multiplication, division and remainder operators have the same level of precedence.

2. Addition and subtraction operations are applied next. If an expression contains several such operations, the operators are applied from left to right. Addition and subtraction operators have the same level of precedence.

These rules enable Swift to apply operators in the correct order. When we say that operators are applied from left to right, we're referring to their **associativity**. Some operators associate from right to left and some do not have associativity (such as the comparative operators you'll see in Section 2.7). Figure 2.9 summarizes these rules of operator precedence for the arithmetic operators and the assignment operator. See Appendix B, Operator Precedence Chart, for a complete list of operators and their precedence.

Operator(s)	Operation(s)	Order of evaluation (precedence)
* / %	Multiplication Division Remainder	Evaluated first. If there are several operators of this type, they're evaluated from *left to right*.
+ –	Addition Subtraction	Evaluated next. If there are several operators of this type, they're evaluated from *left to right*.
=	Assignment	Evaluated last.

Fig. 2.9 | Precedence of arithmetic operators.

2.7 Decision Making: The if Conditional Statement and the Comparative Operators

A **condition** is an expression that can be **true** or **false**. This section introduces the **if condition statement** (also called a **branch statement**) to make a decision based on a condition's value. If the condition in an if statement is *true*, the body of the if statement executes. If the condition is *false*, the body does not execute.

Conditions in if statements can be formed by using the **comparative operators** (==, !=, >, <, >= and <=) summarized in Fig. 2.10. These operators all have the same level of precedence and do not have associativity. In addition to the operators in Fig. 2.10, Swift also provides the === (identical to) and !== (not identical to) operators, which we discuss in Section 3.4.

Algebraic operator	Comparative operator	Sample condition	Meaning of condition
=	==	x == y	x is equal to y
≠	!=	x != y	x is not equal to y
>	>	x > y	x is greater than y
<	<	x < y	x is less than y
≥	>=	x >= y	x is greater than or equal to y
≤	<=	x <= y	x is less than or equal to y

Fig. 2.10 | Comparative operators.

Figure 2.11 uses six if statements to compare two integers. If the condition in any of these statements is *true*, the statement associated with that if statement executes; otherwise, the statement is skipped.

```
1   // fig02-11: Compare integers using if statements
2   // and the comparative operators
3   let number1 = 1000
4   let number2 = 2000
5
6   if number1 == number2 {
7       println("\(number1) == \(number2)")
8   }
9
10  if number1 != number2 {
11      println("\(number1) != \(number2)")
12  }
13
14  if number1 < number2 {
15      println("\(number1) < \(number2)")
16  }
17
18  if number1 > number2 {
19      println("\(number1) > \(number2)")
20  }
21
22  if number1 <= number2 {
23      println("\(number1) <= \(number2)")
24  }
25
```

Fig. 2.11 | Compare integers using if statements and the comparative operators. (Part 1 of 2.)

```
26   if number1 >= number2 {
27       println("\(number1) >= \(number2)")
28   }
```

Sample output with number1 set to 1000 and number2 set to 2000

```
1000 != 2000
1000 < 2000
1000 <= 2000
```

Sample output after changing number1 to 777 and number2 to 777

```
777 == 777
777 <= 777
777 >= 777
```

Sample output after changing number1 to 2000 and number2 to 1000

```
2000 != 1000
2000 > 1000
2000 >= 1000
```

Fig. 2.11 | Compare integers using if statements and the comparative operators. (Part 2 of 2.)

Lines 3–4 declare Int constants number1 and number2, which store the values 1000 and 2000, respectively. Lines 6–8 compare the values of number1 and number2 to determine whether they're equal. An if statement always begins with keyword if, followed by a condition and *required* set of braces ({}) containing the statements to execute if the condition is true. Unlike other C-based languages, Swift does not require that an if statement's condition be enclosed in parentheses.

Indenting the body statement is not required, but improves the program's readability. Line 7 executes only if the numbers stored in number1 and number2 are equal. The if statements in lines 10–12, 14–16, 18–20, 22–24 and 26–28 compare number1 and number2 using the operators !=, <, >, <= and >=, respectively. If the condition in one or more of the if statements is *true*, the corresponding body statement executes.

Error-Prevention Tip 2.1
Unlike some other languages, Swift requires braces for an if statement's body, even if the body contains only one statement. This is one of several Swift requirements that eliminate common errors that occur in C-based languages.

Error-Prevention Tip 2.2
Unlike some other languages, it is not possible in Swift to accidentally use = where == should be used. This is one of several Swift language features that eliminate common errors that occur in C-based languages.

The Empty Statement

In most C-based languages, a semicolon (;) by itself represents the empty statement. In those languages, an empty statement can be used as the one-statement body of a control statement. In the context of an if statement, that could lead to logic errors. For example, in C, the following code always executes *bodyStatement*, because the if statement's body is the empty statement (;) that follows the if's condition:

```
if (condition) ;
    bodyStatement
```

Because if statements and other control statements in Swift require braces ({}) around their bodies, the preceding code in Swift is a compilation error. An empty control-statement body is represented as empty braces ({}) in Swift.

Swift Keywords
For a complete list of Swift keywords, see Appendix A, Keywords. For your convenience, Apple organizes the keywords into several categories:

*   Keywords used in declarations.

*   Keywords used in statements.

*   Keywords used in expressions and types.

*   Keywords reserved in particular contexts, known as *context-sensitive keywords*.

Operators Discussed So Far
Figure 2.12 shows the operators discussed so far in decreasing order of precedence. Appendix B, Operator Precedence Chart, provides the complete list of operators. The assignment operator, =, associates from *right to left*. However, unlike other C-based languages, it does not return a value—so an expression like x = y = 0 is a compilation error.

Operators						Associativity	Type
*	/	%				left to right	multiplicative
+	-					left to right	additive
==	!=	<	<=	>	>=	none	comparative
=						right to left	assignment

Fig. 2.12 | Precedence and associativity of operators discussed.

2.8 Wrap-Up
In this chapter, we presented Swift fundamentals, including displaying data on the screen, performing calculations and making decisions. You declared constants and variables and saw that Swift can infer their types from provided initializer values. We presented Swift's arithmetic operators, discussed the fact that they automatically check for arithmetic overflow and mentioned that there are corresponding overflow operators that allow overflow to occur. We also introduced the boolean and numeric types. Finally, we demonstrated decision making with the if conditional statement and the comparative operators. In Chapter 3, you'll implement your own class and create and manipulate objects of that class.

Introduction to Classes, Objects, Methods and Functions

Objectives

In this chapter you'll:

- Define a class and use it to create an object.
- Implement a class's attributes as properties.
- Specify a `private` property setter that can be used only within the property's class.
- Implement a class's behaviors as methods.
- Use an initializer to initialize an object's properties when the object is created.
- Call an object's methods to make them perform their tasks.
- Understand how local variables and constants of a method differ from properties.
- Understand the difference between value types and reference types
- Use an `NSDecimalFormatter` from the Cocoa and Cocoa Touch Foundation framework to format numeric values as currency.

3.1 Introduction

In Chapter 2, you worked with built-in Swift types (`Int` and `String`) and functions (`print` and `println`). Throughout the book, you'll use many more preexisting Swift types and functions, as well as capabilities of the Cocoa and Cocoa Touch libraries. In this chapter, you'll create your own types in the form of classes. Each new class you create becomes a new type that can be used to define variables and create objects. In later chapters, you'll also create new `struct` and `enum` types.

In this chapter, we create and use a simple bank-account class—`Account`. This class maintains as attributes the account holder's name and balance, and provides behaviors for querying the balance, making deposits (which increase the balance) and making withdrawals (which decrease the balance). We also discuss the differences between value types and reference types.

Floating-Point Numbers

In Chapter 2 we used the data type `Int` to represent integers. In this chapter, we use data type `Double` to represent an `Account`'s `balance` as a number that can contain a decimal *point*—such numbers are called **floating-point numbers** (e.g., 43.95 or –129.8873).

Swift provides two built-in types for storing floating-point numbers in memory— `Float` and `Double`. Variables of type **`Float`** represent **single-precision floating-point numbers** and might have as few as *six significant digits*. Variables of type **`Double`** represent **double-precision floating-point numbers**. These require *twice* as much memory as `Float` variables and have a minimum of *15 significant digits*.

Most programmers represent floating-point numbers with type `Double`. In fact, Swift treats all floating-point literals you type in a program's source code (such as 7.33 and 0.0975) as `Double` values by default.

NSDecimalNumber Class

In later chapters, we'll represent monetary amounts precisely with the Cocoa and Cocoa Touch Foundation framework class `NSDecimalNumber`—as you should do when writing business-critical applications that process monetary amounts. We demonstrate `NSDecimal-Number` in Section 8.10.

3.2 Account Class

We present and discuss the Account class's code in Figs. 3.1–3.5. In Section 3.3, we present a simple program that creates and uses Account objects to demonstrate Account's capabilities. The project for this example has two Swift files—Account.swift contains Account's definition and main.swift (Section 3.3) contains the app that uses class Account. We could have defined class Account in main.swift as well, but classes are generally defined in their own files to make the code easier to reuse and maintain. To add a new Swift file to your project, select **File > New > File…**, then select **Swift File** from the **Source** category.

To run the final project, click the **Run button** (▶) on the Xcode toolbar or press ⌘ + R. The results will be displayed in the **Debug** area at the bottom of the Xcode window (as you saw in Fig. 1.9).

3.2.1 Defining a Class

Line 4 (Fig. 3.1) begins a **class definition** for class Account. The **class** keyword introduces a class definition and is immediately followed by the class name (Account).

```
1   // fig03-01-11: Account.swift
2   // Account class with name and balance properties,
3   // an initializer and deposit and withdraw methods
4   public class Account {
```

Fig. 3.1 | Account class definition.

Class Names Are Identifiers
Class names are *identifiers* that use the *camel-case* naming scheme we discussed in Chapter 2, but, by convention, class names begin with an initial uppercase letter.

Class Body
A **left brace** (at the end of line 4), {, begins the body of every class definition. A corresponding **right brace** (at line 39 in Fig. 3.5), }, ends each class definition. By convention, the contents of a class's body are indented.

Error-Prevention Tip 3.1
A class must be defined before you use it; otherwise, you'll receive errors indicating that you're using an undeclared type. In an Xcode project, if you define a class in a separate .swift file, the IDE allows you to use it in the project's other source-code files.

Access Modifiers public, internal and private
Class Account's definition begins with the keyword **public** (line 4), which is one of Swift's three **access modifiers** (public, internal and private). A class that's declared public can be reused in other apps—for example, the features in the Swift Standard Library are declared public so that you can use them in your apps. A class that's declared **internal** can be used only by other code in the *same project*—internal is the default access specifier if you do not provide one. A class that's declared **private** can be used only in the *file* in which its defined. Though we do not reuse class Account outside this chapter's example, we chose to declare it public so that it can potentially be reused.

Software Engineering Observation 3.1

If a class should be reusable in other apps, declare the class public. *If a class is used only in the files of the project in which it's defined, use the default access* internal. *If a class is used only in the file in which it's defined, declare the class* private.

Software Engineering Observation 3.2

Access modifiers public, internal *and* private *are different from access modifiers in related object-oriented programming languages such as Java, C# and C++. We discuss more about Swift's access modifiers in Section 3.5.*

3.2.2 Defining a Class Attribute as a Stored Property

Different accounts typically have different names and balances. For this reason, class Account contains a name property (Fig. 3.2) and a balance property (Fig. 3.3). Figure 3.2 defines the **stored property** name—such properties enable you to store and retrieve values in an object of a class. Each object has its *own* copy of the class's stored properties. Swift stored properties are similar to C# properties and to *instance variables* with corresponding *set* and *get* methods in Java and C++.

```
5    public var name: String = "" // properties must be initialized
6
```

Fig. 3.2 | Account class stored property name.

Accessing a Stored Property

A class's properties are defined like other constants and variables, but inside the class's body. The property in Fig. 3.2 is a variable (var) stored property of type String that's initialized with an empty String. A variable property is *read/write*—it allows you to get the property's value from an object of the class and store a value in an object of the class.

You use an object's identifier and a dot (.)—known as *dot syntax*—to access a property. Consider an Account object named account1. In the statement:

```
account1.name = "Jane Green" // uses the setter to set the name
```

the expression account1.name uses the property's *setter* to store the String "Jane Green" in the account1 object. In the statement:

```
println(account1.name) // uses the getter to get the name
```

the expression account1.name uses the property's *getter* to retrieve the String "Jane Green" from the account1 object so that it can be displayed with println.

You may also define constant properties in a class with let. A constant property is *read only*—it provides only a *getter* for retrieving the value and is used for a value that does not change after it's initialized.

Error-Prevention Tip 3.2

The Swift compiler will issue a compilation error if you attempt to use the value of an uninitialized constant or variable. This helps you avoid dangerous execution-time logic errors.

A Class's **public** *Properties May Be Accessed Throughout the Class and by Clients of the Class*

The name property is defined as public (line 5). A class's public properties (and other public members) are *publicly accessible.* They can be accessed throughout the class's definition *and* by any code that uses objects of the class—the class's so-called *client code* (like main.swift, which you'll see in Section 3.3). A class's internal members can be accessed via an object of the class anywhere in the app in which the class is defined. A class's private members can be used only in the file that defines the class.

Software Engineering Observation 3.3

A private *class's members are implicitly* private. *A* public *or* internal *class's members are implicitly* internal.

Computed Properties

Swift also provides **computed properties** that do not store data—rather, they manipulate other properties. For example, a Circle class could have a stored property radius and computed properties diameter, circumference and area that would calculate the diameter, circumference and area, respectively, using the stored property radius in the calculations. We'll define a computed property in Section 6.9.1 and discuss them in more detail in Chapter 8.

3.2.3 Defining a public Stored Property with a private Setter

As you saw in Section 3.2.2, a variable property has a *getter* and a *setter*. If a variable property is public, the client code can use the *getter* to get the property's value and the *setter to* modify its value. Though the client code *should* be able to check the balance, the balance should be modifiable *only* within class Account, so we can ensure the client code does not modify the balance incorrectly. For this scenario, you can declare that the property's *setter* is private. Line 8 (Fig. 3.3) defines the public variable stored property named balance of type Double and initializes it with the value 0.0. The notation private(set) between the public and var keywords indicates that balance's *setter* is private and thus can be used only by code in the same file as class Account.

```
7    // balance is public, but its setter can be used only in class Account
8    public private(set) var balance: Double = 0.0
9
```

Fig. 3.3 | Account class stored properties.

3.2.4 Initializing a Class's Properties with init

Swift does not provide default values for a class's properties—you *must* initialize them before they're used. Lines 5 and 8 (Figs. 3.2–3.3) specify default values for both of Account's properties. But what if you want to provide different values for the name and balance when you *create* an Account object? Each class you define can optionally provide an *initializer* with parameters that can be used to initialize a new object of a class. In fact, Swift requires an initializer call for *every* object that's created, so this is the ideal point to initialize an object's properties. For a class that does not explicitly define any initializers, the compiler defines a **default initializer** (with no parameters) that initializes the class's properties to the default values specified in their definitions. Initializers are like constructors in most other object-oriented programming languages.

Error-Prevention Tip 3.3

Unlike many other object-oriented languages, a Swift class's properties do not receive default values if they're not initialized. You must always provide an initial value for each property, either in its definition or in the class's initializer(s); otherwise, compilation errors occur.

Initializer Definition

Lines 11–19 (Fig. 3.4) define class Account's public initializer—only the public class members are accessible when the class is reused outside the project in which it's defined. Each initializer's name is the keyword init, which is followed by a parameter list enclosed in required parentheses, then the initializer's body enclosed in braces ({ and }). The parameter list optionally contains a comma-separated list of parameters with type annotations. The argument values passed to the initializer's parameters initialize the properties for a particular object of the class. As you'll see in Chapter 8, classes can have multiple initializers—this is called *overloading* and enables objects of a class to be initialized in different ways. The initializer for class Account provides a name parameter of type String and a balance parameter of type Double, representing the account holder's name and starting balance, respectively.

```
10      // initializer
11      public init(name: String, balance: Double) {
12          self.name = name
13
14          // validate that balance is greater than 0.0; if not,
15          // property balance keeps its initial value of 0.0
16          if balance > 0.0 {
17              self.balance = balance
18          }
19      }
20
```

Fig. 3.4 | Account class initializer.

Each parameter must be declared with a type annotation specifying the type of the expected argument. When you create a new Account object (as you'll see in Section 3.3), you'll pass as arguments the account holder's name (a String) and starting balance (a Double)—the initializer will receive those values in the parameters name and balance, respectively. The initializer assigns the parameter name to the property name (line 12) and validates the parameter balance, assigning it to the property balance (line 17) only if the corresponding argument is greater than 0.0—otherwise, property balance retains its default value of 0.0 that was specified in its definition (line 8 of Fig. 3.3).

Parameters Are Local to Their Defining Initializer, Method or Function
Parameters are local to the initializer, method or function in which they're defined, as are
any variables and constants defined in the body of an initializer, method or function. If a
local variable or constant has the same name as a property, using the variable or constant
in the body refers to the local variable or constant rather than the property—the local identifier *shadows* the property. You use the keyword `self` (like `this` in other popular object-
oriented languages) to refer to the shadowed property explicitly, as shown on the left side
of the assignments in lines 12 and 17 (Fig. 3.4).

Software Engineering Observation 3.4

*We could have avoided the need for keyword `self` here by choosing different names for
the parameters in line 11, but using the `self` keyword as shown in lines 12 and 17 is a
widely accepted practice to minimize the proliferation of identifier names.*

There's No Default Initializer in a Class That Defines an Initializer
If you define an initializer for a class, the compiler will *not* create a *default initializer* for
that class. In that case, you will not be able to create an `Account` object with the expression
`Account()`—unless the custom initializer you define takes *no* parameters.

Software Engineering Observation 3.5

*Unless default initialization of your class's properties is acceptable, provide a custom
initializer to ensure that your properties are properly initialized with meaningful values
when each new object of your class is created.*

Software Engineering Observation 3.6

*You cannot call methods from initializers before all of the object's stored properties all have
values—we'll explain why in Chapter 10, Inheritance, Polymorphism and Protocols.*

3.2.5 Defining a Class's Behaviors as Methods

Class `Account` defines two `public` methods (Fig. 3.5) for manipulating the `balance`:

- Method `deposit` (lines 22–27) ensures that the deposit amount is positive and,
  if so, adds the amount to the `balance`.

- Method `withdraw` (lines 30–38) ensures that the withdrawal amount is positive
  and that subtracting that amount from the balance will not overdraw the account,
  and, if so, subtracts the amount from the `balance`.

```
21    // deposit (add) a valid amount into the Account
22    public func deposit(amount: Double) {
23        // if amount is valid, add it to the balance
24        if amount > 0.0 {
25            balance = balance + amount
26        }
27    }
28
```

Fig. 3.5 | Account class methods deposit and withdraw. (Part 1 of 2.)

```
29      // withdraw (subtract) a valid amount from the Account
30      public func withdraw(amount: Double) {
31          // if amount is valid, and the balance will not
32          // become negative, subtract it from the balance
33          if amount > 0.0 {
34              if balance - amount >= 0.0 {
35                  balance = balance - amount
36              }
37          }
38      }
39  }
```

Fig. 3.5 | Account class methods deposit and withdraw. (Part 2 of 2.)

Defining a Method
A method definition begins with the keyword **func** (lines 22 and 30) followed by the method's name and parameter list enclosed in required parentheses, then the method's body enclosed in braces ({ and }). Like an initializer, the parameter list optionally contains a comma-separated list of parameters with type annotations. Methods deposit and withdraw each receive one parameter of type Double representing the amount to deposit or withdraw, respectively.

Return Type of a Method
A method may also specify a return type by following the parameter list with -> and the type of the value the method returns. A method that does not specify a return type does not return a value, as is the case for methods deposit and withdraw in class Account. Methods with return values use **return** statements to pass results back to their callers. As you'll see, Swift methods and functions can return more than one value at a time via a *tuple*, which you'll learn about in Chapter 5.

Initializers Cannot Return Values
An important difference between initializers and methods is that *initializers cannot return values*, so they *cannot* specify a return type.

A Method Defined Outside a Type Definition Is a Function
If a method is defined outside a class (or struct or enum), then it's a function (sometimes called a *free function* or *global function*)—println and print are two of the many functions defined in the Swift Standard Library. We define a function in Section 3.3.3.

3.3 Creating and Using Account Objects

Next, we present main.swift, which demonstrates class Account's capabilities. We present the code in Figs. 3.6–3.11 and, as appropriate, show the output produced by the statements in each figure.

3.3.1 Importing the Foundation Framework

A great strength of the iOS 8 and OS X Yosemite platforms is their rich set of predefined capabilities that you can *reuse* rather than "reinventing the wheel." These capabilities are grouped into **frameworks**. To use features from the iOS 8 and OS X Yosemite frameworks, you must *import* them into your Swift code. Throughout this app, we display an Account's balance in a locale-specific currency format. To do so, we use an object of the Foundation framework's NSNumberFormatter class. In Fig. 3.6, line 4 is an import decla-ration indicating that the program uses predefined capabilities from the Foundation framework. All import declarations must appear before any other Swift code (except com-ments) in your source-code files.

```
1   // fig03-01-11: main.swift
2   // Using class Account's init method to initialize an Account's
3   // name property when the Account object is created
4   import Foundation // use Cocoa/Cocoa Touch Foundation Framework
5
```

Fig. 3.6 | Importing a framework for use in Swift code.

3.3.2 Creating and Configuring an NSNumberFormatter to Format Currency Values

Line 7 (Fig. 3.7) creates an NSNumberFormatter object. Unlike many other object-orient-ed programming languages, Swift does not have a new operator for creating an object. In-stead, you simply follow the class name with parentheses. Arguments, if any, for initializing the object's properties are specified as a comma-separated list inside the paren-theses. Line 8 uses the dot (.) syntax to access and set the NSNumberFormatter object's numberStyle property to the enum constant NSNumberFormatterStyle.CurrencyStyle, indicating that the formatter object produces locale-specific currency Strings (we'll say more about enums in later chapters).

```
6   // create and configure an NSNumberFormatter for currency values
7   var formatter = NSNumberFormatter()
8   formatter.numberStyle = NSNumberFormatterStyle.CurrencyStyle
9
```

Fig. 3.7 | Creating and configuring an NSNumberFormatter object.

Xcode *Quick Help Inspector*

When you place the cursor in your source code (either in a playground or in the **Editor** area of a project), you can use the **Quick Help** inspector to get *context-sensitive help*—documen-tation that's based on the cursor position in the source code. For example, clicking in a class name shows a description of the class, and clicking in a property name shows a de-scription of the property. The **Quick Help** inspector also provides links to more detailed documentation that often shows code snippets in both Swift and Objective-C, so you can see how the selected item is used in each language. You can view the **Quick Help** inspector in Xcode's **Utilities** area or by selecting **View > Utilities > Show Quick Help Inspector**. You can also hold the *option* key and click an item to view pop-up quick help for that item.

Jump to Definition *Option in the Xcode Editor*

In an Xcode project, you can hold the *control* key and click an item in your source code, then select **Jump To Definition** to jump to that item's definition. For Swift Standard Library types and functions, this displays a file containing their declarations and explanatory comments.

3.3.3 Defining a Function—formatAccountString

Figure 3.8 defines a function formatAccountString, which we use throughout main.swift to create a formatted String representation of an Account's name and balance. In main.swift, statements that are defined outside any function execute in sequence when the program begins execution. Statements in a function, however, execute only when that function is *called*.

```
10   // function to return String representation of an Account's information
11   func formatAccountString(account: Account) -> String {
12       return account.name + "'s balance: " +
13           formatter.stringFromNumber(account.balance)!
14   }
15
```

Fig. 3.8 | Function to display an Account's information.

Function formatAccountString receives an Account object and returns a String (specified by the return type in line 11) containing the name and balance property values in the Account object. Line 13 uses the formatter object's **stringFromNumber** method to get a locale-specific, currency-formatted string representing the balance. We use the + operator in lines 12 and 13 to concatenate the name String, the literal "'s balance: " and the String returned by stringFromNumber.

The **return** statement passes the concatenated String back to the caller. For example, when the value is returned to the println statement in line 21 of Fig. 3.9, the statement displays the returned String.

It's possible that stringFromNumber will be unable to produce a formatted String. For cases in which a method might sometimes—but not always—return a value, Swift allows a method to return an **optional**, which is either a value of the specified type or nil to indicate the absence of a value (similar to null or NULL in some programming languages). An optional is indicated by following a type with a ?—stringFromNumber's return type is actually String? (an optional String). The exclamation point (!) at the end of line 13 tells Swift to assume that the optional String returned by stringFromNumber contains an actual String value (not nil) and so lines 12–13 can return that value. Note, however, that if the optional String contains nil, a runtime error will occur and the program will stop executing. We discuss optionals and how to check them for nil beginning in Section 6.9.5.

3.3.4 Creating Objects and Calling an Initializer

Lines 17–18 (Fig. 3.9) create and initialize two Account objects and assign them to account1 and account2. When you implicitly invoke a class's initializer, you must specify each parameter's name and a colon (:) before the corresponding argument value, as in lines 17–18). Lines 21–22 display the results of calling function formatAccountString to get String representations of the Account objects' contents after they're initialized—the corresponding output is shown below Fig. 3.9.

```
16   // create two Account objects
17   let account1 = Account(name: "Jane Green", balance: 50.00)
18   let account2 = Account(name: "John Blue", balance: -7.53)
19
20   // display initial balance of each Account
21   println(formatAccountString(account1))
22   println(formatAccountString(account2))
23
```

```
Jane Green's balance: $50.00
John Blue's balance: $0.00
```

Fig. 3.9 | Creating and manipulating an Account object.

3.3.5 Calling Methods on Objects—Depositing into Account Objects

Figure 3.10 demonstrates depositing into each Account (lines 29 and 37) to show that each Account maintains its own copy of the balance property. When calling a method, if it has only one parameter, you simply pass the argument value in the parentheses of the method call. If a method has more than one parameter, each argument after the first must be preceded by the parameter's name and a colon (:)—we discuss the reasoning for this in Section 5.9. After each deposit, we display both Account objects to emphasize that only one Account object's balance is modified by each call to deposit.

```
24   // test Account's deposit method
25   var depositAmount = 25.53
26
27   println("\ndepositing " + formatter.stringFromNumber(depositAmount) +
28       " into account1\n")
29   account1.deposit(depositAmount)
30
31   println(formatAccountString(account1))
32   println(formatAccountString(account2))
33
34   depositAmount = 123.45
35   println("\ndepositing " + formatter.stringFromNumber(depositAmount) +
36       " into account2\n")
37   account2.deposit(depositAmount)
38
39   println(formatAccountString(account1))
40   println(formatAccountString(account2))
41
```

Fig. 3.10 | Depositing into Account objects. (Part I of 2.)

```
depositing $25.53 into account1

Jane Green's balance: $75.53
John Blue's balance: $0.00

depositing $123.45 into account2

Jane Green's balance: $75.53
John Blue's balance: $123.45
```

Fig. 3.10 | Depositing into Account objects. (Part 2 of 2.)

3.3.6 Calling Methods on Objects—Withdrawing from Account Objects

Figure 3.11 demonstrates withdrawing from each Account (lines 47 and 55). Once again, like deposit, method withdraw has only one parameter, so you simply pass the argument value in the parentheses of the method call. After each withdrawal, we display both Account objects.

```
42   // test Account's withdraw method
43   var withdrawalAmount = 14.27
44
45   println("\nwithdrawing " + formatter.stringFromNumber(withdrawalAmount) +
46       " from account1\n")
47   account1.withdraw(withdrawalAmount)
48
49   println(formatAccountString(account1))
50   println(formatAccountString(account2))
51
52   withdrawalAmount = 100.00
53   println("\nwithdrawing " + formatter.stringFromNumber(withdrawalAmount) +
54       " from account2\n")
55   account2.withdraw(withdrawalAmount)
56
57   println(formatAccountString(account1))
58   println(formatAccountString(account2))
```

```
withdrawing $14.27 from account1

Jane Green's balance: $61.26
John Blue's balance: $123.45

withdrawing $100.00 from account2

Jane Green's balance: $61.26
John Blue's balance: $23.45
```

Fig. 3.11 | Withdrawing from Account objects.

3.4 Value Types vs. Reference Types

Swift's types are either **value types** or **reference types**. In Chapter 2, you worked with variables of type Int—one of the value types. Swift's numeric types, Bool type and String type are all values types, as are all struct and enum types (which we discuss in later chapters).

Value Types

A value-type constant's or variable's value is *copied* when it's passed to or returned from a function or method, when it's assigned to another variable or when it's used to initialize a constant. Note that Swift's Strings are value types—in most other object-oriented languages, Strings are reference types.

Reference Types

All class types are reference types. A constant or variable of a reference type (often called a **reference**) is said to **refer to an object**. Conceptually this means that the constant or variable stores the object's *location*. Unlike Objective-C, C and C++, though, that location is not the *actual* memory address of the object, rather it's a *handle* that enables you to locate the object so you can interact with it. Line 7 of Fig. 3.7:

```
var formatter = NSNumberFormatter()
```

creates an object of class NSNumberFormatter, then assigns to the variable formatter a *reference* to that NSNumberFormatter object. Similarly, line 17 of Fig. 3.9:

```
let account1 = Account(name: "Jane Green", balance: 50.00)
```

creates an object of class Account, then initializes the constant account1 with a *reference* to that Account object.

Objects That Are Assigned to Constants Are Not Constant Objects

Even though account1 and account2 in Fig. 3.9 were defined as *constants*, this does *not* make the Account objects themselves constants—assigning an object to a constant simply means that the constant always *refers to* the *same* object. You can still use a reference-type constant to access read/write properties and to call methods that modify the referenced object, as we did throughout main.swift in Section 3.3.

Assigning References

Objects of reference types are *not copied*. If you assign to a reference-type variable another variable or a constant of the same type, then both *refer to the same object* in memory. The same is true if you initialize a reference-type constant with another variable or a constant of the same type.

Identical to (===) and Not Identical to (!==) Operators

Section 2.7 introduced Swift's comparative operators. One key difference between value types and reference types is comparing for equality and inequality. Only value-type constants and variables can be compared with == and !=.

You can compare reference-type constants and variables to determine whether they *refer to the same object* by using the === (identical to) and !== (not identical to) operators.

If you have two `Account` constants (or variables) `account1` and `account2` that refer to the same `Account` object, the condition

```
account1 === account2
```

returns `true`. If those constants refer to *separate* `Account` objects (even though they might have the *same contents*), the preceding condition returns `false`. Similarly, `!==` returns `true` if its operands refer to *different* objects and `false` if they refer to the *same* object.

3.5 Software Engineering with Access Modifiers

As we've mentioned, Swift's `public`, `internal` and `private` access modifiers work differently than access modifiers in languages like Java, C# and C++. In Swift, they are scope based, rather than type based. In this section, we discuss Swift's access modifiers in more detail and provide guidelines for using them.

Files and Modules

In Swift, groups of related files are compiled into a **module**. For example, the source-code files that implement an app are defined in an app project and compiled into a single module. Similarly, you can define the files for related reusable software components in a framework project and those files, too, will be compiled into a module. Modules can be *imported* into other projects for reuse, just as we did with the `Foundation` framework in Section 3.3.

Access Modifiers Can Be Applied to Many Swift Code Elements

Swift's access modifiers enable you to restrict access to various code elements based on the *source-code file* or *module* in which those elements are defined. For example:

- You can declare a function `private` so it can be used *only* in its defining file.
- You can declare a function `internal` so it can be used only in the module in which it's defined—`internal` is also the default access modifier if you don't explicitly provide one.
- You can declare a function `public` so it can be used in its defining module *and* in any module that imports the defining module.

These concepts apply to every language element that can be defined at the top level of a source-code file, such as variables, constants, classes, functions and other language elements that you'll see in later chapters.

Access Modifiers in a Class

Even a class's members are accessible as we described above. If you define a `private` class member in Java, C# or C++, that member is known *only* within its *defining class*. In Swift, however, a `private` class member can be accessed by the class's other members *and* in any other Swift code defined in the *same source-code file*. To prevent any code outside a class from accessing the class's `private` members—and to get the benefit of what `private` offers in languages such as Java, C# and C++—you must define the class in a file *by itself*. Doing so enables you to enforce encapsulation—that is, to *hide* the class's implementation details from the other source code in your module and any module into which your module is imported. For example, for this chapter's `Account` class, defining the class in its own file enabled us to ensure that client code could not access the `balance` property's `private` *setter*.

Software Engineering Observation 3.7

In the Swift documentation, Apple says that access modifiers are primarily for developers creating reusable frameworks and that most app developers can use the default `internal` access throughout their app code. Nevertheless, if you want to encapsulate class members, you should define your classes (and similarly other new types) in their own files and declare the appropriate class members `private`—that's what we do throughout this book.

Access Modifier Resources

For more information on access modifiers, see the Swift blog post on *Access Control*:

```
https://developer.apple.com/swift/blog/?id=5
```

and *The Swift Programming Language* book's Access Control chapter:

```
http://bit.ly/SwiftAccessControl
```

3.6 Wrap-Up

In this chapter, you created a class and objects of that class, then called methods of those objects to perform useful actions, such as depositing money into or withdrawing money from an `Account`.

We introduced the access modifiers `public`, `internal` and `private`, and you defined a `public` class, with `public` properties, a `public` initializer and `public` methods, that could be reused in other apps.

You defined read/write stored properties to maintain data for each object of a class. You also created a read/write property with a `private set` so that the property's *setter* could be used only within class `Account`, not by the class's clients. This enabled the class to control all updates to the `balance` internally (where they could be validated) and to prevent clients from accidentally modifying the `Account`'s `balance`. We discussed computed properties that operate on a class's other properties, but do not themselves store any data.

You used keyword `init` to create an initializer that allowed a client to specify the initial values for a new `Account` object's properties. We discussed that Swift requires an initializer call for every new object that's created. We also discussed the default initializer that the compiler creates for a class that does not explicitly define one. You defined and called methods to operate on the class's properties.

We discussed the differences between calling functions, methods and initializers. You learned that classes are reference types, and we presented various differences between value types and reference types. All non-class types in Swift are value types. Finally, we discussed access modifiers in more detail.

In Chapter 4, we discuss Swift's conditional statements and loop statements, which specify the order in which a program's actions are performed. We also present Swift's arithmetic assignment operators, increment and decrement operators, and logical operators.

4

Control Statements; Assignment, Increment and Logical Operators

Objectives

In this chapter you'll:

- Use the `if` and `if...else` conditional statements to choose between alternative actions.

- Use the compound assignment operators and the increment and decrement operators.

- Use the `switch` conditional statement to choose among multiple statements to execute.

- Use the `while`, `do...while`, `for...in` and `for` loop statements to execute statements in a program repeatedly.

- Use the closed-range operator (`...`), half-open range operator (`..<`) and global `stride` functions to produce ranges of values.

- Use the `break` and `continue` statements to alter the flow of control.

- Use the logical operators to form complex conditional expressions in control statements.

4.1 Introduction

In this chapter, we revisit the if conditional statement and introduce the if...else conditional statement. Next, we review the compound assignment, increment and decrement operators. We then introduce switch conditional statements—as you'll see, the cases in switch are much more flexible than in other C-based programming languages. We demonstrate the while, do...while, for...in and for and loop statements, then introduce the break and continue program-control statements. Finally, we present the logical operators for creating more complex conditions.

4.2 Control Statements

Sequential Execution by Default
Unless directed otherwise, statements execute one after the other in the order in which they're written—that is, in sequence.

Conditional Statements
Swift has three types of conditional statements. The if statement is a **single-selection statement** because it selects or ignores a *single* action (or a single group of actions). The if...else statement is called a **double-selection statement** because it selects between two different actions (or groups of actions). The switch statement is called a **multiple-selec-**

tion statement because it selects among many different actions (or groups of actions). You may also use nested `if...else` statements for multiple selection.

Loop Statements

Swift provides four loop statements (also called iteration statements) that enable programs to perform statements repeatedly as long as a condition (called the loop-continuation condition) remains true. The loop statements are the `while`, `do...while`, `for...in` and `for` statements. The `while` and `for` statements perform the statement(s) in their bodies zero or more times—if the loop-continuation condition is initially `false`, the statement(s) will not execute. The `for...in` statement iterates through a collection of values (e.g., the range of `Int` values from 1 to 5), performing the statement(s) in its body once for each value in the collection. The `do...while` statement performs the statement(s) in its body one or more times. The words `if`, `else`, `switch`, `while`, `do`, `for` and `in` are keywords. A complete list of keywords can be found in Appendix A.

Summary of Control Statements

Swift's single-entry/single-exit control statements make it easy to build programs—we simply connect the exit point of one to the entry point of the next. We call this control-statement stacking. The only other way in which control statements may be connected is control-statement nesting—which occurs when one control statement appears inside another. Thus, algorithms in Swift programs are constructed from only three kinds of control statements (sequential execution, conditionals and loops), combined in only two ways (stacking and nesting).

Error-Prevention Tip 4.1

Unlike other languages, Swift requires braces for every control statement's body, even if the body contains only one statement. This is one of several Swift requirements that eliminate common errors that occur in other languages.

4.3   `if` Conditional Statement

Programs use conditional statements to choose among alternative courses of action. For example, suppose that the passing grade on an exam is 60. The statement

```
if studentGrade >= 60 {
    println("Passed")
}
```

determines whether the condition `studentGrade >= 60` is true. If so, "`Passed`" is printed, and the next statement in order is performed. If the condition is `false`, the printing statement is ignored, and the next in order is performed. The indentation of the second line of this conditional statement is optional, but recommended.

4.4   `if...else` Conditional Statement

The `if` statement performs an action (or group of actions) only when the condition is `true`; otherwise, the action is skipped. The `if...else` statement allows you to specify an action (or group of actions) to perform when the condition is `true` and another action (or group of actions) when the condition is `false`. For example, the statement

```
if studentGrade >= 60 {
    println("Passed")
} else {
    println("Failed")
}
```

prints "Passed" if studentGrade is greater than or equal to 60, but prints "Failed" if it's less than 60. In either case, after printing occurs, the next statement in sequence is performed. The body of the else is also indented (by convention).

Nested if...else Statements

Multiple cases can be tested by placing if...else statements inside other if...else statements to create nested if...else statements. For example, the following nested if...else statement prints A for exam grades greater than or equal to 90, B for grades 80 to 89, C for grades 70 to 79, D for grades 60 to 69 and F for all other grades:

```
if studentGrade >= 90 {
    println("A")
} else {
    if studentGrade >= 80 {
        println("B")
    } else {
        if studentGrade >= 70 {
            println("C")
        } else {
            if studentGrade >= 60 {
                println("D")
            } else {
                println("F")
            }
        }
    }
}
```

If variable studentGrade is greater than or equal to 90, the first four conditions in the nested if...else statement will be true, but only the statement in the if part of the *first* if...else statement will execute. After that statement executes, the else part of the "outermost" if...else statement is skipped. Many programmers prefer to write the preceding nested if...else statement as

```
if studentGrade >= 90 {
    println("A")
} else if studentGrade >= 80 {
    println("B")
} else if studentGrade >= 70 {
    println("C")
} else if studentGrade >= 60 {
    println("D")
} else {
    println("F")
}
```

The two forms are identical except for the spacing and indentation, which the compiler ignores. The latter form avoids deep indentation of the code, which often forces lines to wrap.

Error-Prevention Tip 4.2

In many C-based languages, braces are required only for multistatement bodies. In those languages, the compiler always associates an else *with the immediately preceding* if *unless told to do otherwise by the placement of optional braces ({ and }). This can lead to what is referred to as the dangling-else problem. Swift eliminates this problem because braces are required around every statement body, even if it contains only one statement.*

Ternary Conditional Operator (?:)

The **ternary conditional operator** (**?:**) can be used in place of an if...else statement. This can make your code shorter and clearer. The conditional operator is the only operator that takes three operands. The first operand (to the left of the ?) is a **Bool** expression (i.e., a condition that evaluates to a Bool value—true or false), the second operand (between the ? and :) is the value of the conditional expression if the Bool expression is true and the third operand (to the right of the :) is the value of the conditional expression if the Bool expression evaluates to false. For example, the statement

```
println(studentGrade >= 60 ? "Passed" : "Failed")
```

prints the value of the conditional-expression argument, which evaluates to "Passed" if the Bool expression studentGrade >= 60 is true and to "Failed" if it's false. Thus, this statement with the conditional operator performs essentially the same function as the if...else statement shown earlier in this section. The precedence of the conditional operator is low, so the entire conditional expression is normally placed in parentheses. We'll see that conditional expressions can be used in some situations where if...else statements cannot.

Error-Prevention Tip 4.3

The ?: *operator's second and third operands must have the same type; otherwise, a compilation error occurs. This is another Swift feature that eliminates common errors.*

4.5 Compound Assignment Operators

The **compound assignment operators** abbreviate assignment expressions. Statements like

variable = variable   operator   expression

where *operator* is one of the binary operators +, -, *, / or % (or others we discuss later in the text) can be written in the form

variable   operator= expression

For example, you can abbreviate the statement

```
c = c + 3
```

with the **addition compound assignment operator**, +=, as

```
c += 3
```

The += operator adds the value of the expression on its right to the value of the variable on its left and stores the result in the variable on the left of the operator. Thus, the assignment expression c += 3 adds 3 to c. The += operator can also be used to concatenate Strings. Figure 4.1 shows the arithmetic compound assignment operators, sample expressions using the operators and explanations of what the operators do. As with the arithmetic operators introduced in Chapter 2, the operators in Fig. 4.1 terminate the program if arithmetic overflow occurs. None of the assignment operators returns a value, so assignment expressions cannot be used in larger expressions.

Assignment operator	Sample expression	Explanation	Assigns
Assume: Int c = 3, d = 5, e = 4, f = 6, g = 12			
+=	c += 7	c = c + 7	10 to c
-=	d -= 4	d = d - 4	1 to d
*=	e *= 5	e = e * 5	20 to e
/=	f /= 3	f = f / 3	2 to f
%=	g %= 9	g = g % 9	3 to g

Fig. 4.1 | Arithmetic compound assignment operators.

4.6 Increment and Decrement Operators

Swift provides two unary operators (summarized in Fig. 4.2) for adding 1 to or subtracting 1 from the value of a numeric variable. These are the unary **increment operator**, ++, and the unary **decrement operator**, --. A program can increment by 1 the value of a variable called c using the increment operator, ++, rather than the expression c = c + 1 or c += 1. An increment or decrement operator that's prefixed to (placed before) a variable is referred to as the **prefix increment** or **prefix decrement operator**, respectively. An increment or decrement operator that's postfixed to (placed after) a variable is referred to as the **postfix increment** or **postfix decrement operator**, respectively.

Operator	Operator name	Sample expression	Explanation
++	prefix increment	++a	Increment a by 1, then use the new value of a in the expression in which a resides.
++	postfix increment	a++	Use the current value of a in the expression in which a resides, then increment a by 1.
--	prefix decrement	--b	Decrement b by 1, then use the new value of b in the expression in which b resides.
--	postfix decrement	b--	Use the current value of b in the expression in which b resides, then decrement b by 1.

Fig. 4.2 | Increment and decrement operators.

Using the prefix increment (or decrement) operator to add 1 to (or subtract 1 from) a variable is known as **preincrementing** (or **predecrementing**). This causes the variable to be incremented (decremented) by 1; then the new value of the variable is used in the expression in which it appears. Using the postfix increment (or decrement) operator to add

1 to (or subtract 1 from) a variable is known as **postincrementing** (or **postdecrementing**). This causes the current value of the variable to be used in the expression in which it appears; then the variable's value is incremented (decremented) by 1. Unlike binary operators, the unary increment and decrement operators must be placed next to their operands, with no intervening spaces; otherwise, a compilation error occurs.

Good Programming Practice 4.1

The Swift documentation recommends that you always use the prefix forms of ++ and -- unless you explicitly need the postfix forms.

When incrementing or decrementing a variable in a statement by itself, the prefix increment and postfix increment forms have the same effect, and the prefix decrement and postfix decrement forms have the same effect. It's only when a variable appears in the context of a larger expression that preincrementing and postincrementing the variable have different effects (and similarly for predecrementing and postdecrementing).

Common Programming Error 4.1

Attempting to use the increment or decrement operator on an expression other than one to which a value can be assigned is a syntax error. For example, writing ++(x + 1) is a syntax error, because (x + 1) is not a variable.

Difference Between Prefix Increment and Postfix Increment Operators

Figure 4.3 demonstrates the difference between the prefix increment and postfix increment versions of the ++ increment operator. The decrement operator (--) works similarly.

```
1   // fig04-03: Prefix increment and postfix increment operators.
2
3   // demonstrate postfix increment operator
4   var c = 5
5   println("c before postincrement: \(c)") // prints 5
6   println("    postincrementing c: \(c++)") // prints 5
7   println(" c after postincrement: \(c)") // prints 6
8
9   println() // skip a line
10
11  // demonstrate prefix increment operator
12  c = 5
13  println(" c before preincrement: \(c)") // prints 5
14  println("     preincrementing c: \(++c)") // prints 6
15  println("  c after preincrement: \(c)") // prints 6
```

```
c before postincrement: 5
    postincrementing c: 5
 c after postincrement: 6

 c before preincrement: 5
     preincrementing c: 6
  c after preincrement: 6
```

Fig. 4.3 | Prefix increment and postfix increment operators.

Line 4 initializes the variable c to 5, and line 5 outputs c's initial value. Line 6 outputs the value of the expression c++. This expression postincrements the variable c, so c's *original* value (5) is output, then c's value is incremented (to 6). Thus, line 6 outputs c's initial value (5) again. Line 7 outputs c's new value (6) to prove that the variable's value was indeed incremented in line 11.

Line 12 resets c's value to 5, and line 13 outputs c's value. Line 14 outputs the value of the expression ++c. This expression preincrements c, so its value is incremented; then the *new* value (6) is output. Line 15 outputs c's value again to show that the value of c is still 6 after line 14 executes.

4.7 switch Conditional Statement

The **switch conditional statement** performs different actions based on the possible values of a **control expression**. Unlike many other C-based languages, you can use values of any type for the control expression, including tuples (which we introduce Chapter 5).

4.7.1 Using a switch Statement to Convert Numeric Grades to Letter Grades

Figure 4.4 uses a switch conditional statement (lines 7–20 in function convertToLetter-Grade) to convert numeric grades in the range 0 to 100 to their equivalent letter grades. A grade in the range 90–100 represents A, 80–89 represents B, 70–79 represents C, 60–69 represents D and 0–59 represents F.

```
1   // fig04-04: Converting numeric grades to letter grades with switch
2
3   // function to return a numeric grade's letter equivalent
4   func convertToLetterGrade(grade: Int) -> String {
5       var letterGrade = "Invalid grade"
6
7       switch grade {
8       case 90...100: // grade was 90-100
9           letterGrade = "A"
10      case 80...89: // grade was between 80 and 89
11          letterGrade = "B"
12      case 70...79: // grade was between 70 and 79
13          letterGrade = "C"
14      case 60...69: // grade was between 60 and 69
15          letterGrade = "D"
16      case 0...59: // grade was between 0 and 59
17          letterGrade = "F"
18      default: // grade was out of range
19          break
20      }
21
22      return letterGrade
23  }
24
```

Fig. 4.4 | Converting numeric grades to letter grades with the switch conditional statement. (Part 1 of 2.)

```
25   println("Letter grade for 100: \(convertToLetterGrade(100))")
26   println("Letter grade for 95: \(convertToLetterGrade(95))")
27   println("Letter grade for 89: \(convertToLetterGrade(89))")
28   println("Letter grade for 70: \(convertToLetterGrade(70))")
29   println("Letter grade for 63: \(convertToLetterGrade(63))")
30   println("Letter grade for 32: \(convertToLetterGrade(32))")
31   println("Letter grade for -1: \(convertToLetterGrade(-1))")
32   println("Letter grade for 101: \(convertToLetterGrade(101))")
```

```
Letter grade for 100: A
Letter grade for 95:  A
Letter grade for 89:  B
Letter grade for 70:  C
Letter grade for 63:  D
Letter grade for 32:  F
Letter grade for -1:  Invalid grade
Letter grade for 101: Invalid grade
```

Fig. 4.4 | Converting numeric grades to letter grades with the switch conditional statement. (Part 2 of 2.)

4.7.2 Specifying Grade Ranges with the Closed-Range Operator (. . .)

The switch statement (lines 7–20) determines which letter grade to return. The statement consists of the switch keyword, followed by a control expression and a body in braces. The body contains a sequence of **case labels** and an optional **default case**. Every case *must* contain at least one statement. Braces are not required around multiple statements in a case.

When the flow of control reaches the switch, the program evaluates the control expression (grade) and compares its value with the *pattern* in each case label. In this example, each pattern is a range of values specified with the closed range operator (. . .), which creates a sequential collection of Int values. For example, the expression 80...89 in line 10 represents the sequential collection 80, 81, 82, 83, 84, 85, 86, 87, 88 and 89, so any grade in the range 80–89 matches the case at line 10. Once a match occurs, the statement (or statements) in that case's body execute (line 11 assigns "B" to letter-Grade), then the switch terminates and program control continues with the first statement after the switch (line 22).

Operator ... is known as the closed range operator because both the starting and ending values in the expression 80...89 are included in the collection. Swift also provides the half-open range operator (..<) for which the ending value in the range is *not* included in the sequential collection—so the expression 1..<5 produces four values containing 1 (the first value in the range), 2, 3 and 4.

4.7.3 The default Case

The cases in lines 8–17 explicitly test for grade values from 0–100. A switch statement's cases must be *exhaustive*, covering every possible value for the control expression; otherwise, a compilation error occurs. If the cases are not exhaustive, you *must* provide the default case, which must appear last in the switch's body

For invalid grades, the default case (lines 18–19) executes. In this example, for any invalid grade, we want the letterGrade to maintain its initial value "Invalid grade", which will be returned at line 22. If you want to do nothing in any case or the default case, simply place a break statement as the only statement in the case's body (line 19)—this terminates the switch immediately and allows you to satisfy the requirement that every case *must* have at least one statement in its body.

> **Error-Prevention Tip 4.4**
> *In a switch statement, you must test all possible values of the control expression or provide a default case. This is another of Swift's features that help eliminate common errors.*

4.7.4 Other Patterns in the case Label

A case's patterns may include:

* A single value (or object) of any type.
* A comma-separated list of values.
* A closed range (using . . .) or half-open range (using . .<).
* Tuples (which we begin discussing in the next chapter).
* Various combinations of these patterns in a comma-separated list.

Each case may also include an optional *guard condition* that's specified with a **where** clause followed by a condition. For example, the following case tests for grades in the range 90–100 (these correspond to the letter grade A):

```
case let aGrade where aGrade >= 90 && aGrade <= 100:
```

This creates a **value binding** that assigns the control expression's value to the constant aGrade for use in the where clause.

4.7.5 No Automatic Fall Through as in Other C-Based Languages

In most C-based languages, without break statements at the end of each case, each time a match occurs, the statements for that case and subsequent cases execute until a break statement or the end of the switch is encountered. This is often referred to as "falling through" to the statements in subsequent cases. Swift does not allow fall through unless you explicitly use the statement

```
fallthrough
```

as the last statement in a case.

In Chapter 10, Inheritance, Polymorphism and Protocols, we present a more elegant way to implement switch logic—we use the technique of polymorphism to create programs that are often clearer, easier to maintain and easier to extend than programs using switch logic.

4.8 while Loop Statement

A loop statement allows you to specify that a program should repeat an action while some condition remains *true*. As an example of Swift's **while loop statement**, consider a program segment that finds the first power of 3 larger than 100. Suppose that the Int variable product is initialized to 3. After the following while statement executes, product contains the result:

```
while product <= 100 {
    product = 3 * product
}
```

Each iteration of the while statement multiplies product by 3, so product takes on the values 9, 27, 81 and 243 successively. When product becomes 243, product <= 100 becomes false. This terminates the loop, so the final value of product is 243. At this point, program execution continues with the next statement after the while statement.

4.9 do...while Loop Statement

The **do...while loop statement** is similar to the while statement. In the while, the program tests the loop-continuation condition at the beginning of the loop, before executing the loop's body; if the condition is false, the body never executes. The do...while statement tests the loop-continuation condition *after* executing the loop's body; therefore, the body always executes at least once. Figure 4.5 uses a do...while to output the numbers 1– 10. Upon entering the do...while statement, line 5 outputs counter's value and line 6 increments counter. Then the program evaluates the loop-continuation test (line 7). If the condition is true, the loop continues at the first body statement (line 5). If the condition is false, the loop terminates and the program continues at line 9.

```
1   // fig04-05: do...while loop statement
2   var counter = 1
3
4   do {
5       print("\(counter)   ")
6       ++counter
7   } while counter <= 10
8
9   println()
```

```
1  2  3  4  5  6  7  8  9  10
```

Fig. 4.5 | do...while loop statement.

4.10 for...in Loop Statement and the Range Operators

The **for...in statement** iterates through a collection of values without using a counter, thus avoiding various common errors, such as off-by-one errors. In Section 4.11, we show the for statement that is commonly used for counter-controlled looping and will point out other common errors.

The syntax of a for...in statement is:

```
for item in collection {
    statements
}
```

During each iteration of the loop, the statement assigns *item* one value from the *collection* of values and the loop terminates when the entire collection has been processed. The type of the parameter is inferred from the types of the collection's elements. As the next example illustrates, the *item* represents successive values in the collection on successive loop iterations.

4.10.1 Iterating Over Collections of Values with Closed Ranges, Half-Open Ranges and the Global `stride` Function

Over the next several chapters, you'll see that the `for...in` statement can be used with different types of collections. In this section, we iterate over sequential collections of Int values created with the closed-range operator (`...`), the half-open range operator (`..<`) and the global `stride` functions (discussed shortly).

Iterating Over a Closed Range
The `for...in` loop with the closed range `1...5`

```
for count in 1...5 {
    print("\(count) ")
}
```

prints the collection of five values containing 1 (the first value in the range), 2, 3, 4 and 5 (the last value in the range). Each iteration of the loop assigns one value from the collection to count. [*Note:* The ... notation we use when referring to the `for...in` statement is simply an ellipsis; the ... as used in the range `1...5` is the closed-range operator.]

If you don't need to use the range's values in the loop's body, you can write:

```
for _ in 1...5 {
    statements
}
```

to indicate that the loop should iterate the specified number of times, but ignore the actual range values.

Iterating Over a Closed Range
The `for...in` loop with the half-open range `1..<5`

```
for count in 1..<5 {
    print("\(count) ")
}
```

prints the collection of *four* values containing 1 (the first value in the range), 2, 3 and 4 (the last value in the range, which is less than 5).

Iterating Over a Closed Range Produced by Global Function `stride`
The closed range and half-open range operators each produce ranges of values in *increasing* order that increment by *one*. You can use Swift's global `stride` functions to produce ranges with any increments or decrements. For example, the `for...in` loop

```
for count in stride(from: 11, through: 1, by: -2) {
    print("\(count) ")
}
```

uses the closed-range `stride` function to specify a decreasing closed range of values. This loop prints the collection of six values containing 11 (the from argument), 9, 7, 5, 3 and 1 (the through argument), decrementing by 2 (the by argument) each time.

Iterating Over a Half-Open Range Produced by Global Function stride
A second version of function stride produces half-open ranges. The for...in loop

```
for count in stride(from: 10, to: 50, by: 10) {
    print("\(count) ")
}
```

uses the half-open range stride function to specify an increasing half-open range of values
that terminates *before* 50 (the to argument). This loop prints the collection of *only four*
values—10 (the from argument), 20, 30 and 40 (the largest value *less than* the to argument)—incrementing by 10 (the by argument) each time.

4.10.2 Compound-Interest Calculations with for...in

Let's use the for...in statement to compute compound interest. Consider the following
problem:

> *A person invests $1,000 in a savings account yielding 5% interest. Assuming that all
> the interest is left on deposit, calculate and print the amount of money in the account
> at the end of each year for 5 years.*

The solution to this problem (Fig. 4.6) involves a loop that performs a calculation for each
of the 5 years the money remains on deposit. Lines 5–9 define function rightAligned-
String (discussed shortly), which we use to right align the values displayed in the output's
right column. Lines 12–13 define and configure an NSNumberFormatter for formatting locale-specific currency values. Line 15 defines the variable amount that stores the initial in-
vestment amount (the Double value 1000.0) and during each loop iteration stores the
amount on deposit at the end of a given year. Line 16 defines the constant rate (the Double value 0.05), representing the 5% interest rate. Both amount and rate are used in the
calculation at line 25.

```
 1   // fig04-06: Compound-interest calculations with the for...in statement
 2   import Foundation
 3
 4   // format a String right aligned in a field
 5   func rightAlignedString(string: String, fieldWidth: Int) -> String {
 6       let spaces: Int = fieldWidth - countElements(string)
 7       let padding = String(count: spaces, repeatedValue: Character(" "))
 8       return padding + string
 9   }
10
11   // create and configure an NSNumberFormatter for currency values
12   var formatter = NSNumberFormatter()
13   formatter.numberStyle = NSNumberFormatterStyle.CurrencyStyle
14
15   var amount = 1000.0 // initial amount before interest
16   let rate = 0.05 // interest rate
17
18   // display headers
19   println(String(format:"%@%@", "Year",
20       rightAlignedString("Amount on deposit", 20)))
```

Fig. 4.6 | Compound-interest calculations with the for...in statement. (Part 1 of 2.)

```
21
22    // calculate amount on deposit for each of ten years
23    for year in 1...5 {
24        // calculate new amount for specified year
25        amount *= (1.0 + rate)
26
27        // display the year and the amount
28        println(String(format:"%4d%@", year
29            rightAlignedString(formatter.stringFromNumber(amount)!, 20)))
30    }
```

```
Year    Amount on deposit
  1          $1,050.00
  2          $1,102.50
  3          $1,157.63
  4          $1,215.51
  5          $1,276.28
```

Fig. 4.6 | Compound-interest calculations with the for...in statement. (Part 2 of 2.)

4.10.3 Formatting Strings with Field Widths and Justification

Lines 19–20 output the headers for two columns of output. The first column displays the year and the second column the amount on deposit at the end of that year. The String type provides the capabilities of the Foundation framework's NSString class, which includes various formatting features such as NSString method stringWithFormat. The Swift equivalent of calling stringWithFormat is:

String(format:*formatString*, *arguments*)

which creates a String object with the formatting specified by the first argument and the contents specified by the remaining arguments.

The format parameter is a **format string** that may consist of **fixed text** and **format specifiers**. Fixed text is output just as it would be by print or println. Each format specifier is a placeholder for a corresponding argument's value and specifies the type of data to output. Format specifiers also may include optional formatting information.

Format specifiers begin with a percent sign (%) followed by a character that represents the *data type*. The format specifier %@ is a placeholder for a String representation of the corresponding argument. The format string in line 19 specifies that the resulting String should contain the String representations of two corresponding arguments—one for each format specifier. The value of the first argument after the format string is placed at the first format specifier's position. The value of each subsequent argument is placed at the position of the next format specifier in the format string. So this example substitutes "Year" for the first %@ and value returned by the call to rightAlignedString for the second %@.

Function rightAlignedString (lines 5–9) receives a String and an Int and returns a right-aligned String (possibly preceded by space characters) that contains the number of characters specified by the Int argument. Line 6 uses the Swift global **countElements** function to determine the number of characters in the String argument, then line 7 creates a String of spaces to append to rightAlignedString's first argument. The String initializer called in line 7 receives as its count argument the number of characters the

`String` should contain (`spaces`), and as its `repeatedValue` argument a character that is repeated the number of times specified by the first argument. The expression `Character(" ")` is the Swift way to represent the space character.

4.10.4 Performing the Interest Calculations

The `for...in` statement (lines 23–30) executes its body 5 times, varying the year from 1 to 5 in increments of 1 (as specified by the closed range `1...5`). During each iteration of the loop, line 25 calculates the amount on deposit at the end of the given year—Swift does not have an exponentiation operator, so we simply multiply the current amount by `1.0 + rate` to determine the new amount on deposit at the end of the given year. Lines 28–29 then display two columns containing the `year` and the right-aligned, currency-formatted `amount`.

In the format specifier `%4d` (`d` represents an `Int` value), the integer 4 between the `%` and the conversion character `d` indicates that the value should be formatted with a field width of 4—that is, the value will occupy four character positions. If the value is less than four character positions wide, the value is right aligned in the field by default. If the value were more than four character positions wide, the field width would be extended to accommodate the entire value. To output values left justified, simply precede the field width with the minus sign (–) formatting flag (e.g., `%-4d`). Field widths are not supported for the `%@` format specifier—that's why we created function n `rightAlignedString` in this example.

The body of the `for...in` statement contains the calculation `1.0 + rate`. This calculation produces the *same* result each time through the loop, so repeating it in every iteration of the loop is wasteful—you can perform this calculation in a statement before the loop, assign it to a constant, then use the constant in the calculation at line 25.

Performance Tip 4.1
In loops, avoid calculations for which the result never changes—such calculations should typically be placed before the loop. Today's compilers typically move such calculations before the loop.

4.10.5 A Warning about Displaying Rounded Values

The variable `amount` and the constant `rate` are inferred to be of type `Double` in this example. We're dealing with fractional parts of dollars and thus need a type that allows decimal points in its values. Unfortunately, floating-point numbers can cause trouble. Here's a simple explanation of what can go wrong when using `Double` (or `Float`) to represent dollar amounts (assuming that dollar amounts are displayed with two digits to the right of the decimal point): Two `Double` dollar amounts stored in the machine could be 14.234 (which would normally be rounded to 14.23 for display purposes) and 18.673 (which would normally be rounded to 18.67 for display purposes). When these amounts are added, they produce the internal sum 32.907, which would normally be rounded to 32.91 for display purposes. Thus, your output could appear as

```
  14.23
+ 18.67
-------
  32.91
```

but a person adding the individual numbers as displayed would expect the sum to be 32.90.

Error-Prevention Tip 4.5

Do not use variables of type Double (or Float) to perform precise monetary calculations. The imprecision of floating-point numbers can lead to errors. The Foundation framework provides class NSDecimalNumber for this purpose, which we demonstrate in Fig. 8.14.

4.11 for Loop Statement

The while statement can be used to implement any counter-controlled loop. The **for loop statement** specifies the details of counter-controlled looping in a single line of code. Figure 4.7 uses a for statement to output the even numbers from 2 through 20.

Error-Prevention Tip 4.6

Use the for... in statement to simplify counter-controlled loops. This makes the code more readable and eliminates several error possibilities, such as improperly specifying the control variable's initial value, the loop-continuation test or the increment expression. In addition, each value in the for... in statement's collection is assigned to a constant, so it cannot accidentally be modified in the loop's body—a potential logic error that might occur with a for statement's mutable control variable.

```
1   // fig04-07: Counter-controlled loop with the for statement.
2
3   // for statement header includes initialization,
4   // loop-continuation condition and increment
5   for var counter = 2; counter <= 20; counter += 2 {
6       print("\(counter)  ")
7   }
8
9   println()
```

```
2   4   6   8   10   12   14   16   18   20
```

Fig. 4.7 | Counter-controlled loop with the for statement.

When the for statement (lines 5–7) begins executing, the control variable counter is declared and initialized to 2. Next, the program checks the loop-continuation condition, counter <= 20, which is between the two required semicolons. Because the initial value of counter is 2, the condition initially is true, so the body statement (line 6) displays control variable counter's value (2). After executing the loop's body, the program executes the increment expression counter += 2, which appears to the right of the second semicolon. Then the loop-continuation test is performed again to determine whether the program should continue with the next iteration of the loop. At this point, the control variable's value is 4, so the condition is still true (the final value is not exceeded)—thus, the program performs the body statement again (i.e., the next iteration of the loop). This process continues until the even integers 2 through 20 have been displayed and the counter's value becomes 22, causing the loop-continuation test to fail and looping to terminate (after 10 iterations of the loop body). Then the program performs the first statement after the for (line 9).

4.11.1 General Format of a for Statement

The general format of the for statement is

```
for initialization; loopContinuationCondition; increment {
    statement
}
```

where the *initialization* expression names the loop's control variable and provides its initial value, *loopContinuationCondition* determines whether the loop should continue executing and *increment* modifies the control variable's value, so that the loop-continuation condition eventually becomes false. The two semicolons in the for header are required. Unlike other C-based languages, the *initialization*, *loopContinuationCondition* and *increment* expressions are not required to be placed in a set of parentheses. If the loop-continuation condition is initially false, the program does *not* execute the for statement's body. Instead, execution proceeds with the statement following the for.

4.11.2 Scope of a for Statement's Control Variable

If the *initialization* expression in the for header defines the control variable (i.e., the control variable's name is preceded by var, as in Fig. 4.7), the control variable's scope is *only* that for statement—it will not exist outside it. Section 5.7 discusses scope in more detail.

4.11.3 Expressions in a for Statement's Header Are Optional

All three expressions in a for header are optional. If the *loopContinuationCondition* is omitted, Swift assumes that the loop-continuation condition is *always true*, thus creating an infinite loop. You might omit the *initialization* expression if the program defines and initializes the control variable before the loop. You might omit the *increment* expression if the program calculates the increment with statements in the loop's body or if no increment is needed. The increment expression in a for acts as if it were a standalone statement at the end of the for's body. Therefore, the following expressions

```
counter = counter + 1
counter += 1
++counter
counter++
```

are equivalent increment expressions in a for statement. If the variable being incremented does not appear in a larger expression, preincrementing and postincrementing have the *same* effect.

4.12 break and continue Statements

In addition to conditional and loop statements, Swift provides statements break and continue (presented in this section and Appendix C) to alter the flow of control. The preceding section showed how break can be used to indicate that a case in a switch statement should not perform a task. This section discusses how to use break in loop statements.

4.12.1 break Statement Example

The **break** statement, when executed in a loop, causes *immediate* exit from that statement. Execution continues with the first statement after the control statement. Common uses of the break statement are to escape early from a loop. Figure 4.8 demonstrates a break state-ment exiting a for...in statement. When the if statement nested at lines 3–5 in the for...in statement (lines 2–8) detects that count is 5, the break statement at line 4 exe-cutes. This terminates the for...in statement, and the program proceeds to line 10. The loop fully executes its body only four times instead of 10.

```
1   // fig04-08: break statement exiting a for...in statement
2   for count in 1...10 { // supposed to loop 10 times
3       if (count == 5) {
4           break // terminates loop if count is 5
5       }
6
7       print("\(count)  ")
8   }
9
10  println()
```

```
1 2 3 4
```

Fig. 4.8 | break statement exiting a for...in statement.

4.12.2 continue Statement Example

The **continue** statement, when executed in a loop, skips the remaining statements in the loop body and proceeds with the next iteration of the loop. In while and do...while state-ments, the program evaluates the loop-continuation test immediately after the continue statement executes. In a for statement, the increment expression executes, then the pro-gram evaluates the loop-continuation test. In a for...in statement, the statement proceeds to the next iteration of the loop and uses the next value in the range over which the state-ment is iterating. Figure 4.9 uses continue (line 4) to skip the statement at line 7 when the nested if determines that count's value is 5. When the continue statement executes, program control continues with the next value in the range 1...10—in this case 6.

```
1   // fig04-09: continue statement exiting a for...in statement
2   for count in 1...10 { // supposed to loop 10 times
3       if (count == 5) {
4           continue // move to next iteration of the loop
5       }
6
7       print("\(count)  ")
8   }
9
10  println()
```

```
1 2 3 4 6 7 8 9 10
```

Fig. 4.9 | continue statement terminating an iteration of a for...in statement.

Software Engineering Observation 4.1

Some programmers feel that break and continue violate structured programming. Since the same effects are achievable with structured programming techniques, these programmers do not use break or continue.

Software Engineering Observation 4.2

There's a tension between achieving quality software engineering and achieving the best-performing software. Sometimes one of these goals is achieved at the expense of the other. For all but the most performance-intensive situations, apply the following rule: First, make your code simple and correct; then make it fast and small, but only if necessary.

4.13 Logical Operators

The if, if...else, while, do...while, for and for...in statements each require a condition to determine how to continue a program's flow of control. Simple conditions are expressed in terms of the comparative operators ==, !=, >, <, >= and <=, and each expression tests only one condition. Previously, to test multiple conditions in the process of making a decision, we performed these tests in separate statements or in nested if or if...else statements. Swift's **logical operators** enable you to form more complex conditions by combining simple conditions. The logical operators are && (logical AND), || (logical OR) and logical NOT (!).

4.13.1 Logical AND (&&) Operator

Suppose we wish to ensure at some point in a program that two conditions are *both* true before we choose a certain path of execution. In this case, we can use the && (logical AND) operator, as follows:

```
if gender == "Female" && age >= 65 {
    ++seniorFemales
}
```

This if statement contains two simple conditions. The condition gender == "Female" compares variable gender to "Female" to determine whether a person is female. The condition age >= 65 might be evaluated to determine whether a person is a senior citizen. The if statement considers the combined condition

```
gender == "Female" && age >= 65
```

which is true if and only if *both* simple conditions are true. In this case, the if statement's body increments seniorFemales by 1. If either or both of the simple conditions are false, the program skips the increment. Some programmers find that the preceding combined condition is more readable when *redundant* parentheses are added, as in:

```
(gender == "Female") && (age >= 65)
```

The truth table in Fig. 4.10 summarizes the && operator. The table shows all four possible combinations of false and true values for *expression1* and *expression2*. Swift evaluates to false or true all expressions that include relational operators, equality operators or logical operators.

expression1	expression2	expression1 && expression2
false	false	false
false	true	false
true	false	false
true	true	true

Fig. 4.10 | && (logical AND) operator truth table.

4.13.2 Logical OR (| |) Operator

Now suppose we wish to ensure that *either or both* of two conditions are true before we choose a certain path of execution. In this case, we use the | | (**logical OR**) operator, as in the following program segment:

```
if (semesterAverage >= 90) || (finalExam >= 90) {
    println("Student grade is A")
}
```

This statement also contains two simple conditions. The condition semesterAverage >= 90 evaluates to determine whether the student deserves an A in the course because of a solid performance throughout the semester. The condition finalExam >= 90 evaluates to determine whether the student deserves an A in the course because of an outstanding performance on the final exam. The if statement then considers the combined condition

```
(semesterAverage >= 90) || (finalExam >= 90)
```

and awards the student an A if *either or both* of the simple conditions are true. The only time the message "Student grade is A" is *not* printed is when *both* of the simple conditions are *false*. Figure 4.11 is a truth table for operator logical OR (| |). Operator && has a higher precedence than operator | |. Both operators associate from left to right.

expression1	expression2	expression1 || expression2
false	false	false
false	true	true
true	false	true
true	true	true

Fig. 4.11 | | | (logical OR) operator truth table.

4.13.3 Short-Circuit Evaluation of Complex Conditions

The parts of an expression containing && or | | operators are evaluated *only* until it's known whether the condition is true or false. Thus, evaluation of the expression

```
(gender == FEMALE) && (age >= 65)
```

stops immediately if gender *is not* equal to FEMALE (i.e., the entire expression is false) but continues if gender *is* equal to FEMALE (i.e., the entire expression could still be true if the condition age >= 65 is true). This feature of logical AND and logical OR expressions is called short-circuit evaluation.

Common Programming Error 4.2

In expressions using operator &&, a condition—we'll call this the dependent condition— *may require another condition to be true for the evaluation of the dependent condition to be meaningful. In this case, the dependent condition should be placed after the && operator to prevent errors. Consider the expression (i != 0) && (10 / i == 2). The dependent condition (10 / i == 2) must appear after the && operator to prevent the possibility of division by zero.*

Error-Prevention Tip 4.7

For clarity, avoid expressions with side effects in conditions. They can make code harder to understand and can lead to subtle logic errors.

4.13.4 Logical NOT (!) Operator

The unary ! (logical NOT) operator "reverses" the meaning of a condition. The operator is placed *before* a condition to choose a path of execution if the original condition (without the logical negation operator) is false, as in the program segment

```
if !(age > 65) {
    println("Age is less than or equal to 65")
}
```

which executes the println call only if age is not greater than 65. The parentheses around age > 65 are needed because the ! operator has a *higher* precedence than the > operator.

In most cases, you can avoid using logical negation by expressing the condition differently with an appropriate comparative operator. For example, the previous condition may also be written as follows:

```
if age <= 65 {
    println("Age is less than or equal to 65")
}
```

This flexibility can help you express a condition in a more convenient manner. Figure 4.12 is a truth table for the logical negation operator.

expression	!expression
false	true
true	false

Fig. 4.12 | ! (logical NOT) operator truth table.

Precedence and Associativity of the Operators Presented So Far
Figure 4.13 shows the precedence and associativity of the Swift operators introduced so far. The operators are shown from top to bottom in decreasing order of precedence.

Operators	Associativity	Type
++ --	right to left	unary postfix
++ -- + - ! (*type*)	right to left	unary prefix
* / %	left to right	multiplicative
+ -	left to right	additive
< <= > >= == !=	left to right	comparative
&&	left to right	logical AND
||	left to right	logical OR
?:	right to left	ternary conditional
= += -= *= /= %=	right to left	assignment

Fig. 4.13 | Precedence/associativity of the operators discussed so far.

4.14 Wrap-Up

In this chapter, we presented control statements. Only three types of control statements—sequence, conditional and loop—are needed to develop any program. We demonstrated the if, if...else and switch conditional statements, and the while, do...while, for...in and for loop statements. We introduced the compound assignment operators and the increment and decrement operators. You used the break statement to immediately terminate a loop and used a continue statement to terminate a loop's current iteration and proceed with the next iteration. We also introduced the logical operators. In Chapter 5, we examine functions and methods in greater depth.

5

Functions and Methods: A Deeper Look; **enum**s and Tuples

Objectives

In this chapter you'll:

- Learn about Swift modules (for software reuse).
- Define functions with multiple parameters.
- Use random-number generation to implement a game-playing app.
- Use **enum** types to create sets of named constants.
- Return multiple values from a function via a tuple, pass a tuple to a function and access a tuple's elements.
- Learn how an identifier's scope limits its visibility to specific parts of a program.
- Create overloaded functions.
- Learn how local and external parameter names are used in function and method calls.
- Use default parameter values in function calls.
- Pass method arguments by value and by reference.
- Define a recursive function.
- Define a nested function.

5.1 Introduction

We introduced functions and methods in Chapter 3. The key distinction between a function and a method is that any function defined *in a type* is a method.

In this chapter, we begin by discussing modules, which Swift uses to package related software components for reuse. We introduce Darwin—Apple's UNIX-based core of OS X and iOS—and import Darwin features (such as a C-based random-number-generation function) for use in apps.

We discuss random-number generation and develop a version of a popular casino dice game. That example demonstrates basic enum types for creating named constants that improve the readability of the code. You'll see that Swift's enum constants can have values, but that's not required. The example also presents tuples—collections of values of the same or different types. We return multiple values from a function via a tuple, pass a tuple to a function and access a tuple's elements via both names and indices.

Next, we discuss Swift's scope rules. Then, we introduce the concept of *overloading*. You'll frequently see identically named functions or, within a type, identically named methods. This overloading is used to implement functions or methods that perform similar tasks but with different types and/or different numbers of parameters. This chapter demonstrates overloading with functions, and you'll see examples of method overloading in later chapters.

We discuss the differences between calling functions and methods and present the concepts of local vs. external parameter names. As you'll see, external parameter names must be used in a function call to label all of the corresponding arguments. This is another distinction between functions and methods—by default, methods require their second and subsequent arguments to be labeled with parameter names. This has to do with the similarities between how methods are named in Objective-C and Swift, which we discuss in Section 5.9. We also mention how to disable this feature when calling methods. Parameter names are always required in initializer calls.

We use a default parameter value that the compiler inserts in a function call if you do not provide the corresponding argument when the function is called. We discuss how value- and reference-type arguments are passed to methods, then demonstrate how to pass arguments by reference using the keyword `inout`. You'll write recursive functions (functions that call themselves) and nested functions.

Many of the features presented as functions in this chapter also apply to methods and initializers in the new types you create. We'll point out key differences between functions, methods and initializers.

5.2 Modules in Swift

Swift apps are written by combining new functions and types, properties, methods, classes, `structs` (Chapter 9) and `enums` (introduced in Section 5.6 and discussed in more detail in Chapter 9) with predefined capabilities in the Swift Standard Library, the Cocoa and Cocoa Touch frameworks, and other class libraries. Figure 5.1 overviews some functions, types and protocols (similar to interfaces in other languages) from the Swift Standard Library. You can locate additional information about Swift Standard Library types and functions in the *Swift Standard Library Reference* at

```
http://bit.ly/SwiftStandardLibrary
```

At the time of this writing, the *Swift Standard Library Reference* is not yet complete. There are many other built-in free functions (sometimes called global functions), but only a few are currently listed. Similarly, there are other protocols not yet included in the reference, but mentioned in other Swift documentation (e.g., `Hashable` and `DebugPrintable`).

Feature	Description
Types	
Array	This type is used to represent arrays—collections of related data items. Type `Array` provides many initializers, properties, methods and operators for performing common array manipulations. Chapter 6 discusses type `Array` in detail.
Dictionary	A `Dictionary` maps unique *keys* to *values*—for example, an employee's ID number can be mapped to one employee's information. Type `Dictionary` provides many initializers, properties, methods and operators for performing common manipulations of key–value pairs. Chapter 7 discusses type `Dictionary` in detail.
Boolean and numeric types	As you've seen, Swift provides type `Bool` and integer and floating-point numeric types (Fig. 2.6). These are the equivalent of what many programming languages refer to as the built-in, primitive or fundamental types.
String	`String`s are collections of characters. Type `String` provides many initializers, properties, methods and operators for performing common `String` manipulations. We present details of type `String` throughout the book.
Protocols	
Comparable	An item that is `Comparable` can be compared with another item of the same type using the < operator. `String`s and all of Swift's integer and floating-point numeric types are `Comparable`. We discuss how to make your own types `Comparable` in Chapter 12, Operator Overloading and Subscripts.

Fig. 5.1 | Some Swift Standard Library features. (Part 1 of 2.)

Feature	Description
Equatable	An item that is Equatable can be compared with another item of the same type using the == operator. Bools, Strings and all of Swift's numeric types are Equatable. We discuss how to make your own types Equatable in Chapter 12.
Printable	Any item that is Printable has a description property that returns a String representation of the item—similar to some languages' toString or ToString methods. Bools, Strings and all of Swift's numeric types are Printable. We discuss how to make your own types Printable in Chapter 10.
Functions	
print, println	Functions that display text representations of Printable items.
sort, sorted	Functions that sort the contents of Arrays—sort modifies the original Array's contents and sorted returns a new Array containing the sorted contents. Chapter 6 uses these functions to sort Arrays.

Fig. 5.1 | Some Swift Standard Library features, (Part 2 of 2.)

Modules

Related software components in Objective-C are grouped into frameworks (similar to namespaces or packages in other languages) so that they can be reused in Cocoa and Cocoa Touch apps. Swift's equivalent to a framework is a **module.** When you create a Swift project, Xcode places all of the project's Swift code in a module with the same name as your project. If you create a Swift-based Cocoa Framework project or Cocoa Touch Framework project, you can then reuse that framework in Cocoa and Cocoa Touch apps by importing it with the import keyword (as you did with the Foundation framework in Fig. 3.6).

Software Engineering Observation 5.1

Don't try to "reinvent the wheel." When possible, reuse capabilities of the Swift Standard Library, the Cocoa and Cocoa Touch frameworks, and other libraries. This reduces app development time, avoids introducing programming errors and contributes to good app performance.

5.3 Darwin Module—Using Predefined C Functions

Just as your Swift apps can reuse Cocoa and Cocoa Touch frameworks (written largely in Objective-C), they can also reuse C-based UNIX functions (such as arc4random_uniform in Section 5.5) and C Standard Library functions (such as the common C math functions listed in Fig. 5.2) that are built into OS X and iOS. These and many other features of UNIX and C are available via the **Darwin module,** which provides access to the C libraries in Darwin—Apple's open-source UNIX-based core on which the OS X and iOS operating systems are built. To import the Darwin module, use the following import declaration:

```
import Darwin
```

The Darwin module is imported by default into several Cocoa and Cocoa Touch frameworks—such as Foundation, AppKit and UIKit—so that various software components in those frameworks can interact with the underlying operating system.

Method	Description	Example
Throughout this table, x and y are of type Double		
abs(*x*)	absolute value of *x*	abs(23.7) is 23.7 abs(0.0) is 0.0 abs(-23.7) is 23.7
ceil(*x*)	rounds *x* to the smallest integer not less than *x*	ceil(9.2) is 10.0 ceil(-9.8) is -9.0
cos(*x*)	trigonometric cosine of *x* (*x* in radians)	cos(0.0) is 1.0
exp(*x*)	exponential method e^x	exp(1.0) is 2.71828 exp(2.0) is 7.38906
floor(*x*)	rounds *x* to the largest integer not greater than *x*	floor(9.2) is 9.0 floor(-9.8) is -10.0
log(*x*)	natural logarithm of *x* (base *e*)	log(M_E) is 1.0 log(M_E * M_E) is 2.0
max(*x*, *y*)	larger value of *x* and *y*	max(2.3, 12.7) is 12.7 max(-2.3, -12.7) is -2.3
min(*x*, *y*)	smaller value of *x* and *y*	min(2.3, 12.7) is 2.3 min(-2.3, -12.7) is -12.7
pow(*x*, *y*)	*x* raised to the power *y* (i.e., x^y)	pow(2.0, 7.0) is 128.0 pow(9.0, 0.5) is 3.0
sin(*x*)	trigonometric sine of *x* (*x* in radians)	sin(0.0) is 0.0
sqrt(*x*)	square root of *x*	sqrt(900.0) is 30.0
tan(*x*)	trigonometric tangent of *x* (*x* in radians)	tan(0.0) is 0.0

Fig. 5.2 | Some math functions from the C Standard Library.

5.4 Multiple-Parameter Function Definition

In previous chapters, you called functions, methods and initializers with varying numbers of arguments. You also defined functions and methods with only one parameter. In this section, we define and call a function with multiple parameters.

Figure 5.3 defines a function maximum (lines 4–18) that determines and returns the largest of three Double values. Lines 21–23 call maximum with the largest value (3.3) as the first, second or third argument, respectively, to show that the function always returns the largest of its three arguments.

```
1   // fig05-03: Function maximum with three Double parameters.
2
3   // returns the maximum of its three Double parameters
4   func maximum(x: Double, y: Double, z: Double) -> Double {
5       var maximumValue = x // assume x is the largest to start
6
```

Fig. 5.3 | Function maximum with three Double parameters. (Part I of 2.)

```
7        // determine whether y is greater than maximumValue
8        if y > maximumValue {
9            maximumValue = y
10       }
11
12       // determine whether z is greater than maximumValue
13       if z > maximumValue {
14           maximumValue = z
15       }
16
17       return maximumValue;
18   }
19
20   // test function maximum
21   println("Maximum of 3.3, 2.2 and 1.1 is: \(maximum(3.3, 2.2, 1.1))")
22   println("Maximum of 1.1, 3.3 and 2.2 is: \(maximum(1.1, 3.3, 2.2))")
23   println("Maximum of 2.2, 1.1 and 3.3 is: \(maximum(2.2, 1.1, 3.3))")
```

```
Maximum of 3.3, 2.2 and 1.1 is: 3.3
Maximum of 1.1, 3.3 and 2.2 is: 3.3
Maximum of 2.2, 1.1 and 3.3 is: 3.3
```

Fig. 5.3 | Function `maximum` with three `Double` parameters. (Part 2 of 2.)

Function `maximum`

Line 4 indicates that `maximum` requires three `Double` parameters (x, y and z) to accomplish its task and returns a `Double`. There must be one argument in the function call for each parameter in the function definition. Also, each argument must match the type of the corresponding parameter. Parameters are *constants* by default—if you need to modify a parameter's value in the function's body, you must place `var` before the parameter's name.

Common Programming Error 5.1
Declaring method parameters of the same type as x, y: Double *instead of* x: Double, y: Double *is a syntax error—a type is required for each parameter in the parameter list.*

Error-Prevention Tip 5.1
Making parameters constant by default ensures that you do not accidentally modify their values—you must explicitly opt for this functionality by declaring parameters as var.

Three Ways to Return Control from a Function

There are three ways to return control to the statement that calls a function. If the functions's return type is `Void` (that is, it does not return a result), control returns when the function-ending right brace is reached or when the statement

```
return
```

is executed from the functions's body. If the function returns a result, the statement

```
return expression
```

evaluates the *expression*, then returns the result (and control) to the caller (as in line 17).

Swift Function **max**

Swift provides a **max** function that can be used to compare two values of the same Comparable type—all of Swift's numeric types and Strings are Comparable. A second version of max takes a variable number of arguments and is used to compare three or more arguments of the same Comparable type. You'll create your own functions with variable-length parameter lists in Chapter 6, Arrays and an Introduction to Closures. There is no need for us to define our own maximum function, as we could have replaced the maximum calls in lines 21–23 with:

```
max(3.3, 2.2, 1.1)
max(1.1, 3.3, 2.2)
max(2.2, 1.1, 3.3)
```

5.5 Random-Number Generation

We now take a brief diversion into a popular type of programming application—simulation and game playing. In this and the next section, we develop a game-playing program with multiple functions.

The element of chance can be introduced in a program via the **arc4random_uniform** function (a C-based UNIX function from the Darwin module), which produces random unsigned 32-bit integers (UInt32; see Fig. 2.6) from 0 up to but not including an upper bound that you specify as an argument. There's also function **arc4random**, which takes no arguments and returns a random unsigned 32-bit integer in the range 0 (UInt32.min) to 4,294,967,295 (UInt32.max).

Both functions use the RC4 (also called ARCFOUR) random-number generation algorithm (http://en.wikipedia.org/wiki/RC4) and produce **nondeterministic random numbers** that cannot be predicted. To use these functions, you must import the Darwin module (Section 5.3).

> **Error-Prevention Tip 5.2**
> *Functions arc4random_uniform and arc4random cannot produce repeatable random-number sequences. If you require repeatability for testing, use the Darwin module's C function random to obtain the random values and function srandom to seed the random-number generator with the same seed during each program execution. Once you've completed testing, use either arc4random_uniform or arc4random to produce random values.*

Obtaining a Random Value with **arc4random**

The following statement generates a random UInt32 value in the range 0 (UInt32.min) to 4,294,967,295 (UInt32.max):

```
let randomValue = arc4random()
```

Obtaining a Random Value in a Specific Range with **arc4random_uniform**

The range of values produced by arc4random generally differs from the range of values required in a particular app. For example, a program that simulates the rolling of a six-sided die might require random integers in the range 1–6. For cases like this, we'll use the function arc4random_uniform.

To demonstrate arc4random_uniform, let's develop a program that simulates 20 rolls of a six-sided die and displays the value of each roll. First, we use arc4random_uniform to produce random values in the range 0–5, as follows:

```
let face = arc4random_uniform(6)
```

The argument 6 is the upper bound of the values produced and represents the number of unique values to produce (in this case six—0, 1, 2, 3, 4 and 5).

A six-sided die has the numbers 1–6 on its faces, not 0–5. So we shift the range of numbers produced by adding 1 to our previous result, as in

```
let face = 1 + arc4random_uniform(6)
```

Rolling a Six-Sided Die 20 Times

Figure 5.4 shows two sample outputs which confirm that the results of the preceding calculation are integers in the range 1–6, and that each run of the program can produce a *different* sequence of random numbers. Line 2 imports the `Darwin` module to allow the program to access function `arc4random_uniform`—the Swift Standard Library does not have its own random-number-generation capabilities. Line 5 executes 20 times in a loop to roll the die. To run the program multiple times in a playground, simply press *Enter* on a blank line.

```
1   // fig05-04: Shifted and scaled random integers
2   import Darwin  // allow program to use C function arc4random_uniform
3
4   for i in 1...20 {
5       print("\(1 + arc4random_uniform(6)) ")
6   }
```

```
3 3 3 1 1 2 1 2 4 2 2 3 6 2 5 3 4 6 6 1
```

```
6 2 5 1 3 5 2 1 6 5 4 1 6 1 3 3 1 4 3 4
```

Fig. 5.4 | Shifted and scaled random integers.

5.6 Introducing Enumerations and Tuples

One popular game of chance is the dice game known as "craps." In this section, we implement a simple version of the game and introduce Swift's enum and tuple features.

The rules of the game are straightforward:

> *You roll two dice. Each die has six faces, which contain one, two, three, four, five and six spots, respectively. After the dice have come to rest, the sum of the spots on the two upward faces is calculated. If the sum is 7 or 11 on the first throw, you win. If the sum is 2, 3 or 12 on the first throw (called "craps"), you lose (i.e., "the house" wins). If the sum is 4, 5, 6, 8, 9 or 10 on the first throw, that sum becomes your "point." To win, you must continue rolling the dice until you "make your point" (i.e., roll that same point value). You lose by rolling a 7 before making your point.*

The app in Fig. 5.5 simulates the game of craps. Lines 31–74 of the program play the game. The `rollDice` function (lines 19–23) is called to roll the two dice and compute their sum, and the `displayRoll` function (lines 26–28) is called to display the results of a roll. The four sample outputs show winning on the first roll, losing on the first roll, winning on a subsequent roll and losing on a subsequent roll, respectively.

```
 1  // fig05-05: Simulating the dice game craps
 2  import Darwin
 3
 4  // enum representing game status constants (no raw type)
 5  enum Status {
 6      case Continue, Won, Lost
 7  }
 8
 9  // enum with Int constants representing common dice totals
10  enum DiceNames: Int {
11      case SnakeEyes = 2
12      case Trey = 3
13      case Seven = 7
14      case YoLeven = 11
15      case BoxCars = 12
16  }
17
18  // function that rolls two dice and returns them and their sum as a tuple
19  func rollDice() -> (die1: Int, die2: Int, sum: Int) {
20      let die1 = Int(1 + arc4random_uniform(6)) // first die roll
21      let die2 = Int(1 + arc4random_uniform(6)) // second die roll
22      return (die1, die2, die1 + die2)
23  }
24
25  // function to display a roll of the dice
26  func displayRoll(roll: (Int, Int, Int)) {
27      println("Player rolled \(roll.0) + \(roll.1) = \(roll.2)")
28  }
29
30  // play one game of craps
31  var myPoint = 0 // point if no win or loss on first roll
32  var gameStatus = Status.Continue // can contain Continue, Won or Lost
33
34  var roll = rollDice() // first roll of the dice
35  displayRoll(roll) // display the two dice and the sum
36
37  // determine game status and point based on first roll
38  switch roll.sum {
39      // win on first roll
40      case DiceNames.Seven.rawValue, DiceNames.YoLeven.rawValue:
41          gameStatus = Status.Won
42      // lose on first roll
43      case DiceNames.SnakeEyes.rawValue, DiceNames.Trey.rawValue,
44          DiceNames.BoxCars.rawValue:
45          gameStatus = Status.Lost
46      // did not win or lose, so remember point
47      default:
48          gameStatus = Status.Continue // game is not over
49          myPoint = roll.sum // remember the point
50          println("Point is \(myPoint)")
51  }
52
```

Fig. 5.5 | Simulating the dice game craps. (Part I of 2.)

```
53   // while game is not complete
54   while gameStatus == Status.Continue
55   {
56       roll = rollDice() // first roll of the dice
57       displayRoll(roll) // display the two dice and the sum
58
59       // determine game status
60       if roll.sum == myPoint { // won by making point
61           gameStatus = Status.Won
62       } else {
63           if (roll.sum == DiceNames.Seven.rawValue) { // lost by rolling 7
64               gameStatus = Status.Lost
65           }
66       }
67   }
68
69   // display won or lost message
70   if gameStatus == Status.Won {
71       println("Player wins")
72   } else {
73       println("Player loses")
74   }
```

```
Player rolled 2 + 5 = 7
Player wins
```

```
Player rolled 2 + 1 = 3
Player loses
```

```
Player rolled 2 + 4 = 6
Point is 6
Player rolled 3 + 1 = 4
Player rolled 5 + 5 = 10
Player rolled 6 + 1 = 7
Player loses
```

```
Player rolled 4 + 6 = 10
Point is 10
Player rolled 1 + 3 = 4
Player rolled 1 + 3 = 4
Player rolled 2 + 3 = 5
Player rolled 4 + 4 = 8
Player rolled 6 + 6 = 12
Player rolled 4 + 4 = 8
Player rolled 4 + 5 = 9
Player rolled 2 + 6 = 8
Player rolled 6 + 6 = 12
Player rolled 6 + 4 = 10
Player wins
```

Fig. 5.5 | Simulating the dice game craps. (Part 2 of 2.)

The Game's Logic

The game is reasonably involved. The player may win or lose on the first roll, or may win or lose on any subsequent roll. Lines 31–74 contain the logic for one complete game of craps. Variable myPoint (line 31) stores the "point" if the player does not win or lose on the first roll. Variable gameStatus (line 32) maintains the game status. Variable roll (created at line 34 and assigned a new value at line 56) stores the most recent roll of the dice. Variable myPoint is initialized to 0 so the program can compile. If you do not initialize myPoint, the compiler issues an error, because myPoint is not assigned a value in every case of the switch statement—thus, the app could try to use myPoint before it's assigned a value. By contrast, gameStatus does not require initialization because it's assigned a value in every branch of the switch statement—thus, it's guaranteed to be initialized before it's used.

Error-Prevention Tip 5.3
Initialize every variable when it's defined.

The First Roll

Line 34 calls function rollDice, which picks two random values from 1 to 6 and returns both values and their sum. Line 35 calls function displayRoll to display the value of the first die, the value of the second die and the sum of the dice. We explain the details of rollDice's return value and displayRoll's argument in Sections 5.6.2– and 5.6.3, respectively. Next, the program enters the switch statement at lines 38–51, which uses the sum of the dice to determine whether the game has been won or lost, or whether it should continue with another roll.

Additional Rolls of the Dice

If we're still trying to "make our point" (i.e., the game is continuing from a prior roll), the loop in lines 54–67 executes. Line 56 rolls the dice again. Lines 60–66 determine whether the game was won or lost on the most recent roll—if not, the game continues. When the game completes, lines 70—74 display a message indicating whether the player won or lost, and the app terminates.

5.6.1 Introducing Enumeration (enum) Types

In this section, we introduce basic enumeration features—more details are presented in Chapter 9, Structures, Enumerations and Nested Types.

Status Enumeration

The Status type (lines 5–7) is an enumeration that declares a set of constants represented by identifiers. An enumeration is introduced by the keyword enum and a type name (in this case, Status). As with a class, braces ({ and }) delimit the enum's body. Inside the braces is a case containing a comma-separated list of enumeration constants. The enum constant names must be unique. Unlike enums in other C-based programming languages, a Swift enum's constants do not have values by default—the constants themselves are the values. Sometimes it's useful for each constant to have a so-called raw value, as in the DiceNames enum (lines 10–16) that we discuss momentarily.

Variables and constants of type Status can be assigned only constants defined in the Status enum. When the game is won, the app sets variable gameStatus to Status.Won (lines 41 and 61). When the game is lost, the app sets gameStatus to Status.Lost (lines 45 and 64). Otherwise, the app sets gameStatus to Status.Continue (line 48) to indicate that the dice must be rolled again. If a variable has an enum type, you can assign enum constants to the variable using the shorthand notation:

variableName = *.EnumConstantName*

Good Programming Practice 5.1
enum constant names should begin with a capital letter and use camel-case naming.

DiceNames Enumeration

The sums of the dice that would result in a win or loss on the first roll are declared in the DiceNames enumeration in lines 10–16. These are used in the cases of the switch statement (lines 38–51). The identifier names use casino parlance—such as snake eyes (2) and box cars (12)—for these sums. In DiceNames we explicitly assign a value to each constant's name. When an enum's constants require values (known as **raw values**), you must specify the enum's **raw type**—that is, the type used to represent each constant's value. Line 10 indicates that DiceNames's raw type is Int, so each constant's type is also Int. The raw type can be any of Swift's numeric types, type String or type Character.

Constants that are assigned explicit values are typically defined in a separate cases for readability (as in lines 11–15), but this is not required. We could have written the Dice-Names enumeration as:

```
enum DiceNames: Int {
    case SnakeEyes = 2, Trey = 3, Seven = 7, YoLeven = 11,
        BoxCars = 12
}
```

If an enum type's constants represent sequential integer values, they can be defined as a comma-separated list in one case, as in:

```
enum Months: Int {
    case January = 1, February, March, April, May, June, July,
        August, September, October, November, December
}
```

In Months, each subsequent constant after January has a value one higher than the value of the previous constant, so February is 2, March is 3, etc. So, we could have defined the DiceNames constants SnakeEyes and Trey in one case as:

```
case SnakeEyes = 2, Trey
```

The raw values of an enum's constants must be unique. In an enum with one of the integer numeric types, if the first constant is unassigned, the compiler gives it the value 0.

Good Programming Practice 5.2
Using enumeration constants (like Months.January, Months.February, etc.) rather than literal integer values (such as 1, 2, etc.) makes code easier to read and maintain.

5.6.2 Tuples and Multiple Function Return Values

In the rules of the game, the player must roll two dice on the first roll and must do the same on all subsequent rolls. Function rollDice (lines 19–23) rolls the dice and computes their sum. Function rollDice is declared once, but it's called from two places (lines 34 and 56). The function takes no arguments. Each time it's called, rollDice returns *three values* (the two die values and the sum of the dice) as a **tuple**—an arbitrary collection of values that can be of the same or different types. In function rollDice's return type

```
(die1: Int, die2: Int, sum: Int)
```

die1, die2 and sum are names that can be used to access the returned tuple's elements.

> **Good Programming Practice 5.3**
> *You're not required to specify names for each element of a tuple, but doing so makes the code more readable.*

The sum of the dice can be calculated using the values of the tuple elements die1 and die2. We chose to include sum in the tuple because there are multiple locations in the program where we use the sum of the dice. Rather than recalculating the sum each time, we calculate it once in rollDice, return it as part of the tuple, then simply use the tuple's sum element as necessary in the rest of the code.

Composing a Tuple
To return a tuple containing multiple values from a function, you **compose** it by wrapping the values in parentheses, as in the return statement (line 22).

Accessing a Tuple's Elements
When a tuple specifies names for its elements, you can access them by name using the dot (.) syntax. Line 34 assigns the tuple returned by rollDice to the variable roll, which is inferred to have the tuple type (Int, Int, Int). The switch statement's control expression (line 38) uses roll.sum to get the sum of the dice from the returned tuple.

Decomposing a Tuple
You can also **decompose** a tuple into individual variables or constants. For example, the statement

```
let (die1, die2, sum) = rollDice()
```

assigns the three values in the tuple to the constants die1, die2 and sum, respectively. When decomposing a tuple, if you need only some of the values, you can ignore individual values with the underscore character (_), as in:

```
let (_, _, sum) = rollDice()
```

Explicit Casts Are Required for Numeric Conversions
Unlike many other programming languages, Swift does *not* allow implicit conversions between numeric types. To prevent a compilation error when you use a value of one numeric type where a different numeric type is expected, the compiler requires you to cast the value to the required type to force the conversion. This enables you to "take control" from the compiler. You essentially say, "I know this conversion might lose information, but for my purposes here, that's fine."

Function `rollDice` returns a tuple containing `Int` values; however, the random numbers returned by function `arc4random_uniform` are of type `UInt32`. To convert these to type `Int`, you must use an `Int` cast as shown in line 20:

```
let die1 = Int(1 + arc4random_uniform(6)) // first die roll
```

The cast `Int(1 + arc4random_uniform(6))` creates a *temporary* `Int` copy of the argument in parentheses.

Error-Prevention Tip 5.4
Each numeric type represents a different range of values. Disallowing implicit conversions—thus forcing you to use explicit casts for numeric conversions—prevents unintentional conversions between types. This is another Swift feature that eliminates errors.

Common Programming Error 5.2
Converting a numeric-type value to a value of another numeric type may change the value. For example, converting a `Double` value to an `Int` value may introduce truncation errors (loss of the fractional part) in the result.

5.6.3 Tuples as Function Arguments

After each call to `rollDice`, the program calls function `displayRoll` (lines 35 and 57) to display the two die values and the sum of the dice. The function (lines 26–28) receives one parameter (roll) which has the tuple type `(Int, Int, Int)`. In this case, we did not specify names for the elements in the tuple, so that we could show accessing a tuple's members using indices and dot syntax, as in line 27. The first tuple element has index 0, so `roll.0` evaluates to the first die's value, `roll.1` evaluates to the second die's value and `roll.2` evaluates to their sum.

5.6.4 Accessing the Raw Value of an enum Constant

The `switch` statement at lines 38–51 performs its tasks based on the sum of the dice. Swift does not provide implicit conversions between `enum` constants and numeric types. However, each `enum` constant has a `rawValue` property that returns the constant's raw value. Lines 40, 43 and 44 compare the `Int` sum of the dice to the raw `Int` values of several `DiceNames` constants to determine whether the game was won or lost on the first roll. We use the raw `enum` constant values in this case because there are several sums (4, 5, 6, 8, 9 and 10) that don't correspond to the `DiceName` `enum` constants.

Converting a Value to an enum Constant
You can use an `enum`'s initializer to get the `enum` constant that corresponds to a raw value. For example, using the `Months` enum discussed in Section 5.6.1, the expression

```
Months(rawValue: 2)
```

returns the enum constant `Months.February`. In a program that receives a month as a value in the range 1–12, you could use the `Months` enum's initializer to convert those values to the corresponding `Months` enum constants for use in a `switch`'s cases. Because the argument could be invalid, the actual value returned by the initializer is a `Months?`—an optional value of type `Months`. We discuss this in more depth in Section 9.3.3.

5.7 Scope of Declarations

You've seen declarations of Swift entities, such as classes, methods, properties, variables and parameters. Declarations introduce names that can be used to refer to such Swift entities. The **scope** of a declaration is the portion of the code that can refer to the declared entity by its unqualified name. Such an entity is said to be "in scope" for that portion of the app. This section introduces several important scope issues. The basic scope rules are:

1. The scope of a parameter is the body of the method in which the declaration appears.

2. The scope of a local variable or constant is from the point at which it's defined to the closing right brace (}) of the block containing the definition.

3. The scope of a local variable that appears in the initialization section of a for statement's header is the body of that for statement and the other expressions in the header.

4. The scope of a local variable that receives each value in a for...in statement is the body of that for...in statement.

5. The scope of a method or property of a class is the entire body of the class.

6. A type, function, variable or constant defined outside any other language element has global scope from its point of definition to the end of the file in which the type, function, variable or constant is defined. Types and functions also have module scope—by default, they can be used from other files in the same module or in other apps that import that module, unless they're declared private.

Any block may contain variable declarations. If a local variable, constant or parameter in a method has the same name as a property of a class, the property is hidden until the block terminates. In Chapter 8, we discuss how to access hidden properties via the keyword self. The app in Fig. 5.6 demonstrates the scopes for a global variable, a property of a class and local variables in methods.

```
1   // fig05-06: Demonstrating scopes
2   var x = 5 // global variable x
3
4   class Scope {
5       var x = 1 // property hides global variable x in class Scope
6
7       // create and initialize local variable x during each call
8       func useLocalVariable()
9       {
10          var x = 25 // initialized each time useLocalVariable is called
11
12          println("\nlocal x on entering useLocalVariable is \(x)")
13          ++x // modifies this method's local variable x
14          println("local x before exiting useLocalVariable is \(x)")
15      }
16
```

Fig. 5.6 | Demonstrating scopes. (Part 1 of 2.)

```
17        // modify class Scope's property x during each call
18        func useProperty() {
19            println("\nproperty x on entering useProperty is \(x)")
20            x *= 10 // modifies class Scope's property x
21            println("property x before exiting useProperty is \(x)")
22        }
23    }
24
25    var scope = Scope() // create a Scope object
26
27    println("global variable x when program begins execution is \(x)")
28
29    scope.useLocalVariable()
30    scope.useProperty()
31    scope.useLocalVariable()
32    scope.useProperty()
33
34    println("\nglobal variable x before program terminates is \(x)")
```

```
global variable x when program begins execution is 5

local x on entering useLocalVariable is 25
local x before exiting useLocalVariable is 26

property x on entering useProperty is 1
property x before exiting useProperty is 10

local x on entering useLocalVariable is 25
local x before exiting useLocalVariable is 26

property x on entering useProperty is 10
property x before exiting useProperty is 100

global variable x before program terminates is 5
```

Fig. 5.6 | Demonstrating scopes. (Part 2 of 2.)

Line 2 defines and initializes the global variable x to 5. This variable is hidden in any block or method that declares local variable named x and in any class that defines a property named x. Class Scope (lines 4–23) defines a property x with the value 1 (line 5). We defined the class after the global variable x at line 2 to show that the class's property x hides the global variable.

Line 25 defines an object of class Scope named scope. Line 27 outputs the value of global variable x (whose value is 5). Next, lines 29–32 call Scope methods useLocalVariable (lines 8–15) and useProperty (lines 18–22) that each take no arguments and do not return results. We call each method twice. Method useLocalVariable declares local variable x (line 10). When useLocalVariable is first called (line 29), it creates local variable x and initializes it to 25 (line 10), outputs the value of x (line 12), increments x (line 13) and outputs the value of x again (line 14). When useLocalVariable is called a second time (line 31), it re-creates local variable x and reinitializes it to 25, so the output of each useLocalVariable call is identical.

Method useProperty does not declare any local variables. Therefore, when it refers to x, class Scope's property x (line 5) is used. When method useProperty is first called (line 30), it outputs the value (1) or property x (line 19), multiplies the property x by 10 (line 20) and outputs the value (10) of property x again (line 21) before returning. The next time method useProperty is called (line 32), the property has its modified value, 10, so the method outputs 10, then 100. The app outputs the value of global variable x again (line 34) to show that none of the method calls modified the global variable x, because the methods all referred to variables or properties named x in other scopes.

5.8 Function and Method Overloading

You can define functions of the same name, as long as they have different sets of parameters (determined by the number, types and order of the parameters). This is called **function overloading** and can be used with a type's methods and initializers as well. When an overloaded function is called, the Swift compiler selects the appropriate function by examining the number, types and order of the arguments in the call. Function overloading is commonly used to create several functions with the *same name* that perform the same or similar tasks, but on *different types* or *different numbers of arguments*. For example, Swift function max is overloaded with two versions—one that returns the maximum of two values and one that returns the maximum of three or more values. Our next example demonstrates declaring and invoking overloaded functions. You'll see examples of overloaded initializers in Chapter 8, Classes: A Deeper Look and Extensions.

Declaring Overloaded Functions
In Fig. 5.7, we define overloaded versions of function square—one that calculates the square of an Int (and returns an Int) and one that calculates the square of a Double (and returns a Double). Although these functions have the same name and similar parameter lists and bodies, you can think of them simply as *different* methods. It may help to think of the functions names as "square of Int" and "square of Double," respectively.

```
 1   // fig05-07: Overloaded function definitions
 2
 3   // square function with Int argument
 4   func square(value: Int) -> Int
 5   {
 6       println("Called square with Int argument: \(value)")
 7       return value * value
 8   }
 9
10   // square function with Double argument
11   func square(value: Double) -> Double
12   {
13       println("Called square with Double argument: \(value)")
14       return value * value
15   }
16
17   // test overloaded square functions
18   println("Square of Int 7 is \(square(7))\n")
19   println("Square of Double 7.5 is \(square(7.5))")
```

Fig. 5.7 | Overloaded function definitions. (Part 1 of 2.)

```
Called square with Int argument: 7
Square of Int 7 is 49

Called square with Double argument: 7.5
Square of Double 7.5 is 56.25
```

Fig. 5.7 | Overloaded function definitions. (Part 2 of 2.)

Line 18 invokes method `square` with the argument 7. Literal integer values are treated as type `Int`, so the method call in line 18 invokes the version of `square` at lines 4–8 that specifies an `Int` parameter. Similarly, line 19 invokes `square` with the argument `7.5`. Literal floating-point values are treated as type `Double`, so the method call in line 19 invokes the version of `square` at lines 11–15 that specifies a `Double` parameter. Each function first outputs a line of text to prove that the proper function was called in each case.

The overloaded functions in Fig. 5.7 perform the same calculation, but with two different types. Swift's generics feature provides a mechanism for writing a single "generic function" that can perform the same tasks as an entire set of overloaded functions. We discuss generic functions in Chapter 11, Generics.

Distinguishing Between Overloaded Functions

The compiler distinguishes overloaded functions by their **signature**—a combination of the function's name and the number, types and order of its parameters. The signature also includes the way those parameters are passed, which can be modified by the `inout` keyword (discussed in Section 5.11). If the compiler looked only at method names during compilation, the code in Fig. 5.7 would be *ambiguous*—the compiler would not know how to distinguish between the `square` functions. Internally, the compiler uses signatures to determine whether functions are unique, whether a class's methods are unique and whether a class's initializers are unique.

For example, in Fig. 5.7, the compiler will use the function signatures to distinguish between the "`square` of `Int`" function (the `square` function that specifies an `Int` parameter) and the "`square` of `Double`" function (the `square` function that specifies a `Double` parameter). If a function `someFunction`'s declaration begins as

```
func someFunction(a: Int, b: Double)
```

then that function will have a different signature than the function declared as

```
func someFunction(a: Double, b: Int)
```

The order of the parameter types is important—the compiler considers the preceding two functions to be distinct.

Return Types of Overloaded Functions

In discussing the logical names of functions used by the compiler, we did not mention the return types of the functions. This is because function calls cannot be distinguished by return type. Overloaded functions can have the *same* or *different* return types if the functions have *different* parameter lists. Also, overloaded functions need not have the same number of parameters.

5.9 External Parameter Names

By default, the parameter names you specify in a function definition are local to that function—they're used only in the body of that function to access the function's argument values. You can also define external parameter names that the caller is required to use when a function is called—as is the case for all the arguments to an initializer and any arguments after the first argument in a method call. This can help make the meaning of each argument clear to the programmer calling the function.

For each parameter, you can specify both an external name and a local name by placing the external name before the local name as in:

> *externalName localName*: *type*

or you can specify that the local parameter name should also be used as the external parameter name by placing a # before the local parameter name, as we demonstrate in Fig. 5.8 (line 4). The function power (lines 4–12) calculates the value of its base argument raised to its exponent argument. The two calls to power (lines 15 and 16) each specify the parameter name before each argument. Once you expose an external parameter name, you must label the corresponding argument in a function call with a parameter name and a colon (:); otherwise, a compilation error occurs.

```
1   // fig05-08: External parameter names
2
3   // use iteration to calculate power of base raised to the exponent
4   func power(#base: Int, #exponent: Int) -> Int {
5       var result = 1;
6
7       for i in 1...exponent {
8           result *= base
9       }
10
11      return result
12  }
13
14  // call power with and without default parameter values
15  println("power(base: 10, exponent: 2) = \(power(base: 10, exponent: 2))")
16  println("power(base: 2, exponent: 10) = \(power(base:2, exponent: 10))")
```

```
power(base: 10, exponent: 2) = 100
power(base: 2, exponent: 10) = 1024
```

Fig. 5.8 | External parameter names.

Changing the Default External Parameter Names for an Initializer or Method

By default, the names of an initializer's parameters and the names of a method's parameters for every parameter after the first are used as their external names. You can customize a method's or initializer's external parameter names by specifying your own, using the same syntax we discussed for functions earlier in this section.

Why an External Name Is Not Required for a Method's First Argument
In Objective-C, method calls read like sentences. The method name refers to the first parameter, and each subsequent parameter has a name that's specified as part of the method call. In addition, method and parameter names often include prepositions to help make function calls read like sentences.

Apple wants Swift programmers to use similar naming conventions in their methods. Because the method name should refer to the first parameter, Swift provides only a local parameter name for the first method parameter, then provides local and external parameter names for all subsequent parameters. Using this naming convention, we could reimplement the power function as

```
func raiseBase(base: Int, #toExponent: Int) -> Int
```

In this case, we'd call the function as:

```
raiseBase(10, toExponent: 2)
```

which reads like the sentence, "Raise the base 10 to the exponent 2."

Requiring an External Parameter Name for a Method's First Argument
You can require a method's caller to provide an external parameter name for the method's first argument. To do so, simply precede the parameter name with # to use the local parameter name as the external parameter name or specify an external parameter name.

Passing Method Arguments Without Parameter Names
You can allow a method to be called without labeling its arguments by using an underscore (_) as each parameter's external name.

5.10 Default Parameter Values

Methods can have **default parameters** that allow the caller to vary the number of arguments to pass. A default parameter specifies a **default value** that's assigned to the parameter if the corresponding argument is omitted.

You can create functions with one or more default parameters. *All default parameters must be placed to the right of the function's nonoptional parameters*—that is, at the end of the parameter list. Each default parameter must specify a default value by using an equal (=) sign followed by the value.

When a parameter has a default value, the caller can optionally pass that particular argument. For example, the function

```
func power(base: Int, exponent: Int = 2) -> Int
```

specifies a default second parameter. Any call to power must pass at least an argument for the parameter base, or a compilation error occurs. Optionally, a second argument (for the exponent parameter) can be passed to power. Consider the following calls to power:

```
power() // compilation error--first argument is required
power(10) // calls power with 2 as the second argument
power(10, exponent: 3) // explicitly specifying both arguments
```

The first call generates a compilation error because this function requires a minimum of one argument. The second call is valid because the one required argument (10) is being passed explicitly—the optional exponent is not specified in the method call, so 2 is passed by default. The last call is also valid—10 is passed as the required argument and 3 is passed as the optional argument. A function's default parameter names are automatically external parameter names—when you provide an argument for a default parameter, you *must* specify the default parameter's name with that argument in the function call.

Figure 5.9 demonstrates a default parameter. The program reimplements the power function of Fig. 5.8 without external parameter names and with a default value for its second parameter. Lines 15–16 call function power. Line 15 calls it without the second argument. In this case, the compiler provides the second argument, 2, using the default value specified in line 4, which is not visible to you in the call. Notice that the call to power at line 16 requires the parameter name for the second argument.

```
 1   // fig05-09: Default parameter values
 2
 3   // use iteration to calculate power of base raised to the exponent
 4   func power(base: Int, exponent: Int = 2) -> Int {
 5       var result = 1;
 6
 7       for i in 1...exponent {
 8           result *= base
 9       }
10
11       return result
12   }
13
14   // call power with and without default parameter values
15   println("power(10) = \(power(10))")
16   println("power(2, exponent: 10) = \(power(2, exponent: 10))")
```

```
power(10) = 100
power(2, exponent: 10) = 1024
```

Fig. 5.9 | Default parameter values.

5.11 Passing Arguments by Value or by Reference

Swift allows you to pass arguments to functions by value or by reference. When an argument is passed by *value* (the default for value types in Swift), a *copy* of its value is made and passed to the called function. Changes to the copy do *not* affect the original variable's value in the caller. This prevents the accidental side effects that so greatly hinder the development of correct and reliable software systems. Each argument that's been passed in the programs in this chapter so far has been passed by value. When an argument is passed by *reference*, the caller gives the function the ability to access and modify the caller's original variable.

To pass an object of a class type by reference into a function, simply provide as an argument in the function call the variable that refers to the object. Then, in the function body, reference the object using the parameter name. The parameter refers to the original object in memory, so the called function can access the original object directly.

We've considered value types and reference types. A major difference between them is that value-type variables store *values*, so specifying a value-type variable in a function call passes a *copy* of that value to the method. Reference-type variables store *references to objects*, so specifying a reference-type variable as an argument passes the function a *copy of the reference* that refers to the object. Even though the reference itself is passed by value, the function can still use the reference it receives to interact with—and possibly modify—the original object. Similarly, when returning information from a function via a `return` statement, the function returns a *copy* of the value stored in a value-type variable or a copy of the reference stored in a reference-type variable. When a reference is returned, the caller can use that reference to interact with the returned reference-type object.

inout Parameters

What if you would like to pass a variable by reference so the called function can modify the variable's value in the *caller*? To do this, Swift provides keyword `inout`. Applying `inout` to a parameter declaration allows you to pass a variable to a function *by reference*—the called function will be able to modify the original variable in the caller. It's a compilation error to pass a constant to an `inout` parameter. A function can use multiple `inout` parameters as another way to "return" multiple values to a caller. You can also pass a reference-type variable by reference, which allows you to modify it so that it refers to a *new* object.

Demonstrating an inout Parameter

The app in Fig. 5.10 uses the `inout` keyword to allow a function to modify its `Int` argument. Function `square` (lines 4–6) multiplies its parameter `value` by itself and assigns the result to `value`. The `Int` parameter is preceded with `inout`, which indicates that the argument passed to this method must be an `Int` and that it will be passed by reference. Because the argument is passed by reference, the assignment at line 5 modifies the original argument's value in the caller.

```
 1   // fig05-10: Pass-by-reference with inout parameters
 2
 3   // square function that modifies its argument in the caller
 4   func square(inout value: Int) {
 5      value *= value // squares value of caller's variable
 6   }
 7
 8   // test inout parameter
 9   var x = 5
10   println("Original value of x is \(x)")
11   square(&x)
12   println("Value of x after calling square(&x) is \(x)")
```

```
Original value of x is 5
Value of x after calling square(&x) is 25
```

Fig. 5.10 | Pass-by-reference with inout parameters.

Passing an Argument by Reference

Line 9 initializes variable x to 5. Line 10 displays x's original value. When you pass a variable to a method with a reference parameter, you must precede the argument with an & (line 11)—similar to a pointer in languages like Objective-C, C and C++. After line 11 squares x's value, line 12 displays the new value. Notice that x is now 25.

Software Engineering Observation 5.2

By default, value types are passed by value. Objects of reference types are not passed to methods; rather, references to objects are passed to methods. The references themselves are passed by value. When a method receives a reference to an object, the method can manipulate the object directly, but the reference value cannot be changed to refer to a new object.

5.12 Recursion

Swift supports recursion. A **recursive function** calls itself, either *directly* or *indirectly through another function.*

Recursive Factorial Calculations

Figure 5.11 uses recursion to calculate and display the factorials of the integers from 0 to 10. The recursive function factorial (lines 4–11) first tests to determine whether a terminating condition (line 6) is true. If number is less than or equal to 1 (the base case), factorial returns 1, no further recursion is necessary and the function returns. If number is greater than 1, line 9 expresses the problem as the product of number and a recursive call to factorial evaluating the factorial of number - 1, which is a slightly simpler problem than the original calculation, factorial(number).

```
 1   // fig05-12: Recursive factorial function
 2
 3   // recursive factorial function
 4   func factorial(number: Int64) -> Int64 {
 5       // base case
 6       if number <= 1 {
 7           return 1
 8       } else { // recursion step
 9           return number * factorial(number - 1)
10       }
11   }
12
13   // calculate the factorials of 0 through 10
14   for counter in 0...10 {
15       println("\(counter)! = \(factorial(Int64(counter)))")
16   }
```

```
0! = 1
1! = 1
2! = 2
```

Fig. 5.11 | Recursive factorial function. (Part I of 2.)

```
3! = 6
4! = 24
5! = 120
6! = 720
7! = 5040
8! = 40320
9! = 362880
10! = 3628800
```

Fig. 5.11 | Recursive `factorial` function. (Part 2 of 2.)

Function `factorial` receives a parameter of type `Int64` and returns a result of type `Int64`. As you can see in Fig. 5.11, factorial values become large quickly. We chose `Int64` (which can represent relatively large integers) so that the app could calculate factorials up to 20!. Unfortunately, the function produces large values so quickly that 21! exceeds the maximum value that can be stored in an `Int64` variable, causing an overflow. Due to the restrictions on the integral types, variables of type `Float` or `Double` might ultimately be needed to calculate factorials of larger numbers.

A strength of object-oriented programming languages like Swift is that they can be extended with new types to meet your applications' needs. For example, you could create a type (e.g., `HugeInt`) that supports arbitrarily large integers for use in large-number factorial calculations.

Common Programming Error 5.3

Either omitting the base case or writing the recursion step incorrectly so that it does not converge on the base case will cause infinite recursion, eventually exhausting memory. This error is analogous to the problem of an infinite loop in an iterative (nonrecursive) solution.

5.13 Nested Functions

You can nest function definitions in other function definitions. This can be useful for organizing complex functions. Rather than defining at global scope a utility (helper) function that's called by only one other function, you can nest the utility function's definition in the scope of the function that uses it. This hides it from the rest of your code. For example, an array-sorting function could define a nested `swap` function for swapping elements into sorted order.

If necessary, an enclosing function can return a nested function so that it can be called from other scopes—for example, you could define a function that returns a nested function based on a value passed to the enclosing function (as we do in this section's example). A nested function also has access to the local variables and constants in its enclosing function's scope, including the enclosing function's parameters.

Figure 5.12 contains a mechanical nested-functions example. Function `sortOrder` (lines 4–16), based on the `Bool` parameter `increasingOrder`'s value, returns either the nested function `ascending` (defined at lines 6–8) or the nested function `descending` (defined at lines 11–13). To make the purpose of `sortOrder`'s argument clear, we specified that its parameter name (`increasingOrder`) should also be its external parameter name—thus, each call to `sortOrder` (lines 19 and 28) labels its argument with `increasingOrder`.

```
 1    // fig05-12: Mechanical example of nested functions
 2
 3    // return a function that determines the ordering of two Ints
 4    func sortOrder(#increasingOrder: Bool) -> (Int, Int) -> Bool {
 5        // return true if x and y are in ascending order
 6        func ascending(x: Int, y: Int) -> Bool {
 7            return x < y
 8        }
 9
10        // return true if x and y are in descending order
11        func descending(x: Int, y: Int) -> Bool {
12            return x > y
13        }
14
15        return (increasingOrder ? ascending : descending)
16    }
17
18    // get function for comparing Ints to see if they're in ascending order
19    var order = sortOrder(increasingOrder: true)
20
21    if order(7, 5) {
22        println("7 and 5 are in ascending order")
23    } else {
24        println("7 and 5 are not in ascending order")
25    }
26
27    // get function for comparing Ints to see if they're in descending order
28    order = sortOrder(increasingOrder: false)
29
30    if order(7, 5) {
31        println("7 and 5 are in descending order")
32    } else {
33        println("7 and 5 are not in descending order")
34    }
```

```
7 and 5 are not in ascending order
7 and 5 are in descending order
```

Fig. 5.12 | Mechanical example of nested functions.

Every Function Has a Type and Can Be Treated as Data

Each function you define has a type that's determined by the types of its parameters and by its return type. The return type of function sortOrder is specified as

```
(Int, Int) -> Bool
```

A function type consists of parentheses containing the parameter types, followed by -> and the return type. The preceding type indicates that the value returned by sortOrder is a function type for a function that receives two Int parameters and returns a Bool. Functions ascending and descending meet these requirements.

Because every function has a type, you can assign functions to variables, pass them to functions and methods, and return them from functions and methods. We'll discuss functions as data in more detail in Section 6.7.

Assigning a Function to a Variable and Using the Variable to Call the Function
Line 19 calls function sortOrder with the argument true to indicate that sortOrder
should return the function that determines whether two Ints are in ascending order. The
returned function is assigned to the variable order, which is inferred to have the type

```
(Int, Int) -> Bool
```

Once you've assigned a function to a variable, you can use the variable to call the function,
as shown in line 21. Line 28 calls sortOrder with the argument false to get the function
that determines whether two Ints are in descending order, then line 30 calls that function.

5.14 Wrap-Up

In this chapter, we continued our discussion of functions and methods. We discussed that
Swift automatically creates modules for packaging reusable software components. We introduced Darwin—Apple's UNIX-based core of OS X and iOS—and imported the Darwin module so we could use the random-number generator.

We used enum types to create sets of named constants with and without values for the
constants. You returned multiple values from a function via a tuple, passed a tuple to a
function and accessed a tuple's elements via both names and indices.

We discussed the scope of identifiers. We used overloading to define multiple functions with the same name that performed similar tasks but with different types and/or different numbers of parameters.

We discussed differences in how functions and methods are called, and we presented
the concepts of local parameter names vs. external parameter names. You saw that, when
external parameter names are provided in a function definition, they must be used in the
function call to label the corresponding arguments. You used # to expose a local parameter
name as the external parameter name. We also showed how to disable this feature in
methods—by placing an underscore (_) before the parameter's name—so that parameter
names are not required in a method call.

You specified a default parameter value and saw that the compiler supplied that value
in a function call when you did not explicitly provide an argument for that parameter.

We discussed how value-type and reference-type arguments are passed to methods
and demonstrated how to pass arguments by reference by declaring the parameter as inout
and providing an ampersand (&) before the corresponding argument in a function call. We
demonstrated that Swift supports recursive functions and nested functions.

In Chapter 6, you'll use Arrays to maintain lists and tables of data. You'll also create
functions with variable-length argument lists. We'll continue our discussion of functions
in Chapter 6 which also presents closures—anonymous functions that are typically
defined in the scope of a function or method and commonly passed as arguments to other
functions or methods. As you'll see, a function is a closure with a name. Swift's Array type
provides methods filter, map and reduce that receive closures as arguments—which
enable you to express complex operations in a more concise and elegant manner than with
full function definitions. We'll present additional method and initializer concepts in
Chapters 8–10.

6

Arrays and an Introduction to Closures

Objectives

In this chapter you'll:

- Use Arrays to store and retrieve data.
- Declare, initialize and refer to individual elements of Arrays.
- Iterate through Arrays with the for...in and for loops.
- Use Array methods and the += operator to add elements to Arrays.
- Use Array methods to remove elements from Arrays.
- Sort Arrays with methods sort and sorted.
- Use closures (anonymous functions) as shorthand notation for defining functions and passing them to other functions.
- Use Array methods filter, map and reduce to select elements matching specified criteria, map elements to new values and combine elements into a single value.
- Use optionals when a function might sometimes, but not always, return a value.
- Pass Arrays to functions by value and by reference.
- Define and manipulate multidimensional Arrays.

6.1 Introduction

`Arrays` are data structures consisting of related data items of the same type. Arrays make it convenient to process related groups of values.

In this chapter, you'll see various ways to create and initialize `Arrays`, then several ways to iterate over an `Array`'s elements using the `for...in` and `for` loops. Next, we'll demonstrate the `Array` type's methods and the `+=` operator for adding elements to `Arrays`, methods for inserting elements into `Arrays` and methods for removing elements from `Arrays`. As you'll see, variable `Arrays` are dynamically resizable.

In Section 4.10, you saw how to iterate over ranges with the closed-range and half-open range operators. You can also use those operators in `Array` subscript expressions to manipulate subsets of an `Array`'s elements by selecting, replacing and deleting subsets.

We'll show how to sort `Array` elements with `Array` methods `sort` and `sorted`. Both methods require as an argument a function that's used to compare two `Array` elements to specify their sort order. In this example, we'll introduce Swift's *anonymous function* capability known as *closures*. We'll start by defining a comparison function, then show several progressively shorter versions of that same function using closure syntax. As you'll see, functions have types and closures can be used anywhere a function type is expected. We'll use closures with `Array` methods `filter`, `map` and `reduce`, which enable you to perform Array manipulations without specifying *how* to iterate over an `Array`'s elements—a technique known as *internal iteration*, because the methods hide the iteration details from you, significantly reducing the chance of coding errors and increasing the parallelizability of the code for better performance on today's multi-core architectures.

    We use Arrays to simulate shuffling and dealing playing cards for card-game apps. We demonstrate pass-by-value and pass-by-reference with Arrays and individual Array elements. Next, we discuss multi-dimensional arrays. Finally, we show how to use *variadic parameters* to create functions with variable-length argument lists.

6.2 Arrays

An Array is a group of elements containing values that all have the same type. Arrays are value types, so they're copied when assigned, passed to functions or returned from functions. An Array's elements can be either value types or reference types. Every element of a value-type Array contains a value of the Array's declared element type. Similarly, every element of a reference type Array is a reference to an object of the Array's declared element type. For example, every element of an Int Array is an Int value, and every element of an Array of a class type is a reference to an object of that class.

Logical Array Representation

Figure 6.1 shows a logical representation of a String Array called suits. This Array contains four elements, which you can determine via the read-only **count property**. You refer to an element with the Array name followed by square brackets ([]) containing the element's nonnegative integer index (subscript). An Array's first element has index zero, so you use zero-based counting when iterating over an Array's elements—the elements of Array suit are suit[0], suit[1], suit[2] and suit[3]. The highest index in this Array is 3, which is one less than suit.count.

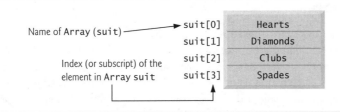

Fig. 6.1 | Four-element Array of Strings named suit.

An Array Can Be a Variable or a Constant

An Array can be defined as a variable (with var) or a constant (with let). You may change an Array's elements, add elements to it or remove elements from it *only* if the Array is defined as a variable.

Array Type Annotations

A program can declare Arrays of any type. Often the type can be inferred by the compiler based on the Array's initializer (as you'll see in Section 6.3), but you also can specify an Array's type with a type annotation. For example,

```
var integers: Array<Int>
```

defines the variable integers as type Array<Int>—an "Array of Int." The type in angle brackets (< and >) is the Array's *element type*. Arrays are *type safe*—only values of the element type may be placed into the Array; values of other types result in compilation errors. Similarly, when you get a value from an Array, the value is guaranteed to be of the Array's element type. Types like Array that specify the types they store or manipulate are **generic types**. We discuss creating your own generic types and generic functions in Chapter 11, Generics.

*Shorthand **Array** Type Annotations*
Swift also provides a shorthand for Array type annotations. For example, you can declare the Array integers as

```
var integers: [Int]
```

with the element type specified in square brackets, which is the preferred idiom. For the rest of this book, we use the shorthand syntax for Array type annotations.

6.3 Creating and Initializing Arrays

Figure 6.2 demonstrates creating an initializing Arrays. For each Array, we also explicitly use the Array type's **description** property (similar to method toString in Java and ToString in C#) to display the Array's String representation—square brackets containing the Array's elements in a comma-separated list. The description property also can be used implicitly for any Printable type (discussed in Section 10.8) by print, println or String interpolation. Each Array in this example is *immutable* (declared as a constant with let), because we do not modify any of the Arrays' elements after they're created.

Error-Prevention Tip 6.1
If an Array's elements do not need to change after the Array is created, then make it constant to prevent accidental modification of its elements.

Performance Tip 6.1
The compiler can perform various optimizations with immutable Arrays, such as preventing unnecessary copy operations.

```
1   // fig06-02.playground: Creating and initializing Arrays
2
3   // create and display an empty Array<Int>
4   let integers1 = [Int]()
5   println("integers1: \(integers1.description)")
6
7   // create and display an Array<Bool> with all elements set to true
8   let booleans = [Bool](count: 5, repeatedValue: true)
9   println("booleans: \(booleans.description)")
10
11  // create and display an empty Array<Int> using an empty initializer list
12  let integers2: [Int] = [] // must specify Array's type
13  println("integers2: \(integers2.description)")
14
```

Fig. 6.2 | Creating and initializing Arrays. (Part 1 of 2.)

```
15   // type inferred as Array<Int> (i.e., [Int]) from initializer list
16   let integers3 = [0, 1, 2, 3, 4]
17   println("integers3: \(integers3.description)")
18
19   // type inferred as Array<String> (i.e., [String]) from initializer list
20   let strings2 =
21      ["red", "orange", "yellow", "green", "blue", "indigo", "violet"]
22   println("strings: \(strings2.description)")
23
24   // creating a new Array by concatenating existing Arrays with +
25   let integers4 = integers3 + integers3
26   println("integers4: \(integers4.description)")
27
28   // concatenating an existing Array and an Array literal with +
29   let integers5 = integers3 + [5, 6, 7, 8, 9]
30   println("integers5: \(integers5.description)")
```

```
integers1: []
booleans: [true, true, true, true, true],
integers2: []
integers3: [0, 1, 2, 3, 4]
strings: [red, orange, yellow, green, blue, indigo, violet]
integers4: [0, 1, 2, 3, 4, 0, 1, 2, 3, 4]
integers5: [0, 1, 2, 3, 4, 5, 6, 7, 8, 9]
```

Fig. 6.2 | Creating and initializing Arrays. (Part 2 of 2.)

Initializing an Empty Array<Int> with the No-Parameter Initializer
Line 4 uses the Array type's *no-parameter initializer* to create an empty Array of Ints. The compiler infers from the right side of the assignment that the constant integers1 is of type [Int] (i.e., Array<Int>). Line 5 displays the Array's description property to show that the Array is empty—this appears in the output as empty square brackets.

Initializing an Array<Bool> with the Two-Parameter Initializer
The Array type also provides a two-parameter initializer that receives the number of elements to create and the value used to initialize all of the elements. Line 8 uses this initializer to create a five-element Array of type [Bool] (i.e., Array<Bool>) in which each element is initialized to true. The type of the constant booleans is inferred from the right side of the assignment.

Creating an Empty Array<Int> with an Array Literal
You can create an Array and initialize its elements with an **Array** literal—a (possibly empty) comma-separated list of expressions enclosed in square brackets. The Array's length is determined by the number of elements in the initializer list. When the compiler encounters an Array definition that includes an Array literal, the compiler sets up the appropriate operations "behind the scenes" to place the elements into the Array.

An empty Array literal ([], line 12) results in an empty Array. In this case, the compiler cannot infer the Array's type, so you must specify the type with a type annotation.

*Creating a Five-Element **Array<Int>** with an **Array** Literal*
Line 16 creates the Array integers3 of Int values using an Array literal. Recall that the Swift compiler treats whole-number literals as type Int by default, so the compiler infers that integers3 is of type [Int] (i.e., Array<Int>).

*Creating a Seven-Element **Array<String>** with an **Array** Literal*
Lines 20–21 create an Array of String values using an Array literal—the compiler infers based on the String values in the Array literal that the constant strings is of type [String] (i.e., Array<String>).

*Creating a New **Array** by Concatenating Existing **Array**s*
Line 25 creates an Array by using the + operator to concatenate its Array operands' contents. In this case, we concatenate two copies of integers3 producing a 10-element Array<Int> containing two copies of the values 0, 1, 2, 3 and 4, as shown in the second to last line of the output.

*Creating a New **Array** by Concatenating an Existing **Array** and an **Array** Literal*
Line 29 creates an Array by using the + operator to concatenate the Array integers3 and the Array literal containing the values 5, 6, 7, 8 and 9. The result is a 10-element Array<Int> containing the values 0 through 9, as shown in the last line of the output.

6.4 Iterating through Arrays

Figure 6.3 creates a five-element Array of Ints (line 4) that's initialized with the even integers from 2 through 10, then demonstrates various ways to iterate through the Array's elements. The Array's type is inferred from the values in the Array literal.

```
1   // fig06-03.playground: Iterating through Array elements
2   import Foundation // to access String formatting features
3
4   let integers = [2, 4, 6, 8, 10]
5   println(
6       "Array integers via description property: \(integers.description)")
7
8   // for...in loop automatically returning each Array element
9   print("\nArray integers via for...in loop: ")
10  for element in integers {
11      print("\(element)   ")
12  }
13
14  // for loop explicitly specifying how to count
15  println("\n\nArray integers selected elements ")
16  println("in column format via counter-controlled for loop")
17  println("Index  Value")
18  for var index = 0; index < integers.count; index += 2 {
19      println(String(format:"%5d%7d", index, integers[index]))
20  }
21
```

Fig. 6.3 | Iterating through Array elements. (Part 1 of 2.)

```
22   // for...in loop with range of indices
23   println("\nArray integers in column format via for...in loop with range")
24   println("Index  Value")
25   for index in 0..<integers.count {
26       println(String(format:"%5d%7d", index, integers[index]))
27   }
28
29   // for...in loop with enumerate global function
30   println(
31       "\nArray integers in column format via for...in loop with enumerate")
32   println("Index  Value")
33   for (index, element) in enumerate(integers) {
34       println(String(format:"%5d%7d", index, element))
35   }
```

```
Array integers via description property: [2, 4, 6, 8, 10]

Array integers via for...in loop: 2  4  6  8  10

Array integers selected elements
in column format via counter-controlled for loop
Index  Value
    0      2
    2      6
    4     10

Array integers in column format via for...in loop with range
Index  Value
    0      2
    1      4
    2      6
    3      8
    4     10

Array integers in column format via for...in loop with enumerate
Index  Value
    0      2
    1      4
    2      6
    3      8
    4     10
```

Fig. 6.3 | Iterating through Array elements. (Part 2 of 2.)

Iterating Over an Array's Elements with for...in

Lines 10–12 use a for...in loop (Section 4.10) to iterate over the elements in the Array integers without using a counter. Each iteration of the loop assigns the next Array element to element (which is implicitly a constant) then displays element's value. Because the loop does not use an explicit counter, it helps you avoid common mistakes, such as off-by-one errors that could result in accessing an element outside the Array's bounds. Also, the control variable in a for...in loop is implicitly a constant, so it cannot be used to modify the Array's elements. In an Array of reference-type elements, though the control variable cannot be used to change which object the element refers to, it *can* be used to invoke methods that change the referenced object's state.

Error-Prevention Tip 6.2
Use a for... in loop to iterate over all the elements of an Array if you do not need to modify the Array's elements.

Iterating Over an **Array**'s Elements with a Counter-Controlled **for**
Lines 18–20 use a counter-controlled for loop to iterate through the *odd* elements of integers by using an increment of 2. Line 19 uses the subscript expression

```
integers[index]
```

to get the value of the element at position index in the integers. If integers were defined as a variable Array, you could use this subscript expression as the target of an assignment to change the element's value (as you'll see in later examples). Though the for and for... in loops each iterate sequentially from a starting value to an ending value, for... in provides an elegant, more concise and less error-prone means for iterating through Arrays.

Error-Prevention Tip 6.3
The for... in loop simplifies the code for iterating through an Array, making the code more readable and eliminating several error possibilities in a for loop, such as improperly specifying the control variable's initial value, the loop-continuation test and the increment expression. Use for... in—in preference to for—to implement all counter-controlled loops and all loops that iterate through an entire Array's elements. For loops that iterate over a range of Int values, use for... in with the closed range or half-open range operators. For loops that require incrementing by more than one or that require counting backwards use for... in with a range produced by global function stride (introduced in Chapter 4).

Error-Prevention Tip 6.4
When using subscript expressions to access an Array's elements, ensure that the index is greater than or equal to 0 and less than the number of elements in the Array. Attempting to access an element outside an Array's bounds results in a runtime error that terminates program execution.

Iterating Over an **Array**'s Elements with **for... in** and a Range of Integers
If you require access to each element's index, you can also use a for... in loop with a range of integers as shown in lines 25–27. In this case, we use the half-open range (..<) operator to iterate over the integers 0 up to, but not including, integers.count (the number of elements in the Array. This is less error prone than a counter-controlled for loop, because for... in does not require a mutable (i.e., modifiable) control variable and you do not need to specify the control variable's increment expression. You could still incorrectly specify the range of integers in a manner that does not iterate over all of the elements or that attempts to access an element outside the Array's bounds. Nevertheless, this is the best way to iterate over an Array's elements if you must use subscript expressions to modify the elements.

Iterating Over an **Array**'s Elements with **for... in** and the **enumerate** Function
If you require access to each element's index and value, but do *not* need to modify the value, the Swift documentation recommends that you use a for... in loop and the global **enumerate** function, as shown in lines 33–35. During each iteration of the loop, enumer-

ate returns a *tuple* containing the current element's index and value. These initialize the constants you specify as a tuple between the for and in keywords in line 33. You can then use these constants in the loop's body to access the current element's index and value.

6.5 Adding and Removing Array Elements

Type Array provides various methods and operators (Fig. 6.4) for adding elements to and removing elements from *variable* Arrays.

Feature	Description
Adding Elements to an **Array**	
append	Adds a new element to the end of an Array.
insert	Inserts a new element at the specified index. The argument passed to this method's atIndex parameter must be greater than or equal to 0 and less than or equal to the Array's size; otherwise, a runtime error occurs and the program terminates. Inserting an element at the index that's equal to the Array's size adds the element to the end of the Array.
+=	Appends all of the right operand's elements to the end of an Array. The right operand is another Array of the same type or an Array literal containing elements of the Array's element type.
Removing Elements from an **Array**	
removeAtIndex	Removes and returns the element at the specified index. The argument passed to this method's index parameter must be greater than or equal to 0 and less than the size of the Array; otherwise, a runtime error occurs and the program terminates.
removeLast	Removes and returns the last element. The Array must contain at least one element; otherwise, a runtime error occurs and the program terminates.
removeAll	Removes all of the elements. The argument passed to this method's keepCapacity parameter (which has the default parameter value false) determines whether the Array's underlying storage should be kept (true) or returned to the system (false).

Fig. 6.4 | Methods and operators for adding elements to and removing elements from Arrays.

Figure 6.5 demonstrates the methods and operator in Fig. 6.4. Function display-Integers (lines 4–7) is used throughout the example to display:

- its Int Array argument's contents.
- the Array's read-only count property—the number of elements currently stored in the array.
- the Array's read-only **capacity** property—the total number of elements the Array can store without reallocating its memory to accommodate more elements.

As you'll see in this example, an Array dynamically resizes itself as necessary when you attempt to add more elements to it. Line 9 creates the empty Array integers of type [Int]. Line 11 displays its initial contents, and its size and capacity, which are both 0 to start. Lines 13–15 demonstrate the read-only Array property **isEmpty**, which returns true if the Array is empty and false otherwise.

```
1   // fig06-05.playground: Adding and removing Array elements
2
3   // display contents, size and capacity of an Array<Int>
4   func displayIntegers(integers: [Int]) {
5       print("contents: \(integers.description)")
6       println("; size=\(integers.count); capacity=\(integers.capacity)")
7   }
8
9   var integers = [Int]() // create an empty variable Array<Int>
10  println("After creating integers")
11  displayIntegers(integers)
12
13  if integers.isEmpty { // true if integers contains 0 elements
14      println("integers is empty")
15  }
16
17  // append each value of i to integers
18  println("\nAppending values 1-5")
19  for i in 1...5 {
20      integers.append(i)
21      displayIntegers(integers)
22  }
23
24  // inserting elements
25  integers.insert(0, atIndex:0)
26  integers.insert(6, atIndex:integers.count)
27  println("\nAfter inserting 0 at index 0 and 6 at integers.count")
28  displayIntegers(integers)
29
30  // appending elements with +=
31  integers += [7, 8, 9]
32  println("\nAfter appending 7, 8 and 9 with +=")
33  displayIntegers(integers)
34
35  // removing element 0 and the last element
36  println("\n\(integers.removeAtIndex(0)) was removed")
37  println("\(integers.removeLast()) was removed")
38  println("After removing element 0 and the last element")
39  displayIntegers(integers)
40
41  // removing all elements
42  integers.removeAll() // by default, element storage is deallocated
43  println("\nAfter removing all remaining elements")
44  displayIntegers(integers)
```

Fig. 6.5 | Adding and removing Array elements. (Part 1 of 2.)

```
After creating integers
contents: []; size=0; capacity=0
integers is empty

Appending values 1-5
contents: [1]; size=1; capacity=2
contents: [1, 2]; size=2; capacity=2
contents: [1, 2, 3]; size=3; capacity=4
contents: [1, 2, 3, 4]; size=4; capacity=4
contents: [1, 2, 3, 4, 5]; size=5; capacity=8

After inserting 0 at index 0 and 6 at integers.count
contents: [0, 1, 2, 3, 4, 5, 6]; size=7; capacity=8

After appending 7, 8 and 9 with +=
contents: [0, 1, 2, 3, 4, 5, 6, 7, 8, 9]; size=10; capacity=16

0 was removed
9 was removed
After removing element 0 and the last element
contents: [1, 2, 3, 4, 5, 6, 7, 8]; size=8; capacity=16

After removing all remaining elements
contents: []; size=0; capacity=0
```

Fig. 6.5 | Adding and removing `Array` elements. (Part 2 of 2.)

Appending Elements with Method **append**

Lines 19–22 call method append to append the Int values 1 through 5 to integers. Each iteration of the loop calls function displayIntegers to show that the Array grows dynamically as necessary to accommodate more elements. After appending 1, the capacity is 2, so one more element can be added before the Array must allocate more memory. After appending 2, the size matches the capacity. When appending 3, the Array reallocates itself, doubling its capacity to 4—again, one more element can be added before the Array must reallocate. After appending 4, the size matches the capacity. Finally, when appending 5, the Array reallocates itself, doubling its capacity to 8—now three more elements can be added before the Array must reallocate.

Performance Tip 6.2

If an Array's capacity cannot accommodate new elements, the Array is reallocated—new memory is created for the Array, the existing elements are copied into the new memory, the new elements are added to the Array and the old memory for the Array is returned to the system. This is particularly expensive for large Arrays. Exponentially doubling an Array's capacity when more memory is required helps Arrays operate efficiently—the Array's capacity quickly grows to the point that reallocations are either infrequent or no longer required.

Performance Tip 6.3

For a large Array in which the count matches the capacity, adding an element doubles the capacity and leaves the Array with many unused elements. Array's **reserveCapacity** *method helps control memory usage. The method receives a minimumCapacity argument and ensures the Array can store at least that many elements. If you know the maximum Array size your program requires, reserve that capacity in advance so that the Array does not need to repeatedly reallocate memory.*

Inserting Elements with Method `insert`

Line 25 calls method `insert` to insert the value 0 at index 0. Line 26 inserts the value 6 at the index that matches the `Array`'s current size—the equivalent of calling `append`. Line 28 displays the `Array`'s contents, size and capacity. Note that the `Array` did not need any re-allocation as the size is still smaller than the capacity.

Appending Elements with Operator `+=`

The `+=` operator can be used to append to an existing `Array` another `Array` of the same type (as in line 31, which appends an `Array` literal to the `Array`). Because we appended three more elements, the `Array` was reallocated—the output shows that the number of elements is 10 and the capacity has doubled again to 16.

Removing Elements with Methods `removeAtIndex` and `removeLast`

Line 36 calls method `removeAtIndex` to remove the Array's first element and line 37 uses `removeLast` to remove the last element. Both methods return the removed element, which we display in the output. Line 39 shows the new contents of the `Array`—note that the capacity is not reduced when elements are removed.

Removing Elements with Method `removeAll`

Finally, line 42 calls method `removeAll` with its default parameter value (false) to remove all of the `Array`'s remaining elements. The output shows that the `Array` now has 0 elements and a capacity of 0—the element storage was returned to the system. Passing the argument `true` would remove the elements but maintain the `Array`'s capacity for subsequently storing additional elements.

6.6 Subscript Expressions with Ranges

Figure 6.6 manipulates subsets of an `Array` by using subscript expressions containing ranges created with the closed range (. . .) and half-open range (. .<) operators. Lines 2–3 create and display the `Array` integers that we use for demonstration purposes.

```
1   // fig06-06.playground: Selecting and assigning to sub-Arrays
2   var integers = [0, 1, 2, 3, 4, 5, 6, 7, 8, 9]
3   println("integers: \(integers.description)")
4
5   // selecting the elements at indices 3...7 in integers
6   let subset = integers[3...7]
7   println("subset of integers: \(subset.description)")
8
9   // replacing the elements at indices 5...9
10  integers[5...9] = [50, 60, 70]
11  println("integers after replacing elements: \(integers.description)")
12
13  // removing the elements at indices 5...7
14  integers[5...7] = []
15  println("integers after removing elements 5-7: \(integers.description)")
```

Fig. 6.6 | Selecting and assigning to sub-Arrays. (Part 1 of 2.)

```
16
17    // removing the elements at indices 0..<2 (i.e., 0 and 1)
18    integers[0..<2] = []
19    println("integers after removing elements 0-1: \(integers.description)")
```

```
integers: [0, 1, 2, 3, 4, 5, 6, 7, 8, 9]
subset of integers: [3, 4, 5, 6, 7]
integers after replacing elements: [0, 1, 2, 3, 4, 50, 60, 70]
integers after removing elements 5-7: [0, 1, 2, 3, 4]
integers after removing elements 0-1: [2, 3, 4]
```

Fig. 6.6 | Selecting and assigning to sub-Arrays. (Part 2 of 2.)

Selecting a Subset of an **Array**

Line 6 selects a subset of Array integers. The subscript expression (integers[3...7]) returns a Slice<Int> (Int is the Array's element type) containing integers' elements at indices 3–7. Line 7 displays the resulting Slice<Int>. Slices and Arrays provide the same capabilities. A Slice represents a view into an Array's elements. Those elements are copied from the Array only if changes are made to the original Array or to the Slice after the Slice is created.

Replacing a Range of **Array** Elements

You can use range-based subscript expressions on the left side of an assignment to replace subsets of a *variable* Array's elements. Line 10 replaces the *five* elements at indices 5–9 with *three* new elements—the assignment's right Array operand can have the same number of elements as, fewer elements than or more elements than the Array subset that's being replaced. The Array now contains eight elements.

A compilation error occurs if the range expression uses indices that are outside the Array's bounds. For this reason, range-based subscript expressions cannot be used to append new elements to an existing Array—instead you must use Array method append or insert.

Deleting a Range of **Array** Elements

You may also use range-based subscript expressions to delete ranges of elements. Line 14 assigns an empty Array literal to integer's elements at indices 5–7, thus deleting the elements and leaving the Array with five elements. Line 18 also removes elements from the Array, this time using a half-open range (..<) operator to specify that the elements at indices 0 and 1 should be removed. After this operation, the Array contains three elements.

6.7 Sorting Arrays; Introduction to Closures

In this section, we introduce closures then use them to specify the sort order when sorting an Array of Strings into ascending or descending order.

6.7.1 Closures and Closure Expressions

A **closure** is an *anonymous function* (i.e., a function with no name)—a shorthand notation that's typically used to:

- pass a function to another function or method (as we'll do in Fig. 6.7).

- return a function from a function or method.
- assign a function to a variable that can be used to call the function at a later time.

Closures support all the features you've learned about functions so far. In fact, a function is actually a closure that has a name. As you'll see throughout this section and in Section 6.8, the Array type has several methods that receive functions as arguments, and closures are a convenient and concise way to specify such arguments.

For cases in which a function's parameter types and return type can be inferred from the context in which it's called, you can define the function as an inline **closure expression**. As you'll see, such expressions can be passed conveniently to functions or methods, like Array methods sort and sorted (discussed momentarily). We introduce closure expressions in Sections 6.7.4—6.7.8, then present additional closure details in the online Other Topics chapter.

6.7.2 Array Methods sort and sorted

The Array type provides methods sort and sorted to order an Array's elements. Method **sort** modifies the existing Array on which it's called, whereas method **sorted** returns a *new* Array containing a *copy* of the original Array's elements in sorted order—the original Array remains unsorted. Both methods require as an argument a function with the type

   (*ElementType*, *ElementType*) -> Bool

The function receives two arguments of the Array's element type and returns a Bool— true if the two elements are in order and false otherwise. For example, to sort an Array of Strings you must supply a function with the type

   (String, String) -> Bool

To sort elements in ascending order, the function must return true if its first argument is less than its second, and to sort in descending order the function must return true if its first argument is greater than its second.

Figure 6.7 demonstrates Array method sorted by calling it first with a named function, then with various progressively shorter closure expressions to show how compact such expressions can be and how the compiler can infer much of the information needed to use a closure expression.

```
1   // fig06-07.playground: Sorting an Array with method sorted and closures
2
3   // return true if s1 < s2
4   func ascendingOrder(s1: String, s2: String) -> Bool {
5       return s1 < s2
6   }
7
8   // Array of color names to sort
9   let colors =
10      ["red", "orange", "yellow", "green", "blue", "indigo", "violet"]
11
12  println("Array colors unsorted:\n\(colors.description)\n")
13
```

Fig. 6.7 | Sorting an Array with method sorted and closures. (Part 1 of 2.)

```
14   // sort ascending: function ascendingOrder
15   let sortedColors1 = colors.sorted(ascendingOrder)
16   println("Array sortedColors1:\n\(sortedColors1.description)\n")
17
18   // sort descending: fully typed closure expression
19   let sortedColors2 =
20       colors.sorted({(s1: String, s2: String) -> Bool in return s1 > s2})
21   println("Array sortedColors2:\n\(sortedColors2.description)\n")
22
23   // sort ascending: inferred types
24   let sortedColors3 = colors.sorted({s1, s2 in return s1 < s2})
25   println("Array sortedColors3:\n\(sortedColors3.description)\n")
26
27   // sort descending: inferred types and implicit return
28   let sortedColors4 = colors.sorted({s1, s2 in s1 > s2})
29   println("Array sortedColors4:\n\(sortedColors4.description)\n")
30
31   // sort ascending: shorthand closure arguments
32   let sortedColors5 = colors.sorted({$0 < $1})
33   println("Array sortedColors5:\n\(sortedColors5.description)\n")
34
35   // sort descending operator function >
36   let sortedColors6 = colors.sorted(>)
37   println("Array sortedColors6:\n\(sortedColors6.description)\n")
38
39   // reversing the elements of an Array
40   let reversed = sortedColors6.reverse()
41   println("Array reversed:\n\(reversed.description)")
```

```
Array colors unsorted:
[red, orange, yellow, green, blue, indigo, violet]

Array sortedColors1:
[blue, green, indigo, orange, red, violet, yellow]

Array sortedColors2:
[yellow, violet, red, orange, indigo, green, blue]

Array sortedColors3:
[blue, green, indigo, orange, red, violet, yellow]

Array sortedColors4:
[yellow, violet, red, orange, indigo, green, blue]

Array sortedColors5:
[blue, green, indigo, orange, red, violet, yellow]

Array sortedColors6:
[yellow, violet, red, orange, indigo, green, blue]

Array reversed:
[blue, green, indigo, orange, red, violet, yellow]
```

Fig. 6.7 | Sorting an Array with method sorted and closures. (Part 2 of 2.)

6.7.3 Sorting with Function `ascendingOrder`

Function `ascendingOrder` (lines 4–6) receives two `String` parameters and returns `true` if the first parameter's value is less than the second. Because the function receives two arguments of the same type (`String`) and returns a `Bool`, it meets the type requirements for the function that must be passed to `Array` method `sorted` or `sort`.

Lines 9–10 define the constant `Array colors`, then line 12 displays the original contents so you can confirm that the `Array` is sorted properly later in the output.

Line 15 calls `Array` method `sorted` with function `ascendingOrder` as an argument then assigns the resulting sorted `Array` to the constant `sortedColors1`. The sorting algorithm implemented by method `sorted` repeatedly calls `sorted`'s argument function with two `Array` elements to determine whether they're in sorted order. If not, method `sorted` reorders the elements. Line 16 displays `sortedColors1` which contains a copy of the original `colors Array`, but with its elements in *ascending* order.

6.7.4 Using a Fully Typed Closure Expression

The rest of this section discusses closure expressions that help method `sorted` determine the sort order of an `Array`'s elements. Lines 19–20 sort `colors` in *descending* order, using a *fully typed closure expression*—that is, one in which the parameter types and return type (if there is one) are explicitly specified. The general syntax for such an expression is:

```
{(ParameterList) -> ReturnType in
    Statements
}
```

The `in` keyword introduces the closure's body. If the closure expression contains only one statement, then you can write it as a single line:

```
{(ParameterList) -> ReturnType in Statement}
```

To define a closure expression with an empty parameter list, specify the parameter list as empty parentheses.

The closure expression in line 20

```
{(s1: String, s2: String) -> Bool in return s1 > s2}
```

receives two `Strings` (`s1` and `s2`) and returns a `Bool` indicating whether `s1` is *greater than* `s2`, so that `Array` method `sorted` can sort the elements in *descending* order. When a method's only argument is a closure, you can eliminate the parentheses and place the closure immediately after the method's name—this is known as a **trailing closure**. Similarly, if a method's last argument is a closure, you can place that closure outside the parentheses.

6.7.5 Using a Closure Expression with Inferred Types

Often, the compiler can infer a closure expression's parameter types and return types from the context in which the closure expression is defined. For the closure expression in line 24

```
{s1, s2 in return s1 < s2}
```

the compiler infers the parameter types and return type from the context. We're sorting an `Array` of `Strings`, so method `sorted` requires a function argument that has the type

```
(String, String) -> Bool
```

The types of parameters s1 and s2 are inferred as String and the return type is inferred as Bool. When using type inference, the parentheses around the parameter list are not required. The preceding closure expression determines whether s1 is *less than* s2, so that Array method sorted can sort the elements in *ascending* order.

6.7.6 Using a Closure Expression with Inferred Types and an Implicit return

When the closure expression's body contains *only* a return statement, the return keyword may be omitted, as in the closure expression at line 28:

```
{s1, s2 in s1 > s2}
```

The result s1 > s2 is *implicitly* returned. Again, the compiler infers the parameters' types as String and the return type as Bool. The preceding closure expression determines whether s1 is *greater than* s2, so Array method sorted sorts the elements in *descending* order.

6.7.7 Using a Closure Expression with Shorthand Argument Names

You may omit a closure expression's parameter list by using Swift's *shorthand argument names*—$0 represents the first argument, $1 the second, etc. The closure expression:

```
{$0 < $1}
```

at line 32 determines whether the first argument ($0) is *less than* the second ($1), so that Array method sorted can sort the elements in *ascending* order.

6.7.8 Using an Operator Function as a Closure Expression

The shortest closure form is an operator function—a function that defines how an operator works for a given type. For example, the String type provides operator functions for the < and > to determine whether one String is less than or greater than another. These functions each take two String parameters (the operator's left and right operands) and return a Bool—exactly what Array method sorted requires as its argument that determines the sorting order. The closure expression > at line 36 helps sort the elements in *descending* order. Two elements of the Array at a time are used as the operands of the > operator, which returns true if they're in sorted order. (We show how to create operator functions for your own types in Chapter 12, Operator Overloading and Subscripts.)

6.7.9 Reversing an Array's Elements

Array method **reverse** (line 40) reverses the order of an Array's elements and returns them as a new Array. If your app requires sorting an Array in both ascending and descending order, you can perform one sort operation, then simply call reverse on the results to get the other sort order.

6.8 Array Methods filter, map and reduce

For each program you write, you typically determine *what* you want to accomplish in a task, then specify precisely *how* to accomplish it. For example, let's assume that *what* you'd like to accomplish is to sum the elements of an Array named values. You might use the following code:

```
var sum = 0

for var index = 0; index < values.count; ++index {
    sum += values[index]
}
```

This loop specifies *how* we'd like to add each `Array` element's value to the `sum`—with a `for` loop that processes each element one at a time, adding each element's value to the `sum`. This iteration technique is known as **external iteration** (because *you* specify how to iterate, *not* the library)—it requires you to explicitly access the elements sequentially from beginning to end. To perform the preceding task, you also create two variables (`sum` and `index`) that are *mutated* repeatedly while the task is performed.

External Iteration Is Error Prone
As we discussed in Section 6.4, there are several opportunities for error with external iteration. In the preceding `for` loop, for example, you could initialize variable `sum` incorrectly, initialize control variable `index` incorrectly, use the wrong loop-continuation condition, increment `index` incorrectly or add each element value to the `sum` incorrectly. You could eliminate the problems with the counter variable index by using a `for...in` loop, but you'd still be expressing precisely *how* to sum the elements.

Internal Iteration
Using `Array` methods and closures, you can specify *what* you want to accomplish in a task, without having to specify *how* to accomplish it—that's exactly what you did with `Array` method `sorted` in Section 6.7. As you'll see in this section, to sum a numeric `Array`'s elements, you can say, "Here's an `Array`, give me the sum of its elements." You do *not* need to specify how to iterate through the elements or declare and use *any* mutable variables. Because the library determines how to access all the elements to perform the task and hides these details from the app programmer, this is known as **internal iteration**.

With internal iteration, a library can determine the best way to accomplish the specified task, possibly optimizing it to use the parallel-processing capabilities of today's multicore architectures—in iOS and OS X apps, this would be accomplished via Apple's Grand Central Dispatch (GCD) libraries. This could significantly improve an app's performance. It's difficult to create parallel tasks that operate correctly if those tasks modify a program's state information (that is, its variable values). So, the capabilities we present here focus on **immutability**—not modifying the data source being processed or any other program state.

Using Array Methods That Perform Internal Iteration
The `Array` type provides methods `filter`, `map` and `reduce` which enable you to perform many common `Array` manipulations using internal iteration:

- Method `filter` returns an `Array` containing only the elements that satisfy a condition—e.g., selecting all the elements of an `Int` `Array` that are greater than 5 or finding all the elements of a `String` `Array` that start with a specified substring.

- Method `map` returns an `Array` in which each element of the original `Array` is mapped to a new value (possibly of a different type)—e.g., mapping numeric values to the squares of those values or mapping `Employee` objects to `String`s containing the `Employee`s' names. The new `Array` has the *same* number of elements as the original `Array`.

- Method **reduce** combines the Array elements into a *single* value using an accumulation function—e.g., summing the elements, summing the squares of the elements or averaging the elements.

Figure 6.8 demonstrates these operations on an Array of Int values. Line 4 creates the Array values and line 6 displays its initial contents.

```
1   // fig06-08.playground: Demonstrating Array methods filter, map and reduce
2
3   // Array of Ints to filter, map and reduce
4   let values = [3, 10, 6, 1, 4, 8, 2, 5, 9, 7]
5
6   println("values: \(values.description)")
7
8   // filter: even values displayed in sorted order
9   let evenValues = values.filter({$0 % 2 == 0}).sorted(<)
10  println("Even values sorted: \(evenValues.description)")
11
12  // map: square each value then sort the squares
13  let squaresOfValues = values.map({$0 * $0}).sorted(<)
14  println("Squares of values sorted: \(squaresOfValues.description)")
15
16  // reduce: sum the elements of values
17  let sumOfValues = values.reduce(0, {$0 + $1})
18  println("Sum of values: \(sumOfValues)")
19
20  // filter, map and reduce: sum the squares of the even integers
21  let sumOfSquares =
22      values.filter({$0 % 2 == 0})
23          .map({$0 * $0})
24          .reduce(0, {$0 + $1})
25  println("Sum of the even value squares: \(sumOfSquares)")
```

```
values: [3, 10, 6, 1, 4, 8, 2, 5, 9, 7]
Even values sorted: [2, 4, 6, 8, 10]
Squares of values sorted: [1, 4, 9, 16, 25, 36, 49, 64, 81, 100]
Sum of values: 55
Sum of the even value squares: 220
```

Fig. 6.8 | Demonstrating Array methods filter, map and reduce.

6.8.1 Filtering an Array

Line 9 in Fig. 6.8 locates the even integers in values, then sorts them in ascending order. Line 10 displays the resulting new Array. You *filter* elements to produce an Array containing elements that match a condition. Method filter's argument is a function that receives one parameter of the Array's element type and returns a Bool indicating whether the function's argument satisfies the condition—in this case, the closure expression

```
{$0 % 2 == 0}
```

returns true if the argument ($0 is the shorthand name for the argument) is divisible by 2. Method filter returns a *constant* Array containing only the matching elements. We then call method `sorted` on the resulting `Array` to arrange the elements in ascending or-der—as specified by the operator function < that's passed to `sorted` as an argument. We must use `sorted` here, rather than `sort`, because `filter` returns a constant `Array`. Method `sort` modifies the `Array` on which it's called, so calling it on the result of `filter` is a com-pilation error.

6.8.2 Mapping an Array's Elements to New Values

Line 13 of Fig. 6.8 maps each element in `values` to the square of that value and sorts the results. Then, line 14 displays the sorted squares. The new feature here is the *mapping* op-eration that takes each value and squares it. Mapping transforms an `Array`'s elements to new values and produces a new constant `Array` containing the resulting elements. Some-times these are of different types from the original stream's elements.

Method map receives a function that receives one value of the `Array`'s element type, maps the element to a new value and returns the result. The closure expression in line 13:

```
{$0 * $0}
```

squares the function's argument ($0) and returns that value, thus mapping it to a new `Int` value. We then call method `sorted` on the resulting `Array` to order the elements in ascend-ing order.

6.8.3 Reducing an Array's Elements to a Single Value

Line 17 of Fig. 6.8 uses `Array` method `reduce` to sum the `Array` `values`' elements. Meth-od `reduce` receives an initial value for the reduction operation and a function that com-bines two values and returns a result.

In line 17, the first argument (0) is a value that helps you begin the reduction opera-tion and the second argument is the closure expression:

```
{$0 + $1}
```

which performs a calculation with two values representing the left and right operands of a binary operator—in this case, adding the values. Evaluation of the reduction proceeds as follows:

- When reduce is first called, $0's value is `reduce`'s first argument (0) and $1's val-ue is the `Array`'s first element (3), producing the sum 3 (0 + 3).

- Method `reduce` then applies its second argument to the current total and the next `Array` element. So the calculation continues with $0 as the current total (3) and $1 as the `Array`'s second element (10), producing the sum 13 (3 + 10).

- Next, the calculation continues with $0 as the current total (13) and $1 as the Ar-ray's third element (6), producing the sum 19 (13 + 6).

This process continues running a total of the `Array`'s values until they've all been used, at which point `reduce` returns the final sum.

Method **reduce**'s First Argument
Method `reduce`'s first argument is typically a value (known as an identity value) that, when combined with an `Array` element using the function in `reduce`'s second argument,

produces that element's original value. For example, when summing the elements, this value is 0 (any value added to 0 results in the original value) and when getting the product of the elements this value is 1 (any value multiplied by 1 results in the original value).

6.8.4 Combining Filtering, Mapping and Reducing

Lines 21–24 of Fig. 6.8 chain together several method calls to combine filtering, mapping and reducing—in this case, to calculate the sums of the squares of Array value's even integers. First, method filter (line 22) returns a new constant Array containing only the even integers. Next, method map (line 23) maps each Int value to the square of that value and returns a constant Array containing the result. Finally, method reduce (line 24) produces a running total of those squared values. Then line 25 displays the result. Note that we could have removed the map call in line 23 by calling reduce as follows:

```
reduce(0, {$0 + $1 * $1})
```

which squares the value $1, then adds it to the running total.

6.9 Card Shuffling and Dealing Simulation; Computed Properties; Optionals

The examples in the chapter thus far have used Arrays containing elements of value types. This section uses random-number generation and an Array of reference-type elements, namely objects representing individual playing cards and an object representing a deck of cards, to develop a class that simulates card shuffling and dealing. This class can then be used to implement applications that play specific card games.

We first develop class Card (Fig. 6.9), which represents a playing card that has a face (e.g., "Ace", "Deuce", "Three", …, "Jack", "Queen", "King") and a suit (e.g., "Hearts", "Diamonds", "Clubs", "Spades"). Next, we develop the DeckOfCards class (Fig. 6.10), which creates a deck of 52 playing cards in which each element is a reference to a Card object. We then build an application (Fig. 6.11) that demonstrates class DeckOfCards's card shuffling and dealing capabilities. This example consists of three Swift files, so we implemented it as an Xcode project, rather than a playground.

6.9.1 Class Card

Class Card (Fig. 6.9) contains two private constant String properties—face and suit—that store the face and suit for a specific Card. The public initializer for the class (lines 8–11) receives two Strings that it uses to initialize face and suit.

```
1   // fig06-09-11: Card.swift
2   // Card class represents a playing card
3   public class Card {
4       private let face: String
5       private let suit: String
6
```

Fig. 6.9 | Card class represents a playing card. (Part 1 of 2.)

```
7      // initializer
8      public init(face: String, suit: String) {
9          self.face = face;
10         self.suit = suit;
11     }
12
13     // computed property that returns String representation of Card
14     public var description: String {
15         get {
16             return face + " of " + suit
17         }
18     }
19  }
```

Fig. 6.9 | Card class represents a playing card. (Part 2 of 2.)

Computed Property **description**

As you learned in Section 3.2.2, a **computed property** does not store data, rather it manipulates a class's other properties. A computed property's **get** accessor returns a computed value, typically based on the values of other properties. A computed property's **set** accessor sets the values of other properties. If a computed property defines both accessors, it is a read-write property. If it defines only a get accessor, it is a read-only property, as is the case for the public read-only property description (lines 14–18). This computed property returns a concatenated String consisting of the Card's face, the String " of " and the Card's suit. A get accessor is defined with the get keyword followed by braces containing the statements that compute and return the property's value. Similarly, a set accessor is defined with the set keyword followed by braces containing the statements that set the values of stored properties.

6.9.2 Class DeckOfCards

Class DeckOfCards (Fig. 6.10) declares a variable Card Array property named deck (line 6) and initializes it as an empty Array. An Array of a reference type is declared like any other Array but stores references to objects of the specified type, rather than values. Class DeckOfCards also declares a private integer property currentCard (line 7) representing the sequence number (0–51) of the next Card to be dealt from the deck Array, and a public constant numberOfCards (line 8) indicating the number of Cards in the deck (52). The constant is public so it can be used in main.swift (Fig. 6.11).

```
1   // fig06-09-11: DeckOfCards.swift
2   // DeckOfCards class represents a deck of playing cards
3   import Darwin
4
5   public class DeckOfCards {
6       private var deck: [Card] = [] // array of Cards
7       private var currentCard: Int = 0 // index of next Card to deal (0-51)
8       public let numberOfCards = 52 // constant # of Cards
9
```

Fig. 6.10 | DeckOfCards class represents a deck of playing cards. (Part 1 of 2.)

```
10        // initializer fills the deck of Cards
11        public init() {
12            let faces = ["Ace", "Deuce", "Three", "Four", "Five", "Six",
13                "Seven", "Eight", "Nine", "Ten", "Jack", "Queen", "King"]
14            let suits = ["Hearts", "Diamonds", "Clubs", "Spades"]
15
16            // populate deck with Card objects
17            for index in 0 ..< numberOfCards {
18                deck.append(
19                    Card(face: faces[index % 13], suit: suits[index / 13]))
20            }
21        }
22
23        // shuffle deck of Cards with one-pass algorithm
24        public func shuffle() {
25            // next call to method dealCard should start at deck[0] again
26            currentCard = 0;
27
28            // Modern Fisher-Yates shuffle: http://bit.ly/FisherYates
29            for first in stride(from: numberOfCards - 1, through: 1, by: -1) {
30                // select a random number between 0 and first
31                let second = Int(arc4random_uniform(UInt32(first + 1)))
32
33                // swap current Card with randomly selected Card
34                let temp = deck[first]
35                deck[first] = deck[second]
36                deck[second] = temp
37            }
38        }
39
40        // deal one Card
41        public func dealCard() -> Card? {
42            // determine whether Cards remain to be dealt
43            if currentCard < deck.count {
44                return deck[currentCard++] // return current Card
45            } else {
46                return nil; // nil indicates that all Cards were dealt
47            }
48        }
49    }
```

Fig. 6.10 | DeckOfCards class represents a deck of playing cards. (Part 2 of 2.)

6.9.3 DeckOfCards Initializer

The class's initializer (lines 11–21) creates the 52 Card objects and appends a reference to each one to the Array deck. In the loop (lines 17–20), each Card is created and initialized with two Strings—one from the faces Array (which contains the Strings "Ace" through "King") and one from the suits Array (which contains the Strings "Hearts", "Diamonds", "Clubs" and "Spades"). The calculation count % 13 always results in a value from 0 to 12 (the 13 indices of the faces Array in lines 12–13), and the calculation count / 13 always results in a value from 0 to 3 (the four indices of the suits Array in line 14). When the deck Array is initialized, it contains the Cards with faces "Ace" through "King" in order for each suit (all 13 "Hearts", then all the "Diamonds", then the "Clubs", then the "Spades"). We use Arrays of Strings to represent the faces and suits in this example. Alternatively, you might want to modify this example to use Arrays of enum constants to represent the faces and suits. In Chapter 9, we discuss additional enum capabilities that enable you to do this.

6.9.4 DeckOfCards Method shuffle

Method shuffle (lines 24–38) shuffles the Cards in the deck. The method uses the modern version of the Fisher-Yates shuffle algorithm described at

```
http://bit.ly/FisherYates
```

The algorithim loops from the last Card's index (represented by first) down to the index 1 (line 29). During each iteration, line 31 chooses a random number in the range 0 through first—the current Card being processed. Recall that arc4random_uniform returns a value from 0 up to, but not including its argument value, so we add 1 to the argument first to ensure that its value is included in the range of possible random values. Next, the Card object at the index first and the randomly selected Card object at index second are swapped in the Array. After the loop terminates, the Card objects are shuffled.

6.9.5 DeckOfCards Method dealCard and Optional Return Values

Method dealCard (lines 41–48) deals one Card in the Array. Recall that currentCard indicates the index of the next Card to be dealt (i.e., the Card at the *top* of the deck). Thus, line 43 compares currentCard to the length of the deck Array. If the deck is not empty (i.e., currentCard is less than 52), line 44 returns the "top" Card and postincrements currentCard to prepare for the next call to dealCard—otherwise, nil is returned to indicate that there are no more cards in the deck.

For cases in which a method might sometimes—but not always—return a value, you can return an **optional**, which is either a value of the specified type or nil. An optional is indicated by following a type with a ?, as in dealCard's return type Card? on line 41. As you'll see in Fig. 6.11, the if statement is used to check whether an optional contains a value and, if so, automatically assign that value to a variable or constant—this is known as **unwrapping** the optional value (Section 6.9.7).

6.9.6 Shuffling and Dealing Cards

Figure 6.11 uses class DeckOfCards to shuffle and deal cards—once using a for...in loop and once using a while loop. Function formatString (lines 5–10) receives the String representation of a Card and returns a String that's formatted to be 19 characters wide so that we can display the cards in columns. Line 6 uses global function **countElements** to determine the number of characters in the first argument, then line 7 creates a String of spaces to append to the first argument. Line 12 creates a DeckOfCards object named myDeckOfCards. The DeckOfCards initializer creates the deck with the 52 Card objects in order by suit and face. Line 13 invokes myDeckOfCards's shuffle method to rearrange the Card objects.

```swift
1   // fig06-09-11: main.swift
2   // Card shuffling and dealing.
3
4   // format a String left aligned in a field
5   func formatString(var string: String, fieldWidth: Int) -> String {
6       let spaces: Int = fieldWidth - countElements(string)
7       let padding = String(count: spaces, repeatedValue: Character(" "))
8       string += padding
9       return string
10  }
11
12  var myDeckOfCards = DeckOfCards()
13  myDeckOfCards.shuffle() // place Cards in random order
14
15  // deal all 52 Cards with for...in
16  for i in 1 ... myDeckOfCards.numberOfCards {
17      if let card = myDeckOfCards.dealCard() { // deal and unwrap Card
18          print(formatString(card.description, 19)) // display Card
19
20          if (i % 4 == 0) { // move to next line after every fourth card
21              println()
22          }
23      }
24  }
25
26  println()
27  myDeckOfCards.shuffle()
28
29  // deal all 52 Cards with while
30  var i = 0
31
32  while let card = myDeckOfCards.dealCard() { // deal and unwrap Card
33      ++i
34      print(formatString(card.description, 19)) // display Card
35
36      if (i % 4 == 0) { // move to next line after every fourth card
37          println()
38      }
39  }
```

Six of Hearts	Three of Clubs	Five of Hearts	Six of Spades
Three of Diamonds	Ten of Clubs	Four of Diamonds	Five of Diamonds
King of Clubs	Ace of Hearts	Seven of Clubs	Eight of Hearts
Four of Hearts	Seven of Diamonds	Eight of Spades	Three of Spades
Nine of Diamonds	Five of Clubs	King of Spades	Five of Spades
Nine of Hearts	King of Hearts	Deuce of Spades	Deuce of Diamonds
Eight of Diamonds	Jack of Clubs	Eight of Clubs	Queen of Hearts
Ace of Clubs	Ten of Hearts	Four of Clubs	Deuce of Hearts
Ten of Diamonds	Seven of Hearts	Jack of Diamonds	Jack of Spades
Deuce of Clubs	Ten of Spades	Queen of Diamonds	Nine of Spades
Six of Diamonds	Ace of Spades	Jack of Hearts	Seven of Spades
Ace of Diamonds	Three of Hearts	King of Diamonds	Six of Clubs
Queen of Spades	Nine of Clubs	Four of Spades	Queen of Clubs

Fig. 6.11 | Card shuffling and dealing. (Part 1 of 2.)

King of Hearts	Eight of Spades	Queen of Spades	Jack of Spades
Seven of Spades	Four of Hearts	Deuce of Spades	Ten of Hearts
Ten of Diamonds	Six of Clubs	Nine of Clubs	Ace of Diamonds
Deuce of Clubs	Ten of Spades	King of Diamonds	Five of Clubs
Eight of Diamonds	Six of Hearts	Four of Spades	Deuce of Hearts
Queen of Hearts	Five of Spades	Nine of Hearts	King of Spades
Eight of Hearts	King of Clubs	Deuce of Diamonds	Ace of Spades
Three of Hearts	Jack of Diamonds	Seven of Diamonds	Four of Clubs
Jack of Clubs	Queen of Clubs	Three of Spades	Three of Diamonds
Eight of Clubs	Nine of Diamonds	Seven of Hearts	Jack of Hearts
Six of Spades	Six of Diamonds	Four of Diamonds	Ace of Hearts
Ten of Clubs	Nine of Spades	Five of Diamonds	Five of Hearts
Ace of Clubs	Seven of Clubs	Three of Clubs	Queen of Diamonds

Fig. 6.11 | Card shuffling and dealing. (Part 2 of 2.)

6.9.7 Unwrapping Optional Values with Optional Binding and the if or while Statements

Lines 16–24 deal all 52 Cards and print their String representations in four columns of 13 Cards each, using function formatString to format each String so it can be displayed left aligned in a 19-character column. The if statement (lines 17–23) deals one Card object by invoking myDeckOfCards's dealCard method, then displays the Card.

Line 17 uses **optional binding** to determine whether a Card was returned and, if so, bind it to a constant (defined with let), but you can also bind to a variable. If dealCard returned nil, the optional does not contain a value and the if condition evaluates to false. If dealCard returned a Card:

- the value is unwrapped from the optional,
- the value is used to initialize the constant card,
- the if condition evaluates to true, and
- the if statement's body executes.

An optional is an object of type **Optional**. Method dealCard's actual return type is Optional<Card>—Optional is a generic type. We discuss type Optional in Section 9.5 and various language features for working with optionals as we use them.

Line 27 reshuffles the Cards, then lines 32–39 deal the Cards using a while statement in which the condition uses optional binding. As with the if statement above, the while statement's condition evaluates to true if dealCard's return value is non-nil; otherwise, the condition evaluates to false and the loop terminates.

6.10 Passing Arrays to Functions

This section demonstrates passing Arrays and individual Array elements as arguments to functions. Swift Arrays are value types, so by default entire Arrays and individual Array elements are passed *by value*—copies are passed to functions. As you'll see, you can use the inout parameters (Section 5.11) to pass entire Arrays or individual elements by reference. Figure 6.12 demonstrates pass-by-value and pass-by-reference with Arrays and Array elements.

Error-Prevention Tip 6.5

The Swift compiler optimizes value-type copy operations, performing them only when necessary.

```
 1   // fig06-12.playground: Passing entire Arrays and individual
 2   // Array elements by value and by reference
 3
 4   // multiply all elements by 2--original Array not modified
 5   func doesNotModifyArray(var values: [Int]) {
 6       for i in 0 ..< values.count {
 7           values[i] *= 2
 8       }
 9   }
10
11   // multiply individual element by 2--original Array not modified
12   func doesNotModifyElement(var element: Int) {
13       element *= 2
14   }
15
16   // multiply all elements by 2--original Array modified
17   func modifyArray(inout values: [Int]) {
18       for i in 0 ..< values.count {
19           values[i] *= 2
20       }
21   }
22
23   // multiply individual element by 2--original Array modified
24   func modifyElement(inout element: Int) {
25       element *= 2
26   }
27
28   var integers = [1, 2, 3, 4, 5]
29
30   // pass entire Array by value
31   println("integers before doesNotModifyArray: \(integers.description)")
32   doesNotModifyArray(integers)
33   println("integers after doesNotModifyArray: \(integers.description)")
34
35   // pass one Array element by value
36   println("\nintegers[3] before doesNotModifyElement: \(integers[3])")
37   doesNotModifyElement(integers[3])
38   println("integers[3] after doesNotModifyElement: \(integers[3])")
39
40   // pass entire Array by reference
41   println("\nintegers before modifyArray: \(integers.description)")
42   modifyArray(&integers) // & indicates pass by reference
43   println("integers after modifyArray: \(integers.description)")
44
45   // pass one Array element by value
46   println("\nintegers[3] before modifyElement: \(integers[3])")
```

Fig. 6.12 | Passing entire Arrays and individual Array elements by value and by reference. (Part 1 of 2.)

```
47   modifyElement(&integers[3]) // & indicates pass by reference
48   println("integers[3] after modifyElement: \(integers[3])")
```

```
integers before doesNotModifyArray: [1, 2, 3, 4, 5]
integers after doesNotModifyArray: [1, 2, 3, 4, 5]

integers[3] before doesNotModifyElement: 4
integers[3] after doesNotModifyElement: 4

integers before modifyArray: [1, 2, 3, 4, 5]
integers after modifyArray: [2, 4, 6, 8, 10]

integers[3] before modifyElement: 8
integers[3] after modifyElement: 16
```

Fig. 6.12 | Passing entire Arrays and individual Array elements by value and by reference. (Part 2 of 2.)

6.10.1 Passing an Entire Array By Value

Line 32 calls function doesNotModifyArray (lines 5–9) to demonstrate passing the entire Array integers (defined at line 28) to a function by value. To pass an entire Array to a function, specify the Array's name as the argument in the function call. Function doesNotModifyArray attempts to modify its argument by multiplying each of the Array's elements by 2 (line 7). Because Arrays are value types, a copy of the original Array is passed to the function and the modifications are performed only on the local copy of the Array. Line 33 outputs the integers, showing the *unmodified* original element values.

Notice that we declared the function's parameter with var (line 5). By default, function parameters are *constants*. If you intend to modify the local copy of a function argument, you must declare the corresponding parameter with var. Otherwise, any attempt to modify the parameter's value results in a compilation error.

6.10.2 Passing One Array Element By Value

Line 37 calls function doesNotModifyElement (lines 12–14) to demonstrate passing an individual element of Array integers to a function by value. Function doesNotModifyElement attempts to modify its argument (integers[3] in line 37) by multiplying the parameter element by 2 (line 13). A copy of integers[3] was passed to the function, so line 13 modifies only the local copy. Lines 36 and 38 show that integers[3] contains the *same* value before and after calling doesNotModifyElement.

6.10.3 Passing an Entire Array By Reference

To pass an entire Array to a function by reference, you must use an inout parameter. Line 42 calls function modifyArray (lines 17–21) to demonstrate passing the entire Array integers to a function by reference. Recall from Section 5.11 that when passing an argument to an inout parameter, you must precede the argument with an ampersand (&)—this tells the compiler that you know you're passing the argument by reference. Like function doesNotModifyArray, function modifyArray multiplies each element of its parameter

Array by 2 (line 19). In this case, the Array was passed by reference, so these changes occur in the original Array integers. Line 41 shows you integers' contents before calling modifyArray and line 43 shows you its *modified* contents.

6.10.4 Passing One Array Element By Reference

Line 47 calls function modifyElement (lines 24–26) to demonstrate passing an individual element of Array integers to a function by reference. Function modifyElement modifies its argument (&integers[3] in line 47) by multiplying the inout parameter element by 2 (line 25). Once again, we pass the argument preceded by an ampersand (&) to indicate that the argument is passed by reference. Line 46 shows the value of integers[3] (8) before calling modifyElement and 48 shows integers[3]'s doubled value (16) after calling modifyElement.

6.11   Notes on Pass-By-Value and Pass-By-Reference

In Swift *all arguments are passed by value* by default. A function call can pass two types of values to a function:

- copies of value types (such as, Ints, Doubles, Strings and Arrays) and
- copies of references to objects of class types—the objects themselves are not passed.

When a function modifies a value-type parameter, changes to the parameter have no effect on the original argument value in the caller. This is also true for reference-type parameters. If you modify a reference-type parameter so that it *refers to another object*, only the *parameter* refers to the new object—the reference stored in the caller's variable still refers to the original object.

    Although an object's reference is passed by value, a function can still interact with the referenced object by calling its functions and accessing its properties using the copy of the object's reference. Since the reference stored in the parameter is a copy of the reference that was passed as an argument, the parameter in the called function and the argument in the caller refer to the *same* object. Thus, with a reference to an object, the called function *can* manipulate the caller's object directly. If a function needs to modify a reference-type variable in the caller to make it refer to another object in memory, then the function must receive the reference-type argument by reference with an inout parameter.

6.12   Multidimensional Arrays

Multidimensional Arrays with two dimensions arrange data in rows and columns. To identify a particular element, you specify two indices. By convention, the first identifies the element's row and the second its column. Multidimensional Arrays can have more than two dimensions. Swift does not support multidimensional Arrays directly; rather it allows you to specify one-dimensional Arrays whose elements are one-dimensional Arrays, thus achieving the same effect and allowing you to create Arrays of any number of dimensions. Figure 6.13 illustrates a two-dimensional Array named a with three rows and four columns (i.e., a three-by-four Array).

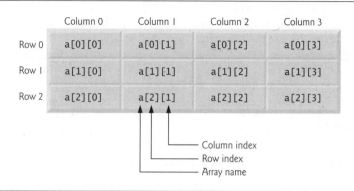

Fig. 6.13 | Two-dimensional Array with three rows and four columns.

Every element in Array a is identified in Fig. 6.13 by a subscript expression of the form a[*row*][*column*]—a is the Array's name, and *row* and *column* are the indices that uniquely identify each element by row and column index. The element names in *row* 0 all have a *first* index of 0, and the element names in *column* 3 all have a *second* index of 3.

Arrays of One-Dimensional Arrays

Like one-dimensional Arrays, multidimensional Arrays can be initialized with Array literals in declarations. A two-dimensional Array b with two rows and two columns could be defined with **nested Array literals** as follows:

```
let b = [[1, 2], [3, 4]]
```

The initial values are grouped by row in square brackets. So 1 and 2 initialize b[0][0] and b[0][1], respectively, and 3 and 4 initialize b[1][0] and b[1][1], respectively. The compiler counts the number of nested Array literals (represented by sets of square brackets within the outer brackets) to determine the number of *rows* in Array b. The compiler counts the values in the nested Array literal for a row to determine the number of *columns* in that row. As you'll see momentarily, this means that rows can have *different* lengths.

Array b in the preceding declaration actually contains two separate one-dimensional Arrays—one with the values in the first nested Array literal [1, 2] and one with the values in the second nested Array literal [3, 4]. Thus, Array b itself is an Array of two elements, each a one-dimensional Array of Ints. Array b's type is inferred as Array<Array<Int>>—the shorthand for this is [[Int]].

Two-Dimensional Arrays with Rows of Different Lengths

The manner in which multidimensional Arrays are represented makes them quite flexible. In fact, the lengths of the rows in an Array are *not* required to be the same. For example,

```
let b = [[1, 2], [3, 4, 5]]
```

creates integer Array b with two elements (determined by the number of nested Array literals) that represent the rows of the two-dimensional Array. Each element of b is a one-dimensional Array of Ints. The Int Array for row 0 is a one-dimensional Array with *two* elements (1 and 2), and the Int Array for row 1 is a one-dimensional Array with *three* elements (3, 4 and 5). Again, Array b's type is inferred as Array<Array<Int>>.

*Creating Two-Dimensional **Arrays** Dynamically*
A multidimensional `Array` can be created dynamically. If you know in advance how many rows you need, you can use the following statement to create the `Array`:

```
var b: [[Int]] = Array(count: 3, repeatedValue: [])
```

This creates a two-dimensional `Array` of `Int`s with three empty rows. For each row, you can then append `Int` values to it, or assign it an `Int` `Array` literal. For example, the statements

```
b[0].append(1)
b[0].append(2)
```

append the values 1 and 2 to row 0, and the statement

```
b[1] = [3, 4, 5]
```

places the values 3, 4 and 5 into row 1. If you do not know the number of rows, you can create the `Array` with the statement

```
var b: [[Int]] = []
```

which creates an empty two-dimensional `Array` of `Int`s. You can then append rows to the `Array` as necessary and use the techniques shown above to specify elements for each row's columns.

*Two-Dimensional **Array** Example: Displaying Element Values*
Figure 6.14 demonstrates initializing two-dimensional `Array`s both with `Array` literals and by dynamically creating `Array`s. We use nested for...in loops to traverse the `Array`s with and without accessing the elements' indices.

```
1   // fig06-14.playground: Creating two-dimensional Arrays
2
3   // display two-dimensional Arrays of Ints by row
4   func outputArray(values: [[Int]]) { // Array<Array<Int>>
5       for row in values {
6           for column in row {
7               print("\(column)  ")
8           }
9
10          println()
11      }
12  }
13
14  // display two-dimensional Arrays of Ints by row using indices
15  func outputArrayWithIndices(values: [[Int]]) { // Array<Array<Int>>
16      for row in 0 ..< values.count {
17          for column in 0 ..< values[row].count {
18              print("\(values[row][column])  ")
19          }
20
21          println()
22      }
23  }
```

Fig. 6.14 | Creating two-dimensional `Array`s. (Part 1 of 2.)

```
24
25   let array1 = [[1, 2, 3], [4, 5, 6]]
26   println("Values in array1 by row")
27   outputArray(array1)
28   println("\nValues in array1 by row using indices")
29   outputArrayWithIndices(array1)
30
31   let array2 = [[1, 2], [3], [4, 5, 6]]
32   println("\nValues in array2 by row")
33   outputArray(array2)
34   println("\nValues in array2 by row using indices")
35   outputArrayWithIndices(array2)
36
37   var array3: [[Int]] = Array(count: 3, repeatedValue: [])
38   array3[0] = [1, 2, 3]
39   array3[1] = [4, 5]
40   array3[2] = [6]
41   println("\nValues in array3 by row")
42   outputArray(array3)
43   println("\nValues in array3 by row using indices")
44   outputArrayWithIndices(array3)
```

```
Values in array1 by row
1  2  3
4  5  6

Values in array1 by row using indices
1  2  3
4  5  6

Values in array2 by row
1  2
3
4  5  6

Values in array2 by row using indices
1  2
3
4  5  6

Values in array3 by row
1  2  3
4  5
6

Values in array3 by row using indices
1  2  3
4  5
6
```

Fig. 6.14 | Creating two-dimentional Arrays. (Part 2 of 2.)

Function *outputArray*

After creating each two-dimensional Array in this example we output its elements row-by-row. Function outputArray's parameter type [[Int]] (line 4) indicates that the function receives a two-dimensional `Array`. The nested `for...in` loops (lines 5–11) output the rows of the two-dimensional `Array`. The outer loop iterates over the rows—the type of `row` is inferred as `[Int]` (`Array<Int>`). The inner loop iterates over the current row's columns and displays its elements—the type of `column` is inferred as the `Array`'s element type `Int`.

Function `outputArrayWithIndices`

Function `outputArrayWithIndices` is similar to function `outputArray` but uses nested `for...in` loops that iterate over the row and column indices. In the outer loop's half-open range (line 16), the expression `values.count` returns the number of rows in the `Array`. In the inner loop, the expression `values[row].count` determines the number of columns in the current row. The inner loops's half-open range expression enables the loop to determine the exact number of columns in each row.

Creating the Two-Dimensional *Arrays*

Line 25 defines `array1` and initializes it with nested `Array` literals in which each row has the same length. The compiler infers from the nested `Array` literals that `array1` is a two-dimensional `Array` of `Int`s with two rows, and initializes the first row with the values 1, 2 and 3, and the second row with the values 4, 5 and 6. Lines 26–29 call functions `output-Array` and `outputArrayWithIndices` to display array1's elements row-by-row.

Line 31 defines `array2` and initializes it with nested `Array` literals in which each row has a different length. The compiler infers from the nested `Array` literals that `array2` is a two-dimensional `Array` of `Int`s with three rows, and initializes the first row with the values 1 and 2, the second row with 3 and the third row with 4, 5 and 6. Lines 32–35 call functions `outputArray` and `outputArrayWithIndices` to display array2's elements.

Finally, lines 37–40 create `array3` as a two-dimensional `Array` of `Int`s. First, line 37 uses `Array`'s two-parameter initializer to create a two-dimensional `Array` of `Int`s with 3 rows in which each row is initialized as an empty `Array` (`[]`). Next, the statements at lines 38–40 assign `Int` `Array` literals to each row of `array3`. We also could have simply appended elements to each row of `array3` to grow the rows dynamically.

6.13 Variadic Parameters

This example is based on the variable-length argument list example we've used in our books for many years. With **variadic parameters**, you can create functions that receive an unspecified number of arguments. A parameter type followed by an **ellipsis** (`...`) indicates that the function receives a variable number of arguments of the specified type. Only one variadic parameter is allowed per function definition and it must be the last parameter in the parameter list.

Figure 6.15 demonstrates function `average` (lines 5–8), which receives a variadic parameter of type `Double`. Swift treats the corresponding arguments as an `Array` of the variadic parameter's type—in this case, `Double`. So, the function body can manipulate the parameter `numbers` as an `Array` of `Double`s. Line 6 uses `Array` method `reduce` (introduced in Section 6.8.3) to total numbers' elements. Line 7 calculates and returns the average by dividing the `total` from line 6 by `numbers.count` (the number of elements). Lines 18, 20 and 22 call `average` with two, three and four arguments, respectively. Because function `average` has a variadic parameter (line 5), it can average as many `Double` arguments as the caller passes. The output shows that each call to function `average` returns the correct value.

```
1   // fig06-15.playground: Variadic parameters
2   import Foundation // for String formatting
3
4   // calculate average
5   func average(numbers: Double...) -> Double {
6       var total = numbers.reduce(0.0, {$0 + $1})
7       return total / Double(numbers.count)
8   }
9
10  var d1 = 10.0
11  var d2 = 15.0
12  var d3 = 20.0
13  var d4 = 30.0
14
15  println(String(format:"d1=%.2f\nd1=%.2f\nd1=%.2f\nd1=%.2f\n",
16      d1, d2, d3, d4))
17  println(String(format:"Average of d1 and d2 is %.2f",
18      average(d1, d2)))
19  println(String(format:"Average of d1, d2 and d3 is %.2f",
20      average(d1, d2, d3)))
21  println(String(format:"Average of d1, d2, d3 and d4 is %.2f",
22      average(d1, d2, d3, d4)))
```

```
d1=10.00
d1=15.00
d1=20.00
d1=30.00

Average of d1 and d2 is 12.50
Average of d1, d2 and d3 is 15.00
Average of d1, d2, d3 and d4 is 18.75
```

Fig. 6.15 | Variadic parameters.

6.14 Wrap-Up

In this chapter, we presented Swift's dynamically resizable Arrays. You saw various ways to create, initialize and iterate over Arrays. We demonstrated the Array type's methods and operator for adding elements to, inserting elements in and removing elements from Arrays.

You used the range operators in Array subscript expressions to select, replace and delete Slices of an Array's elements. You sorted Array elements with Array methods sort and sorted. As you saw, both methods require as an argument a function that's used to compare two Array elements to specify their sort order. You used a named function and various closure forms to specify sorting order. We then used closures with Array methods filter, map and reduce to filter elements that matched a specified condition, map elements to new values and reduce elements to a single value.

We used Arrays to simulate shuffling and dealing playing cards. In the Card class, you created a computed property that returned a concatenated String representation of the face and suit. You defined a method that sometimes, but not always, returned a value by declaring an Optional return type, then used optional binding and the if statement to execute code only if the return value was not `nil`. We demonstrated pass-by-value and pass-by-reference with `Array`s and `Array` elements. Next, we showed how to create and iterate over multidimensional `Array`s. Finally, we demonstrated variadic parameters by creating a function that calculates the average of any number of arguments.

In the next chapter, we continue our coverage of data structures by presenting Swift's `Dictionary` type. Both `Array` and `Dictionary` are generic types. Chapter 11 discusses generics, which enable you to create general models of methods and classes that can be declared once, but used with many different data types.

7

Dictionary

Outline

7.1 Introduction

Chapter 6 presented Swift's built-in `Array` type, which is an *ordered* collection of element values. In this chapter, we'll present Swift's other built-in collection type—`Dictionary`.

7.1.1 What Is a `Dictionary`?

A `Dictionary` is an *unordered* collection of *keys* and *values*—these occur in *key–value pairs*. A `Dictionary` associates values with keys just as a real-world dictionary associates definitions with words. You refer to a particular key to get its value. Because of these associations, `Dictionary` collections are sometimes called *associative arrays*.

Keys must be unique, but multiple keys can have the same value. The keys must all have the same type and the values must all have the same type. The key type can be the same as or different from the value type. We'll say more about what "same type" means in later chapters when we discuss inheritance and protocols.

7.1.2 Dictionary Examples

Figure 7.1 lists `Dictionary` examples with their keys and key types, and their values and value types.

Keys	Key type	Values	Value type
Country names	`String`	Internet country codes	`String`
Decimal numbers	`Int`	Roman numerals	`String`
States	`String`	Agricultural products	Array of `String`
Hospital patients	`String`	Temperature readings	Array of `Double`
Employee numbers	`Int`	Job titles	`String`
Baseball players	`String`	Batting averages	`Double`
Weight exercises	`String`	Weights	`Int`
Metric measurements	`String`	Abbreviations	`String`
Countries	`String`	Capital cities	`String`
Inventory codes	`String`	Quantity in stock	`Int`

Fig. 7.1 | `Dictionary` examples.

7.1.3 Dictionary is a Generic Type

Like `Array`, `Dictionary` is a *generic* type. When you declare an `Array`, you provide the type of the values to be stored in the `Array`. For example, `Array<Double>` (or the shorthand notation `[Double]`) is the type of an `Array` whose values all have the type `Double`.

When you declare a `Dictionary` you specify its key *and* value types. For example, `Dictionary<String, Int>` is the generic notation for the type of a `Dictionary` with `String` keys and `Int` values. This `Dictionary` type also can be written with the preferred shorthand notation `[String : Int]`. More generally, the type

    Dictionary<*keyType*, *valueType*>

can be written with the preferred shorthand notation

    [*keyType* : *valueType*]

7.1.4 Dictionary Is a Value Type

Unlike most other popular object-oriented programming languages, Swift types `Array`, `String` and `Dictionary` are all *value* types, so their objects are passed and assigned by value and copies normally are made.

Performance Tip 7.1

As a performance optimization, Swift—in a manner transparent to the programmer—avoids unnecessary copying of value-type objects.

Performance Tip 7.2

Objective-C's NSArray, NSMutableArray, NSString, NSMutableString, NSDictionary and NSMutableDictionary classes are all reference types. Objects of these classes are passed or assigned by reference—no copies are made.

Software Engineering Observation 7.1

Because Arrays, Strings and Dictionary collections are value types, you always have ownership of their corresponding objects, wherever you are accessing or modifying them. This is particularly important with today's multicore hardware systems, which encourage the use of multithreaded programming.

7.1.5 Dictionary Is Implemented as a Hash Table

Type Dictionary is implemented as a *hash table*. The location at which a key–value pair is placed in a Dictionary is determined by applying a *hashing transformation* to the key, so Dictionary key types must conform to the **Hashable** protocol. Swift's numeric, Bool and String types are all Hashable. The Hashable requirement is enforced by a generic type constraint that's specified for the key type in Dictionary's generic definition. In Chapter 11, Generics, we discuss type constraints in more detail. We explain protocols and protocol conformance in Chapter 10, Inheritance, Polymorphism and Protocols. Though we do not have access to Swift's Dictionary implementation, we discuss how hash tables work in general in Section 7.14, focussing on performance issues.

7.1.6 Dictionary Is Type Safe

Every Dictionary always has a type. You establish a Dictionary's key and value types— and hence the Dictionary's type—by providing the types explicitly or by type inference.

Error-Prevention Tip 7.1

Dictionary collections are type safe—you cannot place keys or values of the wrong type into a Dictionary, nor can you ever get keys or values of the wrong type from one. The Foundation collection types NSDictionary and NSMutableDictionary are not type safe.

7.2 Declaring a Dictionary: Key–Value Pairs and Dictionary Literals

In this section we declare several Dictionary objects (Fig. 7.2) which can hold country names (Strings such as "Argentina", "Finland", "South Africa" and "Nepal") as keys and Internet country codes (two-character Strings such as "ar", "fi", "za" and "np", respectively) as values. We use let to create an *immutable* Dictionary object and var to create several *mutable* Dictionary objects. We also use Dictionary's description property explicitly (lines 20–22) and implicitly (lines 28–30) to print the Dictionary objects.

Good Programming Practice 7.1

Where appropriate, use type inference to make your code more concise. Some programmers, however, feel that explicit typing makes their programs clearer.

```
 1   // Fig. 7.2: fig07_02.playground
 2   // Declaring and printing mutable and immutable Dictionary objects.
 3
 4   // declare immutable Dictionary with traditional generic type syntax
 5   // and a Dictionary literal with one key-value pair
 6   let countryCodes1: Dictionary<String, String> = ["Argentina" : "ar"]
 7
 8   // declare mutable Dictionary with shorthand type syntax
 9   // and a Dictionary literal with multiple key-value pairs
10   var countryCodes2: [String : String] = ["Finland" : "fi",
11       "South Africa" : "za", "Nepal" : "np"]
12
13   // declare mutable Dictionary with type inference and a Dictionary literal
14   var countryCodes3 = ["Argentina" : "ar"] // prefer this approach
15
16   // print with Dictionary description property (from Printable protocol)
17   // Printable protocol's description property returns String
18   // invoke description property explicitly
19   println("PRINT DICTIONARIES USING THE DESCRIPTION PROPERTY EXPLICITLY")
20   println("countryCodes1: \(countryCodes1.description)")
21   println("countryCodes2: \(countryCodes2.description)")
22   println("countryCodes3: \(countryCodes3.description)")
23
24   println()
25
26   // invoke description property implicitly
27   println( "PRINT DICTIONARIES USING THE DESCRIPTION PROPERTY IMPLICITLY")
28   println("countryCodes1: \(countryCodes1)")
29   println("countryCodes2: \(countryCodes2)")
30   println("countryCodes3: \(countryCodes3)")
```

```
PRINT DICTIONARIES USING THE DESCRIPTION PROPERTY EXPLICITLY
countryCodes1: [Argentina: ar]
countryCodes2: [Nepal: np, Finland: fi, South Africa: za]
countryCodes3: [Argentina: ar]

PRINT DICTIONARIES USING THE DESCRIPTION PROPERTY IMPLICITLY
countryCodes1: [Argentina: ar]
countryCodes2: [Nepal: np, Finland: fi, South Africa: za]
countryCodes3: [Argentina: ar]
```

Fig. 7.2 | Declaring and printing mutable and immutable Dictionary objects.

7.2.1 Dictionary Key–Value Pairs and Dictionary Literals

A key–value pair, such as

```
    "Argentina" : "ar"
```

in line 6 consists of a key, followed by a colon (:) and the corresponding value. A **Dictionary** literal—such as in line 6 or lines 10–11—consists of square brackets ([]) containing a comma-separated list of key–value pairs. We'll use the **empty Dictionary literal**, [:], in Fig. 7.3.

7.2.2 Declaring a `Dictionary` with Generics and Explicit Typing

The type annotation for a `Dictionary` is written with generics notation as

```
Dictionary<keyType, valueType>
```

Line 6 in Fig. 7.2 declares a `Dictionary` using this notation and explicit typing:

```
let countryCodes1: Dictionary<String, String> = ["Argentina" : "ar"]
```

Lines 10–11 declare a `Dictionary` using the preferred shorthand type annotation:

```
var countryCodes2: [String : String] = ["Finland" : "fi",
    "South Africa" : "za", "Nepal" : "np"]
```

7.2.3 Declaring a `Dictionary` with Type Inference

Line 14 uses *type inference* for an even more concise `Dictionary` declaration:

```
var countries = ["Argentina": "ar", "Norway": "no"]
```

In this case, the type is inferred from the data in the `Dictionary` literal.

Common Programming Error 7.1

`Dictionary` declarations that use type inference based on a `Dictionary` literal will not compile unless the keys are all of the same type and the values are all of the same type. We'll say more about what "same type" means in later chapters when we discuss inheritance and protocols.

7.2.4 Invoking `Dictionary`'s `description` Property Explicitly and Implicitly

`Dictionary` conforms to the `Printable` protocol, so it has a `description` property which returns a `Dictionary`'s `String` representation. We print all three `Dictionary` objects by *explicitly* accessing the `description` property (lines 20–22), then by *implicitly* accessing it via `String` interpolation (lines 28–30). Again, because `Dictionary` is an *unordered* collection, the order in which `description` produces the key–value pairs does not necessarily match the order in which they're listed in the `Dictionary` literal or, as we'll see, the order in which key–value pairs are added dynamically. We'll soon use `println` inside a `for...in` statement to print a `Dictionary`'s contents one key–value pair at a time. Later, we'll create a generic `printDictionary` function that will print any `Dictionary`, regardless of its key type or value type, as long as those types conform to the `Printable` protocol.

7.3 Declaring and Printing Empty `Dictionary` Objects

Figure 7.3 demonstrates several ways to declare empty `Dictionary` objects. Line 5 declares a mutable empty `Dictionary` with *initializer syntax*—the empty parentheses invoke the `Dictionary` initializer that receives no arguments. Line 8 declares a mutable empty `Dictionary` with an empty `Dictionary` literal, explicit typing and shorthand notation. Line 11 declares an empty `Dictionary`, using the `Dictionary` initializer that receives a `minimumCapacity`—this creates a `Dictionary` that can store up to 10 key–value pairs before it needs to allocate more storage. The compiler guarantees at least the specified `minimumCapacity`, but might reserve more space. The outputs confirm that all three `Dictionary` objects are empty—and that the description property (*implicitly* invoked) prints an empty Dictionary as [:]. Later in the chapter, we'll show several ways to remove all of a Dictionary's key–value pairs. In Fig. 7.7, we'll do it by assigning the empty Dictionary literal to the Dictionary. In Fig. 7.11, we'll do it by calling Dictionary method removeAll.

```
1   // Fig. 7.3: fig07_03.playground
2   // Declaring and printing empty Dictionary objects.
3
4   // declare a mutable empty Dictionary with initializer syntax
5   var countryCodes1 = [String : String]()
6
7   // declare a mutable empty Dictionary with an empty dictionary literal
8   var countryCodes2: [String : String] = [:]
9
10  // declare empty Dictionary with a minimiumCapacity
11  var countryCodes3 = [String : String] (minimumCapacity: 10) // no literal
12
13  // following is an invalid declaration because type inference fails
14  // var countryCodes4 = [:]  // would fail: cannot infer type of Dictionary
15
16  // print each of the empty Dictionary objects
17  println("PRINT EMPTY DICTIONARY OBJECTS")
18  println("countryCodes1 is \(countryCodes1)")
19  println("countryCodes2 is \(countryCodes2)")
20  println("countryCodes3 is \(countryCodes3)")
```

```
PRINT EMPTY DICTIONARY OBJECTS
countryCodes1 is [:]
countryCodes2 is [:]
countryCodes3 is [:]
```

Fig. 7.3 | Declaring and printing empty Dictionary objects.

7.4 Iterating through a Dictionary with for...in

Let's create and use a Dictionary whose String keys are the names of the months and whose Int values are the corresponding numbers of days in each month in a leap year (Fig. 7.4). We'll use for...in statements to iterate through the Dictionary. This example is interesting because it's not limited to a *one-to-one mapping* between keys and values—*many* keys can map to *one* value. For example, April, June, September and November all have 30 days.

```
1   // Fig. 7.4: fig07_04.playground
2   // Iterating through a Dictionary with for...in and tuple decomposition.
3
4   let months = ["January" : 31, "February" : 29,
5       "March" : 31, "April" : 30,  "May" : 31, "June" : 30,
6       "July" : 31, "August" : 31, "September" : 30,
7       "October" : 31, "November" : 30, "December" : 31]
```

Fig. 7.4 | Iterating through a Dictionary with for...in and tuple decomposition. (Part 1 of 2.)

```
 8
 9   // print table of month numbers and names
10   // use for...in to iterate through months Dictionary
11   println("ITERATING THROUGH A DAYS-PER-MONTH-IN-A-LEAP-YEAR DICTIONARY")
12   println("WITH FOR...IN DECOMPOSING KEY-VALUE PAIRS INTO THE TUPLE")
13   println("(monthName, monthDays), THEN PRINTING THE TUPLE ELEMENTS")
14   for (monthName, monthDays) in months {
15       println("\(monthName):  \(monthDays)")
16   }
17
18   println()
19
20   // replace (key, value) form with tuple identifier like monthTuple,
21   // then say monthTuple.0 and monthTuple.1
22   println("ITERATING THROUGH A DAYS-PER-MONTH-IN-A-LEAP-YEAR DICTIONARY")
23   println("WITH FOR...IN USING A TUPLE NAME LIKE monthTuple")
24   println("THEN DECOMPOSING THE TUPLE WITH monthTuple.0 and monthTuple.1")
25   for monthTuple in months {
26       println("\(monthTuple.0):  \(monthTuple.1)")
27   }
```

```
ITERATING THROUGH A DAYS-PER-MONTH-IN-A-LEAP-YEAR DICTIONARY
WITH FOR...IN DECOMPOSING KEY-VALUE PAIRS INTO THE TUPLE
(monthName, monthDays), THEN PRINTING THE TUPLE ELEMENTS
June:  30
September:  30
October:  31
May:  31
February:  29
July:  31
April:  30
March:  31
December:  31
January:  31
August:  31
November:  30

ITERATING THROUGH A DAYS-PER-MONTH-IN-A-LEAP-YEAR DICTIONARY
WITH FOR...IN USING A TUPLE NAME LIKE monthTuple
THEN DECOMPOSING THE TUPLE WITH monthTuple.0 and monthTuple.1
June:  30
September:  30
October:  31
May:  31
February:  29
July:  31
April:  30
March:  31
December:  31
January:  31
August:  31
November:  30
```

Fig. 7.4 | Iterating through a Dictionary with for...in and tuple decomposition. (Part 2 of 2.)

First we define the months Dictionary (lines 4–7) with String keys and Int values—inferred from the Dictionary literal. We use 29 (days) as the value for the key "February" because the example focusses on the days per month in a leap year.

The for...in statement in lines 14–16 iterates through months' key–value pairs. Each iteration decomposes one key–value pair into the tuple (monthName, monthDays) in which the monthName element is the key and the monthDays element is the value. Because Dictionary is an unordered collection, you cannot make any assumptions about the order in which the loop accesses key–value pairs, as the output confirms. The tuple elements monthName and monthValue are implicitly *constants*—we use these in line 15 to output the key–value pairs. We iterate through months again (lines 25–27), this time using the item monthTuple to receive a tuple containing both a key and a value. Line 26 decomposes this into the key and value portions using the tuple element notations monthTuple.0 and monthTuple.1, respectively.

Common Programming Error 7.2
Attempting to modify the key and/or value portion of the tuple item produced on each iteration through of a for...in is a compilation error.

Common Programming Error 7.3
When iterating through a Dictionary, expecting that the key–value pairs will be accessed in key order can lead to logic errors. Dictionary objects are unordered—you cannot even assume that key–value pairs will be retrieved in the order in which they were added.

7.5 General-Purpose Generic Dictionary Printing Function

In Fig. 7.5, we create generic function printDictionary (lines 8–12), which we can use to print any Dictionary, regardless of its key type and value type (as long as those types are Strings or conform to the Printable protocol).

```
1   // Fig. 7.5: fig07_05.playground
2   // Example: Metric weight abbreviations
3
4   // Dictionary with common metric weight abbreviations
5   let metricWeightAbbreviations = ["mg" : "milligram",
6      "g" : "gram",  "kg" : "kilogram", "mt" : "metric ton"]
7
8   func printDictionary<K, V>(dictionary: [K : V]) {
9      for (key, value) in dictionary {
10         println("\(key):  \(value)")
11      }
12   }
13
14   // call the generic display function
15   println("PRINT METRIC WEIGHT ABBREVIATIONS WITH")
16   println("GENERIC printDictionary FUNCTION")
17   printDictionary(metricWeightAbbreviations)
```

Fig. 7.5 | Metric weight abbreviations. (Part 1 of 2.)

```
PRINT METRIC WEIGHT ABBREVIATIONS WITH
GENERIC printDictionary FUNCTION
kg:  kilogram
mt:  metric ton
g:   gram
mg:  milligram
```

Fig. 7.5 | Metric weight abbreviations. (Part 2 of 2.)

Generic Function Syntax

A **generic function** specifies one or more **type parameters** in angle brackets *following* the function name and *before* the function's parameter list. Type parameters are *placeholders* for actual types. In printDictionary, we use the type parameters K and V to represent a Dictionary's key and value types, respectively. Once you've introduced the type parameters, you can use them in the function's parameter list, return type (if any) and body to represent the actual types that the Swift compiler infers from a call to the function. In this case, we use K and V to declare that the function receives as an argument any type of Dictionary. The function's body uses the techniques you learned in Section 7.4 to display the argument's key–value pairs one at a time.

Calling a Generic Function

To call printDictionary (line 17), you simply pass the Dictionary's name, regardless of its key and value types. The compiler infers that the type parameters K and V both represent type String, because metricWeightAbbreviations's keys and values are both Strings. Thus, for this call to printDictionary, the dictionary parameter is a Dictionary of type [String : String] and the types of the tuple elements key and value in line 9 are both String.

If we were to call this function with a Dictionary of type [String : Int], the compiler would infer that the type parameters K and V represent types String and Int. In that case, the function's parameter would be a Dictionary of type [String : Int] and the types of the tuple elements key and value in line 9 would be String and Int, respectively.

Again, notice that the function does not necessarily print the key–value pairs in the order in which they appear in the Dictionary declaration. The version of printDictionary shown here does not print anything for an empty Dictionary. Using the Dictionary property isEmpty (Section 7.7), you could test whether the Dictionary contains any key–value pairs and, if not, display the empty Dictionary literal "[:]".

7.6 Dictionary Equality Operators == and !=

Figure 7.6 demonstrates using the equality operators == (line 17) and != (line 22) to compare two Dictionary objects to determine whether they have identical or different *contents*, respectively. The outputs confirm these relationships.

In Section 3.4, we discussed the related *identity operators* === and !==, which work only for *reference types* (classes), but not for value types like Dictionary. These operators allow you to determine whether two references refer to the *same* or *different* class objects, respectively.

```
 1   // Fig. 7.6: fig07_06.playground
 2   // Dictionary equality operators == and !=
 3   let countryCapitals1 =
 4       ["Belgium" : "Brussels", "Haiti" : "Port-au-Prince"]
 5   println("\ncountryCapitals1: \(countryCapitals1)")
 6
 7   // different Dictionary from countryCapitals1
 8   let countryCapitals2 = ["Nepal" : "Kathmandu", "Uruguay" : "Montevideo"]
 9   println("countryCapitals2: \(countryCapitals2)")
10
11   // same contents as Dictionary countryContents1 but a different object
12   let countryCapitals3 =
13       ["Belgium" : "Brussels", "Haiti" : "Port-au-Prince"]
14   println("countryCapitals3: \(countryCapitals3)")
15
16   // use == operator
17   if countryCapitals1 == countryCapitals3 {
18       print("countryCapitals1 has the same contents as countryCapitals3")
19   }
20
21   // use != operator
22   if countryCapitals1 != countryCapitals2 {
23       print("countryCapitals1 does not have the same contents ")
24       println("as countryCapitals2")
25   }
```

```
countryCapitals1: [Belgium: Brussels, Haiti: Port-au-Prince]
countryCapitals2: [Nepal: Kathmandu, Uruguay: Montevideo]
countryCapitals3: [Belgium: Brussels, Haiti: Port-au-Prince]
countryCapitals1 has the same contents as countryCapitals3
countryCapitals1 does not have the same contents as countryCapitals2
```

Fig. 7.6 | Dictionary equality operators == and !=.

7.7 Dictionary count and isEmpty Properties

You access and modify a Dictionary through its methods and properties, or by using subscript syntax. Figure 7.7 uses Dictionary property **count** (which returns an Int) to determine how many key–value pairs the Dictionary contains and property **isEmpty** (which returns a Bool) to determine whether the Dictionary is empty. Line 6 uses count to determine that countryCodes contains two key–value pairs. Line 9 uses isEmpty to determine that countryCodes is not empty. We then assign the empty Dictionary literal ([:]) to countryCodes to remove all of its key–value pairs (line 15) and confirm that it's empty (line 19).

```
 1   // Fig. 7.7: fig07_07.playground
 2   // Dictionary properties count and isEmpty
 3   var countryCodes = ["Argentina" : "ar", "Jamaica" : "jm"]
 4
```

Fig. 7.7 | Dictionary properties count and isEmpty. (Part 1 of 2.)

```
 5    // Use count property to determine number of key-value pairs in Dictionary
 6    println("\ncountryCodes CONTAINS \(countryCodes.count) KEY-VALUE PAIRS")
 7
 8    // Use method isEmpty to determine if a contryCodes is empty
 9    if countryCodes.isEmpty {
10        println("\nDictionary countryCodes IS EMPTY")
11    } else {
12        println("\nDictionary countryCodes IS NOT EMPTY")
13    }
14
15    countryCodes = [:] // empty the Dictionary using empty Dictionary literal
16
17    // Use method isEmpty to determine if a contryCodes1 is empty
18    println("\nAFTER ASSIGNING [:] TO countryCodes")
19    if countryCodes.isEmpty {
20        println("Dictionary countryCodes IS EMPTY")
21    } else {
22        println("Dictionary countryCodes IS NOT EMPTY")
23    }
```

```
countryCodes CONTAINS 2 KEY-VALUE PAIRS

Dictionary countryCodes IS NOT EMPTY

AFTER ASSIGNING [:] TO countryCodes
Dictionary countryCodes IS EMPTY
```

Fig. 7.7 | Dictionary properties count and isEmpty. (Part 2 of 2.)

7.8 Dictionary Whose Values Are Arrays

Figure 7.8 uses a Dictionary to represent an instructor's grade book. The Dictionary maps each student name (a String) to an Int Array of that student's grades. In each iteration of the loop that displays the data (lines 15–21), a key–value pair is decomposed into the tuple (student, grades) containing one student's name and the corresponding Array containing the student's test scores. Line 16 uses Array method reduce and a closure (as discussed in Section 6.8.3) to total a given student's grades; we then calculate that student's semester average (lines 17–18) by dividing total by the number of grades for that student (grades.count). Lines 17–18 use the format String "%.2f" to print the average with two digits of precision. Lines 24–25 print the overall average of all the students' grades on all exams. Note that the line 16 method call can be further simplified by passing just the + operator function, as in grades.reduce(0, +).

```
 1    // Fig. 7.8: fig07_08.playground
 2    // Instructor's gradebook Dictionary
 3    import Foundation
 4
 5    let gradeBook = [
 6        "Susan" : [92, 85, 100], // name : Array of grades
 7        "Eduardo" : [83, 95, 79],
```

Fig. 7.8 | Instructor's gradebook Dictionary. (Part 1 of 2.)

```
 8       "Azizi" : [91, 89, 82],
 9       "Pantipa" : [97, 91, 92]
10  ]
11  var allGradesTotal = 0.0
12  var allGradesCount = 0
13
14  // uses reduce and a closure
15  for (student, grades) in gradeBook {
16      let total = Double(grades.reduce(0, {$0 + $1}))
17      println("AVERAGE GRADE FOR \(student): " +
18          String(format: "%.2f", total / Double(grades.count)))
19      allGradesTotal += total
20      allGradesCount += grades.count
21  }
22
23  // String formatting
24  println("AVERAGE GRADE FOR ALL STUDENTS: " +
25      String(format: "%.2f", allGradesTotal / Double(allGradesCount)))
```

```
AVERAGE GRADE FOR Eduardo: 85.67
AVERAGE GRADE FOR Pantipa: 93.33
AVERAGE GRADE FOR Susan: 92.33
AVERAGE GRADE FOR Azizi: 87.33
AVERAGE GRADE FOR ALL STUDENTS: 89.67
```

Fig. 7.8 | Instructor's gradebook Dictionary. (Part 2 of 2.)

7.9 Dictionary's keys and values Properties

Figure 7.9 demonstrates Dictionary's keys and values properties. The for statement in lines 13–15 iterates through Dictionary winterMonths' keys. The **keys property** returns a read-only, iterable collection of the Dictionary's keys. Again, the output confirms that those keys were not necessarily returned in the order in which they were added to the Dictionary.

```
 1  // Fig. 7.9: fig07_09.playground
 2  // Dictionary keys and values properties.
 3
 4  let winterMonths =
 5      [12 : "December", 1 : "January", 2 : "February", 3 : "March"]
 6
 7  // print the winterMonths Dictionary
 8  println("winterMonths DICTIONARY IS")
 9  println(winterMonths)
10
11  // print winterMonth's keys
12  println("\nwinterMonths KEYS ARE:")
13  for key in winterMonths.keys {
14      println(key)
15  }
```

Fig. 7.9 | Dictionary keys and values properties. (Part I of 3.)

```
16
17    // print winterMonths values
18    println("\nwinterMonths VALUES ARE:")
19    for value in winterMonths.values {
20        println(value)
21    }
22
23    // use for...in to iterate through the iterable keys collection
24    println("\nfor...in ITERATING THROUGH keys COLLECTION")
25
26    for monthNumber in winterMonths.keys {
27        println("winterMonths[\(monthNumber)] \(winterMonths[monthNumber]!)")
28    }
29
30    println()
31
32    // convert iterable keys collection to an Array and process it
33    println("ARRAY OF winterMonths.keys")
34    let winterMonthsNumbersArray = [Int](winterMonths.keys)
35    for monthNumber in winterMonthsNumbersArray {
36        println("\(monthNumber)   ")
37    }
38
39    println()
40
41    // convert iterable values collection to an Array and process it
42    println("ARRAY OF winterMonths.values")
43    let winterMonthsNamesArray = [String](winterMonths.values)
44    for monthName in winterMonthsNamesArray {
45        println("\(monthName)   ")
46    }
```

```
winterMonths DICTIONARY IS
[12: December, 2: February, 3: March, 1: January]

winterMonths KEYS ARE:
12
2
3
1

winterMonths VALUES ARE:
December
February
March
January

for...in ITERATING THROUGH keys COLLECTION
winterMonths[12] December
winterMonths[2] February
winterMonths[3] March
winterMonths[1] January
```

Fig. 7.9 | Dictionary keys and values properties. (Part 2 of 3.)

```
ARRAY OF winterMonths.keys
12
2
3
1

ARRAY OF winterMonths.values
December
February
March
January
```

Fig. 7.9 | Dictionary keys and values properties. (Part 3 of 3.)

Lines 19–21 use Dictionary's **values** property on winterMonths to return a read-only, iterable collection of winterMonths' values. The output shows that those values were not retrieved in the order in which they were placed in the Dictionary.

Lines 26–28, iterate through the keys collection, printing the key–value pairs, with each line containing "winterMonths[*key*]" (such as winterMonths[12]) and its corresponding month name String *value* (such as "December"). In line 27, we use the exclamation point (!) in the expression winterMonths[monthNumber]! to **force unwrap** the optional returned by the subscript operation—this returns an optional, because the key might not exist in the Dictionary. We'll look at Dictionary subscripting operations in detail in the next section.

You might occasionally need to have Array versions of the iterable keys and values collections. Line 34 uses the notation [Int](winterMonths.keys) to create a new Int Array that's initialized with the elements of the winterMonths.keys collection—you could also use the notation Array(winterMonths.keys). We then iterate through that Array, printing all of winterMonth's keys. Line 43 uses the notation [String](winterMonths.values) to create a new String Array that's initialized with the elements of the winterMonths.values collection—again, you could use the notation Array(winterMonths.values) here. We then iterate through that Array, printing all of winterMonth's values.

7.10 Inserting, Modifying and Removing Key–Value Pairs with Subscripting

Figure 7.10 demonstrates how to use Dictionary subscripting operations, including inserting new key–value pairs, modifying the values associated with keys and removing key–value pairs. The example also demonstrates how to process the optionals that are returned when you get the value for a given Dictionary key. We begin by declaring Dictionary romanNumerals (lines 5–6), then printing it. We intentionally provided the incorrect value 100 for the key "X", which we'll correct in line 13. The sample output confirms the effects of each of the program's subscript operations.

```
1   // Fig. 7.10: fig07_10.playground
2   // Dictionary subscript operations and optionals.
3
```

Fig. 7.10 | Dictionary subscript operations and optionals. (Part 1 of 3.)

```
4    // mutable Dictionary maps Roman numerals to their decimal equivalents
5    var romanNumerals = ["I" : 1, "II" : 2, "III" : 3,
6       "V" : 5, "X" : 100] // 100 should be 10 -- we'll soon correct this
7
8    // print table of Roman numerals and decimal values
9    println("\nDECIMAL EQUIVALENTS OF ROMAN NUMERALS")
10   println(romanNumerals)
11
12   // fix decimal equivalent on Roman numeral "X"
13   romanNumerals["X"] = 10
14   println("\nAFTER CORRECTING VALUE OF KEY \"X\"")
15   println(romanNumerals)
16
17   // use subscripting to add a new key-value pair
18   romanNumerals["L"] = 50
19   println("\nADDED NEW KEY-VALUE PAIR [\"L\" : 50]")
20   println(romanNumerals)
21
22   // use subscripting to assign nil to a key to remove its key-value pair
23   romanNumerals["III"] = nil
24   println("\nAFTER ASSIGNING NIL TO \"III\" TO REMOVE ITS KEY-VALUE PAIR")
25   println(romanNumerals)
26
27   // prints Optional(5)
28   // print "without forced unwrapping" and "with forced unwrapping"
29   println()
30   print("WITHOUT FORCED UNWRAPPING: ")
31   println(romanNumerals["V"]) // Optional because key may not exist
32   print("   WITH FORCED UNWRAPPING: ")
33   println(romanNumerals["V"]!) // Optional because key may not exist
34
35   // result of access attempt with subscripting could be nil if no item
36   let romanSymbol = "III"
37   if let decimalNumber = romanNumerals[romanSymbol] {
38       println("\nDECIMAL: \(decimalNumber)")
39   } else {
40       println("\nromanNumerals DOES NOT CONTAIN: \(romanSymbol)")
41   }
42
43   // use subscripting to add a new key-value pair to an empty Dictionary
44   var romanNumerals1: [String : Int] = [:] // new empty Dictionary
45   romanNumerals1["C"] = 100 // insert key-value pair into empty Dictionary
46   println("\nAFTER ADDING THE KEY-VALUE PAIR [\"C\" : 100] TO")
47   println("THE EMPTY romanNumerals1 DICTIONARY")
48   println("romanNumerals1 IS: \(romanNumerals1)")
49
```

```
DECIMAL EQUIVALENTS OF ROMAN NUMERALS
[X: 100, I: 1, II: 2, V: 5, III: 3]

AFTER CORRECTING VALUE OF KEY "X"
[X: 10, I: 1, II: 2, V: 5, III: 3]
```

Fig. 7.10 | Dictionary subscript operations and optionals. (Part 2 of 3.)

```
ADDED NEW KEY-VALUE PAIR ["L" : 50]
[X: 10, L: 50, I: 1, II: 2, V: 5, III: 3]

AFTER ASSIGNING NIL TO "III" TO REMOVE ITS KEY-VALUE PAIR
[X: 10, L: 50, I: 1, II: 2, V: 5]

WITHOUT FORCED UNWRAPPING: Optional(5)
   WITH FORCED UNWRAPPING: 5

romanNumerals DOES NOT CONTAIN: III

AFTER ADDING THE KEY-VALUE PAIR ["C" : 100] TO
THE EMPTY romanNumerals1 DICTIONARY
romanNumerals1 IS: [C: 100]
```

Fig. 7.10 | `Dictionary` subscript operations and optionals. (Part 3 of 3.)

7.10.1 Updating the Value of an Existing Key–Value Pair

Line 13 corrects the value associated with "X" by assigning 10 to `romanNumerals["X"]`.

Common Programming Error 7.4
When you intend to modify the value associated with an existing key, if you mistype the key, you could inadvertently create a new key–value pair and the value you intended to modify will not be modified.

Common Programming Error 7.5
A compilation error occurs if you attempt to modify an immutable `Dictionary` *(declared with* `let`*) by adding a new key–value pair, changing the value in a key–value pair or deleting a key–value pair.*

7.10.2 Adding a New Key–Value Pair

Line 18 adds a new key–value pair by assigning 50 to `romanNumerals["L"]`—previously the key "L" was not in the `Dictionary`.

7.10.3 Removing a Key–Value Pair

Line 23 removes the key–value pair "III" : 3 by assigning `nil` to `romanNumerals["III"]`. The output confirms the removal. Assigning `nil` to a nonexistent key is not an error—it simply does nothing.

7.10.4 Subscripting Returns an Optional Value

When you use subscripting to attempt to retrieve a value for a given key, an optional is returned because that key may not exist. Line 31 demonstrates this by printing the value returned by `romanNumerals["V"]`. Because `romanNumerals` is a `Dictionary` of type `[String : Int]`, `romanNumerals["V"]` returns an `Int?` (that is, optional `Int`) containing the key's corresponding value or `nil` if the key is not in the `Dictionary`. In the output, the `Int?` value appears as `Optional(5)` indicating that the returned value is an optional containing the `Int` value 5.

To manipulate the value for a given key, you must first extract it from the optional—this is known as unwrapping the value. Line 33 prints `romanNumerals["V"]!`—the exclamation point ! *force unwraps* the optional, which extracts the `Int` value 5 from the `Int?` object.

Common Programming Error 7.6
When you force unwrap an optional, it must be non-`nil`; otherwise, a runtime error occurs.

Error-Prevention Tip 7.2
Unless you know with absolute certainty that an optional will never contain `nil`, you should use optional binding (introduced in Section 6.9.7) to unwrap an optional.

7.10.5 Processing an Optional Value

The statement in lines 37–41 use *optional binding* to unwrap an optional only if its value is not `nil`. Recall from Section 6.9.7 that the `if` condition is `false` if the optional contains `nil`, in which case the `else` part of the `if...else` statement executes. Otherwise, the optional's value is unwrapped and assigned to the constant `decimalNumber` for use in the `if` part of the `if...else` statement.

7.10.6 Inserting a New Key–Value Pair in an Empty Dictionary

Line 44 creates an empty `Dictionary`. In line 45, we show that when you assign a value to a key that doesn't exist, a new key–value pair is created. The explicit `Dictionary` type annotation is required in line 44, because the compiler cannot infer the `Dictionary`'s type from the empty `Dictionary` literal.

7.11 Inserting, Removing and Modifying Key–Value Pairs

In the previous section, we used `Dictionary` subscripting operations to manipulate a `Dictionary`'s contents. Figure 7.11 uses `Dictionary` methods `updateValue`, `removeValueForKey` and `removeAll` to perform equivalent manipulations, several of which involve processing optional values.

Creating Empty Dictionary countryCodes
Line 5 declares the empty `Dictionary` countryCodes. We cannot simply say

```
var countryCodes = [:]
```

as there's insufficient information for the compiler to infer countryCodes's type from the literal `[:]`. We print countryCodes to confirm the effect of each of the method operations we describe in the next several sections.

```
1   // Fig. 7.11: fig07_11.playground
2   // Dictionary methods updateValue, removeValueForKey and removeAll
3
```

Fig. 7.11 | Dictionary methods updateValue, removeValueForKey and removeAll. (Part 1 of 3.)

```
 4   // Start with empty Dictionary
 5   var countryCodes : [String : String] = [:]
 6
 7   // method updateValue
 8   // add a new key-value pair with method updateValue
 9   // handle optional return of previous value (of type String?)
10   if let previous = countryCodes.updateValue("za", forKey: "South Africa") {
11       println("PREVIOUS VALUE FOR KEY \"South Africa\" WAS \(previous)")
12   } else {
13       println("KEY \"South Africa\" IS NEW")
14   }
15
16   println("countryCodes: \(countryCodes)\n")
17
18   // add a second key-value pair
19   // "ar" is incorrect for "Australia" should be "au" -- we'll fix below
20   // handle optional return of previous value (of type String?)
21   if let previous = countryCodes.updateValue("ar", forKey: "Australia") {
22       println("PREVIOUS VALUE FOR KEY \"Australia\" WAS \(previous)")
23   } else {
24       println("KEY \"Australia\" IS NEW")
25   }
26
27   println("countryCodes: \(countryCodes)\n")
28
29   // update existing value (correct Australia's code from "ar" to "au"
30   // handle optional return of previous value (of type String?)
31   println("CORRECTED \"Australia\" COUNTRY CODE FROM \"ar\" TO \"au\"")
32   if let previous = countryCodes.updateValue("au", forKey: "Australia") {
33       println("PREVIOUS VALUE FOR KEY \"Australia\" WAS \"\(previous)\"")
34   } else {
35       println("KEY \"Australia\" IS NEW")
36   }
37
38   println("countryCodes: \(countryCodes)\n")
39
40   // method removeValueForKey
41   // remove existing key-value pair
42   // handle optional return (of type String?)
43   if let previous = countryCodes.removeValueForKey("South Africa") {
44       print("KEY-VALUE PAIR \"South Africa\": ")
45       println("\"\(previous)\" WAS REMOVED")
46   } else {
47       println("KEY \"South Africa\" WAS NOT IN DICTIONARY")
48   }
49
50   println("countryCodes: \(countryCodes)\n")
51
52   // attempt to remove non-existing value
53   // handle nil return
54   if let previous = countryCodes.removeValueForKey("Paraguay") {
55       println("KEY-VALUE PAIR \"Paraguay\": \"\(previous)\" WAS REMOVED")
```

Fig. 7.11 | Dictionary methods updateValue, removeValueForKey and removeAll. (Part 2 of 3.)

```
56    } else {
57        println("KEY \"Paraguay\" IS NOT IN DICTIONARY")
58    }
59
60    println("countryCodes: \(countryCodes)\n")
61
62    // method removaAll
63    countryCodes.removeAll(keepCapacity: true)
64    if countryCodes.isEmpty {
65        println("DICTIONARY countryCodes IS EMPTY")
66    }
67
68    println("countryCodes: \(countryCodes)\n")
```

```
KEY "South Africa" IS NEW
countryCodes: [South Africa: za]

KEY "Australia" IS NEW
countryCodes: [South Africa: za, Australia: ar]

CORRECTED "Australia" COUNTRY CODE FROM "ar" TO "au"
PREVIOUS VALUE FOR KEY "Australia" WAS "ar"
countryCodes: [South Africa: za, Australia: au]

KEY-VALUE PAIR "South Africa": "za" WAS REMOVED
countryCodes: [Australia: au]

KEY "Paraguay" IS NOT IN DICTIONARY
countryCodes: [Australia: au]

DICTIONARY countryCodes IS EMPTY
countryCodes: [:]
```

Fig. 7.11 | Dictionary methods updateValue, removeValueForKey and removeAll. (Part 3 of 3.)

7.11.1 Inserting a Key–Value Pair with Dictionary Method updateValue

When you use subscripting to add or update a key–value pair, you receive no indication as to whether the Dictionary already contained that key. If you need this information, Dictionary method **updateValue** returns an optional containing nil if the key is new, or it returns the key's previous value if the key already exists.

Line 10 uses updateValue to add the key–value pair "South Africa" : "za" to countryCodes. That key does not exist, so updateValue adds the new key–value pair and returns an optional containing nil. The condition in line 10 evaluates to false and the else part of the if...else statement executes.

Line 21 uses updateValue to add the key–value pair "Australia" : "ar". The value "ar" is incorrect— we'll replace it with the correct value "au" in the next section. The condition in line 21 once again evaluates to false and the else part of the if...else statement executes.

7.11.2 Updating a Key–Value Pair with `Dictionary` Method `updateValue`

Line 32 again calls `updateValue`, this time to update the incorrect value "ar" that we associated with the key "Australia" (line 21). That exists, so `updateValue` updates the value for that key and returns an optional containing the previous value ("ar"). The condition in line 32 evaluates to `true` and the `if` part of the `if...else` statement executes. The output confirms that the value was corrected.

7.11.3 Removing a Key–Value Pair with `Dictionary` Method `removeValueForKey`

When you use subscripting to remove a key–value pair, you receive no indication as to whether the `Dictionary` already contained that key. If you need this information, `Dictionary` method **`removeValueForKey`** returns an optional containing the key's corresponding value if the key existed, or `nil` otherwise. Line 43 calls `removeValueForKey` to remove the key–value pair associated with the key "South Africa". This key already existed, so the condition in line 43 evaluates to `true` and the `if` part of the `if...else` statement executes.

7.11.4 Attempting to Remove a Nonexistent Key–Value Pair with Method `removeValueForKey`

The call to `removeValueForKey` in line 54 attempts to remove a key–value pair for a nonexistent key, so `removeValueForKey` returns an optional containing `nil` and the condition in line 54 evaluates to `false`.

7.11.5 Emptying a `Dictionary` with Method `removeAll`

Line 63 uses `Dictionary` method **`removeAll`** to empty the `countryCodes` `Dictionary`. This method receives a `Bool` argument (`keepCapacity`) that indicates whether to keep the memory that's already allocated to the `Dictionary`. The argument's default value is `false`, so calling `removeAll` with no arguments releases the `Dictionary`'s memory—in this case, we pass `true` to retain the `Dictionary`'s memory. The output confirms that there are no more key–value pairs in `countryCodes`.

Performance Tip 7.3

If you intend to reuse a `Dictionary`, then for performance reasons you might want to specify `keepCapacity: true` when calling `removeAll` to eliminate the overhead of deallocating and reallocating the memory.

7.12 Building a `Dictionary` Dynamically: Word Counts in a `String`

Figure 7.12 uses a `Dictionary` to count the number of occurrences of each word in a `String`. Function `padString` (lines 6–10) is similar to function `rightAlignedString` in Fig. 4.6—`padString` helps neatly align the program's output. Lines 7–9 could also be implemented with the following call to `NSString` method `stringByPaddingToLength`:

```
return string.stringByPaddingToLength(
    width, withString: " ", startingAtIndex: 0)
```

Lines 12–13 create a `String` that will be broken into its individual words (i.e., tokenized) for counting purposes. Recall that if you import the Foundation framework (line 3), you can use all of `NSString`'s methods on Swift Strings. Line 16 tokenizes the `String` sentence by calling `NSString` method **componentsSeparatedByString**, which separates the words using the delimiter provided in the method's `String` argument—a space in this case—and returns a `String` Array.

```
1   // Fig. 7.12: fig07_12.playground
2   // Tokenizing a string and producing word counts
3   import Foundation
4
5   // format a String left aligned in a field width
6   func padString(string: String, # width: Int) -> String {
7       let spaces: Int = width - countElements(string)
8       let padding = String(count: spaces, repeatedValue: Character(" "))
9       return string + padding
10  }
11
12  let sentence = "this is a sample sentence with several words " +
13      "this is another sample sentence with some different words"
14
15  // tokenize the sentence string
16  let words = sentence.componentsSeparatedByString(" ")
17
18  // summarize word counts
19  var wordCounts: [String : Int] = [:] // empty Dictionary
20
21  // summarize occurrences of each word
22  for word in words {
23      // if word in Dictionary, increment count; otherwise, add it
24      if let count = wordCounts[word] {
25          wordCounts[word] = count + 1 // increment count
26      } else {
27          wordCounts[word] = 1 // add word to Dictionary
28      }
29  }
30
31  // display the wordCounts contents
32  println("THE STRING \"\(sentence)\" CONTAINS:\n")
33  println(padString("WORD", width: 15) + "COUNT")
34
35  for (word, count) in wordCounts {
36      println(String(format: "%@%5d", padString(word, width: 15), count))
37  }
38
39  println("\nNUMBER OF KEYS IN WORDCOUNTS DICTIONARY: \(wordCounts.count)")
```

```
THE STRING "this is a sample sentence with several words this is another sam-
ple sentence with some different words" CONTAINS:
```

Fig. 7.12 | Tokenizing a `String` and producing word counts. (Part 1 of 2.)

```
WORD            COUNT
several          1
words            2
a                1
this             2
sample           2
another          1
some             1
different        1
with             2
sentence         2
is               2

NUMBER OF KEYS IN WORDCOUNTS DICTIONARY: 11
```

Fig. 7.12 | Tokenizing a String and producing word counts. (Part 2 of 2.)

Line 19 creates an empty Dictionary. The Dictionary's keys are Strings that hold the separate words, and its values are Ints that hold counts of how many times each word appears in the String sentence. Lines 22–29 iterate through the Array words. For each word, line 24 uses *optional binding* to determine whether that word (the key) is already in the Dictionary. If so, line 25 increments that word's count (the value) in the Dictionary; otherwise, line 27 inserts a new key–value pair for that word with a count of 1.

Lines 32–37 summarize the results by displaying the original value of the sentence followed by two columns that display each word and its corresponding count, respectively. The for...in statement (lines 35–37) iterates through the Dictionary's key–value pairs. Each key and value is decomposed into the tuple (word, count), then displayed (line 36).

7.13 Bridging Between Dictionary and Foundation Classes

You'll often pass Swift objects into and receive Swift objects from methods of classes written in Objective-C, such as those in the Cocoa and Cocoa Touch frameworks. Swift's numeric types and its String, Array and Dictionary types can all be used in contexts where their Objective-C equivalents are expected. Similarly, the Objective-C equivalents (NSString, NSMutableString, NSArray, NSMutableArray, NSDictionary, NSMutableDictionary and Objective-C numeric types), when returned to your Swift code, are *automatically* treated as their Swift counterparts. This mechanism—known as **bridging**—is transparent to you. In fact, when you look at the Swift version of the Cocoa and Cocoa Touch documentation online or in Xcode, you'll see the Swift types, not the Objective-C types for cases in which this bridging occurs. For example, the NSString method componentsSeparatedByString that we used in Fig. 7.12 actually returns an NSArray containing NSStrings. However, when you click the method name in Xcode and view its help in the **Quick Help** inspector, the return type is specified as [String]. We'll say more about bridging later in the book—for additional details, see Apple's *Using Swift with Cocoa and Objective-C* at:

```
http://bit.ly/UsingSwiftWithObjC
```

7.14 Hash Tables and Hashing

We've mentioned that `Dictionary` collections are implemented as hash tables. This section briefly discusses the general operation of hash tables and hashing mechanisms for the benefit of readers who have not studied these topics. We emphasize how hash tables achieve high performance.

Software Engineering Observation 7.2

`Dictionary` objects enable you to use sophisticated hashing mechanisms without having to implement your own—a classic benefit of software reuse.

When Are `Dictionary` Collections with Hashing More Appropriate Than `Arrays`?
Programs typically need to store and retrieve data items, such as `Array` values and `Dictionary` key–value pairs, efficiently. Such operations with `Array`s are efficient if some aspect of your data directly matches a numerical key value and if the keys are *unique* and *tightly packed*, so they can be used as `Array` subscripts.

Suppose you have 100 employees and intend to use their nine-digit social security numbers as keys—this would require an `Array` with close to a billion elements. A program having an `Array` that large could achieve high performance for both storing and retrieving employee data simply by using the social security number as the `Array` index. But using that much memory is impractical for the vast majority of applications that use social security numbers as keys.

Numerous applications have this problem—either the keys are of the wrong type (i.e., not positive integers that map easily to a "tight" range of memory locations) or they're of the right type but *sparsely* spread over a *huge range*. What's needed is a high-speed scheme for converting keys such as social security numbers, inventory part numbers and and even nonnumeric keys into unique memory locations over a specified range. Then, when an application needs to store a data item, the scheme transforms the application's key rapidly into a memory location, and the item is stored at that location. Retrieval is accomplished the same way—once the application has a key for which it wants to retrieve a data item, the *same* hashing transformation is applied again with the same key—this determines the memory location where the data is stored and the item is then retrieved.

The scheme we describe here is the basis of the technique called **hashing**. Why the name? When we transform a key into a memory location, the key's bits are essentially *scrambled*, forming a kind of "mishmashed," or hashed, number. The number actually has no real significance beyond its usefulness in storing and retrieving data items, such as a `Dictionary`'s key–value pairs.

Performance Tip 7.4

For applications similar to those that use social security numbers for keys but with a relatively small number of people, a small `Dictionary` will give you efficient memory utilization and rapid insertion, updating, retrieval and removal of key–value pairs.

Collisions
A glitch in the scheme is called a *collision*—this occurs when two different keys "hash into" the *same* memory location. Because we cannot store two values in the same place, we need to find alternative locations for all values beyond the first that hash to a particular memory

location. There are many schemes for doing this. One is to "hash again"—you simply apply the *same* hashing transformation to the result of the first transformation to provide the next candidate location in memory. The hashing process is designed to spread the values randomly throughout the range of memory locations in the table, so the assumption is that after a collision an available cell will be found with just one or a few hashes.

Another scheme hashes once to find the first candidate location. If that one is occupied, successive locations are simply searched in order until an available one is found. Retrieval works the same way: The key is hashed once to determine the initial location and check whether it contains the desired data. If it does, the search is finished. If it does not, successive locations are searched linearly until the desired data is found.

The most popular solution to hash-table collisions is to have each location of the table be a hash "bucket," typically a linked list of all the key–value pairs that hash to that location. The trick is to keep those lists short, because such linear searching is slow.

Software Engineering Observation 7.3

Two objects have that have the same hash value might not be equal; however, if two objects are equal, they will have the same hash value.

Hash Table Load Factor and Performance

A hash table's *load factor* affects the performance of hashing schemes. The load factor is the ratio of the number of *occupied* locations in the table to its *total* number of locations. The closer this ratio gets to 1.0, the greater the chance of collisions and the less efficient the hash table operations become.

Performance Tip 7.5

The load factor in a hash table is a classic example of a space–time trade-off: By increasing the load factor, we get better memory utilization, but the program runs slower, due to increased hashing collisions. By decreasing the load factor, we get better program speed, because of reduced hashing collisions, but memory utilization is poorer.

Because each value has an associated key, `Dictionary` collections take up more space than `Arrays` (where the keys are implicitly the subscripts and the values are the `Array` elements). Nevertheless, `Dictionary` collections provide fast lookup capabilities, often requiring only one hashing operation.

Performance Tip 7.6

Despite the fact that `Dictionary` entries are unordered, hashing still makes `Dictionary` operations fast.

7.15 Wrap-Up

In this chapter we discussed Swift's other built-in collection type—`Dictionary`. We defined what a `Dictionary` is, presented several examples, explained that `Dictionary` is a generic type and a value type, and that `Dictionary` is type safe.

We mentioned that `Dictionary` collections are implemented as hash tables, and for that reason their keys must conform to the `Hashable` protocol. We discussed how hash tables operate in general and explained how to declare and initialize `Dictionary` objects.

We showed the syntax of key–value pairs and showed how to use them to compose `Dictionary` literals for initializing `Dictionary` objects. We declared `Dictionary` objects with generics notation, showed an equivalent shorthand notation and simplified the declaration further by using type inference.

You used subscripting to retrieve the value that corresponds to a given key, and to update, add and remove key–value pairs. You learned that any attempt to retrieve the value for a particular key could fail, so retrieving a value for a given key returns an optional. You also used the `Dictionary` methods `updateValue` to update the value associated with a given key, `removeValueForKey` to remove a key–value pair and `removeAll` to remove all of a `Dictionary`'s key–value pairs.

You created an empty `Dictionary` by using initializer syntax and the empty `Dictionary` literal `[:]`. You used `Dictionary` properties `count` and `isEmpty` to determine the number of key–value pairs and whether a `Dictionary` is empty, respectively.

We created a `Dictionary` specifying its `minimumCapacity` and saw that when we remove all of the key–value pairs from a `Dictionary`, we can use `keepCapacity` to retain its memory for performance reasons should we need to add new key–value pairs.

You iterated through `Dictionary` objects with `for...in`. You used the `keys` and `values` properties to obtain iterable collections of the `Dictionary`'s keys and values, respectively, and learned how to convert these collections to `Arrays`, if needed. You also used the `keys` collection to iterate through a `Dictionary`'s key–value pairs.

We mentioned that Swift bridges between Swift `Dictionary` collections and Cocoa and Cocoa Touch Foundation classes `NSDictionary` and `NSMutableDictionary` (neither of which is type safe). In the next chapter, we begin our deeper treatment of object-oriented programming in Swift. We take a deeper look at building classes and creating robust class definitions. We'll also introduce Swift's `extensions`, which enable you to add features to existing types. Many of the capabilities you'll learn in Chapter 8 are also available in Swift's structure and enumeration types (Chapter 9).

8

Classes: A Deeper Look and Extensions

Objectives

In this chapter you'll:

- Take a deeper look at classes.
- Use stored properties and computed properties.
- Use `willSet` and `didSet` property observers with stored properties.
- Initialize stored properties with default initializers, designated initializers, convenience initializers and failable initializers.
- Add capabilities to a class via `extension`s.
- Create a read-write computed property with `get` and `set` accessors.
- Understand composition and the *has-a* relationship.
- Use `NSDecimalNumber` for precise monetary calculations.
- Understand automatic reference counting.
- Understand deinitializers.
- Use type properties and type methods.
- Learn how lazy stored properties can boost performance.

8.1 Introduction

We now take a deeper look at building classes and creating robust class definitions. Many of the capabilities you'll learn in this chapter are also available in Swift's structure and enumeration types. In Chapter 9, Structures, Enumerations and Nested Types, we'll explain the close relationships between classes, structures and enumerations, and when to prefer each in your apps. We'll also consider structure-specific and enumeration-specific limitations.

Property Observers and Data Validation
We begin by introducing stored properties with property observers (Section 8.2). As you'll see, when a property is assigned a new value, property observers enable code to execute before and after the property's value changes. We'll demonstrate how you can use property observers to validate a property's new value and, if it's invalid, restore the property's original value.

Designated and Convenience Initializers
You've seen that you can declare your own initializer to specify how objects of a class should be initialized. In this chapter, we'll show that you can overload initializers to enable objects to be initialized several ways, based on different sets of arguments. As we'll discuss in Section 8.3, Swift has two types of initializers—*designated initializers* that must initialize all of a class's stored properties and *convenience initializers* that call designated initializers, typically to provide common values for specific initializer arguments.

Failable Initializers

Sometimes it's useful to *prevent* an object from being created if the initializer receives invalid data. This is the purpose of Swift's *failable initializers* (Section 8.4). We'll show that when you invoke a failable initializer, it returns an *optional* of the class's type containing a properly initialized object or `nil` if initialization fails.

Extensions

Objective-C enabled programmers to add new features to existing classes via *categories*. In Section 8.5, we introduce a similar capability called `extensions`, which you can use to enhance your *existing* custom class, structure and enumeration types, as well as *existing* types from the Swift Standard Library and the Cocoa and Cocoa Touch Frameworks. As you'll see in this and subsequent chapters, most features that you can define directly in a type also can be defined via `extensions`.

Read-Write Computed Properties

So far, we've shown several read-only computed properties. In Section 8.6, we'll demonstrate that computed properties can be read-write and provide both `get` *and* `set` accessors. We'll use this feature to create a `Circle` class with a `radius` stored property and computed properties that use the radius to calculate the `diameter`, `circumference` and `area`. Those computed properties will each provide a `set` accessor that updates the `radius` when those properties are assigned new values.

Composition

In earlier chapters, we created classes that contained stored properties of value types (e.g., class `Account` in Chapter 3) and reference types (e.g., class `DeckOfCards` in Section 6.9.2). Creating classes that contain objects of value types or references to objects of class types is known as composition. Section 8.7 formalizes this concept and demonstrates a class that contains stored properties of both value and reference types. Section 8.7's example also introduces the Foundation framework classes `NSDate` and `NSDateFormatter`. An `NSDate` stores date and time data. An `NSDateFormatter` is used to create *locale-specific* date and time `Strings` and to create `NSDates` from `Strings` containing dates and times.

Automatic Reference Counting and Deinitializers

Unlike some languages, Swift manages the memory of reference-type objects for you via *automatic reference counting (ARC)*—when there are no more "strong" references to an object, the runtime removes it from memory. Section 8.8 discusses ARC fundamentals and introduces Swift's different types of references. Section 8.9 discusses deinitializers, which are called by the runtime just before a reference-type object is deallocated. We show an example of a deinitializer in Section 8.11.

NSDecimalNumbers for Precise Monetary Calculations

In Section 4.10.2, we demonstrated compound-interest calculations with `Double` values and mentioned that precise monetary calculations should be performed with `NSDecimalNumbers`. Section 8.10 reimplements the example of Section 4.10.2 using `NSDecimalNumbers`.

Type Properties and Type Methods

You can define properties that are accessed directly on a type. Such properties are *shared* by *all* objects of the type, rather than each object having its own separate copies of the properties. Similarly, you can define methods that are called directly on a type, rather than on a particular object of the type. Section 8.11 demonstrates how to implement such capabilities with type properties and type methods.

Lazy Stored Properties

Sometimes it's helpful to defer a stored property's initialization until that property is first used. Section 8.12 discusses how you can do this via `lazy` stored properties. Such properties can help prevent unnecessary initialization, improving performance.

8.2 Time Class: Default Initializers and Property Observers

Our first example presents a simple `Time` class that represents the time of day. We use this class to introduce *default initializers* and *property observers*. The example consists of two files—`Time.swift` (Fig. 8.1) containing class `Time` and `main.swift` (Fig. 8.2) containing code that tests class `Time`'s features. The example's output appears in Fig. 8.2.

Time Class Declaration

Class `Time`'s has three variable stored properties—`hour` (lines 5–15), `minute` (lines 18–28) and `second` (lines 31–41). These properties represent the time in *universal-time* format—the 24-hour clock format in which hours are in the range 0–23, and minutes and seconds are each in the range 0–59. Class `Time` also provides the read-only computed properties `universalDescription` (lines 44–46) and `description` (lines 49–53). (In Chapter 10, Inheritance, Polymorphism and Protocols, we'll discuss the `Printable` protocol's `description` property and how to make any type work with `String` interpolation and the `print` and `println` functions.) Class `Time` and all of its properties are declared `public`—these are the **public services** that the class provides to its clients.

Software Engineering Observation 8.1

Throughout this chapter, we design our classes for reuse. For this reason, the classes are declared `public`, and their members are declared `public`, unless they should be hidden from client code. Recall that—in a given source-code file—anything declared `private` is accessible only in that file, anything declared `internal` is accessible throughout the module and anything declared `public` is accessible throughout the module and wherever that module is imported.

Software Engineering Observation 8.2

When appropriate, provide `public` properties and methods to change and retrieve the values of `private` properties. This architecture helps hide the implementation of a class from its clients, which improves program modifiability.

```
1  // Fig. 8.1: Time.swift (TimeClass.xcodeproj)
2  // Time class with default initializer and property observers
3  public class Time {
```

Fig. 8.1 | Time class with default initializer and property observers. (Part 1 of 2.)

```
 4      // an hour value in the range 0-23
 5      public var hour: Int = 0 {
 6          willSet {
 7              println("hour is \(hour); setting it to \(newValue)")
 8          }
 9          didSet {
10              if hour < 0 || hour > 23 {
11                  println("hour invalid, resetting to \(oldValue)")
12                  hour = oldValue
13              }
14          }
15      }
16
17      // a minute value in the range 0-59
18      public var minute: Int = 0 {
19          willSet {
20              println("minute is \(minute); setting it to \(newValue)")
21          }
22          didSet {
23              if minute < 0 || minute > 59 {
24                  println("minute invalid, resetting to \(oldValue)")
25                  minute = oldValue
26              }
27          }
28      }
29
30      // a second value in the range 0-59
31      public var second: Int = 0 {
32          willSet {
33              println("second is \(second); setting it to \(newValue)")
34          }
35          didSet {
36              if second < 0 || second > 59 {
37                  println("second invalid, resetting to \(oldValue)")
38                  second = oldValue
39              }
40          }
41      }
42
43      // convert to String in universal-time format (HH:MM:SS)
44      public var universalDescription: String {
45          return String(format: "%02d:%02d:%02d", hour, minute, second)
46      }
47
48      // convert to String in standard-time format (H:MM:SS AM or PM)
49      public var description: String {
50          return String(format: "%d:%02d:%02d %@",
51              ((hour == 0 || hour == 12) ? 12 : hour % 12),
52              minute, second, (hour < 12 ? "AM" : "PM"))
53      }
54  }
```

Fig. 8.1 | Time class with default initializer and property observers. (Part 2 of 2.)

8.2.1 Stored Property Initialization and the Default Initializer

Recall from Section 3.2.4 that Swift does not provide default values for a class's stored properties—before they're used, you *must* initialize them either in their definitions or in an initializer. The only exception is for stored properties of *optional* types, which are initialized to nil by default. For each of class Time's stored properties, we provided our own default value of 0, as specified in lines 5, 18 and 31. When all stored properties are defined with default values *and* the class does *not* define an initializer, recall that the compiler supplies a *default initializer* (with no parameters) that sets the stored properties to the default values specified in their definitions.

8.2.2 willSet and didSet Property Observers for Stored Properties

Sometimes, your code should be notified when an object's stored property is about to change or has changed. For example, in an iOS or OS X app, after a property changes you might want to update the app's UI with new data. (We show how to build iOS apps in Chapters 13–14 and in our book *iOS 8 for Programmers: An App-Driven Approach with Swift*.) For such cases, you can define **willSet** and **didSet property observers** that are invoked when a property *is about to be assigned* a new value and *after the new value has been assigned*, respectively. You can add one or both of these property observers to any variable stored property, including global or local variables, which are also stored properties.

Defining Property Observers
To define a property observer, enclose it in braces ({ and }) after the property, as in lines 5–15, which define the stored property hour to be of type Int with a default initial value of 0. In this case, we provide both willSet (lines 6–8) and didSet (lines 9–14) property observers. When you define a willSet property observer, it receives a constant with the default name newValue that represents the value that's *about to be* assigned to the property. Similarly, a didSet property observer receives a constant with the default name oldValue that represents the property's value *before* the assignment. In both cases, you can specify a custom name for the constant by enclosing the name in parentheses between the willSet or didSet keyword and the opening left brace ({) of the property observer's body.

Common Programming Error 8.1
For a stored property with property observers, you must explicitly specify a type annotation by placing a colon and a type to the right of the property's name; otherwise, a compilation error occurs.

willSet Property Observers for Properties **hour, minute** *and* **second**
To demonstrate when a willSet property observer executes, each willSet observer (lines 6–8, 19–21 and 32–34) simply outputs the corresponding property's current value and the newValue that's about to be assigned to the property.

didSet Property Observers for Properties **hour, minute** *and* **second**
Assigning a value to a property in its didSet property observer replaces the property's value. This enables you to use the didSet property observers (lines 9–14, 22–27 and 35–40) to *validate* the new value that was assigned to the hour, minute or second property, respectively. For each property, if its new value is invalid, we assign to the property the didSet ob-

server's oldValue constant—this restores the property's original value. If the new value is invalid, we also display a line of output showing that the didSet observer executed.

Software Engineering Observation 8.3
Unlike many object-oriented languages, Swift does not have exception handling. Validation is typically performed with property observers and failable initializers (Section 8.4).

Software Engineering Observation 8.4
You can define property observers for any stored property, whether it's a member of a type, a global stored property or a local stored property.

Property Observers Do Not Execute During Initialization
A property's observers do *not* execute when you assign a default value to the property in its definition, nor do they execute when you assign a value to the property in an initializer. *After* an object has already been initialized, however, the property's observers execute every time that property is assigned a value—even if the value is the same as the property's current value.

Implicit Use of self
As you learned in Chapter 3, every object can access its own members with keyword self. Throughout this example's Time class, we did not use self. However, each mention of hour, minute and second implicitly uses self to access the property on the current Time object being manipulated.

8.2.3 Computed Read-Only Properties universalDescription and description
Recall from Section 3.2.2 that computed properties do not store data—rather, they are calculated when needed. Also, recall from Section 6.9.1 that a computed property with only a get accessor is *read only*. When you provide only a get accessor for a computed property, you can use the shorthand notation for read-only computed properties in which you eliminate the get keyword and the braces. Class Time's universalDescription and description properties (lines 44–53) each use this shorthand notation. In Section 8.6, we demonstrate a read-write computed property.

universalDescription Computed Property
The read-only computed property universalDescription (lines 44–46) returns a String in *universal-time* format (i.e., 24-hour clock format), consisting of two digits each for the hour, minute and second. The 0 flag in a format specifier (e.g., "%02d") displays leading zeros for a value that doesn't use all the character positions in the specified field width. For example, if the time were 1:30:07 PM, the method would return 13:30:07. Line 45 creates a String containing the formatted hour, minute and second values, each with two digits and possibly a leading 0 (specified with the 0 flag).

description Computed Property
The read-only computed property description (lines 49–53) returns a String in *standard-time* format, consisting of the hour, minute and second values separated by colons and followed by AM or PM (e.g., 11:30:17 AM or 1:27:06 PM). Once again, we format the

minute and second as two-digit values, with leading zeros if necessary. Line 51 uses a ternary conditional operator (?:) to determine the value for hour in the String—if the hour is 0 or 12 (midnight or noon), 12 is inserted into the String; otherwise, a value from 1 to 11 is inserted. The conditional operator in line 52 determines whether the String should contain "AM" or "PM".

8.2.4 Using Class Time

Figure 8.2 demonstrates class Time. Lines 6–9 define a global function displayTime that receives a String and a Time object, then displays the String and the values of the Time's universalDescription and description properties, each on a line by itself. We use this function throughout the example to show the Time object's value after each operation. Of course, lines 7–8 could also use String interpolation to assemble the output String.

```
1   // Fig. 8.2: main.swift (TimeClass.xcodeproj)
2   // Testing class Time
3   import Foundation
4
5   // displays a Time object in 24-hour and 12-hour formats
6   func displayTime(header: String, time: Time) {
7       println(String(format: "%@\nUniversal time: %@\nStandard time: %@\n",
8           header, time.universalDescription, time.description))
9   }
10
11  // create and initialize a Time object
12  let time = Time() // invokes Time default initializer
13  displayTime("AFTER TIME OBJECT IS CREATED", time)
14
15  // change time then display new time
16  println("SETTING A NEW TIME")
17  time.hour = 13
18  time.minute = 27
19  time.second = 6
20  displayTime("\nAFTER SETTING NEW HOUR, MINUTE, AND SECOND VALUES", time)
21
22  // attempt to set time with invalid values
23  println("ATTEMPTING TO SET INVALID PROPERTY VALUES")
24  time.hour = 99
25  time.minute = 99
26  time.second = 99
27  displayTime("\nAFTER ATTEMPTING TO SET INVALID VALUES", time)
```

```
AFTER TIME OBJECT IS CREATED
Universal time: 00:00:00
Standard time: 12:00:00 AM

SETTING A NEW TIME
hour is 0; setting it to 13
minute is 0; setting it to 27
second is 0; setting it to 6
```

Fig. 8.2 | Testing class Time. (Part 1 of 2.)

```
AFTER SETTING NEW HOUR, MINUTE, AND SECOND VALUES
Universal time: 13:27:06
Standard time: 1:27:06 PM

ATTEMPTING TO SET INVALID PROPERTY VALUES
hour is 13; setting it to 99
hour invalid, resetting to 13
minute is 27; setting it to 99
minute invalid, resetting to 27
second is 6; setting it to 99
second invalid, resetting to 6

AFTER ATTEMPTING TO SET INVALID VALUES
Universal time: 13:27:06
Standard time: 1:27:06 PM
```

Fig. 8.2 | Testing class Time. (Part 2 of 2.)

Creating a *Time* Object and Displaying Its Initial Value

Line 12 creates a Time object named time using the class's default initializer. To confirm that the Time object is created and initialized properly, line 13 calls displayTime to display the Time object's universalDescription and description property values, which return the Time in universal-time format and standard-time format, respectively. Notice that when the object is initialized, the willSet and didSet property observers do *not* execute.

Changing the *Time*

Lines 17–19 change time by modifying its hour, minute and second properties. The output shows that each property's willSet executes *before* the new value is set. Line 20 calls displayTime again to confirm that time was set correctly.

Setting Invalid Values for a *Time* Object's Properties

To illustrate that Time's hour, minute and second properties' didSet observers *validate* new values that are assigned to the properties, lines 24–26 assign each property the *invalid* value 99. When this occurs, each property's didSet displays a line of text indicating that the new value is invalid and *resets the property's original value*. Line 27 calls displayTime again to confirm that time was restored to its original value before the invalid values were assigned to its properties.

Foundation Class *NSDate*

Several of this chapter's remaining examples demonstrate Swift concepts using variations of the class Time that we introduced in this example. In iOS and OS X development, rather than building your own time (or date) class, you'll typically reuse the Foundation framework's NSDate class (as we'll do in Section 8.7)—objects of this class can store both times and dates. In addition, you'll often use the Foundation framework's NSDateFormatter class, which provides various capabilities, including formatting NSDates as date and time Strings and creating NSDates from Strings containing dates and times.

8.3 Designated and Convenience Initializers in Class Time

As you know, you can declare your own initializer to specify how objects of a class should be initialized. Next, we demonstrate a Time class with several **overloaded initializers** that enable objects to be initialized with different sets of arguments. As we'll discuss, Swift has two types of initializers—designated initializers (Section 8.3.2) and convenience initializers (Section 8.3.3).

8.3.1 Class Time with Overloaded Initializers

Figure 8.3 presents an updated Time class with overloaded initializers. Lines 5–29 define the hour, minute and second stored properties, and lines 58–67 define the read-only computed properties universalDescription and description. For this and the remaining Time classes in this chapter, we removed the stored properties' willSet property observers and the output statements in the didSet property observers—the willSets and the output statements in the didSets were used in the first example simply to demonstrate when property observers execute. Lines 32–55 define the initializers (discussed in the next two sections).

```
1   // Fig. 8.3: Time.swift (TimeInitializers.xcodeproj)
2   // Time class with overloaded designated and convenience initializers.
3   public class Time {
4       // an hour value in the range 0-23
5       public var hour: Int = 0 {
6           didSet {
7               if hour < 0 || hour > 23 {
8                   hour = oldValue
9               }
10          }
11      }
12
13      // a minute value in the range 0-59
14      public var minute: Int = 0 {
15          didSet {
16              if minute < 0 || minute > 59 {
17                  minute = oldValue
18              }
19          }
20      }
21
22      // a second value in the range 0-59
23      public var second: Int = 0 {
24          didSet {
25              if second < 0 || second > 59 {
26                  second = oldValue
27              }
28          }
29      }
30
```

Fig. 8.3 | Time class with overloaded designated and convenience initializers. (Part 1 of 2.)

```
31    // designated initializer: sets each stored property to default value
32    public init() { } // empty body
33
34    // designated initializer: sets stored properties to specified values
35    public init(hour: Int, minute: Int, second: Int) {
36        self.hour = hour
37        self.minute = minute
38        self.second = second
39    }
40
41    // convenience initializer: hour supplied, minute and second set to 0
42    public convenience init(hour: Int) {
43        self.init(hour: hour, minute: 0, second: 0)
44    }
45
46    // convenience initializer: hour and minute supplied, second set to 0
47    public convenience init(hour: Int, minute: Int) {
48        self.init(hour: hour, minute: minute, second: 0)
49    }
50
51    // convenience initializer: another Time object supplied
52    public convenience init(time: Time) {
53        self.init(hour: time.hour, minute: time.minute,
54            second: time.second)
55    }
56
57    // convert to String in universal-time format (HH:MM:SS)
58    public var universalDescription: String {
59        return String(format: "%02d:%02d:%02d", hour, minute, second)
60    }
61
62    // convert to String in standard-time format (H:MM:SS AM or PM)
63    public var description: String {
64        return String(format: "%d:%02d:%02d %@",
65            ((hour == 0 || hour == 12) ? 12 : hour % 12),
66            minute, second, (hour < 12 ? "AM" : "PM"))
67    }
68 }
```

Fig. 8.3 | Time class with overloaded designated and `convenience` initializers. (Part 2 of 2.)

8.3.2 Designated Initializers

Swift divides initializers into two categories:

- **Designated initializers** ensure that *all* of the class's stored properties receive initial values—either by using the default values assigned to the stored properties in their definitions or by explicitly assigning values to the properties.

- **Convenience initializers** call the class's designated initializers to set the class's stored properties. These are typically used to provide common values for certain designated initializer arguments, giving client code more flexibility when creating objects of the class. Convenience initializers are *not* required to initialize every stored property, because they *must* call a designated initializer before doing anything else.

Each class you define *must* have a designated initializer. In a class with no initializers (e.g., class Time in Fig. 8.1), the designated initializer is the default initializer provided by the compiler. You can define several overloaded designated initializers, provided that each ensures all of the class's stored properties are initialized.

Error-Prevention Tip 8.1
Every stored property must be initialized either in its definition or in every designated initializer of the class; otherwise, a compilation error occurs.

Error-Prevention Tip 8.2
Every convenience initializer must call a designated initializer in the same class either directly or via another convenience initializer; otherwise, a compilation error occurs.

Error-Prevention Tip 8.3
Initializers cannot manipulate properties or call methods that manipulate properties until every property of the class has an initial value; otherwise, a compilation error occurs. This ensures that all properties are initialized before they're used.

Class *Time*'s Overloaded Designated Initializers

In Fig. 8.1, class Time's default initializer set hour, minute and second to their default 0 values (i.e., midnight in universal time). The default initializer does not enable the class's clients to initialize a Time object with custom values. The Time class in Fig. 8.3 defines a designated initializer (lines 35–39) that receives three Int arguments for the hour, minute and second, respectively, and uses them to initialize the stored properties.

Once you define any initializers in a class, the compiler no longer provides the default initializer. In this case, you must declare a no-argument initializer (line 32) if default initialization is required. Like a default initializer, a no-argument initializer is invoked with empty parentheses. If we omit the no-argument initializer, clients of this class would not be able to create a Time object with the expression Time(). The no-argument initializer defined here has an *empty body*, so it initializes the stored properties with their default values. As you can see, to overload designated initializers, you provide multiple initializer definitions with different signatures.

8.3.3 Convenience Initializers and Initializer Delegation with self

In other object-oriented languages, it's common for overloaded constructors to call a single constructor in the same class. This reduces code duplication and makes the constructors easier to maintain, modify and debug. In Swift, this is accomplished with convenience initializers that call a designated initializer—this is known as *delegating* work to a designated initializer. A convenience initializer's definition is preceded with the **convenience** keyword (as in Fig. 8.3, lines 42, 47 and 52). Before a convenience initializer manipulates the class's stored properties, it must call one of the class's designated initializers, either directly or via another convenience initializer. To delegate to another initializer, you use the self keyword as shown in lines 43, 48 and 53.

Class *Time*'s Overloaded Convenience Initializers

The convenience initializer in lines 42–44 receives one Int representing the hour, which is passed along with 0 for the minute and second to the three-argument designated initializer at lines 35–39. The convenience initializer in lines 47–49 receives two Ints representing the hour and minute, which are passed with 0 for the second to the three-argument designated initializer at lines 35–39. The convenience initializer in lines 52–55 receives an existing Time object, then invokes the three-argument designated initializer with that Time object's hour, minute and second property values—this is similar to a *copy constructor* in some other object-oriented languages.

Note Regarding Class Time's No-Argument Initializer
Class Time's no-argument initializer also could have been defined as a convenience initializer that passes 0 for the hour, minute and second to the three-argument designated initializer.

8.3.4 Using Class Time's Designated and Convenience Initializers

Figure 8.4 demonstrates each of class Time's designated and convenience initializers (lines 12–17). Line 12 invokes the Time no-argument designated initializer that initializes the t1 object to a Time's default values (i.e., midnight). Lines 13–17 demonstrate passing arguments to the other Time initializers:

- Line 13 invokes the single-argument convenience initializer that receives an Int (lines 42–44 of Fig. 8.3).

- Line 14 invokes the two-argument convenience initializer (lines 47–49 of Fig. 8.3).

- Line 15 invokes the three-argument designated initializer (lines 35–39 of Fig. 8.3.)

- Line 16 invokes the single-argument convenience initializer that receives an existing Time object (lines 52–55 of Fig. 8.3).

- Finally, line 17 once again invokes the three-argument designated initializer, but with invalid values for the hour, minute and second.

Next, the app displays the String representations of each Time object to confirm that it was initialized properly (lines 20–25). Notice that the Time object t6 contains invalid values for the hour, minute and second. Recall from Section 8.2, that property observers do not execute during initialization, thus it's possible with this example's Time class to initialize a Time object with invalid values for the hour, minute and second properties. In Section 8.4, we'll show how to validate initializer arguments with failable initializers. We'll use this technique to prevent a Time object from being created with invalid data.

```
1   // Fig. 8.4: main.swift (TimeInitializers.xcodeproj)
2   // Testing class Time's designated and convenience initializers
3   import Foundation
4
5   // displays a Time object in 24-hour and 12-hour formats
6   func displayTime(header: String, time: Time) {
7       println(String(format: "%@\n    %@\n    %@",
8           header, time.universalDescription, time.description))
9   }
```

Fig. 8.4 | Testing class Time's designated and convenience initializers. (Part 1 of 2.)

```
10
11    // create and initialize Time objects
12    let t1 = Time() // 00:00:00
13    let t2 = Time(hour: 2) // 02:00:00
14    let t3 = Time(hour: 21, minute: 34) // 21:34:00
15    let t4 = Time(hour: 12, minute: 25, second: 42) // 12:25:42
16    let t5 = Time(time: t4) // 12:25:42
17    let t6 = Time(hour: 99, minute: 99, second: 99) // invalid values
18
19    println("OBJECT: INITIALIZED WITH")
20    displayTime("t1: all default arguments", t1)
21    displayTime("t2: hour; default minute and second", t2)
22    displayTime("t3: hour and minute; default second", t3)
23    displayTime("t4: hour, minute and second", t4)
24    displayTime("t5: Time object t4", t5)
25    displayTime("t6: all invalid arguments (no validation)", t6)
```

```
OBJECT: INITIALIZED WITH
t1: all default arguments
    00:00:00
    12:00:00 AM
t2: hour; default minute and second
    02:00:00
    2:00:00 AM
t3: hour and minute; default second
    21:34:00
    9:34:00 PM
t4: hour, minute and second
    12:25:42
    12:25:42 PM
t5: Time object t4
    12:25:42
    12:25:42 PM
t6: all invalid arguments (no validation)
    99:99:99
    3:99:99 PM —— The value 3 is the result of the calculation hour % 12 (Fig. 8.3, line 65) with an hour of 99.
```

Fig. 8.4 | Testing class Time's designated and convenience initializers. (Part 2 of 2.)

8.4 Failable Initializers in Class Time

In the preceding example, we showed that it's possible to initialize a Time object with invalid data. We could have implemented the three-argument designated initializer in Fig. 8.3 to ensure that each argument was in range and, if not, set the corresponding property to a default value (such as 0). However, a better option would be to *prevent* the object from being created in the first place—similar to throwing an exception from a constructor in some object-oriented languages. This is the purpose of Swift's **failable initializers**. When you invoke a failable initializer, it returns an *optional* of the class's type—if the object is initialized properly, the optional contains an object of that type; otherwise, it contains nil. Figure 8.5 shows a version of class Time with failable initializers that validate a Time object's initial values and return nil if any of them are invalid. We'll explain the syntax for creating failable initializers in Sections 8.4.1– and 8.4.3.

```
1   // Fig. 8.5: Time.swift (TimeFailableInitializers.xcodeproj)
2   // Time class with failable initializers
3   public class Time {
4       // an hour value in the range 0-23
5       public var hour: Int = 0 {
6           didSet {
7               if hour < 0 || hour > 23 {
8                   hour = oldValue
9               }
10          }
11      }
12
13      // a minute value in the range 0-59
14      public var minute: Int = 0 {
15          didSet {
16              if minute < 0 || minute > 59 {
17                  minute = oldValue
18              }
19          }
20      }
21
22      // a second value in the range 0-59
23      public var second: Int = 0 {
24          didSet {
25              if second < 0 || second > 59 {
26                  second = oldValue
27              }
28          }
29      }
30
31      // designated initializer; not failable, because this initializer
32      // implicitly uses the stored properties' default values
33      public init() { } // empty body
34
35      // failable designated initializer
36      // returns nil if any argument is invalid
37      public init?(hour: Int, minute: Int, second: Int) {
38          self.hour = hour
39          self.minute = minute
40          self.second = second
41
42          if hour < 0 || hour > 23 || minute < 0 || minute > 59 ||
43              second < 0 || second > 59 {
44
45              return nil // initialization failed
46          }
47      }
48
49      // convenience initializer: hour supplied, minute and second set to 0
50      public convenience init?(hour: Int) {
51          self.init(hour: hour, minute: 0, second: 0)
52      }
53
```

Fig. 8.5 | Time class with failable initializers. (Part 1 of 2.)

```
54    // convenience initializer: hour and minute supplied, second set to 0
55    public convenience init?(hour: Int, minute: Int) {
56        self.init(hour: hour, minute: minute, second: 0)
57    }
58
59    // convenience initializer: use values from existing Time object;
60    // implicitly unwrapped failable initializer; all arguments
61    // are valid so failable designated initializer cannot fail
62    public convenience init!(time: Time) {
63        self.init(hour: time.hour, minute: time.minute,
64            second: time.second)
65    }
66
67    // convert to String in universal-time format (HH:MM:SS)
68    public var universalDescription: String {
69        return String(format: "%02d:%02d:%02d", hour, minute, second)
70    }
71
72    // convert to String in standard-time format (H:MM:SS AM or PM)
73    public var description: String {
74        return String(format: "%d:%02d:%02d %@",
75            ((hour == 0 || hour == 12) ? 12 : hour % 12),
76            minute, second, (hour < 12 ? "AM" : "PM"))
77    }
78 }
```

Fig. 8.5 | Time class with failable initializers. (Part 2 of 2.)

8.4.1 Failable Designated Initializers

Designated and convenience initializers can be failable. Lines 37–47 define class Time's three-argument designated initializer as failable. Such initializers are named init?—in class Time, the ? indicates that the initializer's result is a Time? (an optional Time). As in Fig. 8.3, we assign the initializer's argument values to the corresponding stored properties (Fig. 8.5, lines 38–40). Lines 42–46 then validate the values that were assigned to the stored properties. If any of them is invalid, line 45 returns nil; otherwise, initialization completes successfully. The client code can then manipulate the returned optional value with optional binding or optional chaining (as you'll see in Section 8.4.4).[1] We did not make class Time's no-argument initializer (line 33) failable, because it sets the stored properties to their default values—thus, it initializes a Time object to a valid default time (midnight).

8.4.2 Failable Convenience Initializers

Any convenience initializer that delegates to a failable initializer must itself be defined as a failable initializer, as is the case with the initializers in lines 50–52 and 55–57. Each delegates to the three-argument failable designated initializer. Note that when you delegate to a failable initializer you do *not* include the ? in the self.init call (lines 51 and 56).

---

1. Currently, you cannot return nil from a failable initializer unless all of the class's stored properties have values. According to Apple's Swift team, this is considered a bug and will be fixed in a future Swift release (https://devforums.apple.com/message/1062922#1062922).

Common Programming Error 8.2

A compilation error occurs if you define in the same class both failable and nonfailable initializers with the same signature.

8.4.3 Implicitly Unwrapped Failable Initializers

Lines 62–65 define a failable convenience initializer that receives as its argument an existing Time object. Because the argument object already exists, it must have been initialized with a valid time and the property observers ensure that the object cannot be set to invalid values. Thus, we can guarantee that the designated initializer called in lines 63–64 will not fail. For this reason, we define the initializer in 62–65 as an *implicitly unwrapped failable initializer—init!*. This initializer returns a Time!—an implicitly unwrapped Time object.

Common Programming Error 8.3

A compilation error occurs if a nonfailable initializer delegates to a failable initializer defined with init?.

Common Programming Error 8.4

A runtime error occurs if a nonfailable initializer delegates to a failable initializer defined with init! and the resulting optional contains nil.

8.4.4 Invoking Failable Initializers

The program of Fig. 8.6 tests three of class Time's failable initializers:

- Line 6 invokes class Time's three-argument failable designated initializer with three invalid values and uses optional binding to determine whether the object was created. In this case, the initializer returns nil because at least one of its arguments is out of range, so line 9 indicates that the initializer failed.

- Line 13 invokes class Time's one-argument failable convenience initializer—passing an invalid hour value—and uses optional binding to determine whether the object was created. Again, the initializer returns nil because at least one of its arguments is out of range, so line 16 indicates that the initializer failed.

- Line 20 invokes class Time's three-argument failable designated initializer with three valid values. In this case, the object is created and initialized, so line 20 unwraps the optional result and line 21 displays the Time object's description. Next, line 25 invokes class Time's implicitly unwrapped failable convenience initializer, passing the existing time3 object as an argument. Because time3 already exists, it always contains a valid time. The initializer copies the values of time3's stored properties into the time4 object. Line 26 the uses time4—an implicitly unwrapped Time object—to display the new Time's description.

Common Programming Error 8.5

If the implicitly unwrapped optional returned by init! contains nil and you attempt to access its members, a runtime error occurs.

```
1   // Fig. 8.6: main.swift (TimeFailableInitializers.xcodeproj)
2   // Testing class Time's failable initializers
3   import Foundation
4
5   // attempt to create a Time object with failable designated initializer
6   if let time1 = Time(hour: 99, minute: 99, second: 99) {
7       println("Time is \(time1.description)")
8   } else {
9       println("time1: initializer failed due to invalid arguments")
10  }
11
12  // attempt to create a Time object with a failable convenience initializer
13  if let time2 = Time(hour: 99) {
14      println("Time is \(time2.description)")
15  } else {
16      println("time2: initializer failed due to invalid argument")
17  }
18
19  // create a Time object, then use it to initialize another Time object
20  if let time3 = Time(hour: 16, minute: 4, second: 0) {
21      println("time3 is \(time3.description)")
22
23      // attempt to create a Time object with an implicitly
24      // unwrapped failable convenience initializer
25      let time4 = Time(time: time3)
26      println("time4 is \(time4.description)")
27  }
```

```
time1: initializer failed due to invalid arguments
time2: initializer failed due to invalid argument
time3 is 4:04:00 PM
time4 is 4:04:00 PM
```

Fig. 8.6 | Testing class Time's failable initializers.

8.5 Extensions to Class Time

Objective-C enables programmers to add new methods to existing classes via *categories*. Swift provides a similar capability called **extensions**, which you can use to add features to your *existing* custom class, structure and enumeration types, as well as *existing* types (like Int, String, Array, etc.) from the Swift Standard Library and the Cocoa and Cocoa Touch Frameworks. The primary differences betwen Objective-C categories and Swift extensions are that extensions do not have names and that extensions can be used to add methods and more to an existing type. In this section, we'll use class extensions to add computed properties and convenience initializers to a class. You can also use class extensions to:

- add methods.
- add subscripts ([]; shown in Chapter 12, Operator Overloading and Subscripts).
- add protocol conformance (demonstrated in Section 10.8).
- add nested types (that is, classes, structs or enums defined in the scope of other types).

- add computed properties and computed type properties.

- add type methods.

In addition to the items mentioned above, you can use extensions with structs (Chapter 9) to add stored type properties. Stored properties and designated intializers, however, must be defined directly in a type.

Common Programming Error 8.6

Compilation errors occur if you attempt to use an extension to redefine existing capabilities, add property observers to existing stored properties, or add stored properties or designated initializers.

8.5.1 Class Time with Extensions

For demonstration purposes in Fig. 8.7, we reorganize class Time from Fig. 8.3 so that the class definition contains only the stored properties and designated initializers (Fig. 8.3, lines 3–40). We define one extension containing just the convenience initializers (Fig. 8.7, lines 43–59) and another extension containing just the computed properties (Fig. 8.7, lines 62–74). An extension has the following syntax:

```
extension NameOfTypeToExtend {
    // method, computed property and convenience initializers
}
```

Software Engineering Observation 8.5

Programmers often use extensions to organize their code into related groups of functionality to make the code easier to maintain.

```swift
1   // Fig. 8.7: Time.swift (TimeExtension.xcodeproj)
2   // Time class with extensions
3   public class Time {
4       // an hour value in the range 0-23
5       public var hour: Int = 0 {
6           didSet {
7               if hour < 0 || hour > 23 {
8                   hour = oldValue
9               }
10          }
11      }
12
13      // a minute value in the range 0-59
14      public var minute: Int = 0 {
15          didSet {
16              if minute < 0 || minute > 59 {
17                  minute = oldValue
18              }
19          }
20      }
21
```

Fig. 8.7 | Time class with extensions. (Part I of 2.)

```
22          // a second value in the range 0-59
23          public var second: Int = 0 {
24              didSet {
25                  if second < 0 || second > 59 {
26                      second = oldValue
27                  }
28              }
29          }
30
31          // designated initializer
32          public init() { } // empty body
33
34          // designated initializer
35          public init(hour: Int, minute: Int, second: Int) {
36              self.hour = hour
37              self.minute = minute
38              self.second = second
39          }
40  }
41
42  // extension to class Time containing convenience initializers
43  extension Time {
44          // convenience initializer: hour supplied, minute and second set to 0
45          public convenience init(hour: Int) {
46              self.init(hour: hour, minute: 0, second: 0)
47          }
48
49          // convenience initializer: hour and minute supplied, second set to 0
50          public convenience init(hour: Int, minute: Int) {
51              self.init(hour: hour, minute: minute, second: 0)
52          }
53
54          // convenience initializer: use values from existing Time object
55          public convenience init(time: Time) {
56              self.init(hour: time.hour, minute: time.minute,
57                  second: time.second)
58          }
59  }
60
61  // extensions for String representations of a Time
62  extension Time {
63          // convert to String in universal-time format (HH:MM:SS)
64          public var universalDescription: String {
65              return String(format: "%02d:%02d:%02d", hour, minute, second)
66          }
67
68          // convert to String in standard-time format (H:MM:SS AM or PM)
69          public var description: String {
70              return String(format: "%d:%02d:%02d %@",
71                  ((hour == 0 || hour == 12) ? 12 : hour % 12),
72                  minute, second, (hour < 12 ? "AM" : "PM"))
73          }
74  }
```

Fig. 8.7 | Time class with extensions. (Part 2 of 2.)

8.5.2 Testing Class Time's Extensions

Figure 8.8 is the program of Fig. 8.4 without the initializer call that passed all invalid values. Line 8 uses the computed properties defined in the extension at lines 62–74 of Fig. 8.7. Lines 13, 14 and 16 use the convenience initializers defined in the extension at lines 43–59 of Fig. 8.7. As you can see from the program's output, the computed properties and convenience initializers work exactly as they did when they were defined directly in the Time class of Fig. 8.3.

```
 1   // Fig. 8.8: main.swift (TimeExtension.xcodeproj)
 2   // Testing class Time's extensions
 3   import Foundation
 4
 5   // displays a Time object in 24-hour and 12-hour formats
 6   func displayTime(header: String, time: Time) {
 7       println(String(format:"%@\n   %@\n   %@",
 8           header, time.universalDescription, time.description))
 9   }
10
11   // create and initialize Time objects
12   let t1 = Time() // 00:00:00
13   let t2 = Time(hour: 2) // 02:00:00
14   let t3 = Time(hour: 21, minute: 34) // 21:34:00
15   let t4 = Time(hour: 12, minute: 25, second: 42) // 12:25:42
16   let t5 = Time(time: t4) // 12:25:42
17
18   println("OBJECT: INITIALIZED WITH")
19   displayTime("t1: all default arguments", t1)
20   displayTime("t2: hour; default minute and second", t2)
21   displayTime("t3: hour and minute; default second", t3)
22   displayTime("t4: hour, minute and second", t4)
23   displayTime("t5: Time object t4", t5)
```

```
OBJECT: INITIALIZED WITH
t1: all default arguments
   00:00:00
   12:00:00 AM
t2: hour; default minute and second
   02:00:00
   2:00:00 AM
t3: hour and minute; default second
   21:34:00
   9:34:00 PM
t4: hour, minute and second
   12:25:42
   12:25:42 PM
t5: Time object t4
   12:25:42
   12:25:42 PM
```

Fig. 8.8 | Testing class Time's extensions.

8.5.3 Extensions and Access Modifiers

Though the class and its extensions are defined in the same source-code file here, that's not required. However, the usual access-modifier restrictions apply:

- If you define an extension in the same *file* as the type it extends, then the extension has access to all the members of that type.

- If you define an extension in the same *module* but a separate source-code file from the type it extends, then the extension has access to all the public and internal members of that type.

If you define an extension in a separate module from the type it extends, then the extension has access only to the type's public members.

8.6 Read-Write Computed Properties

Computed properties do not provide their own storage. Rather, they perform tasks that compute values, possibly using the type's other members. For example, in a Rectangle type with width and height properties, you could define computed properties to calculate the area or perimeter from the Rectangle's width and height. In Chapter 3, we introduced computed properties and demonstrated read-only computed properties that provide only a get accessor for obtaining a value. In Section 8.2.3, we also showed a read-only computed property's shorthand notation in which you can eliminate the get keyword and the property's braces.

In this section, we demonstrate read-write computed properties that provide both get and set accessors—a computed property's set accessor typically changes the value of a stored property. Figure 8.9 defines a class Circle with a radius stored property (line 6) that has a default value of 0.0 and read-write computed properties diameter (lines 9–16), circumference (lines 19–26) and area (lines 29–36) that enable the client code to get or set a Circle's diameter, circumference and area, respectively. As you'll see, when you *set* one of these computed properties, the Circle's radius is recalculated accordingly.

```
1   // Fig. 8.9: Circle.swift (Circle.xcodeproj)
2   // Circle class with read-write computed properties
3   import Darwin
4
5   public class Circle {
6       public var radius: Double = 0.0
7
8       // computes diameter or sets radius based on new diameter
9       public var diameter: Double {
10          get {
11              return 2.0 * radius
12          }
13          set {
14              radius = newValue / 2.0
15          }
16      }
```

Fig. 8.9 | Circle class with read-write computed properties. (Part 1 of 2.)

```
17
18      // computes circumference or sets radius based on new circumference
19      public var circumference: Double {
20          get {
21              return M_PI * diameter
22          }
23          set {
24              radius = newValue / (2.0 * M_PI)
25          }
26      }
27
28      // computes area or sets radius based on new area
29      public var area: Double {
30          get {
31              return M_PI * radius * radius
32          }
33          set {
34              radius = sqrt(newValue / M_PI)
35          }
36      }
37  }
```

Fig. 8.9 | `Circle` class with read-write computed properties. (Part 2 of 2.)

Defining Read-Write Computed Properties

Recall that a computed property is always defined with var (lines 9, 19 and 29) and must provide a type annotation to specify the property's type. The read-write diameter computed property's get accessor (lines 10–12) returns the result of the diameter calculation in line 11. The set accessor (lines 13–15) determines the new radius via the calculation in line 14. By default, the value assigned to the computed property is placed in the constant newValue, which the set accessor can then use to access the new value. You may also provide a custom name for the new value in a set accessor, as in:

```
set(customNewValueName) {
    // code that sets a new value--typically for a stored property
}
```

Lines 19–26 define the computed property circumference's get and set accessors. The get accessor (lines 20–22) uses the constant M_PI from the Darwin module to represent the mathematical constant PI, and returns the result of multiplying PI by the Circle's diameter *computed* property. The set accessor determines the new radius via the calculation in line 24.

Lines 29–36 define the computed property area's get and set accessors. The get accessor (lines 30–32) returns the result of the area calculation in line 31. The set accessor (lines 33–35) uses the sqrt function from the Darwin module to calculate the new radius (line 34).

Using Class Circle's Read-Write Computed Property

The program of Fig. 8.10 creates a Circle object (line 12), then sets its stored property radius to 10.0 (line 13). Lines 15–16 then display the values of the radius and the computed properties diameter, circumference and area (by calling the function display-

Circle defined in lines 5–10). Next, line 18 assigns a new value to the computed property diameter. At this point, the diameter property's set accessor *recalculates* the radius. Lines 19–20 then display the updated radius, diameter, circumference and area. Next, line 22 assigns a new value to the computed property area. Then, the area property's set accessor recalculates the radius and lines 23–24 display the updated radius, diameter, circumference and area. Finally, line 26 assigns a new value to the computed property circumference. The circumference property's set accessor recalculates the radius, then lines 27–28 once again display the updated radius, diameter, circumference and area.

```
1   // Fig. 8.10: main.swift (Circle.xcodeproj)
2   // Using read-write computed properties
3
4   // displays a Circle's data
5   func displayCircle(circle: Circle) {
6       println("Radius: \(circle.radius)")
7       println("Diameter: \(circle.diameter)")
8       println("Circumference: \(circle.circumference)")
9       println("Area: \(circle.area)")
10  }
11
12  let circle = Circle()
13  circle.radius = 10.0
14
15  println("CIRCLE AFTER SETTING RADIUS TO 10.0")
16  displayCircle(circle)
17
18  circle.diameter = 10.0
19  println("\nCIRCLE AFTER SETTING DIAMETER TO 10.0")
20  displayCircle(circle)
21
22  circle.area = 10.0
23  println("\nCIRCLE AFTER SETTING AREA TO 10.0")
24  displayCircle(circle)
25
26  circle.circumference = 10.0
27  println("\nCIRCLE AFTER SETTING CIRCUMFERENCE TO 10.0")
28  displayCircle(circle)
```

```
CIRCLE AFTER SETTING RADIUS TO 10.0
Radius: 10.0
Diameter: 20.0
Circumference: 62.8318530717959
Area: 314.159265358979

CIRCLE AFTER SETTING DIAMETER TO 10.0
Radius: 5.0
Diameter: 10.0
Circumference: 31.4159265358979
Area: 78.5398163397448
```

Fig. 8.10 | Using read-write computed properties. (Part 1 of 2.)

```
CIRCLE AFTER SETTING AREA TO 10.0
Radius: 1.78412411615277
Diameter: 3.56824823230554
Circumference: 11.2099824327959
Area: 10.0

CIRCLE AFTER SETTING CIRCUMFERENCE TO 10.0
Radius: 1.59154943091895
Diameter: 3.18309886183791
Circumference: 10.0
Area: 7.95774715459477
```

Fig. 8.10 | Using read-write computed properties. (Part 2 of 2.)

8.7 Composition

A class may contain stored properties that are:

- references to objects of other class types (such as custom classes you define or classes from the Cocoa and Cocoa Touch frameworks), or

- objects of value types (such as custom structure or enumerations types you define or the Swift Standard Library's numeric, String, Array and Dictionary types).

This is called **composition** and is sometimes referred to as a *has-a* **relationship**. For example, an AlarmClock object needs to know the current time *and* the time when it's supposed to sound its alarm, so it's reasonable to include *two* Time stored properties in an Alarm-Clock object. Similarly, a car *has-a* steering wheel, a brake pedal and an accelerator pedal.

8.7.1 Class Employee

The following composition example contains class Employee (Fig. 8.11) and main.swift (Fig. 8.13). Class Employee (Fig. 8.11) has stored instance properties firstName, last-Name, birthDate and hireDate—an Employee *has a* first name, *has a* last name, *has a* birth date and *has a* hire date. Members firstName and lastName are objects of type String—a value type. Members birthDate and hireDate are *references to objects* of the Foundation framework class **NSDate**—a reference type. This demonstrates that a class can have as stored properties objects of value types (structures and enumerations) and references to objects of class types.

> ### Software Engineering Observation 8.6
> *In C++, composition creates a type that physically contains objects of other types. In Objective-C, Java, C# and Swift, a property of a class type references an object that's stored elsewhere in memory.*

```
1  // Fig. 8.11: Employee.swift (Composition.xcodeproj)
2  // Employee class composed of Strings and NSDates
3  import Foundation
4
```

Fig. 8.11 | Employee class composed of Strings and NSDates. (Part 1 of 2.)

```
5   public class Employee {
6       public var firstName: String
7       public var lastName: String
8       public var birthDate: NSDate
9       public var hireDate: NSDate
10
11      // designated initializer
12      public init(firstName: String, lastName: String,
13          birthDate: NSDate, hireDate: NSDate) {
14
15          self.firstName = firstName
16          self.lastName = lastName
17          self.birthDate = birthDate
18          self.hireDate = hireDate
19      }
20
21      // return String representation of an Employee
22      public var description: String {
23          let formatter = NSDateFormatter() // used to format dates
24          formatter.timeStyle = NSDateFormatterStyle.NoStyle // no time
25          formatter.dateStyle = NSDateFormatterStyle.LongStyle
26          formatter.locale = NSLocale.currentLocale()
27
28          return String(format: "%@, %@\nHired: %@\nBorn: %@",
29              lastName, firstName, formatter.stringFromDate(hireDate),
30              formatter.stringFromDate(birthDate))
31      }
32  }
```

Fig. 8.11 | Employee class composed of `Strings` and `NSDates`. (Part 2 of 2.)

Employee *Initializer*

The Employee designated initializer (lines 12–19 of Fig. 8.11) takes four parameters representing the first name, last name, birth date and hire date, and assigns them to the corresponding stored properties.

Employee description *Property*

Class Employee's description computed property (lines 22–31) returns a String containing the employee's name and the *locale-specific* String representations of its two NS-Dates. To obtain the locale-specific String representation of an NSDate, we first create an object of class NSDateFormatter (line 23) and configure its timeStyle, dateStyle and locale properties (lines 24–26). The NSDateFormatterStyle enumeration constant NoStyle (line 24) indicates that the formatted NSDate should not include time information. The NSDateFormatterStyle enumeration constant LongStyle (line 25) indicates that the date should be formatted in a style that includes the complete month name, day and year. Line 26 indicates that formatting should be performed based on the *locale* of the computer on which the program executes. Lines 29 and 30 create the locale-specific date Strings by calling the NSDateFormatter's **stringFromDate** method. For the complete list of NSDateFormatterStyle constants and their purposes, see:

> http://bit.ly/NSDateFormatterStyle

Employee *Object in Memory*

Figure 8.12 is a conceptual diagram illustrating an Employee object and its stored properties in memory. For value-type properties like the Strings firstName and lastName, the property values reside in the Employee object. For reference-type properties like the NSDates birthDate and hireDate, the Employee object contains only references to those objects—that is, values indicating *where* these NSDate objects can be found in memory. These references are represented by the arrows in the diagram. Though references are not "raw" memory addresses like pointers in Objective-C, C++ or C, references still serve the same purpose (but more safely).

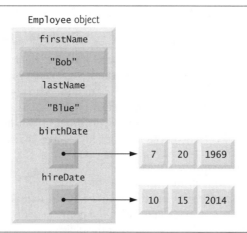

Fig. 8.12 | Conceptual representation of an Employee object in memory.

8.7.2 Testing Class Employee

The program in Fig. 8.13 demonstrates class Employee and using NSDateFormatter to create NSDate objects from String representations of the dates.

```
1  // Fig. 8.13: main.swift (Composition.xcodeproj)
2  // Composition demonstration.
3  import Foundation
4
5  let dateFormatter = NSDateFormatter()
6  dateFormatter.dateFormat = "yyyy-MM-dd" // "2015-07-04" is July 4, 2015
7
8  let birthDate = dateFormatter.dateFromString("1969-07-20")!
9  let hireDate = dateFormatter.dateFromString("2014-10-15")!
10 let employee = Employee(firstName: "Bob", lastName: "Blue",
11    birthDate: birthDate, hireDate: hireDate)
12 println(employee.description)
```

```
Blue, Bob
Hired: October 15, 2014
Born: July 20, 1969
```

Fig. 8.13 | Composition demonstration,

Creating NSDates from Strings Representing Dates

In addition to formatting NSDates as Strings, class NSDateFormatter can be used to create NSDates from Strings by using method **dateFromString** (Fig. 8.13, lines 8–9). Line 5 creates an NSDateFormatter and line 6 sets its **dateFormat** property to specify how a date's String representation should be formatted so it can be properly converted to an NSDate by dateFromString. In this case, the date should be a four-digit year (yyyy), a dash, a two-digit month (MM), a dash and a two-digit day (dd). The symbols like yyyy, MM and dd used to specify date formats are based on the Unicode Technical Standard #35, which you can read at:

```
http://www.unicode.org/reports/tr35/
```

The date-specific formatting codes are discussed at:

```
http://www.unicode.org/reports/tr35/tr35-dates.html#Contents
```

Lines 8 and 9 create the NSDates that we'll use to initialize an Employee's birth date and hire date, respectively. NSDateFormatter method dateFromString returns an NSDate?, because converting a String to an NSDate could fail if the String is not in the correct format. For simplicity in this example, we force unwrap the NSDates, because we know we provided correctly formatted dates. However, you should typically use optional binding to ensure that method dateFromString returned an NSDate object, rather than nil.

Creating and Displaying an Employee

Lines 10–11 create an Employee and initialize its properties with two Strings (representing the Employee's first and last names) and two NSDate objects (representing the birth date and hire date). Line 12 uses the Employee's description property to display the values of the Employee's stored properties and demonstrate that the object was initialized properly.

8.8 Automatic Reference Counting, Strong References and Weak References

Swift manages the memory for your app's reference-type objects using dynamically allocated memory and **automatic reference counting** (ARC), which keeps track of how many references there are to a given object. When an object's *reference count* becomes 0, the runtime invokes the object's *deinitializer* (discussed in Section 8.9), then immediately deallocates the object, removing it from memory.

Strong References

Property attributes can specify whether a property changes an object's reference count. By default, properties create **strong references** to objects. Every strong reference created causes an object's reference count to be incremented by 1. So, every time you assign an object to a var property or use an object to initialize a let property, the object's reference count is incremented by 1. When a strong reference no longer refers to an object, its reference count is decremented by 1. This occurs, for example, when a local property goes out of scope or a var property is assigned nil or a different object. The code that manages incrementing and decrementing the reference counts is inserted by the Swift compiler.

weak References

Swift also supports **weak** properties (introduced in Chapter 14, **Tip Calculator** App) that do not increment an object's reference count. If an object is referenced *only* by weak properties, then the object can be removed from memory. A weak property is one that can refer to an object or can have the value nil. If a property will always refer to an object (i.e., it will never go out of scope or be assigned nil), but should *not* increment that object's reference count, you should declare the property **unowned** instead. You can learn more about ARC at

```
http://bit.ly/SwiftARC
```

Error-Prevention Tip 8.4

Strong reference cycles occur when one object has a strong reference to another and vice versa. ARC can never remove such objects from memory, because their reference counts will always be at least one. For such cases, you can use weak or unowned properties to prevent strong reference cycles.

Error-Prevention Tip 8.5

The runtime sets a weak reference to nil automatically when the referenced object is deallocated. This prevents the kinds of "dangling pointer" issues encountered in languages like Objective-C, C and C++.

8.9 Deinitializers

When a reference-type object's reference count becomes 0 (i.e., there are no more strong references to that object), the runtime automatically invokes the object's **deinitializer** to perform **termination housekeeping** before the object's memory is reclaimed, so the memory may be reused to hold new objects. *The deinitializer itself does not actually release the object's memory*—the runtime does this when deinitialization completes. Typically, a deinitializer frees resources used by the object. For example, you could use a deinitializer to close files, database connections or network connections. For an iOS or OS X app in which an object receives notifications from the operating system or another app, you might use a deinitializer to unregister the object so that it no longer receives those notifications.

Each class has one deinitializer, which is defined with the **deinit** keyword, as in:

```
deinit {
    // statements to execute before the object is deallocated
}
```

Because the runtime does not deallocate an object (i.e., remove it from memory) until deinitialization is complete, all of the object's data is accessible in the deinitializer.

Even though deinitializers have not been defined for the classes presented so far, *every class has a deinitializer*. If you do not *explicitly* define a deinitializer, the compiler defines an "empty" deinitializer. [*Note:* In Section 10.11, we'll discuss that such an *implicitly* created deinitializer does, in fact, perform important operations on class-type objects that are created through inheritance.]

8.10 Using NSDecimalNumber for Precise Monetary Calculations

In Section 4.10.2, we demonstrated monetary calculations using Double values and mentioned the fact that any application that performs monetary calculations should instead use Foundation framework class **NSDecimalNumber**.

Figure 8.14 reimplements the interest calculation example of Fig. 4.6 using NSDecimalNumbers to perform the calculations. We also produce *locale-specific* currency Strings using NSNumberFormatter type method localizedStringFromNumber (lines 25–26). This method returns a String in the specified format (in this case, CurrencyStyle from the NSNumberFormatterStyle enum).

```
1   // Fig. 8.14: CompoundInterest.playground
2   // Compound-interest calculations with NSDecimalNumber
3   import Foundation
4
5   // format a String right aligned in a field
6   func rightAlignedString(string: String, fieldWidth: Int) -> String {
7       let spaces: Int = fieldWidth - countElements(string)
8       let padding = String(count: spaces, repeatedValue: Character(" "))
9       return padding + string
10  }
11
12  var amount = NSDecimalNumber(string: "1000.00") // amount before interest
13  let rate = NSDecimalNumber(string: "0.05") // interest rate
14
15  // display headers
16  println(String(format: "%@%@", "Year",
17      rightAlignedString("Amount on deposit", 20)))
18
19  // calculate amount on deposit for each of five years
20  for year in 1...5 {
21      // calculate new amount for specified year
22      amount = amount.decimalNumberByMultiplyingBy(
23          rate.decimalNumberByAdding(NSDecimalNumber.one()))
24
25      let formattedAmount = NSNumberFormatter.localizedStringFromNumber(
26          amount, numberStyle: .CurrencyStyle)
27
28      // display the year and the amount
29      println(String(format: "%4d%@", year,
30          rightAlignedString(formattedAmount, 20)))
31  }
```

```
Year   Amount on deposit
   1        $1,050.00
   2        $1,102.50
   3        $1,157.62
   4        $1,215.51
   5        $1,276.28
```

Fig. 8.14 | Compound-interest calculations with NSDecimalNumber.

Performing the Interest Calculations with **NSDecimalNumber**
Lines 12–13 declare and initialize NSDecimalNumber variable amount and constant rate using the NSDecimalNumber initializer that receives a String representing the number.

Lines 22–23 perform the interest calculation using NSDecimalNumber methods **decimal-NumberByMultiplyingBy** and **decimalNumberByAdding**. The statement evaluates as follows:

1. First, the expression at line 23 adds 1 to the rate to produce an NSDecimalNumber containing 1.05—this is equivalent to 1.0 + rate in line 25 of Fig. 4.6. The NS-DecimalNumber type method **one** returns an NSDecimalNumber containing the value 1. Class NSDecimalNumber also provides the method **zero** (0).

2. Next, NSDecimalNumber method decimalNumberByMultiplyingBy is called on the amount object to multiply the current amount by the result of *Step 1*, then the resulting NSDecimalNumber is assigned to the amount reference. This is equivalent to line 25 of Fig. 4.6.

Lines 25–26 create a *locale-specific* currency String representing the amount. Lines 29–30 display the year and amount on deposit at the end of that year.

As you can see in this example, NSDecimalNumber arithmetic is verbose due to the lengths of the method names used to perform calculations. In Chapter 12, Operator Overloading and Subscripts, we'll define overloaded operators for NSDecimalNumbers that enable you to perform NSDecimalNumber arithmetic more concisely and conveniently using the +, -, * and / operators.

Rounding *NSDecimalNumber* Values

In addition to precise calculations, NSDecimalNumber also gives you control over how values are *rounded*. By default all calculations assume that the results do not need more than 38 significant digits (including the digits after the decimal separator) and round as necessary based on that assumption. For example, if a given value cannot be represented exactly—such as the result of 1 divided by 3, which is 0.3333333…—the result will round to 38 significant digits.

Though we do not use them in this example, class NSDecimalNumber has methods that perform calculations with the rounding behavior you specify. You may also change the default behavior for all NSDecimalNumber calculations. For more information, see Apple's NSDecimalNumber Class Reference at

```
http://bit.ly/NSDecimalNumberClass
```

8.11 Type Properties and Type Methods

Every object of a class has its own copy of the class's stored properties. In certain cases, only *one* copy of a particular property should be *shared* by all objects of a type. These are known as **type properties** and are often called *class variables* or *static variables* in other object-oriented programming languages. Similarly, you can define methods that are called directly on a type, rather than on a particular object of the type. These are known as **type methods**—often called *class methods* or *static methods* in other object-oriented programming languages. At the time of this writing, Swift classes support type methods and *computed* type properties, but not *stored* type properties. In Chapter 9, we'll show that structure and enumeration types support type methods, computed type properties *and* stored type properties.

Software Engineering Observation 8.7

Although most methods execute on specific objects in response to method calls, this is not always the case. Sometimes a method performs a task that does not depend on the contents of any object. Such a method can be defined as a type method that applies to the class in which it's defined as a whole. It's not uncommon for a class to contain a group of type methods to perform common tasks.

8.11.1 Type Scope

Type properties and type methods have *type scope*—they are visible to one another in the type that defines them. As you'll see in the next program, you access type properties and type methods by qualifying the member name with the type name and a dot (.) separator. In the body of a type property or type method, you can reference other type properties and type methods directly by name or by preceding them with self and a dot (.) separator—in the context of a type property or type method, self refers to the type, rather than an object of the type. This differs from most other object-oriented languages, which disallow use of self or this (depending on the language) in class methods.

Software Engineering Observation 8.8

Type properties and methods exist, and can be used, even if no objects of that class have been instantiated. For this reason, a type property or type method cannot access the type's other members—often called instance properties or instance methods.

Common Programming Error 8.7

A compilation error occurs if a type property or type method attempts to use an instance property or instance method.

8.11.2 Motivating Type Properties

Let's consider a case in which type properties are useful. Suppose that we have a video game with Martians and other space creatures. Each Martian tends to be brave and willing to attack other space creatures when the Martian is aware that at least four other Martians are present. If fewer than five Martians are present, each of them becomes cowardly. Thus, each Martian needs to know the martianCount. We could endow class Martian with martianCount as an *instance property*. If we do this, then every Martian will have *a separate copy* of the instance property, and every time we create a new Martian, we'll have to update the martianCount in *every* Martian object. This wastes space with the redundant copies, wastes time in updating the separate copies and is error prone. Instead, we declare martianCount to be a *type property*, making martianCount classwide data. Every Martian can see the martianCount, but only *one* copy of the martianCount is maintained. This saves space. We save time by having the Martian initializer increment the type property martianCount. There's only one copy, so we do not have to increment separate copies for each Martian object.

Software Engineering Observation 8.9

Use a type property when all objects of a class must use the same copy of the variable.

8.11.3 Creating Type Properties and Type Methods in Classes

Our next program contains Employee.swift (Fig. 8.15) and main.swift (Fig. 8.16). In Fig. 8.15, line 5 defines the private *global* variable employeeCount (with the default value 0), which maintains a count of the number of Employee objects currently in memory. We made this variable a private global because Swift classes currently do not support stored type properties—this variable is visible only in Employee.swift. Making the variable private ensures that it can be used only by other code in Employee.swift—in this case, just class Employee. For each Employee the program creates, line 13 in the Employee initializer increments the employeeCount. When the runtime is about to deallocate an Employee, the Employee deinitializer executes and line 19 decrements the employeeCount.

```
1   // Fig. 8.15: Employee.swift (TypeMethodsAndProperties.xcodeproj)
2   // Employee class with a type property and type method
3
4   // global because classes do not yet support stored type properties
5   private var employeeCount: Int = 0
6
7   public class Employee {
8       public var name: String
9
10      // designated initializer
11      public init(name: String) {
12          self.name = name
13          ++employeeCount // increment global private variable
14          println("Employee init: \(name); count = \(Employee.getCount())")
15      }
16
17      // deinitializer
18      deinit {
19          --employeeCount // decrement global private variable
20          println("Employee deinit: \(name); count = \(Employee.count)")
21      }
22
23      // computed read-only type property
24      public class var count: Int {
25          return employeeCount
26      }
27
28      // type method
29      public class func getCount() -> Int {
30          return self.count
31      }
32  }
```

Fig. 8.15 | Employee class with a type property and type method.

Defining Type Properties and Type Methods in a Class
Lines 24–26 and 29–31 define the count read-only computed type property and the get-Count type method, respectively. Like computed instance properties, computed type properties also can be read-write properties with get and set accessors.

The type property count and method getCount each return the current number of Employees in memory—we define both in this example to show the syntax of type properties and methods. In classes, type properties and methods are declared with the class keyword, as shown on lines 24 and 29. (As you'll see in Chapter 9, structures and enumerations use the static keyword instead.)

The count type property simply returns the global variable employeeCount's value (line 25). To demonstrate that type properties and type methods can access other type properties and type methods of the class, the getCount type method returns the value of the count type property (line 30). Again, using self in a type property's or type method's body references the *type*, not an object of the type. Within a type property or type method, you can invoke the class's other type properties and type methods directly by name, so the expression self.count also can be written simply as count.

Accessing Type Properties and Type Methods from a Class's Other Members
As each Employee is initialized, line 14 in class Employee's initializer displays a line of text containing the Employee's name and the current number of Employees in memory. The statement calls the type method getCount to obtain the employeeCount. When accessing a type property or type method from a class's other members, you specify the class name followed by a dot (.) separator and the name of the type property or type method. The same notation is used to access a type property or type method from the class's client code (as you'll see in Section 8.11.4). As each Employee is about to be deallocated, line 20 in class Employee's deinitializer displays a line of text containing the Employee's name and the number of Employees that will be in memory after the Employee is deallocated. In this case, the statement uses the type property count to obtain the employeeCount.

8.11.4 Using Type Properties and Type Methods
In main.swift (Fig. 8.16), the function createEmployees (lines 5–14) will be called to create two Employee objects (lines 7–8) and display the number of Employees in memory (lines 11–13). When createEmployees terminates, the local constants e1 and e2 are discarded—remember that a local constant or variable exists *only* until the block in which it's defined completes execution. Because e1 and e2 were the only references to the Employee objects created in lines 7–8, these objects' reference counts are decremented to 0. As you'll see in the program's output, the two Employee objects are deallocated when the function terminates.

```
1   // Fig. 8.16: main.swift (TypeMethodsAndProperties.xcodeproj)
2   // Demonstrating type methods and properties
3
4   // function that creates two Employees
5   func createEmployees() {
6       // create two Employees; count should be 2
7       let e1 = Employee(name: "Susan Baker")
8       let e2 = Employee(name: "Bob Blue")
9
```

Fig. 8.16 | Demonstrating type methods and properties. (Part 1 of 2.)

```
10        // show that Employee count is 2 after creating two Employees
11        println("\nEMPLOYEES AFTER INSTANTIATION")
12        println("   via type property: \(Employee.count)")
13        println("   via type method: \(Employee.getCount())\n")
14   }
15
16   // show that Employee count is 0 before creating Employees
17   println("EMPLOYEES BEFORE INSTANTIATION")
18   println("   via type property: \(Employee.count)")
19   println("   via type method: \(Employee.getCount())\n")
20
21   createEmployees()
22
23   // show that count is 0 after Employees' references counts go to 0
24   println("\nEMPLOYEES AFTER ARC")
25   println("   via type property: \(Employee.count)")
26   println("   via type method: \(Employee.getCount())")
```

```
EMPLOYEES BEFORE INSTANTIATION
   via type property: 0
   via type method: 0

Employee init: Susan Baker; count = 1
Employee init: Bob Blue; count = 2

EMPLOYEES AFTER INSTANTIATION
   via type property: 2
   via type method: 2

Employee deinit: Bob Blue; count = 1
Employee deinit: Susan Baker; count = 0

EMPLOYEES AFTER ARC
   via type property: 0
   via type method: 0
```

Fig. 8.16 | Demonstrating type methods and properties. (Part 2 of 2.)

In this example, first lines 17–19 use class Employee's type property count and type method getCount to display the number of Employees in memory *before* any are created. Next, line 21 calls the createEmployees function. As each Employee is created, its initializer outputs the Employee's name and the total number of Employees in memory. Lines 11–13 in createEmployees show that there are now two Employees. Then the createEmployees function terminates and the Employees are deallocated. The output shows that each Employee's deinitializer executes and that the number of Employees is decremented to 0. Finally, lines 24–26 use class Employee's type property count and type method getCount to display the number of Employees in memory after they are all deallocated.

8.12 Lazy Stored Properties and Delayed Initialization

Sometimes it's helpful to defer a stored property's initialization until that property is used. That's the purpose of **lazy stored properties**. Such properties can help prevent unnecessary initialization or improve initialization performance. You'd typically declare as `lazy` a property for which initialization requires:

- compute-intensive calculations that might never be needed,
- downloading large amounts of data that might never be needed or
- resources that might not be available until after the object containing the `lazy` stored property is created.

This is particularly important in mobile apps, in which app start-up time is important. Users want their mobile apps to begin executing quickly, so deferring complex initialization until the app is running can increase performance from a user-interaction perspective. If a `lazy` property is not used in a particular program, its initialization never executes.

Performance Tip 8.1

A downside of `lazy` stored properties is that there could be an initialization delay at a later time when performance is of the essence. For example, in an action-intensive game, you'd typically perform complex initialization (such as loading large images or complex 3D graphics) before game play begins to ensure that the user does not see performance delays during game play.

A `lazy` stored property must be a `var` property, because its value will not be known until a later time. Constant stored properties *must* receive a value *before* initialization completes, so they cannot be declared `lazy`. Unlike other stored properties, `lazy` stored properties cannot have property observers.

The value assigned to a `lazy` stored property is typically:

- the result of creating an object,
- the value returned by a method, property or function, or
- the value returned by a closure that performs the initialization tasks.

For example, when you create a data-driven iOS or OS X app that uses Core Data for database access, Xcode generates various `lazy` stored properties. These are initialized by closures that perform various tasks related to database initialization and loading objects into memory for data access. Because these tasks can be time consuming for large databases, these `lazy` stored properties are initialized only when they're used. We demonstrate database access with Core Data in Chapter 8 of our book *iOS 8 for Programmers: An App-Driven Approach with Swift.* You can read more about `lazy` stored properties at:

```
http://bit.ly/SwiftStoredProperties
```

Performance Tip 8.2

Global variables and constants are initialized lazily when they're used for the first time, even though they're not defined with the `lazy` keyword. Local variables and constants are initialized when they're defined.

8.13 Wrap-Up

In this chapter, we took a deeper look at building robust classes. We introduced stored properties with property observers that execute before and after a stored property's value changes. We used a `didSet` property observer to validate a property's new value and restore the property's original value if the new one was invalid.

We showed how to overload initializers to enable objects to be initialized in several ways, based on different sets of arguments. You learned that Swift has designated initializers that must initialize all of a class's stored properties and convenience initializers that call designated initializers, typically to provide common values for specific initializer arguments. We demonstrated how to use failable initializers and implicitly unwrapped failable initializers to prevent an object from being created if an initializer receives invalid data.

We used `extensions` to enhance an existing custom class with new features and indicated that you can use `extensions` to enhance any existing type, including classes from the Swift Standard Library and the Cocoa and Cocoa Touch frameworks. We showed read-write computed properties that provide both `get` and `set` accessors, and used their `set` accessors to update a stored property when the computed properties were assigned new values.

We discussed composition (the *has-a* relationship) and showed that a class's stored properties can be of value types and reference types. We also introduced the Foundation framework classes `NSDate` and `NSDateFormatter` for date and time manipulation.

You learned that Swift manages the memory of reference-type objects for you via automatic reference counting (ARC), which deallocates an object when there are no more strong references to it. We also introduced Swift's weak and unowned reference types, which do not affect an object's reference count. We then considered deinitializers, which are called by the runtime just before a reference-type object is deallocated. We demonstrated precise monetary calculations with `NSDecimalNumbers`.

We showed how to define type properties that are accessed directly on a type and shared by all objects of a class, and how to define type methods that are called on a type, rather than an object of a type. We also mentioned that classes do not currently support stored type properties. Finally, you learned that a `lazy` stored property defers initialization until that property is used.

Many of the class capabilities you saw in this chapter also are supported by structure and enumeration types. In Chapter 9, we'll explain the close relationships among classes, structures and enumerations, and when to prefer each in your apps. We'll also point out structure-specific and enumeration-specific limitations.

9

Structures, Enumerations and Nested Types

Objectives

In this chapter you'll:

- Use **structs** and **enums**.

- Understand the similarities and differences among classes, **structs** and **enums**.

- Use memberwise initializers with **structs**.

- Create nonmutating and **mutating** methods.

- Add capabilities to a **struct** (or **enum**) via **extensions**.

- Understand type methods, computed type properties and stored type properties for **structs** and **enums**, and use stored type properties in **enums**.

- Understand when to prefer **structs**, **enums** or classes in your apps.

- Use **enums** with associated values.

- Learn how Swift's optionals are implemented as an **enum** with associated values.

9.1 Introduction

Many of the class capabilities you saw in Chapter 8 are also supported by structure (struct) and enumeration (enum) types. In this chapter, we demonstrate the close relationships among classes, structures and enumerations, then discuss when to prefer each in your apps. We'll also point out structure-specific and enumeration-specific limitations.

Swift Standard Library struct Types

You've been working with struct types throughout this book. All of the Swift Standard Library's numeric types (e.g., Int, Float, Double, etc.) and the Bool, String, Array and Dictionary types are implemented as structs and hence are *value* types. If you need to pass a value-type object to a function or method *by reference*, you must define its corresponding parameter with the inout keyword (introduced in Section 5.11).

Software Engineering Observation 9.1

Because value-type objects are copied, you always have exclusive ownership of those objects, wherever you're accessing or modifying them. This is particularly important with today's multicore hardware systems, which encourage the use of multithreaded programming. For new types, this can influence your choice of using a struct or enum in preference to a class.

Performance Tip 9.1

Recall that Swift avoids unnecessary copying of value-type objects in a manner transparent to the programmer.

Prefer Constants and Immutability By Default

In general, you should follow the *principle of least privilege* when defining objects—use constants declared with let unless it's necessary for your code to modify an object. In fact, Swift prefers immutability *by default*. For example:

- All function, method and initializer parameters are treated as *constants* by default, unless you specify otherwise by declaring them with var or inout.

- The *item* that receives a value in each iteration of a for...in statement is a *constant* by default, unless you declare the item's identifier with with var.

- Methods in struct and enum types *cannot* modify objects of those types by default—you must explicitly declare them mutating (as you'll see in Section 9.2.4) to allow such modifications.

When you define a constant *value-type* object with `let`, the compiler *disallows* all operations on that object that would modify its data. Thus, even *variable* properties of constant value-type objects are treated as constants. So, for example, if you create a constant `Array` that contains elements of a value type, you cannot change the values after the `Array` is initialized. As we've discussed previously, however, if a constant property *refers* to an object of a *class* type, the referenced object *can* be modified, but the reference itself cannot.

Software Engineering Observation 9.2

Classes can be designed for immutability. To do so, provide initializers that set a new object's properties and do not expose to the client code any method, property or subscript that allows the client code to modify an object of the class.

9.2 Structure Definitions

Figure 9.1 reimplements the Time class from Section 8.5 as a `struct` to demonstrate similarities and differences between classes and `struct`s. We discuss the Time `struct` and its extensions in Sections 9.2.1—9.2.4, then present a test program in Section 9.2.5 that demonstrates `struct`-object initialization, `struct`-object assignment and calling `struct` methods that modify `struct` objects.

```
1   // Fig. 9.1: Time.swift (TimeStructure.xcodeproj)
2   // Time struct with default and memberwise initializers, and extensions
3   public struct Time {
4       // an hour value in the range 0-23
5       public var hour: Int = 0 {
6           didSet {
7               if hour < 0 || hour > 23 {
8                   hour = oldValue
9               }
10          }
11      }
12
13      // a minute value in the range 0-59
14      public var minute: Int = 0 {
15          didSet {
16              if minute < 0 || minute > 59 {
17                  minute = oldValue
18              }
19          }
20      }
21
22      // a second value in the range 0-59
23      public var second: Int = 0 {
24          didSet {
25              if second < 0 || second > 59 {
26                  second = oldValue
27              }
28          }
29      }
30  }
```

Fig. 9.1 | Time struct with default and memberwise initializers, and extensions. (Part 1 of 3.)

```
31
32   // extension to struct Time containing additional initializers
33   extension Time {
34       // initializer: hour supplied, minute and second set to 0
35       public init(hour: Int) {
36           self.init(hour: hour, minute: 0, second: 0)
37       }
38
39       // initializer: hour and minute supplied, second set to 0
40       public init(hour: Int, minute: Int) {
41           self.init(hour: hour, minute: minute, second: 0)
42       }
43   }
44
45   // extension to struct Time for String representations
46   extension Time {
47       // convert to String in universal-time format (HH:MM:SS)
48       public var universalDescription: String {
49           return String(format: "%02d:%02d:%02d", hour, minute, second)
50       }
51
52       // convert to String in standard-time format (H:MM:SS AM or PM)
53       public var description: String {
54           return String(format: "%d:%02d:%02d %@",
55               ((hour == 0 || hour == 12) ? 12 : hour % 12),
56               minute, second, (hour < 12 ? "AM" : "PM"))
57       }
58   }
59
60   // extension to struct Time for adding hours, minutes or seconds to a Time
61   extension Time {
62       // add an Int to the hour
63       public mutating func addHours(increment: Int) {
64           hour = (hour + increment) % 24
65       }
66
67       // add an Int to the minute
68       public mutating func addMinutes(increment: Int) {
69           // possibly increment the hour
70           if minute + increment > 59 {
71               addHours((minute + increment) / 60)
72           }
73
74           minute = (minute + increment) % 60
75       }
76
77       // add an Int to the second
78       public mutating func addSeconds(increment: Int) {
79           // possibly increment the minute
80           if second + increment > 59 {
81               addMinutes((second + increment) / 60)
82           }
83
```

Fig. 9.1 | Time struct with default and memberwise initializers, and extensions. (Part 2 of 3.)

```
84            second = (second + increment) % 60
85        }
86    }
```

Fig. 9.1 | `Time struct` with default and memberwise initializers, and extensions. (Part 3 of 3.)

9.2.1 Time struct Definition with Default and Memberwise Initializers

Like classes, `struct`s can define stored and computed properties, methods, computed type properties, type methods, subscripts (Chapter 12) and initializers. Unlike classes, `struct`s:

- *can* define *stored* type properties,
- do *not* have deinitializers,
- are *not* managed with ARC because they're allocated on the stack (unless they are composed into a class object; we discussed composition in Section 8.7), and
- *cannot* be used in inheritance hierarchies (as we'll discuss in Chapter 10, Inheritance, Polymorphism and Protocols).

In this example, the `Time struct` (lines 3–30) defines only three `public` stored properties—hour, `minute` and `second`—each with a `didSet` property observer that validates the value assigned to the corresponding property. As with class initialization, these property observers do *not* execute during `struct` initialization.

Default Initializer

Like classes, the compiler defines a *default initializer* for a `struct` *only* if you provide default values for all its stored properties *and* you do not define any initializers. The default initializer has no parameters and sets the stored properties to their default values.

Memberwise Initializer

For `struct`s with no explicitly defined initializers, the compiler *always* generates a **memberwise initializer** with parameters for each of the `struct`'s stored properties. The parameters have the same names and types as the `struct`'s stored properties. In addition, the parameters are defined in the same order as the property definitions in the `struct`. So, for the `struct` Time, the compiler generates the following memberwise initializer:

```
init(hour: Int, minute: Int, second: Int) {
    self.hour = hour
    self.minute = minute
    self.second = second
}
```

in which the parameter's values are assigned to the corresponding stored properties. You can use this initializer to create a `Time` object as follows:

```
let time = Time(hour: 15, minute: 30, second: 45)
```

9.2.2 Custom Initializers extension to struct Time

As with classes, you can define custom `struct` initializers and overload them. Unlike classes, however, `struct` initializers are not separated into designated and convenience initializers, so you do not use the convenience keyword when overloading initializers that delegate to other initializers.

If you define *any* custom initializers directly in a struct's definition, the compiler will *not* generate default or memberwise initializers. However, if you place custom initializers in an extension, the compiler still generates default and memberwise initializers—of course, the default initializer will be generated only if all the stored properties have default values. Placing custom struct initializers in an extension enables the custom initializers to *delegate* their work to the autogenerated memberwise initializer.

Software Engineering Observation 9.3

Typically, custom initializers for a struct type should be placed in extensions. This enables the compiler to generate the default and memberwise initializers. Also, the custom initializers can then delegate to the memberwise initializer.

For the reasons above, we define struct Time's custom initializers in an extension (Fig. 9.1, lines 33–43). We provided two custom initializers:

- one that receives an Int to initialize the hour and provides default 0 values for the minute and second (lines 35–37), and

- one that receives two Int values to initialize the hour and minute, and provides a default 0 value for the second (lines 40–42).

The custom initializers delegate their work to the autogenerated memberwise initializer using self.init, as shown in lines 36 and 41.

We do not define a three-parameter initializer since the compiler generates struct Time's memberwise initializer. Also, we do not define an initializer that receives a Time object as an argument. Instead, we take advantage of Swift's ability to memberwise copy a value-type object with = during initialization or assignment. Consider the statement

```
let t1 = t2
```

which initializes the Time object t1 with the existing Time object t2—each member of t2 is copied into the corresponding member in t1. This is equivalent to calling the memberwise initializer and passing the values of the existing t2 object's stored properties as follows:

```
let t1 = Time(hour: t2.hour, minute: t2.minute, second: t2.second)
```

9.2.3 Computed Properties extension to struct Time

Like the extensions to class Time in Section 8.5, lines 46–58 define an extension to struct Time containing the universalDescription and description computed properties that return String representations of a Time.

9.2.4 Mutating Methods extension to struct Time

By default, a struct's methods are *not* allowed to modify a struct object's properties. Any struct method that modifies a struct object's properties must be defined as **mutating** (as in lines 63, 68 and 78). Such methods can be defined directly in the struct definition or can be added to the struct type via an extension, as we did in lines 61–86. The methods addHours (lines 63–65), addMinutes (lines 68–75) and addSeconds (line 78–85) add an Int value to a Time's hour, minute or second, respectively.

Software Engineering Observation 9.4

The compiler prevents all attempts to modify a constant value-type object after it's initialized—thus, a mutating struct *method cannot be invoked on a constant* struct *object, nor can you assign values to a constant* struct *object's properties. This differs from reference-type objects. When you define a reference-type constant, the reference always refers to the same object, but the object itself can still be modified via its properties and methods.*

9.2.5 Testing the Time struct

Figure 9.2 demonstrates the Time struct's capabilities. Lines 12–16 demonstrate each of Time's initializers.

- Line 12 invokes the Time *default initializer* that sets the t1 object to its default value (i.e., midnight). The object t1 is defined as a var so we can modify it later.

- Line 13 invokes the *single-argument initializer* that receives an Int representing the hour (lines 35–37 of Fig. 9.1).

- Line 14 invokes the *two-argument initializer* that receives two Ints representing the hour and minute (lines 40–42 of Fig. 9.1).

- Line 15 invokes the *three-argument memberwise initializer* that the compiler *autogenerated* for struct Time.

- Line 16 initializes the new object t5 with the *existing object* t4—this statement memberwise copies the t4 object's stored-property values into the corresponding stored properties of t5.

Next, the app displays the String representations of each Time object to confirm that it was initialized properly (lines 19–23).

```
1   // Fig. 9.2: main.swift (TimeStructure.xcodeproj)
2   // Testing struct Time
3   import Foundation
4
5   // displays a Time object in 24-hour and 12-hour formats
6   func displayTime(header: String, time: Time) {
7       println(String(format:"%@\n   %@\n   %@",
8           header, time.universalDescription, time.description))
9   }
10
11  // create and initialize Time objects
12  var t1 = Time() // 00:00:00
13  let t2 = Time(hour: 2) // 02:00:00
14  let t3 = Time(hour: 21, minute: 34) // 21:34:00
15  let t4 = Time(hour: 12, minute: 25, second: 42) // 12:25:42
16  let t5 = t4 // 12:25:42; initializes t5 with copies of t6's members
17
18  println("OBJECT: INITIALIZED WITH")
19  displayTime("t1: all default arguments", t1)
20  displayTime("t2: hour; default minute and second", t2)
21  displayTime("t3: hour and minute; default second", t3)
```

Fig. 9.2 | Testing struct Time. (Part 1 of 2.)

```
22   displayTime("t4: hour, minute and second", t4)
23   displayTime("t5: Time object t4", t5)
24
25   println("\nASSIGNING STRUCT OBJECTS")
26   t1 = t5 // copies t5's members into t1's members
27   displayTime("after t1 = t5, t1 is", t1)
28
29   println("\nADDING TO A TIME")
30   var t6 = Time(hour: 23, minute: 59, second: 58)
31   println("t6 is initially: \(t6.description)")
32   t6.addSeconds(7) // increment the time by 7 seconds
33   println("t6 after adding 7 seconds is: \(t6.description)")
```

```
OBJECT: INITIALIZED WITH
t1: all default arguments
    00:00:00
    12:00:00 AM
t2: hour; default minute and second
    02:00:00
    2:00:00 AM
t3: hour and minute; default second
    21:34:00
    9:34:00 PM
t4: hour, minute and second
    12:25:42
    12:25:42 PM
t5: Time object t4
    12:25:42
    12:25:42 PM

ASSIGNING STRUCT OBJECTS
after t1 = t5, t1 is
    12:25:42
    12:25:42 PM

ADDING TO A TIME
t6 is initially: 11:59:58 PM
t6 after adding 7 seconds is: 12:00:05 AM
```

Fig. 9.2 | Testing struct Time. (Part 2 of 2.)

Assigning **struct** *Objects*

Line 26 assigns the struct object t5 to the variable struct object t1. For class types, this would result in two references to the *same* object. For struct and enum value types, however, assignment *copies* the right operand into the left operand. Line 27 shows that t1 and t5 contain the same time. Again, the compiler might not *actually* copy t5 into t1.

Performance Tip 9.2
The Swift compiler optimizes copy operations so that they're performed only if the copy is modified in your code—this is known as copy-on-write.

Calling **mutating** *Methods on* **struct** *Objects*

Line 30 creates the variable Time object t6, initializing it to 11:59:58 PM. Line 32 then calls the mutating method addSeconds to add seven seconds to the time. This increments the time past midnight, so addSeconds also calls addMinute to update the minute, and addMinutes also calls addHours to update the hour. Line 33 displays t6's time to confirm that it was incremented correctly.

9.3 Enumerations and Nested Types

Section 5.6.1 introduced enum types. In that section, you learned that an enum declares a set of constants represented by identifiers and that, unlike other C-based programming languages, a Swift enum's constants do *not* have values by default—the constants themselves *are* the values. You also saw that you can specify the underlying type of an enum type's constants and provide a *unique* raw value for each constant (which can be accessed via the constant's compiler-generated rawValue property). In an enum with underlying raw values of an *integer* numeric type:

- Each constant must have a unique integer raw value.

- By default each constant's value is one higher than the previous constant's value.

- The compiler implicitly assigns the first constant the raw value 0 and the subsequent constants the values 1, 2, 3, etc.

- For any constant that's explicitly assigned a value, the compiler implicitly assigns the subsequent constants values that increment from the assigned value (as we'll show in lines 32–33 of Fig. 9.3).

Software Engineering Observation 9.5

In most programming languages, enums can have only integer underlying types. In a Swift enum, however, you can specify as the underlying type String, Character or any of Swift's integer or floating-point types. For noninteger underlying types, you must assign a unique raw value to each constant in the enumeration.

Except for stored type properties, enums support the same capabilities as structs. In this section, to demonstrate additional enum and struct features, we'll reimplement our card shuffling and dealing simulation from Section 6.9. In this version, we'll use structs rather than classes to define the types Card and DeckOfCards (though these could still be classes here, too). We'll also define the 13 card faces and four card suits as constants in enum types. Finally, we'll introduce nested types and stored type properties for value types (again, classes do not yet support stored type properties). In Section 9.4, we'll discuss guidelines for choosing among classes, structs and enums when you define new types.

9.3.1 Card struct with Nested Suit and Face enum Types

In some cases, a type's primary purpose is to support another type. In such cases, it's common to define the supporting type as a **nested type**—that is, a type defined in the body of another class, struct or enum. As with other members of a type, a nested type can be defined as public, internal (the default) or private to control its scope. Figure 9.3 defines the struct type Card with two supporting nested types—the enum Suit (line 15–28) and the enum Face (lines 31–48). Like class Card in Section 6.9.1, struct Card contains the stored properties face and suit; however, in this example, they have the enum types Face and Suit, respectively. When you know in advance the finite set of values a type can assume—such as the faces and suits in a deck of cards—enums should be used to represent the values. Because Card is now a struct, we do not need to define an initializer—the compiler-generated memberwise initializer will suffice.

```swift
1   // Fig. 9.3: Card.swift (CardShufflingAndDealing.xcodeproj)
2   // Card struct represents a playing card as a Face and a Suit
3   public struct Card {
4       public let face: Face
5       public let suit: Suit
6
7       // computed property that returns String representation of Card
8       public var description: String {
9           get {
10              return face.description + " of " + suit.description
11          }
12      }
13
14      // enumeration of the four suits in a standard deck of playing cards
15      public enum Suit: String {
16          case Hearts = "Hearts"
17          case Diamonds = "Diamonds"
18          case Clubs = "Clubs"
19          case Spades = "Spades"
20
21          // stored type property: Array of all Suit constants
22          public static let values = [Hearts, Diamonds, Clubs, Spades]
23
24          // returns the raw value of a given constant
25          public var description: String {
26              return self.rawValue
27          }
28      }
29
30      // enumeration of the 13 faces in a standard deck of playing cards
31      public enum Face: Int {
32          case Ace = 1, Two, Three, Four, Five, Six, Seven, Eight, Nine,
33              Ten, Jack, Queen, King
34
35          // stored type property: Array of all Face constants
36          public static let values = [Ace, Two, Three, Four, Five, Six,
37              Seven, Eight, Nine, Ten, Jack, Queen, King]
38
39          // stored type property: String representations of Face constants
40          private static let nameStrings = ["Ace", "Two", "Three", "Four",
41              "Five", "Six", "Seven", "Eight", "Nine", "Ten", "Jack",
42              "Queen", "King"]
43
44          // returns a String from the nameStrings stored type property
45          public var description: String {
46              return Face.nameStrings[self.rawValue - 1]
47          }
48      }
49  }
```

Fig. 9.3 | Card struct represents a playing card as a Face and a Suit.

Nested **enum** Type `Suit`

Lines 15–28 define the nested enum type `Suit`, which contains four constants representing the suits in a standard playing-card deck. Line 15 specifies that each constant has type `String` and lines 16–19 define each constant and its *raw* `String` value. Recall that each enum constant's definition is introduced with the `case` keyword, though you can also define multiple constants in a comma-separated list as in:

```
case Hearts = "Hearts", Diamonds = "Diamonds", Clubs = "Clubs",
    Spades = "Spades"
```

Unlike enums in some languages (like Java), Swift does *not* provide a way to iterate over an enum's collection of constants. However, you can easily add such a capability to an enum by defining as a **stored type property** an `Array` containing the constants, such as the `values` Array in line 22. Type properties and methods for value types (`struct`s and enums) are defined with the **static keyword** (as opposed to the `class` keyword in classes). In Section 9.3.2, we'll use this `Array` to iterate through the `Suit`s when creating a deck of `Card`s.

Software Engineering Observation 9.6

You must provide an initial value for every stored type property—types do not have "type initializers."

Software Engineering Observation 9.7

Stored (instance) properties are not allowed in enum types.

Lines 25–27 define a `description` computed property that returns a `String` representation of a `Suit` constant. Since each `Suit` constant is already a `String`, we simply return the constant's `rawValue` (introduced in Section 5.6.4). When an `enum` type is defined with an underlying type for its constants, then the compiler autogenerates the `rawValue` property for each constant.

Nested **enum** Type `Face`

Lines 31–48 define the nested enum type `Face`, which contains 13 constants representing the faces in a standard playing-card deck. Each constant has the underlying type `Int` (line 31). We defined all of this enum's constants in a comma-separated list in a single `case` (lines 32–33). The first constant (`Ace`) is explicitly assigned the value 1 (line 32) and the compiler implicitly assigns each subsequent constant a value one higher than the previous constant. So the `Face` constants have *consecutive* `Int` values in the range 1–13. Of course, for certain card games an Ace can have the value 1 or 11 (e.g., Blackjack), and in other card games an Ace can be both the lowest and highest card. The card game's logic would need to account for these special cases.

Once again, we'd like to iterate through the `Face` constants when initializing a deck of `Card`s. For this reason, lines 36–37 define as a stored type property the `values` Array containing all 13 constants.

The `description` computed property (lines 45–47) returns a `String` representation of a given `Face` constant. To help do this, we define as a `private` stored type property the `nameStrings` Array containing `String` representations of each constant's name. Line 46 calculates the index into the nameStrings Array by using the Face constant's rawValue. Since the constants' rawValues range from 1 to 13, we subtract one from the rawValue to calculate the proper index.

Using enum Constants in switch Statements

You can use enum constants in a switch statement's cases. If you have a variable of type Suit named suit, the following switch performs a task based on the various Suit constants:

```
switch suit {
    case .Hearts:
        // task to perform for Hearts
    case .Diamonds:
        // task to perform for Diamonds
    case .Clubs:
        // task to perform for Clubs
    case .Spades:
        // task to perform for Spades
}
```

Swift *infers* from the control expression's type that the value in each case *must* be a Suit, so you're not required to qualify each constant's name with Suit.

If you place such a switch statement *inside* an instance property or method of an enum type (i.e., not a type property or type method), you can specify the control expression as self, as in the folloing reimplementation of Suit's description computed property (Fig. 9.3, lines 25–27):

```
var description: String {
    switch self {
        case .Hearts:
            return "Hearts"
        case .Diamonds:
            return "Diamonds"
        case .Clubs:
            return "Clubs"
        case .Spades:
            return "Spades"
    }
}
```

The keyword self indicates that the switch should compare to each case the value of the Suit constant on which the description property is invoked. So the statement:

```
println(Card.Suit.Diamonds.description)
```

would display the String "Diamonds".

9.3.2 DeckOfCards struct

We made only minor changes to class DeckOfCards (Fig. 6.10) to create the struct DeckOfCards (Fig. 9.4)—the changes are highlighted. Because the type is now defined as a struct, any method that modifies the properties of a DeckOfCards object must be defined as mutating (lines 21 and 38). We once again import the Darwin module to access the arc4random_uniform function for random-number generation.

```
1   // Fig. 9.4: DeckOfCards.swift (CardShufflingAndDealing.xcodeproj)
2   // DeckOfCards struct represents a deck of playing cards
3   import Darwin
4
5   public struct DeckOfCards {
6       private var deck: [Card] = [] // array of Cards
7       private var currentCard: Int = 0 // index of next Card to deal (0-51)
8       public let numberOfCards = 52 // constant # of Cards
9
10      // initializer fills the deck of Cards
11      public init() {
12          // populate deck with Card objects
13          for face in Card.Face.values {
14              for suit in Card.Suit.values {
15                  deck.append(Card(face: face, suit: suit))
16              }
17          }
18      }
19
20      // shuffle deck of Cards with one-pass algorithm
21      public mutating func shuffle() {
22          // next call to method dealCard should start at deck[0] again
23          currentCard = 0;
24
25          // Modern Fisher-Yates shuffle: http://bit.ly/FisherYates
26          for first in stride(from: numberOfCards - 1, through: 1, by: -1) {
27              // select a random number between 0 and first
28              let second = Int(arc4random_uniform(UInt32(first + 1)))
29
30              // swap current Card with randomly selected Card
31              let temp = deck[first]
32              deck[first] = deck[second]
33              deck[second] = temp
34          }
35      }
36
37      // deal one Card
38      public mutating func dealCard() -> Card? {
39          // determine whether Cards remain to be dealt
40          if currentCard < deck.count {
41              return deck[currentCard++] // return current Card
42          } else {
43              return nil; // nil indicates that all Cards were dealt
44          }
45      }
46  }
```

Fig. 9.4 | DeckOfCards struct represents a deck of playing cards.

*Initializing a **DeckOfCards** Object*

Lines 11–18 define the DeckOfCards initializer, which uses a nested for statement to create the 52 Card struct objects. The outer for statement (lines 13–17) iterates through all the Face constants in the stored type property Card.Face.values. Because the enum Face is a nested type in the struct Card, we must *fully qualify* the nested type's name (Face) with its outer type's name (Card) to access the stored type property values. Similarly, the inner for statement (lines 14–16) iterates through all the Suit constants in the stored type property Card.Suit.values. Each iteration of the nested for statement initializes a Card by passing its memberwise initializer the current Face and Suit.

9.3.3 Testing the struct Types Card and DeckOfCards, and the enum Types Suit and Face

The program of Fig. 9.5 demonstrates the struct DeckOfCards and features of the Face and Suit enums. The first part of the output demonstrates that shuffling and dealing an object of the DeckOfCards struct type works identically to the DeckOfCards class in Fig. 6.10. One key difference between the programs is the call to dealCard (Fig. 9.5, line 18). Though this method call is identical to the corresponding one in Fig. 6.11, dealCard in the DeckOfCards struct returns a *copy* of a Card object because Card is a value type.

```swift
1   // Fig. 9.5: main.swift (CardShufflingAndDealing.xcodeproj)
2   // Card shuffling and dealing.
3
4   // format a String left aligned in a field
5   func formatString(var string: String, fieldWidth: Int) -> String {
6       let spaces: Int = fieldWidth - countElements(string)
7       let padding = String(count: spaces, repeatedValue: Character(" "))
8       string += padding
9       return string
10  }
11
12  var myDeckOfCards = DeckOfCards()
13
14  myDeckOfCards.shuffle() // place Cards in random order
15  println("SHUFFLED DECK OF CARDS")
16  var i = 0 // used to determine when to start new output line
17
18  while let card = myDeckOfCards.dealCard() { // deal and unwrap Card
19      ++i
20      print(formatString(card.description, 19)) // display Card
21
22      if (i % 4 == 0) { // move to next line after every fourth card
23          println()
24      }
25  }
26
27  println("\nDESCRIPTIONS AND RAW VALUES OF THE FACE ENUM CONSTANTS")
28  for face in Card.Face.values {
29      println("\(face.description) = \(face.rawValue)")
30  }
31
32  println("\nRAW VALUES OF THE SUIT ENUM CONSTANTS")
33  for suit in Card.Suit.values {
34      println("\(suit.rawValue)")
35  }
```

Fig. 9.5 | Card shuffling and dealing. (Part 1 of 3.)

```
36
37   println("\nCREATING FACES FROM RAW VALUES")
38   for i in 1...14 {
39       if let face = Card.Face(rawValue: i) {
40           println("\(i) is \(face.description)'s raw value")
41       } else {
42           println("There is no Face constant for the raw value \(i)")
43       }
44   }
```

```
SHUFFLED DECK OF CARDS
Three of Spades     Three of Clubs      Six of Spades       Six of Clubs
Queen of Clubs      Nine of Clubs       Ace of Hearts       Seven of Spades
Six of Diamonds     Queen of Hearts     Four of Hearts      Five of Diamonds
Two of Diamonds     Four of Spades      Seven of Diamonds   Jack of Diamonds
Queen of Diamonds   Eight of Hearts     King of Clubs       Eight of Clubs
Ten of Clubs        Ace of Spades       Five of Hearts      Five of Clubs
Nine of Diamonds    Ace of Clubs        Ten of Spades       King of Diamonds
Jack of Spades      Ace of Diamonds     Two of Clubs        Ten of Hearts
Jack of Hearts      Four of Clubs       Two of Spades       King of Hearts
Nine of Spades      Three of Hearts     King of Spades      Two of Hearts
Queen of Spades     Ten of Diamonds     Jack of Clubs       Eight of Spades
Six of Hearts       Nine of Hearts      Five of Spades      Seven of Hearts
Three of Diamonds   Seven of Clubs      Eight of Diamonds   Four of Diamonds

DESCRIPTIONS AND RAW VALUES OF THE FACE ENUM CONSTANTS
Ace = 1
Two = 2
Three = 3
Four = 4
Five = 5
Six = 6
Seven = 7
Eight = 8
Nine = 9
Ten = 10
Jack = 11
Queen = 12
King = 13

RAW VALUES OF THE SUIT ENUM CONSTANTS
Hearts
Diamonds
Clubs
Spades

CREATING FACES FROM RAW VALUES
1 is Ace's raw value
2 is Two's raw value
3 is Three's raw value
4 is Four's raw value
5 is Five's raw value
6 is Six's raw value
```

Fig. 9.5 | Card shuffling and dealing. (Part 2 of 3.)

```
7 is Seven's raw value
8 is Eight's raw value
9 is Nine's raw value
10 is Ten's raw value
11 is Jack's raw value
12 is Queen's raw value
13 is King's raw value
There is no Face constant for the raw value 14
```

Fig. 9.5 | Card shuffling and dealing. (Part 3 of 3.)

Accessing **enum** Constant Properties

Lines 28–30 in Fig. 9.5 iterate through the Face enum's constants and display each constant's description and rawValue. Similarly, lines 33–35 iterate through the Suit enum's constants and display each constant's rawValue.

Creating an **enum** Constant from a Raw Value

For an enum with an underlying type, the compiler generates an initializer that receives a constant's raw value and, if that value exists in the enum, returns the corresponding constant. This is why raw values must be unique for constants in a given enum type. Because the raw value might not exist in the enum, this initializer is *failable* (init?). Lines 38–44 demonstrate the Face enum's failable initializer by attempting to create Face constants for the values in the *closed range* 1...14—the value 14 is invalid. If the argument to the Face enum's initializer is invalid, the initializer returns nil. So each iteration of the loop uses *optional binding* (line 39) to determine whether the expression

```
Card.Face(rawValue: i)
```

returns a valid Face constant. If so, line 40 displays the argument that was passed to the initializer and the String representation of that constant. When 14 is passed to the initializer, the optional binding at line 39 evaluates to false (because 14 is not a valid raw value for a Face enum constant) and line 42 indicates that there is no constant for the value 14.

9.4 Choosing Among Structures, Enumerations and Classes in Your Apps

When designing a new type, your choice of class, struct or enum might be dictated to you by the context in which the type will be used. For example, in iOS or OS X apps, new types often must be classses because they must *inherit* from existing Cocoa or Cocoa Touch framework classes (and only classes can inherit from other classes). Doing so ensures that your new class has the functionality that's required for interacting with these frameworks and for integrating your apps with iOS or OS X. We'll discuss inheritance in Chapter 10. In Chapter 14's iOS app, we'll inherit from the Cocoa Touch framework class UIViewController, which provides the basic capabilities for displaying an iOS app's user interface.

Guidelines

If the context for your type does *not require* a class, you can follow these guidelines for choosing the kind of type to use:

- Use an enum if your type should have *value semantics* and represents a *well-known, finite* set of values. For example, in Section 9.3's card-shuffling program, we used enums named `Suit` and `Face` to represent the four suits and 13 faces, respectively, in a deck of cards.

- Use a `struct` if your type should have *value semantics* and does not represent a finite set of values. Typically `struct` types contain small numbers of value-type properties (such as the `Card struct` in Section 9.3).

Software Engineering Observation 9.8

It's possible for a struct type to contain references to objects of class types, but this is discouraged. Copying a struct object that contains references to class objects creates multiple references to those class objects and can lead to unexpected results.

- Use a class if your type should have *reference semantics* or should *inherit* implementation details—such as initializer, property and method definitions—from an existing class. Also, if your type uses resources that require clean-up via a deinitializer—such as database connections, network connections, etc.—you must use a class, because only classes can have deinitializers.

- As we said in **Software Engineering Observation 9.1**, because value-type objects are copied, you always have exclusive ownership of those objects, wherever you're accessing or modifying them. This is particularly important with today's multicore hardware systems, which encourage the use of multithreaded programming. If you're defining a new type in a multithreaded application, you might prefer using a `struct` or enum to a class.

Apple Documentation on Value Types vs. Reference Types and Using Classes vs. Structures
For more information on value vs. reference types, see Apple's Swift team blog post:

```
https://developer.apple.com/swift/blog/?id=10
```

For more information regarding when to choose classes vs. structs, see the Classes and Structures chapter of Apple's *Swift Programming Language* book:

```
http://bit.ly/SwiftClassVsStruct
```

9.5 Associated Values for enums

You can specify that an enum constant should have one or more **associated values** that are stored with the constant when you assign it to a variable of the enum type—enums with associated values are similar to `unions` in C. The associated values' required types are specified as a tuple following the constant's name, as in:

```
case ConstantName(Type1, Type2, ...)
```

You've actually been using enum constants with associated values extensively throughout this book. Swift's optionals are implemented as the generic enum type `Optional<T>`—T is a placeholder for the type of the value, if any, stored in the `Optional`. That value is actually an associated value for one of `Optional<T>`'s constants. So for an `Int?` (that is, an `Optional<Int>`), the placeholder T represents an associated value of type `Int`, and for a `String?`, the placeholder T represents an associated value of type `String`.

Common Programming Error 9.1

A compilation error occurs if you specify a raw value type for an enum that contains constants with associated values.

The enum type Optional<T> has two constants:

* The enum constant None for an Optional that *does not contain* a value.

* The enum constant Some(T) for an optional that *contains* a value. The *one-element tuple*, (T), contains Some's associated value—the Optional's underlying value.

When you use optional binding or optional chaining to check whether an Optional contains a value, Swift calls the Optional's map method to check the Optional's value. If the value is Some, the map method returns Some's associated value; otherwise, if the Optional's value is None, map returns nil.

Demonstrating Associated Values with Optional<Int>

Figure 9.6 demonstrates associated values using optionals of type Int?. You've already used optionals with optional binding or optional chaining, so this example explicitly uses Optional<T>'s Some and None constants to check whether an Optional contains a value.

```
1   // Fig. 9.6: AssociatedValues.playground
2   // Demonstrating associated values with the Optional<T> enum type
3
4   // accesses an Optional Int's Some and None constants
5   func displayOptionalViaEnumConstants(string: String, optionalInt: Int?) {
6       switch optionalInt {
7           case .Some(let value):
8               println("The optional \(string) contains the Int \(value)")
9           case .None:
10              println("The optional \(string) contains nil")
11      }
12  }
13
14  // create Optional Int values
15  let emptyInt1 = Optional<Int>() // uses init() to set emptyInt1 to nil
16  let emptyInt2: Int? = nil // uses init(nil) to set emptyInt2 to nil
17
18  let filledInt1 = Optional<Int>(7) // uses init(7) to set filledInt1 to 7
19  let filledInt2: Int? = 11 // uses init(11) to set filledInt2 to 11
20
21  // display Optional contents by accessing constants Some and None
22  displayOptionalViaEnumConstants("emptyInt1", emptyInt1)
23  displayOptionalViaEnumConstants("emptyInt2", emptyInt2)
24  displayOptionalViaEnumConstants("filledInt1", filledInt1)
25  displayOptionalViaEnumConstants("filledInt2", filledInt2)
```

```
The optional emptyInt1 contains nil
The optional emptyInt2 contains nil
The optional filledInt1 contains the Int 7
The optional filledInt2 contains the Int 11
```

Fig. 9.6 | Demonstrating associated values with the Optional<T> enum type.

Creating `Optionals`

Lines 15–19 create several optional `Int` constants and initialize them with various `Optional<T>` initializers:

- Line 15 explicitly uses `Optional<T>`'s no-argument initializer to create the `emptyInt1` and initialize it to `nil`. The compiler infers `emptyInt1`'s type as `Int?` (the shorthand for `Optional<Int>`).

- Line 16 implicitly uses `Optional<T>`'s initializer that receives the `nil` literal to create the constant `emptyInt2` of type `Int?` and initialize it to `nil`.

- Line 18 explicitly uses `Optional<T>`'s initializer that receives the `Some` constant's associated value (the `Int` value 7 in this case) to create the constant `filledInt1` of type `Int?`.

- Line 19 implicitly uses `Optional<T>`'s initializer that receives the `Some` constant's associated value (the `Int` value 11 in this case) to create the constant `filledInt2` of type `Int?`.

Displaying `Optional` *Values by Using* `switch` *with the* **Some** *and* **None** *Constants*

Next, lines 22–25 call the function `displayOptionalViaEnumConstants` (lines 5–12) to determine whether each `Int?` contains a value and display an appropriate line of text. The `switch`'s control expression (line 6) is `optionalInt`—the `Int?` passed as the function's second argument. The argument's value is either the constant `Some` or `None`:

- If the value is `Some`, the `Int?` *contains* an `Int` value. Because we provided a tuple in the `case` (line 7), the `Some` constant's associated value tuple is decomposed and its one element is placed into the constant `value` (declared in line 7). We then display the `value` in line 8.

- If the value is `None`, `optionalInt` *does not contain* a value (i.e., the optional is `nil`), so line 10 displays that the optional contains `nil`.

For the optionals in lines 15–16, the function `displayOptionalViaEnumConstants` indicates that each optional contains `nil`. For the optionals in lines 18–19, the function displays each optional's associated value—7 and 11, respectively.

9.6 Wrap-Up

In this chapter, you saw that many of the class capabilities in Chapter 8 also are supported by `struct` and `enum` types. We demonstrated the close relationships among classes, `struct`s and `enum`s, and pointed out their differences.

You learned that, like classes, `struct`s can define stored properties, methods, computed type properties, type methods, subcripts and initializers. You also learned that, unlike classes, `struct`s and `enum`s can define stored type properties, do not have deinitializers, are not managed with ARC and cannot be used in inheritance hierarchies. We used a `struct`'s compiler-generated default and memberwise initializers, and discussed why you should define custom `struct` initializers in an `extension`.

We reimplemented the card-shuffling-and-dealing case study from Section 6.9, using `struct`s, `enum`s and nested types. We demonstrated stored type properties for value types in the context of the `Face` and `Suit` `enum` types.

We provided guidelines for how to choose whether to implement a new type as a `class`, `struct` or `enum`. Finally, we introduced enum types with associated values and demonstrated how Swift's optionals are implemented using such `enum` types.

In the next chapter, we continue our discussion of object-oriented programming by introducing inheritance, a form of software reuse in which a new class is created by absorbing an existing class's capabilities and customizing them and/or adding new ones. We explain and demonstrate polymorphism, which processes objects inherited from the same superclass, either directly or indirectly, as if they were all objects of the superclass, and show how this can simplify programming. Finally, we demonstrate protocols, which are particularly useful for assigning common capabilities to disparate `class`, `struct` and `enum` types. Protocols can even be used to implement polymorphic behavior across value-type and reference-type objects in the same program.

10

Inheritance, Polymorphism and Protocols

Objectives

In this chapter you'll:

- Use inheritance to develop new classes that absorb the attributes and behaviors of existing classes.

- Understand superclasses and subclasses and the relationship between them.

- Access superclass members with **super** from a subclass.

- Learn how initializers and deinitializers are used and when they run in inheritance hierarchies.

- Create a hierarchy of **Employee** classes and use them in a polymorphic payroll system that calculates each **Employee**'s earnings in a subclass-specific manner.

- Learn how access modifiers affect what a subclass can inherit from a superclass.

- Create a custom protocol to assign common capabilities to possibly disparate types.

- Use a protocol to create a polymorphic accounts-payable system that calculates payment amounts for employee and invoice objects.

10.1 Introduction

This chapter continues our discussion of object-oriented programming by introducing **inheritance**, a form of *software reuse* in which a new class is created by absorbing an existing class's capabilities (i.e., initializers, properties and methods) and customizing them with new or modified capabilities. With inheritance, you can save time during program development and build better software by reusing proven, high-quality classes, as you'll commonly do with classes from Apple's Cocoa and Cocoa Touch frameworks. Unlike object-oriented programming languages such as Objective-C, Java, C# and Visual Basic, Swift does not have a common superclass from which all classes inherit basic capabilities. Swift's value types (i.e., structs and enums) do not support inheritance.

10.1.1 Superclasses and Subclasses

When creating a class, rather than declaring completely new members, you can designate that the new class *inherits* the members of an existing class. The existing class is called the **superclass**, and the new class is the **subclass**. A subclass can add its own properties, initializers and methods, and it can customize the ones it inherits. Therefore, a subclass is *more* *specific* than its superclass and represents a more *specialized group of objects*. Each superclass can have many subclasses. Each subclass has exactly one superclass. To demonstrate inheritance, we provide a simple example that shows how to create a new class from an existing one, how to add new features and how to customize existing features.

10.1.2 Polymorphism

We explain and demonstrate **polymorphism**, which enables you to conveniently program "in the general" rather than "in the specific." In particular, polymorphism enables you to write programs which process objects that share the same superclass, either directly or indirectly, as if they were all objects of the superclass; this can simplify programming.

Consider the following example of polymorphism. Suppose we create a program that simulates the movement of several types of animals, represented by the classes Fish, Frog and Bird. Suppose that each class inherits from superclass Animal, which contains a method move and maintains an animal's current location as *x-y* coordinate properties. Each subclass implements its own specialized version of method move. Our program maintains an Animal array containing references to objects of the various Animal subclasses. To simulate the animals' movements, the program invokes on each object the *same* method once per second—namely, move. Each specific type of Animal responds to a move call in its own way—a Fish might swim three feet, a Frog might jump five feet and a Bird might fly ten feet. Each object knows how to modify its *x-y* coordinates appropriately for its specific type of movement. Relying on each object to know how to "do the right thing" (i.e., do what's appropriate for that type of object) in response to the *same* method call is the key concept of polymorphism. The *same* method call (in this case, move) sent to a *variety* of objects has *many forms* of results—hence the term polymorphism.

We present a payroll application that polymorphically calculates the weekly pay of several different types of employees using each employee's earnings property. Though each employee's earnings are calculated in a *specific* way, polymorphism allows us to process the employees conveniently "in the *general*." As you'll soon see, when we invoke each employee's earnings property (regardless of the employee's type), the correct earnings subclass calculation is performed, due to Swift's polymorphic capabilities.

10.1.3 Implementing for Extensibility

With inheritance and polymorphism, we can design and implement systems that are easily *extensible*—new classes can be added with little or no modification to the general portions of the program, as long as the new classes are part of the inheritance hierarchy that the program processes generally. The new classes simply "plug right in." The only parts of a program that must be altered are those that require direct knowledge of the new classes. For example, if we inherit from class Animal to create class Tortoise (which might respond to a move call by crawling one inch), we need to write only the Tortoise class and the part of the simulation that instantiates a Tortoise object. The portions of the simulation that tell each Animal to move can remain the same.

10.1.4 Programming in the Specific

Occasionally, when performing polymorphic processing, we need to program "in the *specific*." In the polymorphic payroll application, we also demonstrate that a program can determine an object's type at *execution time* and act on that object accordingly. We'll use this technique to give 10% raises to all employees of one particular type.

10.1.5 Protocols

In Chapter 7, we introduced type `Dictionary` and mentioned that a `Dictionary`'s keys must conform to the `Hashable` protocol. We also discussed `Dictionary`'s `description` property, which comes from the `Printable` protocol. Protocols are particularly useful for assigning *common* capabilities to *disparate* `class`, `struct` and enum types. This allows objects of these types to be processed polymorphically, because objects of types that "conform to" the *same* protocol have the capabilities described by that protocol. We create a custom protocol, then modify the employee-payroll application to build a more generalized accounts-payable application that calculates payments due for company employees *and* invoice amounts for goods and services purchased by the company. As you'll see, the application uses protocol-type variables to polymorphically process objects of disparate employee and invoice types that conform to the protocol.

10.2 Superclasses and Subclasses

Inheritance creates an *is-a* **relationship** between classes. This enables an object of a subclass to be treated as an object of its superclass. For example, a car *is a* vehicle. Figure 10.1 lists several additional examples of superclasses and subclasses—superclasses tend to be *more general* and subclasses tend to be *more specific*. Superclass objects *cannot* be treated as objects of their subclasses—although all cars are vehicles, *not* all vehicles are cars.

Superclass	Subclasses
Vehicle	A Car *is a* Vehicle
	A Plane *is a* Vehicle
Student	A GraduateStudent *is a* Student
	An UndergraduateStudent *is a* Student
Shape	A Circle *is a* Shape
	A Triangle *is a* Shape
Loan	A CarLoan *is a* Loan
	A HomeImprovementLoan *is a* Loan
BankAccount	A CheckingAccount *is a* BankAccount
	A SavingsAccount *is a* BankAccount

Fig. 10.1 | Inheritance examples.

Because every subclass object *is an* object of its superclass, and one superclass can have *many* subclasses, the set of objects represented by a superclass is typically larger than the set of objects represented by any of its subclasses. For example, the *superclass* Vehicle represents *all* vehicles, including cars, trucks, boats, planes and the like. By contrast, *subclass* Car represents a smaller, more specific subset of vehicles.

10.3 An Inheritance Hierarchy: CommunityMembers

The Unified Modeling Language (UML; uml.org) is a widely used, industry-standard graphical scheme for modeling object-oriented systems. UML diagrams help systems designers specify a system in a concise, graphical, programming-language-independent manner, before programmers implement the system in a specific programming language.

Figure 10.2 shows a sample UML class diagram of an **inheritance hierarchy**. A college community has thousands of community members, including employees, students and alumni. Employees are either faculty members or staff members. Faculty members are either administrators (such as deans and department chairpersons) or teachers. The hierarchy could contain many other classes. For example, students can be graduate or undergraduate students. Undergraduate students can be freshmen, sophomores, juniors or seniors.

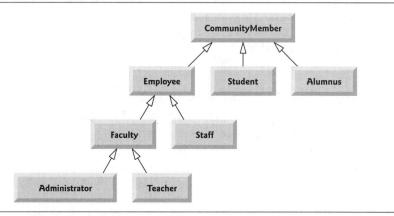

Fig. 10.2 | Inheritance hierarchy for university CommunityMembers.

Each arrow in the inheritance hierarchy represents an *is-a* relationship. As we follow the arrows *upward*, we can state, for instance, that "an Employee *is a* CommunityMember" and "a Teacher *is a* Faculty member." A **direct superclass** is the class from which a subclass explicitly inherits. An **indirect superclass** is inherited from two or more levels up in the **class hierarchy**. So, class CommunityMember is the *direct* superclass of Employee, Student and Alumnus, and is an *indirect* superclass of all the other classes in the diagram. Starting from the bottom of the diagram, you can follow the arrows and apply the *is-a* relationship up to the topmost superclass. For example, an Administrator *is a* Faculty member, *is an* Employee and ultimately *is a* CommunityMember.

10.4 Case Study: Using Inheritance to Create Related Employee Types

In this section, we use an inheritance hierarchy containing types of employees in a company's payroll app to demonstrate the relationship between a superclass and its subclass. All employees of the company have a lot in common—for example, each has a name and gets paid—but *commission employees* (who will be represented as objects of a superclass) are paid a percentage of their sales, while *base-salaried commission employees* (who will be represented as objects of a subclass) receive a base salary *plus* a percentage of their sales. First, we present the *superclass* CommissionEmployee. Next, we create a *subclass* BasePlusCommissionEmployee that inherits from class CommissionEmployee. Then we present an app that creates CommissionEmployee and BasePlusCommissionEmployee objects and shows that a BasePlusCommissionEmployee has all the capabilities of the superclass *and* the subclass, but calculates its earnings differently. In Section 10.5, we discuss how access modifiers determine the classes from which a subclass can inherit and which superclass members are inherited.

Utility Functions Used in Each of This Chapter's Examples
In each of this chapter's example projects, we include the file UtilityFunctions.swift (Fig. 10.3), which contains functions that we use for numeric formatting throughout this chapter's examples.

```
1   // Fig. 10.3: UtilityFunctions.Swift
2   // Locale-specific currency and percentage formatting functions
3   import Foundation
4
5   // convert a numeric value to localized percent string
6   public func formatAsPercent(number: NSNumber) -> String {
7       let percentFormatter = NSNumberFormatter()
8       percentFormatter.numberStyle = .PercentStyle
9       percentFormatter.minimumFractionDigits = 2
10      percentFormatter.locale = NSLocale.currentLocale()
11      return percentFormatter.stringFromNumber(number)!
12  }
13
14  // convert a numeric value to localized currency string
15  func formatAsCurrency(number: NSNumber) -> String {
16      return NSNumberFormatter.localizedStringFromNumber(
17          number, numberStyle: .CurrencyStyle)
18  }
```

Fig. 10.3 | Locale-specific currency and percentage formatting functions.

Function formatAsPercent (lines 6–12) formats a number as a *locale-specific* percentage String. First the function creates an NSNumberFormatter object and configures its numberStyle, minimumFractionDigits and locale properties, so that any number formatted with this object is a percentage with two digits to the right of the decimal separator (a symbol that depends on the locale). NSNumberFormatter's stringFromNumber method (line 11) returns a String? that's nil if the argument cannot be converted. For this chapter's examples, we assume that the argument is converted correctly, so we force unwrap the String? with ! before returning it.

Function formatAsCurrency (lines 15–18) formats a number as a locale-specific currency String using NSNumberFormatter type method localizedStringFromNumber, which returns a locale-specific String in the specified format (CurrencyStyle from the NSNumberFormatterStyle enum). We could have used localizedStringFromNumber in function formatAsPercent to produce a percentage String (using the PercentStyle constant from the NSNumberFormatterStyle enum), but the default behavior for formatting percentages rounds to the nearest integer. We preferred to display percentages with two digits to the right of the decimal separator.

10.4.1 Superclass CommissionEmployee

We begin by defining superclass CommissionEmployee (Fig. 10.4), which contains:

- the stored properties name, grossSales and commissionRate (lines 6–8)[1]—each defined as an implicitly unwrapped optional,

- a *failable initializer* (init?, lines 11–27) to set the stored properties' values if their initial values are all valid, and

- computed property earnings (lines 30–32), which calculates a CommissionEmployee's earnings by using NSDecimalNumber method decimalNumberByMultiplyingBy to multiply the commissionRate by the grossSales, and

- computed property description (lines 35–40), which uses a CommissionEmployee's stored properties to create a String containing the CommissionEmployee's information. [*Note:* In Chapter 7, we mentioned that description is a property of the Printable protocol. In this example and the one in Section 10.7, we define our own description property in each class. In Section 10.8, we'll show how to make all employee types conform to the Printable protocol.]

Except for final classes (discussed in Section 10.10), every class you create potentially can be a superclass. In Swift, a class hierarchy's topmost superclass is known as the **base class**, so class CommissionEmployee is this example's base class.

```
1   // Fig. 10.4: CommissionEmployee.swift
2   // CommissionEmployee superclass is the hierarchy's base class
3   import Foundation
4
5   public class CommissionEmployee {
6       public var name: String!
7       public var grossSales: NSDecimalNumber!
8       public var commissionRate: NSDecimalNumber!
9
10      // failable initializer
11      public init?(name: String, grossSales: NSDecimalNumber,
12          commissionRate: NSDecimalNumber) {
13
14          // if any arguments are invalid, return nil
15          if name.isEmpty ||
16              (grossSales.compare(NSDecimalNumber.zero()) ==
17                  NSComparisonResult.OrderedAscending) ||
18              (commissionRate.compare(NSDecimalNumber.zero()) ==
19                  NSComparisonResult.OrderedAscending) {
20
21              return nil // an initializer argument was invalid, so fail
22          }
23
```

Fig. 10.4 | CommissionEmployee superclass is the hierarchy's base class. (Part 1 of 2.)

---

1. Class CommissionEmployee's stored properties are implicitly unwrapped optionals. Recall from Chapter 8 that we do this to avoid a known compiler bug for failable initializers at the time of this writing. Currently, you cannot return nil from a failable initializer unless all of the type's stored properties have values. Optionals are initialized to nil by default, which satisfies this requirement.

```
24              self.name = name
25              self.grossSales = grossSales
26              self.commissionRate = commissionRate
27          }
28
29          // earnings computed property
30          public var earnings: NSDecimalNumber {
31              return commissionRate.decimalNumberByMultiplyingBy(grossSales)
32          }
33
34          // description computed property
35          public var description: String {
36              return String(format:"%@: %@\n%@: %@\n%@: %@",
37                  "Commission Employee", name,
38                  "Gross Sales", formatAsCurrency(grossSales),
39                  "Commission Rate", formatAsPercent(commissionRate))
40          }
41      }
```

Fig. 10.4 | CommissionEmployee superclass is the hierarchy's base class. (Part 2 of 2.)

10.4.2 Subclass BasePlusCommissionEmployee

Most of a BasePlusCommissionEmployee's capabilities are similar, if not identical, to a CommissionEmployee's (Fig. 10.4). Both classes require properties for the name, gross sales and commission rate, and capabilities for manipulating that data. In this example, each class has an initializer, computed properties and the ability to manipulate the stored properties' values (and could have methods, though neither class does in this example). To create class BasePlusCommissionEmployee *without* using inheritance, we probably would have *copied* the code from class CommissionEmployee and *pasted* it into class BasePlusCommissionEmployee, then modified the new class to include a base salary property, and the capabilities that manipulate the base salary, including new implementations of the initializer and the earnings and description properties. This *copy-and-paste approach* is often tedious and error prone. Worse yet, it can spread many physical copies of the same code (including errors) throughout a system, creating a code-maintenance nightmare. Using inheritance, we can "absorb" class CommissionEmployee's features into class BasePlusCommissionEmployee—also, any changes to a superclass propagate to all of its subclasses.

Class *BasePlusCommissionEmployee*
The subclass BasePlusCommissionEmployee (Fig. 10.5) *inherits* most of its capabilities from base class CommissionEmployee. To inherit from an existing class, you follow the new class's name with a colon (:) and the superclass's name (as in line 5).

```
1   // Fig. 10.5: BasePlusCommissionEmployee.swift
2   // BasePlusCommissionEmployee class inherits from class CommissionEmployee
3   import Foundation
4
```

Fig. 10.5 | BasePlusCommissionEmployee class inherits from class CommissionEmployee. (Part 1 of 2.)

```
5   public class BasePlusCommissionEmployee : CommissionEmployee {
6       public var baseSalary: NSDecimalNumber!
7
8       // failable initializer
9       public init?(name: String, grossSales: NSDecimalNumber,
10          commissionRate: NSDecimalNumber, baseSalary: NSDecimalNumber)
11      {
12          super.init(name: name, grossSales: grossSales,
13              commissionRate: commissionRate)
14
15          // validate baseSalary
16          if baseSalary.compare(NSDecimalNumber.zero()) ==
17              NSComparisonResult.OrderedAscending {
18
19              return nil // baseSalary was invalid, so fail
20          }
21
22          self.baseSalary = baseSalary
23      }
24
25      // earnings computed property
26      public override var earnings: NSDecimalNumber {
27          return baseSalary.decimalNumberByAdding(super.earnings)
28      }
29
30      // description computed property
31      public override var description: String {
32          return String(format: "%@ %@\n%@: %@",
33              "Base-Salaried", super.description, "Base Salary",
34              formatAsCurrency(baseSalary))
35      }
36  }
```

Fig. 10.5 | BasePlusCommissionEmployee class inherits from class CommissionEmployee. (Part 2 of 2.)

A BasePlusCommissionEmployee *is a* CommissionEmployee, because inheritance enables the subclass to absorb class CommissionEmployee's capabilities. Class BasePlusCommissionEmployee also has:

- the stored property baseSalary (line 6)—an implicitly unwrapped optional,

- a failable initializer (lines 9–23) to set a BasePlusCommissionEmployee's baseSalary and the inherited stored properties from class CommissionEmployee,

- a customized version of the computed property earnings (lines 26–28), and

- a customized version of computed property description (lines 31–35).

BasePlusCommissionEmployee *Initializer*
Recall that a class's stored properties *must* be initialized—either in their definitions, or via a designated initializer. A subclass initializer is responsible for:

- initializing the stored properties defined in the subclass,

- calling one of its superclass's *designated initializers* to set the inherited properties' values,

- setting the subclass properties' values, and

- possibly changing the values of inherited properties that were set by the superclass's initializer.

To call a superclass initializer, you precede the call with the keyword **super** and a dot (.), as shown in lines 12–13. Since this is a call to a *failable* initializer in class CommissionEmployee, the remainder of the BasePlusCommissionEmployee initializer executes *only* if CommissionEmployee's initializer does *not* return nil. In that case, lines 16–20 validate the baseSalary. If it's valid, line 22 assigns the value to the baseSalary property.

Statement Order in a Subclass Initializer

In many object-oriented programming languages, a constructor's *first* step must be an implicit or explicit call to the superclass's constructor. Swift initializers perform their tasks in a slightly different order. We summarize this here and discuss the issues in more detail in Section 10.11:

- When creating a subclass object, each subclass stored property must be initialized *before* the superclass initializer is called. In class BasePlusCommissionEmployee, the baseSalary property is an *optional*, so it's automatically initialized to nil before the superclass initializer is called in lines 12–13. Any non-optional stored property explicitly must be assigned a value, either in its definition or in the initializer before the superclass initializer is called.

- A subclass initializer can manipulate superclass properties only *after* the superclass initializer executes. This ensures that all superclass properties have values *before* the subclass initializer can use or change their values. In addition, this ensures that the superclass initializer does not change an property's value after the subclass initializer sets it.

Section 10.11 discusses Swift's *two-phase initialization process*, the tasks that the compiler performs to ensure that each object gets initialized properly and how these tasks affect initializers in inheritance hierarchies.

Overriding the Computed Property **earnings**

Class BasePlusCommissionEmployee's earnings property (lines 26–28) overrides class CommissionEmployee's earnings property (Fig. 10.4, lines 30–32) to calculate the earnings of a BasePlusCommissionEmployee. The overridden version obtains the commission portion of the BasePlusCommissionEmployee's earnings (i.e., grossSales times commissionRate) by using the expression super.earnings (Fig. 10.5, line 27) to get superclass CommissionEmployee's earnings property. BasePlusCommissionEmployee's earnings property then adds that value to the baseSalary to calculate the BasePlusCommissionEmployee's total earnings. To invoke an overridden superclass property or method—place the keyword super and a dot (.) before the superclass property or method name, as in line 27. By having BasePlusCommissionEmployee's earnings property use CommissionEmployee's earnings property to calculate part of a BasePlusCommissionEmployee's earnings, we *avoid duplicating the code and reduce code-maintenance problems.*

Line 26 uses the required keyword **override** to indicate that the earnings property *overrides* an *existing* superclass property. When overriding a superclass property, the subclass property must have the same name and type. The override keyword helps the compiler prevent common errors. For example, if you inadvertently spell the earnings property's name incorrectly in the subclass, the compiler will flag this as an error because the superclass does not contain a property with the same name.

Similarly, a subclass method or initializer defined with override must have the same signature as a superclass method or initializer, respectively. Another common overriding error is declaring the wrong number or types of parameters in a method's or initializer's parameter list. Without the override keyword, this would create an *unintentional overload* of the superclass method or initializer. When the compiler encounters a method or initializer defined with override, it compares the method's or initializer's signature with those in the superclass. If there isn't an *exact* match, the compiler issues an error message.

Error-Prevention Tip 10.1

You must define overridden superclass members with override *to help the compiler ensure that you're overriding them correctly. If you unintentionally override a superclass member without the* override *keyword, the compiler generates an error—this helps prevent accidental overrides.*

Software Engineering Observation 10.1

A subclass can override any of its superclass's instance properties, computed type properties, instance methods, type methods, subscripts (discussed in Chapter 12) and designated initializers. (At the time of this writing, stored type properties are not yet supported for classes.)

Overriding the Computed Property description

BasePlusCommissionEmployee's description property (lines 31–36) overrides class CommissionEmployee's description property (Fig. 10.4, lines 35–40) to return a String representation that's appropriate for a BasePlusCommissionEmployee. The subclass creates part of a BasePlusCommissionEmployee object's String representation by creating a formatted String containing "Base-Salaried" followed by the String returned by CommissionEmployee's description property (via the expression super.description in Fig. 10.5, line 33) and the remainder of a BasePlusCommissionEmployee object's String representation (i.e., the base salary). Again, we'll discuss the Printable protocol and its description property in Section 10.8.

10.4.3 Testing the Class Hierarchy

Figure 10.6 tests classes CommissionEmployee and BasePlusCommissionEmployee. Lines 6–9 create a CommissionEmployee object and invoke CommissionEmployee's initializer with "Sue Jones" as the name, 10000.00 as the gross sales amount ($10,000) and 0.06 (i.e., 6%) as the commission rate. Lines 14–17 use CommissionEmployee's properties to retrieve the object's data for output. Lines 19–20 assign new values to the object's grossSales and commissionRate properties. Then, lines 22–23 output the updated CommissionEmployee's String representation and earnings. Note the use of optional binding in line 12 to unwrap the CommissionEmployee? returned by lines 7–9.

```swift
1   // Fig. 10.6: main.swift
2   // Testing the CommissionEmployee-BasePlusCommissionEmployee hierarchy
3   import Foundation
4
5   // create and test a CommissionEmployee
6   let commissionEmployee =
7       CommissionEmployee(name: "Sue Jones",
8           grossSales:NSDecimalNumber(string: "10000.00"),
9           commissionRate: NSDecimalNumber(string: "0.06"))
10
11  // get commission employee data
12  if let employee = commissionEmployee {
13      println("COMMISSIONEMPLOYEE DATA VIA PROPERTIES")
14      println("Name: \(employee.name)")
15      println("Gross Sales: \(formatAsCurrency(employee.grossSales))")
16      println("Commission Rate: \(employee.commissionRate)")
17      println("Earnings: \(formatAsCurrency(employee.earnings))")
18
19      employee.grossSales = NSDecimalNumber(string: "5000.00")
20      employee.commissionRate = NSDecimalNumber(string: "0.10")
21      println("\nAFTER UPDATING GROSSSALES AND COMMISSIONRATE")
22      println(employee.description)
23      println("Updated Earnings: \(formatAsCurrency(employee.earnings))")
24  }
25
26  // create and test a BasePlusCommissionEmployee
27  let basePlusCommissionEmployee =
28      BasePlusCommissionEmployee(name: "Bob Lewis",
29          grossSales:NSDecimalNumber(string: "5000.00"),
30          commissionRate: NSDecimalNumber(string: "0.04"),
31          baseSalary: NSDecimalNumber(string: "300.00"))
32
33  // get commission employee data
34  if let employee = basePlusCommissionEmployee {
35      println("\nBASEPLUSCOMMISSIONEMPLOYEE DATA VIA PROPERTIES")
36      println("Name: \(employee.name)")
37      println("Gross Sales: \(formatAsCurrency(employee.grossSales))")
38      println("Commission Rate: \(employee.commissionRate)")
39      println("Base Salary: \(formatAsCurrency(employee.baseSalary))")
40      println("Earnings: \(formatAsCurrency(employee.earnings))")
41
42      employee.baseSalary = NSDecimalNumber(string: "1000.00")
43      println("\nAFTER UPDATING BASESALARY")
44      println(employee.description)
45      println("Updated Earnings: \(formatAsCurrency(employee.earnings))")
46  }
```

```
COMMISSIONEMPLOYEE DATA VIA PROPERTIES
Name: Sue Jones
Gross Sales: $10,000.00
Commission Rate: 6.00%
Earnings: $600.00
```

Fig. 10.6 | Testing the CommissionEmployee–BasePlusCommissionEmployee hierarchy. (Part 1 of 2.)

```
AFTER UPDATING GROSSSALES AND COMMISSIONRATE
Commission Employee: Sue Jones
Gross Sales: $5,000.00
Commission Rate: 10.00%
Updated Earnings: $500.00

BASEPLUSCOMMISSIONEMPLOYEE DATA VIA PROPERTIES
Name: Bob Lewis
Gross Sales: $5,000.00
Commission Rate: 4.00%
Base Salary: $300.00
Earnings: $500.00

AFTER UPDATING BASESALARY
Base-Salaried Commission Employee: Bob Lewis
Gross Sales: $5,000.00
Commission Rate: 4.00%
Base Salary: $1,000.00
Updated Earnings: $1,200.00
```

Fig. 10.6 | Testing the `CommissionEmployee–BasePlusCommissionEmployee` hierarchy. (Part 2 of 2.)

Lines 27–31 create a `BasePlusCommissionEmployee` object and pass `"Bob Lewis"`, `5000.00`, `0.04` and `300.00` to the initializer as the name, gross sales, commission rate and base salary, respectively. Lines 36–40 use `BasePlusCommissionEmployee`'s properties to output the object's data. Notice that we're able to access *all* of the `public` properties of classes `CommissionEmployee` *and* `BasePlusCommissionEmployee` here. Line 40 calculates and displays the `BasePlusCommissionEmployee`'s earnings. Because this property is accessed on a `BasePlusCommissionEmployee` object, the *subclass version* of the property executes. Next, line 42 modifies the `baseSalary` property. Lines 44–45 output the updated data using the `BasePlusCommissionEmployee`'s description and earnings properties. Again, because these properties are accessed on a `BasePlusCommissionEmployee` object, the *subclass versions* of these properties execute. Also, note the use of optional binding in line 34 to unwrap the `BasePlusCommissionEmployee?` returned by lines 27–31.

10.5 Access Modifiers in Inheritance Hierarchies

Recall from Section 3.5 that Swift's `public`, `internal` (the default) and `private` access modifiers restrict access to functions, types and type members based on their scope, which is determined by the *source-code file* or *module* in which those elements are defined:

- Any `private` element is accessible *only* in its defining *source-code file*.
- Any `internal` element is accessible throughout its defining *module* (e.g., an app or framework).
- Any `public` element is accessible in its defining module *and* in any module that imports the defining module.

The compiler generates error messages if you try to access any element that's not accessible in a given scope. These rules affect whether you can use a class as a superclass and, if you can, which superclass members are inherited:

- If a class is accessible in a given scope, then you can inherit from it. So, you can inherit from a `private` class defined in the *same source-code file*, from an `internal` class defined in the *same module*, or from a `public` class defined in the *same module* or an *imported module*.

- A subclass cannot be more accessible than its superclass, because the inherited superclass members might not be accessible in all scopes where the subclass is accessible.

- If a subclass and superclass are defined in the *same source-code file*, the subclass inherits all of the superclass's `private`, `internal` and `public` members.

- If a subclass and superclass are defined in the *same module*, the subclass inherits the superclass's `internal` and `public` members.

- If a subclass and superclass are defined in *separate modules* and the subclass's module *imports* the superclass's module, the subclass inherits *only* the superclass's `public` members.

A subclass can override any inherited superclass designated initializer, property, method or subscript as necessary.

Software Engineering Observation 10.2

In the Swift documentation, Apple says that access modifiers are primarily for developers creating reusable frameworks and that most app developers can use the default `internal` access throughout their app code. Nevertheless, if you want to encapsulate specific members of a `class`, `struct` or `enum`, you should define that type in its own file and define as `private` any members that should not be accessible outside that type's definition.

10.6 Introduction to Polymorphism: A Polymorphic Video Game Discussion

Suppose we design a video game that manipulates objects of many different types, including objects of classes `Martian`, `Venusian`, `Plutonian`, `SpaceShip` and `LaserBeam`. Imagine that each class inherits from the common superclass called `SpaceObject`, which contains method `draw`. Each subclass implements this method in a manner appropriate to that class. A screen-manager program maintains a collection (for example, a `SpaceObject Array`) of references to objects of the various classes. To refresh the screen, the screen manager periodically sends each object the same method call, `draw`. However, each object responds in a unique way. For example, a `Martian` object might *draw itself* in green with the appropriate number of antennae. A `SpaceShip` object might *draw itself* as a bright silver flying saucer. A `LaserBeam` object might *draw itself* as a bright red beam across the screen. Once again, the same method call (in this case, `draw`) sent to a variety of objects of classes in the same hierarchy has *many forms* of results, hence the term *polymorphism*.

A screen manager might use polymorphism to make the system extensible, facilitating adding new classes with minimal modifications to the system's code. Suppose that we want to add `Mercurian` objects to our video game. To do so, we must build a class `Mercurian` that inherits from `SpaceObject` and provides its own `draw` method implementation. When objects of class `Mercurian` appear in the `SpaceObject` collection, the screen-manager code invokes method `draw`, exactly as it does for the other objects in the collection, *regardless* of their types. So the new `Mercurian` class simply *plugs right in* without any modification of the screen-manager code by the programmer. Thus, without modifying the system (other than to build new classes and modify the code that creates new objects), programmers can use polymorphism to include types that were not envisioned when the system was created.

10.7 Case Study: Payroll System Class Hierarchy Using Polymorphism

Let's reexamine the `CommissionEmployee`–`BasePlusCommissionEmployee` hierarchy that we explored in Section 10.4. Now we use polymorphism to perform payroll calculations based on the type of employee. We create an enhanced employee hierarchy to solve the following problem:

> *A company pays its employees on a weekly basis. The employees are of three types: Salaried employees are paid a fixed weekly salary regardless of the number of hours worked, commission employees are paid a percentage of their sales, and base-plus-commission employees receive a base salary plus a percentage of their sales. The company wants to implement an app that performs its payroll calculations polymorphically.*

The UML class diagram in Fig. 10.7 shows our polymorphic employee inheritance hierarchy. We use the superclass `Employee` to define the common features of all employees in the class hierarchy. The classes that inherit from `Employee` are `SalariedEmployee` and `CommissionEmployee`. Class `BasePlusCommissionEmployee` inherits from `CommissionEmployee`. Unlike many other object-oriented programming languages, Swift does not have abstract classes (we'll say more about this shortly). As we'll discuss in Section 10.8, Swift has protocols, which give you many of the same benefits of abstract classes in other languages.

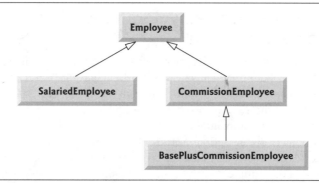

Fig. 10.7 | `Employee` hierarchy UML class diagram.

The following five sections implement the `Employee` class hierarchy. The first four show the superclass `Employee`, the *direct* subclasses `SalariedEmployee` and `CommissionEmployee`, and the *indirect* subclass `BasePlusCommissionEmployee`. The last section shows a test program that builds objects of these classes and processes them polymorphically.

Recall that we include with every project in this chapter the file `UtilityFunctions.swift` (Fig. 10.3) containing functions for currency and percentage formatting.

10.7.1 Base Class Employee

The base class `Employee` defines the set of capabilities that all employees must have. Each employee, regardless of the way his or her earnings are calculated, has a name. So the public property `name` will appear in class `Employee`. Class `Employee` also provides the computed properties `earnings` to return an `Employee`'s earnings and `description` to return an `Employee`'s `String` representation. The property `earnings` certainly applies to all Employees, but each *specific* calculation depends on the type of `Employee`. Each subclass will override `earnings` with an appropriate implementation.

In the test program, we'll maintain an `Array` of `Employee`s, each holding a reference to an object of an `Employee` subclass. Programs typically use base classes and superclasses in this manner to manipulate subclass objects polymorphically. The program we build in Fig. 10.13 iterates through an `Array` of `Employee`s and displays each `Employee`'s earnings *polymorphically*. Providing the `earnings` property in class `Employee` ensures that every subclass of `Employee` has an `earnings` property. Overriding the property in each subclass ensures that the `earnings` is calculated properly for each type of `Employee`. Similarly, each iteration of the loop displays each `Employee`'s `description`. Class `Employee`'s `description` property is defined to return a `String` containing the `Employee`'s name. Each subclass of `Employee` will override the `description` property to create a `String` representation that contains the employee's type (for example, `"Salaried Employee:"`) followed by the rest of the employee's information.

Figure 10.8 shows the hierarchy's four classes of Fig. 10.7 down the left side and the computed properties `earnings` and `description` across the top. For each class, the table shows the desired return value of each computed property. We do not list base class `Employee`'s name property because it's not overridden in any of the subclasses—name is inherited and used "as is" by each subclass.

	earnings computed property	description computed property
Employee	0.0	*name*
Salaried- Employee	weeklySalary	Salaried Employee: *name* Weekly Salary: *weeklySalary*
Commission- Employee	commissionRate * grossSales	Commission Employee: *name* Gross Sales: *grossSales* Commission Rate: *commissionRate*
BasePlus- Commission- Employee	(commissionRate * grossSales) + baseSalary	Base-Salaried Commission Employee: *name* Gross Sales: *grossSales* Commission Rate: *commissionRate* Base Salary: *baseSalary*

Fig. 10.8 | Return values of the computed properties in the `Employee` hierarchy classes.

Class `Employee` (Fig. 10.9) contains:

- a stored property `name` (line 6),

- a failable initializer (lines 9–15) to set the `name`,

- a computed property `earnings` (lines 18–20) that returns `0.0`, and

- a computed property `description` (lines 23–25) that returns an `Employee`'s name.

```
1   // Fig. 10.9: Employee.swift
2   // Employee base class
3   import Foundation
4
5   public class Employee {
6       public var name: String!
7
8       // failable initializer: if name is empty, return nil
9       public init?(name: String) {
10          if name.isEmpty {
11              return nil
12          }
13
14          self.name = name
15      }
16
17      // earnings computed property
18      public var earnings: NSDecimalNumber {
19          return NSDecimalNumber.zero()
20      }
21
22      // description computed property
23      public var description: String {
24          return name
25      }
26  }
```

Fig. 10.9 | `Employee` base class.

Swift Does Not Have Abstract Classes

Why did we define `earnings` to return `0.0`? It does not make sense to provide an implementation of this property in class `Employee`. We cannot calculate the earnings for a *general* `Employee`—we first must know the *specific* `Employee` type to determine how to calculate the earnings. In many object-oriented languages, we'd implement `Employee` as an *abstract class*—that is, one that cannot be instantiated. In addition, we'd define the property `earnings` as an *abstract property* (or *abstract method*, depending on the language)—that is, one that does *not* provide an implementation and *must* be overridden by each *concrete* (i.e., non-abstract) class that inherits from `Employee`. Abstract properties and methods act as placeholders that are "filled in" as appropriate by more specific subclasses. Swift does not have abstract classes, so a base class or superclass like `Employee` must provide *default implementations* for all its properties and methods. Protocols (Section 10.8) provide some of the key benefits of abstract classes.

Rather than returning a legitimate value, you can implement a property or method that should always be overridden. Currently the only way to accomplish this in Swift is to define the property or method such that it *terminates* the program if it's not overridden and is used anywhere in the program. To do so, you use Swift's global **fatalError** function. For example, you can replace line 19 of Fig. 10.9 with

```
fatalError("Must override the earnings property")
```

If the property is ever used—either for an Employee object or for an object of an Employee subclass that does not override the property—Swift will terminate the program and output a message similar to:

```
fatal error: Must override the earnings property: file path/
Employee.swift, line 19
```

where *path* is the location containing the Employee.swift file. As we'll see in Section 10.8, Swift protocols give you many of the same benefits of abstract classes in other languages.

10.7.2 Subclass SalariedEmployee

Class SalariedEmployee (Fig. 10.10) inherits from class Employee (line 5) and overrides the properties earnings (lines 23–25) and description (lines 28–32). The class includes:

- A weeklySalary property (line 6).

- A failable initializer (lines 9–20) that takes a name and a weekly salary as arguments, invokes base class Employee's initializer to initialize the inherited name property, validates the weekly salary (ensuring that it's not less than 0.0) and, if valid, sets the weeklySalary property.

- An overridden computed property earnings (lines 23–25) that returns a SalariedEmployee's earnings.

- An overridden computed property description (lines 28–32) that returns a String including the employee's type, namely, "Salaried Employee:", followed by employee-specific information produced by base class Employee's description property, and the value of SalariedEmployee's weeklySalary property.

If we did *not* override the earnings and description properties, SalariedEmployee would have inherited Employee's versions, which do not properly calculate a SalariedEmployee's earnings or produce a complete String representation of a SalariedEmployee.

```
1   // Fig. 10.10: SalariedEmployee.swift
2   // SalariedEmployee class derived from class Employee
3   import Foundation
4
5   public class SalariedEmployee : Employee {
6       public var weeklySalary: NSDecimalNumber!
7
8       // failable initializer
9       public init?(name: String, weeklySalary: NSDecimalNumber) {
10          super.init(name: name) // initialize inherited property
```

Fig. 10.10 | SalariedEmployee class derived from class Employee. (Part 1 of 2.)

```
11
12          // if any arguments are invalid, return nil
13          if weeklySalary.compare(NSDecimalNumber.zero()) ==
14              NSComparisonResult.OrderedAscending {
15
16              return nil // an initializer argument was invalid, so fail
17          }
18
19          self.weeklySalary = weeklySalary
20      }
21
22      // earnings computed property
23      public override var earnings: NSDecimalNumber {
24          return weeklySalary
25      }
26
27      // description computed property
28      public override var description: String {
29          return String(format: "%@: %@\n%@: %@",
30              "Salaried Employee", super.description,
31              "Weekly Salary", formatAsCurrency(weeklySalary))
32      }
33  }
```

Fig. 10.10 | SalariedEmployee class derived from class Employee. (Part 2 of 2.)

10.7.3 Subclass CommissionEmployee

Class CommissionEmployee (Fig. 10.11) inherits from class Employee (line 5); therefore, CommissionEmployee no longer defines the capabilities that are common to all Employees (such as the name property presented in Section 10.4.1). The class includes:

- Properties grossSales and commissionRate (lines 6–7).

- A failable initializer (lines 10–26) that takes a name, a gross sales amount and a commission rate, invokes base class Employee's initializer to initialize the inherited name property, validates the gross sales and commission rate (ensuring that neither is less than 0.0) and, if valid, sets the grossSales and commissionRate properties.

- An overridden earnings computed property (lines 29–31) that returns a CommissionEmployee's earnings.

- An overridden description computed property (lines 34–39) that returns a String including the employee's type, namely, "Commission Employee:", followed by employee-specific information produced by base class Employee's description property, and the value of CommissionEmployee's grossSales and commissionRate properties.

```
1   // Fig. 10.11: CommissionEmployee.swift
2   // CommissionEmployee class derived from Employee
3   import Foundation
```

Fig. 10.11 | CommissionEmployee class derived from Employee. (Part 1 of 2.)

```
4
5   public class CommissionEmployee : Employee {
6       public var grossSales: NSDecimalNumber!
7       public var commissionRate: NSDecimalNumber!
8
9       // failable initializer
10      public init?(name: String, grossSales: NSDecimalNumber,
11          commissionRate: NSDecimalNumber) {
12
13          super.init(name: name) // initialize inherited property
14
15          // if any arguments are invalid, return nil
16          if (grossSales.compare(NSDecimalNumber.zero()) ==
17                  NSComparisonResult.OrderedAscending) ||
18              (commissionRate.compare(NSDecimalNumber.zero()) ==
19                  NSComparisonResult.OrderedAscending) {
20
21              return nil // an initializer argument was invalid, so fail
22          }
23
24          self.grossSales = grossSales
25          self.commissionRate = commissionRate
26      }
27
28      // earnings computed property
29      public override var earnings: NSDecimalNumber {
30          return commissionRate.decimalNumberByMultiplyingBy(grossSales)
31      }
32
33      // description computed property
34      public override var description: String {
35          return String(format:"%@: %@\n%@: %@\n%@: %@",
36              "Commission Employee", super.description,
37              "Gross Sales", formatAsCurrency(grossSales),
38              "Commission Rate", formatAsPercent(commissionRate))
39      }
40  }
```

Fig. 10.11 | CommissionEmployee class derived from Employee. (Part 2 of 2.)

10.7.4 Indirect Subclass BasePlusCommissionEmployee

Class BasePlusCommissionEmployee (Fig. 10.12) is identical to the version presented in
Fig. 10.5. However, in this example, because BasePlusCommissionEmployee inherits from
CommissionEmployee (line 5), BasePlusCommissionEmployee is also an *indirect* subclass
of Employee. Class BasePlusCommissionEmployee contains:

- Property baseSalary (line 6).
- A failable initializer (lines 9–23) that takes a name, a gross sales amount, a commission rate and a base salary, invokes superclass CommissionEmployee's initializer with the name, grossSales and commissionRate properties, validates the base salary (ensuring that it's not less than 0.0) and, if valid, sets the baseSalary

property. Recall that CommissionEmployee's initializer calls Employee's initializer, so BasePlusCommissionEmployee's initializer begins a *chain of initializer calls* that spans all three levels of the Employee hierarchy.

- An overridden earnings computed property (lines 26–28) that obtains the portion of the employee's earnings based on *commission alone* (i.e., grossSales times commissionRate) by using the expression super.earnings to get superclass CommissionEmployee's earnings property, then adds that value to the baseSalary to calculate the BasePlusCommissionEmployee's total earnings.

- An overridden description computed property (lines 31–35) that returns a String that begins with "Base-Salaried", followed by superclass CommissionEmployee's description property and the value of BasePlusCommissionEmployee's baseSalary property. Recall that CommissionEmployee's description property uses Employee's description property, so accessing a BasePlusCommissionEmployee's description begins a chain that assembles the String representation from the description properties at all three levels of the Employee hierarchy.

```
1   // Fig. 10.12: BasePlusCommissionEmployee.swift
2   // BasePlusCommissionEmployee class derived from CommissionEmployee
3   import Foundation
4
5   public class BasePlusCommissionEmployee : CommissionEmployee {
6       public var baseSalary: NSDecimalNumber!
7
8       // failable initializer
9       public init?(name: String, grossSales: NSDecimalNumber,
10          commissionRate: NSDecimalNumber, baseSalary: NSDecimalNumber)
11      {
12          super.init(name: name, grossSales: grossSales,
13              commissionRate: commissionRate)
14
15          // validate baseSalary
16          if baseSalary.compare(NSDecimalNumber.zero()) ==
17              NSComparisonResult.OrderedAscending {
18
19              return nil // baseSalary was invalid, so fail
20          }
21
22          self.baseSalary = baseSalary
23      }
24
25      // earnings computed property
26      public override var earnings: NSDecimalNumber {
27          return baseSalary.decimalNumberByAdding(super.earnings)
28      }
29
```

Fig. 10.12 | BasePlusCommissionEmployee class derived from CommissionEmployee. (Part 1 of 2.)

```
30        // description computed property
31        public override var description: String {
32            return String(format: "%@ %@\n%@: %@",
33                "Base-Salaried", super.description, "Base Salary",
34                formatAsCurrency(baseSalary))
35        }
36    }
```

Fig. 10.12 | BasePlusCommissionEmployee class derived from CommissionEmployee. (Part 2 of 2.)

10.7.5 Polymorphic Processing

To test our Employee hierarchy, the program in Fig. 10.13 creates an object of each of the subclasses SalariedEmployee, CommissionEmployee and BasePlusCommissionEmployee (lines 6–20). The program manipulates these objects, first via variables of each object's own type, then polymorphically, using an Array of base class Employee references. Lines 23–28 display (*nonpolymorphically*) the String representation and earnings of each of these objects.

```
1   // Fig. 10.13: main.swift
2   // Polymorphic Employee hierarchy
3   import Foundation
4
5   // create a SalariedEmployee
6   let salariedEmployee = SalariedEmployee(name: "John Smith",
7       weeklySalary: NSDecimalNumber(string: "800.00"))!
8
9   // create a CommissionEmployee
10  let commissionEmployee =
11      CommissionEmployee(name: "Sue Jones",
12          grossSales:NSDecimalNumber(string: "10000.00"),
13          commissionRate: NSDecimalNumber(string: "0.06"))!
14
15  // create and test a BasePlusCommissionEmployee
16  let basePlusCommissionEmployee =
17      BasePlusCommissionEmployee(name: "Bob Lewis",
18          grossSales:NSDecimalNumber(string: "5000.00" ),
19          commissionRate: NSDecimalNumber(string: "0.04"),
20          baseSalary: NSDecimalNumber(string: "300.0"))!
21
22  println("EMPLOYEES PROCESSED INDIVIDUALLY\n")
23  print("\(salariedEmployee.description)\nEarned: ")
24  println(formatAsCurrency(salariedEmployee.earnings))
25  print("\n\(commissionEmployee.description)\nEarned: ")
26  println(formatAsCurrency(commissionEmployee.earnings))
27  print("\n\(basePlusCommissionEmployee.description)\nEarned: ")
28  println(formatAsCurrency(basePlusCommissionEmployee.earnings))
29  println()
```

Fig. 10.13 | Polymorphic Employee hierarchy. (Part 1 of 3.)

```
30
31   // create initially empty Array of Employees
32   var employees: [Employee] = []
33
34   // initialize array with Employees
35   employees.append(salariedEmployee)
36   employees.append(commissionEmployee)
37   employees.append(basePlusCommissionEmployee)
38
39   println("\nEMPLOYEES PROCESSED POLYMORPHICALLY\n")
40
41   // display each Employee's description and earnings properties
42   for currentEmployee in employees {
43       println(currentEmployee.description)
44
45       // if BasePlusCommissionEmployee, increase base salary
46       if let employee = currentEmployee as? BasePlusCommissionEmployee {
47           employee.baseSalary =
48               employee.baseSalary.decimalNumberByMultiplyingBy(
49                   NSDecimalNumber(string: "1.1"))
50           print("New base salary with 10% increase is: ")
51           println(formatAsCurrency(employee.baseSalary))
52       }
53
54       println("Earned: \(formatAsCurrency(currentEmployee.earnings))\n")
55   }
```

```
EMPLOYEES PROCESSED INDIVIDUALLY

Salaried Employee: John Smith
Weekly Salary: $800.00
Earned: $800.00

Commission Employee: Sue Jones
Gross Sales: $10,000.00
Commission Rate: 6.00%
Earned: $600.00

Base-Salaried Commission Employee: Bob Lewis
Gross Sales: $5,000.00
Commission Rate: 4.00%
Base Salary: $300.00
Earned: $500.00


EMPLOYEES PROCESSED POLYMORPHICALLY

Salaried Employee: John Smith
Weekly Salary: $800.00
Earned: $800.00
```

Fig. 10.13 | Polymorphic Employee hierarchy. (Part 2 of 3.)

```
Commission Employee: Sue Jones
Gross Sales: $10,000.00
Commission Rate: 6.00%
Earned: $600.00

Base-Salaried Commission Employee: Bob Lewis
Gross Sales: $5,000.00
Commission Rate: 4.00%
Base Salary: $300.00
New base salary with 10% increase is: $330.00
Earned: $530.00
```

Fig. 10.13 | Polymorphic Employee hierarchy. (Part 3 of 3.)

Creating an Array of Base Class Employee Variables

Line 32 creates an initially empty Array of Employees named employees, then lines 35–37 append to the Array the salariedEmployee, commissionEmployee and basePlusCommissionEmployee objects. Recall that Arrays are *type safe*, so only Employees can be placed in an Employee Array. Lines 35–37 are valid statements because, through inheritance, a SalariedEmployee *is an* Employee, a CommissionEmployee *is an* Employee and a BasePlusCommissionEmployee *is an* Employee.

Polymorphically Processing Employees

Lines 42–55 iterate through employees and get each Employee's description (line 43) and earnings (line 54) with Employee variable currentEmployee, which is assigned the reference to a different Employee in the Array during each iteration. The output illustrates that the loop uses the appropriate properties for each type of object—you can compare the results in the second half of the output with the non-polymorphic results in the first half to see that they're identical (except for the BasePlusCommissionEmployee, which we'll discuss momentarily). Each use of description and earnings in the loop is resolved *polymorphically* at execution time, based on the type of the object to which currentEmployee refers. This process is known as **dynamic binding**.

Performing Type-Specific Operations on BasePlusCommissionEmployees

The loop performs special processing on BasePlusCommissionEmployee objects—as we encounter these objects at execution time, we increase their base salary by 10%. When processing objects *polymorphically*, we typically do not need to worry about the *specifics*, but to adjust the base salary, we *do* have to determine the *specific* type of Employee object at *execution time*. Line 46 uses the **as? downcast operator** to determine whether a particular Employee object *is a* BasePlusCommissionEmployee. The as? operator returns an optional of its right operand's type (BasePlusCommissionEmployee?). The optional is non-nil only if the object in the left operand (currentEmployee) has the *is-a* relationship with the type in the right operand (BasePlusCommissionEmployee). This would also be *true* for any object of a BasePlusCommissionEmployee subclass because of the *is-a* relationship a subclass has with its superclass. This downcast is required if we're to invoke subclass BasePlusCommissionEmployee property baseSalary on the current Employee object—*attempting to invoke subclass-only properties or subclass-only methods directly on a superclass* *variable is a compilation error.* Swift also has the **as downcast operator**, which assumes that the left operand has an *is-a* relationship with the type in the right operand.

> **Common Programming Error 10.1**
>
> *Downcasting with the as operator causes a runtime error if the object in the left operand does not have an* is a *relationship with the type specified in the cast operator.*

The *optional-binding* expression in line 46 unwraps the as? operator's optional result if it's non-nil, in which case lines 47–51 perform the special processing required for a BasePlusCommissionEmployee. Lines 47–49 invoke subclass-only property baseSalary to retrieve and update the employee's base salary with the 10% raise.

10.8 Case Study: Creating and Using Custom Protocols

A **protocol** describes a set of capabilities that can be called on an object, but does *not* provide implementations of those capabilities. A protocol may describe properties, methods, initializers, subscripts (Chapter 12) and operators (Chapter 12) for which other types must provide implementations. The capabilities described by a protocol are known as its requirements. Protocols are similar to interfaces in various other object-oriented programming languages. Each class, struct and enum you define can **adopt** any number of protocols, then implement their capabilities—a process known as **conforming** to the protocols. As you'll see in Section 10.8.8, you can also add protocol conformance to existing types via extensions.

10.8.1 Protocol Capabilities Must Be Defined in Each Conforming Type

In Objective-C, it's common to adopt a protocol and implement only a subset of its methods. By default, every capability defined in a Swift protocol *must* be implemened in each type that adopts the protocol; otherwise, a compilation error occurs. Section 10.9.3 discusses the keywords @objc and optional, which can be used to create protocols with members that are not required to be implemented. The @objc keyword is used primarily to mark Swift code that can be used from Objective-C. We discuss this keyword in more detail in the online Other Topics chapter. The optional keyword designates which protocol members are not required in a conforming type.

10.8.2 Protocols and *Is-a* Relationships

Once a type conforms to a protocol, all objects of that type have an *is-a* relationship with the protocol type and are guaranteed to provide the capabilities described by the protocol. Thus, all types that conform to a given protocol can be processed polymorphically (as you'll see in Section 10.8.9). In inheritance hierarchies, if a superclass conforms to a protocol, so do all of its subclasses.

10.8.3 Relating Disparate Types Via Protocols

Protocols are particularly useful for assigning *common functionality to disparate types*. This allows objects of class, struct and enum types that conform to a protocol to be processed polymorphically. For example, an object of any type that conforms to the Printable protocol can be converted to a String with String interpolation or displayed as a String by the print or println functions (as we'll do in the next example).

10.8.4 Accounts-Payable Application

To demonstrate creating and using protocols, we'll modify the payroll app from Section 10.7. Suppose that the company involved wishes to perform several accounting operations in an accounts payable application. In addition to calculating the earnings that must be paid to each employee, the company also wants to calculate the payment due on each of several invoices (that is, bills for goods and services purchased by the company). Though applied to *disparate* things (employees and invoices), both operations have to do with determining some kind of *payment amount*. For an employee, the payment refers to the employee's *earnings*. For an invoice, the payment refers to the *total cost of the goods and services* listed on the invoice. Can we perform such *disparate* calculations in a single application polymorphically? Protocols offer exactly this capability. The next example introduces a `Payable` protocol to describe the functionality of any object that must be capable of being paid and thus must offer a method to determine the proper payment amount due.

10.8.5 Developing a Payable Hierarchy

To build an application that can determine payments for employees and invoices alike, we'll first create protocol `Payable`, containing a single `paymentAmount` property, which returns an amount (as an `NSDecimalNumber`) that must be paid for a `Payable` object. After defining the `Payable` protocol, we'll introduce class `Invoice`, which adopts the protocol and implements its `paymentAmount` property to conform to the protocol. We'll then add `Payable` conformance to the `Employee` hierarchy by using an `extension` (Section 10.8.8). This will make all `Employee` subclasses `Payable` as well. We'll also have `Invoices` and `Employees` conform to the `Printable` protocol—which defines a `description` property that returns a `String`. As you'll see, the `print` and `println` functions can implicitly access a `Printable` object's `description` to display a `String` representation of an object.

Classes `Invoice` and `Employee` both represent things for which the company must be able to calculate a payment amount. Both classes conform to `Payable`, so a program can access the `paymentAmount` property on `Invoice` objects and `Employee` objects alike. This enables the polymorphic processing of `Invoices` and `Employees` required for our accounts payable application.

The class diagram in Fig. 10.14 shows the `Payable` protocol hierarchy used in our accounts payable application. A class diagram models protocol conformance as a dashed arrow with a hollow arrowhead pointing from each conforming class to the protocol. The diagram in Fig. 10.14 indicates that classes `Invoice` and `Employee` conform to the `Payable` protocol.

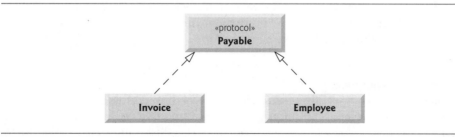

Fig. 10.14 | `Payable` protocol hierarchy class diagram.

10.8.6 Declaring Protocol Payable

Figure 10.15 shows the definition of the Payable protocol (lines 5–7), which contains the instance property paymentAmount (line 6)—i.e., a property that must be accessed through an object of a conforming type. A protocol definition begins with the keyword **protocol** (line 5) and may contain:

- *Instance properties* and *instance methods* that are accessed via an object of a conforming type.

- *Type properties* and *type methods* that are accessed through a type name.

- Initializers.

- Subscripts (Chapter 12).

```
1   // Fig. 10.15: Payable.swift
2   // Payable protocol definition
3   import Foundation
4
5   protocol Payable {
6       var paymentAmount: NSDecimalNumber {get}
7   }
```

Fig. 10.15 | Payable protocol definition.

Properties in a Protocol
Properties are always prefixed with the var keyword. Type properties are always prefixed with class var—even though the keyword static is used to define type properties in struct and enum types. The instance property in line 6 is a *read-only property* as specified by {get}, which indicates that the property must provide a get accessor. You can also require *read-write properties* by following the property name with {get set}. The protocol specifies the property's type, but *not* how to implement it. Conforming types can define *read-only properties* as constants with let or a variables with var, but *read-write properties* must be defined with var. Also, when you define a type that conforms to a protocol, you choose whether to implement a property as a stored property or as a computed property.

Methods in a Protocol
For a method, you specify the method's name, parameter and return type, but no implementation details (i.e., no method body). Like type properties, type methods are always prefixed with the class keyword. For a method that will modify the objects on which it's called, you must precede the method declaration with the mutating keyword. You must also use this keyword when defining the method in a conforming struct or enum type, but not in a conforming class type.

Initializers in a Protocol
Like methods, you can specify initializers in a protocol. If you define a class that conforms to the protocol, you must implement each initializer as a required initializer, unless the class is declared final. This forces subclasses either to inherit the initializers (Section 10.11) or provide appropriate initializer implementations to ensure that the subclasses properly

conform to the protocol. A conforming class can implement a protocol's initializers as either designated or convenience initializers. If a protocol defines *failable initializers*, a conforming type can implement the initializers as failable or nonfailable. *Nonfailable initializers* in a protocol *must* be implemented in a conforming type as nonfailable initializers or implicitly unwrapped failable initializers (i.e., init!).

10.8.7 Creating Class Invoice

We now create class Invoice (Fig. 10.16) to represent an invoice that contains billing information for only one kind of part. The class defines the properties partNumber, partDescription, quantity and price (in lines 6–9). Class Invoice also contains a failable initializer (lines 12–25). Line 5 indicates that class Invoice adopts the protocols Payable and Printable. A type can adopt zero or more protocols. To adopt more than one protocol, you specify the type's name followed by a colon (:) and a comma-separated list of protocol names. In a subclass, the superclass's name must be listed *before* any protocol names. Objects of a type that adopts multiple protocols have the *is-a* relationship with each of the protocol types.

```
1   // Fig. 10.16: Invoice.java
2   // Invoice class that adopts the Payable protocol
3   import Foundation
4
5   public class Invoice : Payable, Printable {
6       let partNumber: String!
7       let partDescription: String!
8       var quantity: Int!
9       var price: NSDecimalNumber!
10
11      // initializer
12      public init?(partNumber: String, partDescription: String,
13          quantity: Int, price: NSDecimalNumber) {
14
15          if partNumber.isEmpty || partDescription.isEmpty ||
16              quantity < 0 || (price.compare(NSDecimalNumber.zero()) ==
17              NSComparisonResult.OrderedAscending) {
18              return nil
19          }
20
21          self.partNumber = partNumber
22          self.partDescription = partDescription
23          self.quantity = quantity
24          self.price = price
25      }
26
27      // conform to the Payable protocol
28      public var paymentAmount: NSDecimalNumber {
29          let quantity = NSDecimalNumber(string: self.quantity.description)
30          return quantity.decimalNumberByMultiplyingBy(price)
31      }
```

Fig. 10.16 | Invoice class that adopts the Payable protocol. (Part 1 of 2.)

```
32
33      // return String representation of Invoice object
34      public var description: String {
35          let pricePerItem = NSNumberFormatter.localizedStringFromNumber(
36              price, numberStyle: .CurrencyStyle)
37          return String(format: "%@:\n%@: %@ (%@) \n%@: %d\n%@: %@",
38              "Invoice", "Part number", partNumber, partDescription,
39              "Quantity", quantity, "Price per item",
40              formatAsCurrency(pricePerItem))
41      }
42  } // end class Invoice
```

Fig. 10.16 | Invoice class that adopts the Payable protocol. (Part 2 of 2.)

*Conforming to the **Payable** Protocol*
To conform to the Payable protocol, class Invoice defines the protocol's paymentAmount property (lines 28–31). The property calculates the total payment required to pay the invoice by multiplying the values of quantity and pricePerItem and returning the result. Implementing paymentAmount in class Invoice satisfies the requirements of the protocol Payable.

*Conforming to the **Printable** Protocol*
To conform to the Printable protocol, class Invoice defines the protocol's description property (lines 34–41). In this case, the property returns a formatted String representation of an Invoice object's data. Implementing description in class Invoice satisfies the requirements of the Printable protocol.

10.8.8 Using extensions to Add Printable and Payable Protocol Conformance to Class Employee

In class Invoice, we specified protocol conformance by adopting protocols, then implementing their requirements directly in the type definition. We now demonstrate how to add protocol conformance to an existing class via extensions. Figure 10.17 shows an updated Employee.swift file that contains the same Employee class from Section 10.7.1 followed by two extensions—one that enables Employees to conform to the Payable protocol and one that enables Employees to conform to the Printable protocol.

```
1   // Fig. 10.17: Employee.swift
2   // Employee class that conforms to the Payable protocol via extensions
3   import Foundation
4
5   public class Employee {
6       public var name: String!
7
8       // failable initializer: if name is empty, return nil
9       public init?(name: String) {
10          if name.isEmpty {
11              return nil
12          }
```

Fig. 10.17 | Employee class that conforms to the Payable protocol via extensions. (Part 1 of 2.)

```
13
14              self.name = name
15         }
16
17         // earnings computed property
18         public var earnings: NSDecimalNumber {
19              return NSDecimalNumber.zero()
20         }
21
22         // description computed property
23         public var description: String {
24              return name
25         }
26  }
27
28  // add Payable conformance to entire Employee hierarchy
29  extension Employee : Payable {
30       var paymentAmount: NSDecimalNumber {
31            return earnings
32       }
33  }
34
35  // add Printable conformance to entire Employee hierarchy; empty
36  // extension because all Employee's already have a description property
37  extension Employee : Printable {}
```

Fig. 10.17 | Employee class that conforms to the Payable protocol via extensions. (Part 2 of 2.)

Conforming to the *Payable* Protocol

To add Payable conformance to class Employee, we define an extension that adopts the protocol (line 29) and implements the paymentAmount property (lines 30–32). The property simply returns an Employee's earnings. As we showed in Section 10.7, Employee is the base class in a hierarchy of several employee types, and each type in the hierarchy overrides earnings to calculate the earnings appropriately. As you'll see in Section 10.8.9, when the paymentAmount property is accessed on an object that *is an* Employee, the appropriate subclass's earnings property will be used to determine the paymentAmount.

Software Engineering Observation 10.3

You can add protocol conformance to any existing type via an extension.

Software Engineering Observation 10.4

When defining a new type, you can choose to build protocol conformance directly into the type or to add protocol conformance via extensions. Some programmers prefer to use extensions, because they separate the protocol conformance code from the rest of the type's code, which can make the code easier to maintain. Apple does not yet have a style guide for Swift programmers and uses both techniques in its own code.

Conforming to the *Printable* Protocol

To conform to the Printable protocol, we must define the protocol's description property, which returns a String. Class Employee already defines a description property that meets this requirement (Fig. 10.17, lines 23–25). In this case, we can add `Printable` conformance to the class by defining an empty protocol as shown in line 37. (The same technique could be used to add `Printable` conformance to our `Card` class in Fig. 6.9.)

Protocol Conformance in Inheritance Hierarchies

When a type conforms to a protocol, the same *is-a* relationship as inheritance applies. When a *superclass* conforms to a protocol, all of its subclasses also conform to that protocol and have the *is-a* relationship with that protocol type. Because we added `Payable` conformance to class `Employee`, we can say that an `Employee` *is a* `Payable` and that objects of any classes that inherit from `Employee`—`SalariedEmployee`, `CommissionEmployee` and `BasePlusCommissionEmployee`—are also `Payable`s. Thus, just as we can assign a `SalariedEmployee`, `CommissionEmployee` or `BasePlusCommissionEmployee` object to a base class `Employee` variable (as we did with an `Employee` Array in Section 10.7.5), we can assign objects of these types to a protocol `Payable` variable. Similarly, class `Invoice` implements `Payable`, so an `Invoice` object also *is a* `Payable`, and we can assign the reference of an `Invoice` object to a `Payable` variable.

Software Engineering Observation 10.5

The is-a *relationship that exists between subclasses and superclasses, and between types that implement protocols and the protocols themselves, holds when passing an object to a method. If a parameter has a superclass type, you also can pass as an argument any object that has the* is-a *relationship with that superclass. Similarly, if a parameter has a protocol type, it can receive an object of any type that implements the protocol.*

10.8.9 Using Protocol `Payable` to Process `Invoices` and `Employees` Polymorphically

Figure 10.18 illustrates that protocol `Payable` can be used to process a set of `Invoices` and `Employees` polymorphically in a single application, even though `Invoices` and `Employees` are otherwise unrelated.

```
1   // Fig. 10.18: main.swift
2   // Processing Payables (Invoices and Employees) polymorphically
3   import Foundation
4
5   // create Array of Payables
6   var payableObjects: [Payable] = [
7       SalariedEmployee(name: "John Smith",
8           weeklySalary: NSDecimalNumber(string: "800.00"))!,
9       Invoice(partNumber: "01234", partDescription: "seat",
10          quantity: 2, price: NSDecimalNumber(string: "375.00"))!,
11      CommissionEmployee(name: "Sue Jones",
12          grossSales: NSDecimalNumber(string: "10000.00"),
13          commissionRate: NSDecimalNumber(string: "0.06"))!,
14      Invoice(partNumber: "56789", partDescription: "tire",
15          quantity: 4, price: NSDecimalNumber(string: "79.95"))!,
```

Fig. 10.18 | Processing `Payables` (`Invoices` and `Employees`) polymorphically. (Part 1 of 2.)

```
16          BasePlusCommissionEmployee(name: "Bob Lewis",
17              grossSales:NSDecimalNumber(string: "5000.00"),
18              commissionRate: NSDecimalNumber(string: "0.04"),
19              baseSalary: NSDecimalNumber(string: "300.0"))!
20      ]
21
22  println("INVOICES AND EMPLOYEES PROCESSED POLYMORPHICALLY\n")
23
24  // display each Payable's description and paymentAmount properties
25  for currentPayable in payableObjects {
26      println(currentPayable) // implicitly uses description property
27      let paymentAmount = formatAsCurrency(currentPayable.paymentAmount)
28      println("Payment Due: \(paymentAmount)\n")
29  }
```

```
INVOICES AND EMPLOYEES PROCESSED POLYMORPHICALLY

Salaried Employee: John Smith
Weekly Salary: $800.00
Payment Due: $800.00

Invoice:
Part number: 01234 (seat)
Quantity: 2
Price per item: $375.00
Payment Due: $750.00

Commission Employee: Sue Jones
Gross Sales: $10,000.00
Commission Rate: 6.00%
Payment Due: $600.00

Invoice:
Part number: 56789 (tire)
Quantity: 4
Price per item: $79.95
Payment Due: $319.80

Base-Salaried Commission Employee: Bob Lewis
Gross Sales: $5,000.00
Commission Rate: 4.00%
Base Salary: $300.00
Payment Due: $500.00
```

Fig. 10.18 | Processing Payables (Invoices and Employees) polymorphically. (Part 2 of 2.)

Lines 6–20 define the Payable Array named payableObjects and initialize it with five Payable objects—a SalariedEmployee, an Invoice, a CommissionEmployee, another Invoice and a BasePlusCommissionEmployee. Objects of all these types are allowed to be assigned to a Payable Array's elements, because they are all Payable:

- Each Invoice *is a* Payable, because class Invoice's definition adopts the protocol.

- A SalariedEmployee *is a* Payable, because a SalariedEmployee *is an* Employee and class Employee conforms to the Payable protocol (via an extension); thus, anything that *is an* Employee also *is a* Payable. This, of course, applies to CommissionEmployee and a BasePlusCommissionEmployee as well.

The type annotation in line 6 is required, because the objects in the Array literal have disparate types.

Lines 25–29 polymorphically process each Payable object in payableObjects. Notice that unlike line 43 in Fig. 10.13, line 26 in Fig. 10.18 does not explicitly pass to println the description of the current object. When a Printable object is passed to function println or print, the function automatically uses its description property's value as the object's String representation; otherwise, a String representation of the object's type is used. Line 27 uses the Payable property paymentAmount to obtain the payment amount for the current object, regardless of the object's actual type. The output reveals that the appropriate type's implementation of properties description and paymentAmount are used for every object in payableObjects.

10.9 Additional Protocol Features

In this section, we summarize additional protocol features, including protocol inheritance, class-only protocols, defining protocols with optional capabilities and protocol composition.

10.9.1 Protocol Inheritance

A protocol can inherit from one or more other protocols. The result is typically a protocol that describes more capabilities that a conforming type must implement. Protocol inheritance can be used to combine the capabilities described by several protocols into a single protocol or to create a new protocol that adds more capabilities. The syntax for protocol inheritance is

```
protocol ProtocolName : InheritedProtocol1, InheritedProtocol2, ... {
    // additional protocol member descriptions
}
```

10.9.2 Class-Only Protocols

If a protocol is meant for use only with reference types (i.e., classes), you can designate it as a **class-only protocol** with the class keyword as follows:

```
protocol ProtocolName : class {
    // protocol member descriptions
}
```

If a class-only protocol also inherits from other protocols, they're placed in a comma-separated list following the class keyword, as in:

```
protocol ProtocolName : class, InheritedProtocol1, InheritedProtocol2, ... {
    // additional protocol member descriptions
}
```

10.9.3 Optional Capabilities in Protocols

By default, a type must define all the members of each Swift protocol the class adopts. As we mentioned earlier, *Objective-C protocols* may contain optional methods that are not required to be implemented. This is commonly the case with the delegate protocols that are used frequently in iOS and OS X user-interface programming. In Swift, class-only protocols may contain optional members. To include optional members, a protocol must be preceded by the @objc keyword, and each optional capability described by the protocol must be preceded by the **optional** keyword.

Because optional capabilities might not be implemented by a conforming class, when you attempt to access optional capabilities on an object of the class, you must use *optional chaining* (following the name of the property or method with ?) to ensure that no runtime errors occur. Also, an optional property returns an optional value of the property's type and an optional method returns an optional of its return type (if any).

10.9.4 Protocol Composition

You can use a **protocol composition** to specify that an object used in a given context—such as an object passed as an argument to a function or method—must conform to multiple protocols. For example, if a function argument should conform to both the Payable and Printable protocols, you can specify the corresponding parameter's type with the keyword protocol and angle brackets (< and >) as follows:

parameterName : **protocol**<Payable, Printable>

In this case, *parameterName* has a temporary protocol type with the combined capabilities of the Payable and Printable protocols.

10.9.5 Common Protocols in Swift

There are dozens of Swift Standard Library protocols. Figure 10.19 overviews a few that we use in this book.

Protocol	Description
Comparable	Swift's comparative operators (<, <=, >, >=, == and !=) introduced in Section 2.7) enable you to compare values of the Swift Standard Library's numeric types and type String. Objects of a type that adopts this protocol also can be compared to one another. For a type that conforms to Comparable, you define overloaded < and == operator functions (Chapter 12) that specify how to compare two objects of that type. The Swift Standard Library uses generic functions (Chapter 11) and your < and == operators to provide implementations of the other comparative operators—for example, the <= operator for your type returns true if both your < and your == operators return true.
Equatable	Objects of a type that adopts the Equatable protocol can be compared to one another to determine if they contain the same values. For a type that conforms to Equatable, you define an overloaded == operator function. The Swift Standard Library uses a generic function and your == operator to provide the != operator's implementation for your type—if your == returns true, the != implementation returns false, and vice versa. The Comparable protocol inherits from Equatable.

Fig. 10.19 | Common protocols from the Swift Standard Library. (Part 1 of 2.)

Protocol	Description
Printable	The Printable protocol (discussed in Section 10.8) defines a description property that returns a String representation of an object. Swift Standard Library's types, including the numeric types and the Bool, String, Array and Dictionary types, conform to this protocol. As we discussed in Section 10.8.9, Swift Standard Library functions print and println each implicitly use a Printable object's description property to display the object's String representation.
Hashable	As you learned in Chapter 7, a Dictionary's keys must conform to the Hashable protocol, which defines an Int property named hashValue. The Hashable protocol inherits from the Equatable protocol, so hash values can be compared to determine whether a key is in the Dictionary. Swift's numeric, Bool and String types are all Hashable.

Fig. 10.19 | Common protocols from the Swift Standard Library. (Part 2 of 2.)

10.10 Using `final` to Prevent Method Overriding and Inheritance

`final` Properties, Methods and Subscripts Cannot Be Overridden
A **final** property, method or subscript in a superclass *cannot* be overridden by a subclass. Because a final implementation can never change, all subclasses are guaranteed to use the superclass's implementation of the property, method or subscript.

`final` Classes Cannot Be Superclasses
A **final** class cannot be used as a superclass. All members of a final class are *implicitly* final. Since a final class cannot be extended, programs that use a final class can rely on the functionality that it provides—for example, making a class final prevents programmers from creating subclasses that might bypass security restrictions.

10.11 Initialization and Deinitialization in Class Hierarchies

Creating a subclass object begins a *chain of initializer calls* through all of that subclass's direct and indirect superclasses to ensure that every stored property in the subclass object is initialized. The last initializer called in the chain is *always* a designated initializer in the base class—the hierarchy's topmost superclass.

10.11.1 Basic Class-Instance Initialization

Swift's rules for initializers in inheritance hierarchies differ from those for constructors in various other object-oriented languages. Before we discuss Swift's rules, recall the following from Chapter 8:

- All of a class's stored properties *must* be initialized—either with values provided by initializers or with default values specified in the properties' definitions.

- Every class *must* have at least one *designated initializer* and can have any number of `convenience` *initializers*.

- If *all* of a class's stored properties specify default values in their definitions *and* you do not define *any* initializers, then the compiler provides a *default initializer.* This no-parameter designated initializer sets the stored properties to their specified default values.

- Every `convenience` initializer must eventually call one of its *own* class's designated initializers—either directly or via another `convenience` initializer.

10.11.2 Initialization in Class Hierarchies

Swift uses a **two-phase initialization process** to ensure that all of a subclass object's stored properties are initialized before the object is used:

- *Phase 1:* When a subclass object is created, a chain of designated-initializer calls ensures that every stored property is given an initial value by a designated initializer from the class in which that stored property was *originally* defined.

Error-Prevention Tip 10.2

Phase 1 *ensures that every stored property has a value before it's used and that a value set by a subclass initializer is not subsequently overwritten by a superclass initializer.*

- *Phase 2:* When the chain of initializer calls returns to the subclass initializer, all the stored properties have initial values. At this point, the subclass initializer can change the initial values of the subclass's inherited stored properties.

Error-Prevention Tip 10.3

Phase 2 *ensures that each subclass can customize the initialization of its inherited stored properties as appropriate.*

Additional Rules for Initializers in Class Hierarchies
With this two-phase initialization process in mind, Swift has additional rules for initializers in class hierarchies:

- A subclass inherits its superclass's initializers if all of the subclass's stored properties specify default values in their definitions *and* you do not define any initializers in the subclass. (Most other object-oriented programming languages do not support constructor inheritance—though C++ added this feature as of C++11.)

- Each subclass designated initializer *must* initialize the subclass's stored properties *first, then* call a superclass *designated initializer* to give values to the inherited stored properties. The superclass designated-initializer call can be an *implicit* call to the default initializer (if any) or an *explicit* call to a designated initializer.

- Only after the inherited stored properties are initialized by a superclass designated initializer can a subclass initializer modify their values.

Given the rules above and in Section 10.11.1, a subclass designated initializer should perform its tasks in the following order:

1. Initialize the subclass's stored properties—either with explicit statements or to the default values specified in the stored properties' definitions. (Remember that optionals are initialized to `nil`, by default.)

2. Call a superclass designated initializer—either implicitly or explicitly.

3. Perform subclass-specific customization of inherited superclass stored properties.

Error-Prevention Tip 10.4

The Swift compiler enforces the initialization rules by generating errors if: 1. A subclass designated initializer does not initialize all of the subclass's stored properties before calling a superclass designated initializer. 2. A subclass initializer attempts to assign a value to an inherited stored property before calling a superclass designated initializer. 3. A subclass `convenience` *initializer attempts to assign a value to a subclass stored property before calling a subclass designated initializer or delegating to another* `convenience` *initializer. 4. An initializer attempts to use the object (`self`) or any of its properties (directly or by calling the class's methods) before Phase 1 of the two-phase initialization process completes.*

10.11.3 Initialization of a BasePlusCommissionEmployee Object

Now that we've presented the rules for initialization in class hierarchies, let's reconsider the initialization of the `BasePlusCommissionEmployee` object created in Fig. 10.6.

Phase 1 of the Two-Phase Initialization Process
When we create a `BasePlusCommissionEmployee` object (Fig. 10.6, lines 27–31), the `BasePlusCommissionEmployee` initializer (Fig. 10.5, lines 9–23) is called. That initializer, before executing its full body code, initializes the `baseSalary` property to its default value (`nil`) then explicitly calls `CommissionEmployee`'s initializer (Fig. 10.5, lines 12–13). Class `CommissionEmployee`'s initializer (Fig. 10.4, lines 11–27) validates and initializes the properties *defined* in class `CommissionEmployee` (Fig. 10.4, lines 6–8) that are *inherited* into the `BasePlusCommissionEmployee`. This completes *Phase 1* of the two-phase initialization process.

Phase 2 of the Two-Phase Initialization Process
When `CommissionEmployee`'s initializer returns control to `BasePlusCommissionEmployee`'s initializer, lines 16–22 of Fig. 10.5 then validate and initialize the subclass stored property `baseSalary`. Though we do not do so here, at this point we could also customize the values of the inherited superclass stored properties.

Software Engineering Observation 10.6

In the `CommissionEmployee`-`BasePlusCommissionEmployee` *example, we chose to set the* `BasePlusCommissionEmployee`'s `baseSalary` *value* after *calling superclass* `CommissionEmployee`'s *failable initializer. When a superclass's failable initializer returns* `nil`, *the subclass failable initializer immediately fails and returns* `nil`. *In this case, there's no need to set* `baseSalary`.

10.11.4 Overriding Initializers and Required Initializers

As with a subclass's overridden properties or methods, you must use the `override` keyword to define a subclass initializer that has the same signature as a superclass designated initializer. The `override` keyword is not required for a subclass initializer that has the same signature as a superclass `convenience` initializer. Superclass `convenience` initializers are accessible to a subclass only if the subclass inherits its superclass's initializers (as discussed in Section 10.11.2).

required Initializers

You can designate that an initializer with a specified signature is required in all subclasses by preceding the superclass initializer's definition with the **required** keyword. Each subclass must provide a definition of a `required` initializer either by explicitly defining it or by inheriting the superclass's initializers (as discussed in Section 10.11.2). If you define any initializers in the subclass, none of the super class initializers are inherited—in this case, you must provide a definition for each `required` superclass initializer. When defining a `required` initializer explicitly in a given subclass, you precede the initializer with `required` rather than `override`.

10.11.5 Deinitialization in Class Hierarchies

Recall from Chapter 8 that each class can define at most one deinitializer (`deinit`) that performs custom cleanup tasks for instances of that class before they're deallocated. When a subclass object is about to be deallocated, first the subclass's deinitializer executes, then it automatically invokes its superclass's deinitializer. This process continues up the class hierarchy until the base class's deinitializer executes. A superclass's deinitializer executes regardless of whether its subclass provides a custom one. Also, because the deinitializer is called before the object is deallocated, all of the object's data is still available for use in the deinitializer. If a class does not provide a deinitializer, the compiler provides one that simply calls the superclass's initializer.

10.12 Wrap-Up

This chapter introduced software reuse via inheritance, which enables a new subclass to absorb an existing superclass's capabilities and customize them with new or modified capabilities. You learned that—unlike object-oriented programming languages such as Java, C# and Visual Basic—Swift does not have a common superclass from which all classes inherit. You also learned that value types (i.e., `struct`s and `enum`s) do not support inheritance.

We used a `CommissionEmployee-BasePlusCommissionEmployee` hierarchy to show that a subclass can add its own properties, initializers and methods, and it can customize the ones it inherits. You learned that each superclass can have many subclasses, but each subclass must have exactly one superclass. We discussed how access modifiers and the `final` keyword affect what a subclass can inherit from a superclass.

We demonstrated polymorphism, which enables you to process objects that share the same superclass, either directly or indirectly, as if they were all objects of the superclass. We discussed that with inheritance and polymorphism, we can design and implement systems that are easily extensible—new classes can be added with little or no modification to the general portions of the program, as long as the new classes are part of the inheritance hierarchy that the program processes generally. The new classes simply "plug right in." The only parts of a program that must be altered are those that require direct knowledge of the new classes. We used an `Employee` hierarchy to create a polymorphic payroll application. In that example, you also saw that you can determine an object's type at execution time and act on that object accordingly.

We introduced protocols and mentioned that they're particularly useful for assigning common capabilities to disparate `class`, `struct` and `enum` types, allowing objects of such types to be processed polymorphically. We then created a custom protocol and modified the employee-payroll application to create a generalized accounts-payable application that calculated payments due for company employees *and* invoice amounts for purchased goods and services.

You learned that you can use `final` to prevent a superclass member from being overridden in a subclass and to prevent a class from being a superclass. Finally, we discussed how initializers and deinitializers work in inheritance hierarchies. In the next chapter, we discuss how to define generic functions and types.

Generics

Objectives

In this chapter you'll:

- Create generic functions and methods that perform identical tasks on arguments of different types.

- Use generic parameter clauses to define type parameters for generic functions and generic types.

- Use inferred type arguments to specialize generic functions.

- Use type constraints to restrict the type arguments that can be used for a given type parameter.

- Understand how to overload generic functions with generic and nongeneric functions.

- Create a generic data structure type that can be used to manipulate objects of any type.

- Use explicit type arguments to specialize a generic type.

11.1 Introduction

Rather than writing separate code to perform identical tasks on different types (e.g., summing an Array of integers vs. summing an Array of floating-point values), generics enable you to write the code once and use *placeholders* to represent the type(s) of data to manipulate. The compiler replaces placeholders with *actual* types when you call a generic function or create an object of a generic type—this is transparent to the programmer. Array (Chapter 6) and Dictionary (Chapter 7) are generic types, and many Swift Standard Library functions, such as print and println, are generic functions. When you use generic functions and types, the compiler performs *type checking* to ensure that you use the functions and types correctly—this is known as compile-time *type safety*. For example, if you create an Array of Ints, then attempt to place a String into that Array, you'll receive a compilation error. In this chapter, we provide motivation for generics and demonstrate how to create your own generic functions, methods and types (classes, structs and enums).

11.2 Motivation for Generic Functions

Overloaded functions are often used to perform *similar* operations on *different* types of data. To help motivate why generics are useful, let's begin with an example (Fig. 11.1) containing overloaded printArray functions (lines 5–11 and 14–20) that print the contents of an Int Array ([Int]) and a Double Array ([Double]), respectively. Both functions mimic the Array output format used by the print function.

The program defines three Arrays (lines 23–25)—the no-element Int Array emptyIntegers, seven-element Int Array integers and four-element Double Array doubles. Then lines 27–33 display the Arrays' contents.

```
1   // Fig. 11.1: OverloadedFunctions.playground
2   // Printing Array elements using overloaded functions.
3
4   // print an Int Array
5   func printArray(values: [Int]) {
6       print("[")
7       for i in 0..<values.count {
8           i < values.count - 1 ? print("\(values[i]), ") : print(values[i])
9       }
10      print("]")
11  }
12
```

Fig. 11.1 | Printing Array elements using overloaded functions. (Part 1 of 2.)

```
13   // print a Double Array
14   func printArray(values: [Double]) {
15       print("[")
16       for i in 0..<values.count {
17           i < values.count - 1 ? print("\(values[i]), ") : print(values[i])
18       }
19       print("]")
20   }
21
22   // create Arrays
23   let emptyIntegers: [Int] = []
24   let integers = [1, 2, 3, 4, 5, 6, 7]
25   let doubles = [1.1, 2.2, 3.3, 4.4]
26
27   print("emptyIntegers contains: ")
28   printArray(emptyIntegers) // pass empty Int Array
29   print("\nintegers contains: ")
30   printArray(integers) // pass Int Array
31   print("\ndoubles contains: ")
32   printArray(doubles) // pass Double Array
33   println()
```

```
emptyIntegers contains: []
integers contains: [1, 2, 3, 4, 5, 6, 7]
doubles contains: [1.1, 2.2, 3.3, 4.4]
```

Fig. 11.1 | Printing `Array` elements using overloaded functions. (Part 2 of 2.)

When the compiler encounters a `printArray` call (lines 28, 30 and 32), it attempts to locate a function definition with the same name and with parameters that *match* the argument types in the call. In this example, each call matches one of the `printArray` definitions. For example, line 30 calls `printArray` with `integers` as its argument. The compiler determines the argument's type (i.e., `[Int]`), locates the `printArray` function that specifies an `[Int]` parameter (lines 5–11), then sets up a call to that function. Similarly, when the compiler encounters the call at line 32, it determines the argument's type (i.e., `[Double]`), locates the `printArray` function that specifies a `[Double]` parameter (lines 14–20), then sets up a call to that function.

Common Features in the Overloaded *printArray* Functions
The only difference between the `printArray` functions is the `Array` type specified for each function's parameter—`[Int]` in line 5 and `[Double]` in line 14. In the next section, rather than separate functions that output `Array`s of type `[Int]` and `[Double]`, we use a single generic function with the notation `[T]` ("`Array` of `T`"), where `T` is a placeholder for the `Array`'s element type. As you'll see, the generic function outputs `Array`s of any type.

11.3 Generic Functions: Implementation and Specialization

If the operations performed by several overloaded functions are *identical* for each argument type (as is the case with the `printArray` functions in Fig. 11.1), the overloaded functions can be more conveniently coded using a generic function. You can write a single generic function definition that uses *placeholders* for the actual types that will be processed, then call the function with arguments of different types. The compiler determines the *actual types* to process, based on the types of the arguments passed to the generic function. At *compilation time*, the compiler ensures the type safety of your code, preventing many runtime errors.

A Generic `printArray` Function

Figure 11.2 reimplements the overloaded printArray functions in Fig. 11.1 with a *single* generic printArray<T> function (lines 5–11 of Fig. 11.2). The function calls in lines 19, 21 and 23 of Fig. 11.2 are identical to those in lines 28, 30 and 32 of Fig. 11.1, and the outputs of the two programs are identical. This demonstrates the expressive power of generics.

```
 1   // Fig. 11.2: GenericFunction.playground
 2   // Printing Array elements using a generic function.
 3
 4   // print an Array
 5   func printArray<T>(values: [T]) {
 6       print("[")
 7       for i in 0..<values.count {
 8           i < values.count - 1 ? print("\(values[i]), ") : print(values[i])
 9       }
10       print("]")
11   }
12
13   // create Arrays
14   let emptyIntegers: [Int] = []
15   let integers = [1, 2, 3, 4, 5, 6, 7]
16   let doubles = [1.1, 2.2, 3.3, 4.4]
17
18   print("emptyIntegers contains: ")
19   printArray(emptyIntegers) // pass empty Int Array
20   print("\nintegers contains: ")
21   printArray(integers) // pass Int Array
22   print("\ndoubles contains: ")
23   printArray(doubles) // pass Double Array
24   println()
```

```
emptyIntegers contains: []
integers contains: [1, 2, 3, 4, 5, 6, 7]
doubles contains: [1.1, 2.2, 3.3, 4.4]
```

Fig. 11.2 | Printing Array elements using a generic function.

Generic Parameter Clause of a Generic Function

Each generic function definition has a **generic parameter clause** (<T> in line 5of Fig. 11.2) that follows the function's name and precedes the function's parameter list—the identifier T is arbitrary but preferred. The generic parameter clause contains one or more **type parameters** in a comma-separated list—printArray has only one type parameter, T (line 5). A type parameter is an identifier that specifies a generic type name. Type parameters can be used to declare the return type, parameter types ([T] in line 5) and local variable and constant types in a generic function's definition.

Type parameters act as *placeholders* for actual types—known as **type arguments**. In this example's generic-function calls (lines 19, 21 and 23), the type arguments are Int, Int and Double, respectively—the Array element types for each Array passed to the function.

The type-parameter names throughout the function definition must be defined in the generic parameter clause. Type-parameter names need not be unique among different generic functions.

Good Programming Practice 11.1

The letter T (for "type") is commonly used as a type parameter, but you might want to use more meaningful names. For example, the generic Dictionary type uses the helpful type-parameter names Key and Value for the types of its keys and values, respectively. Because they represent types, type parameters should be named like classes, structs and enums.

Testing the Generic printArray Function

As in Fig. 11.1, the program of Fig. 11.2 defines three Arrays (lines 14–16)—the no-element Int Array emptyIntegers, seven-element Int Array integers and four-element Double Array doubles. Then lines 18–24 display the Arrays' contents. Each Array is output (implicitly) by calling the *same* generic printArray<T> function (in lines 19, 21 and 23)—once with the argument emptyIntegers, once with the argument integers and once with the argument doubles.

When the compiler encounters line 19, it first determines the type of the argument emptyIntegers (i.e., [Int]) and attempts to locate a function named printArray that specifies one [Int] parameter. There's no such function in this example. Next, the compiler determines whether there's a generic printArray function with a single Array parameter that uses a type parameter to represent the generic Array element type. The compiler determines that printArray<T> (lines 5–11) is a match, then sets up a call to the function, using the actual type Int to replace the placeholder type parameter T. The same process is repeated for the calls to function printArray at lines 21 and 23. The process of replacing type parameters with type arguments at compile time is known as **specialization**.

In addition to setting up the function calls, the compiler also determines whether the operations in the function body can be applied to elements of the Array argument's element type—another example of Swift's type safety. The only operation performed on each Array element in this example is to display its String representation by passing each element to the print function, which uses a Printable[1] object's description property to get the element's String representation. Types Int and Double both conform to the Printable protocol. For objects of non-Printable types, Swift prints the type's fully qualified name—i.e., its module name, a dot (.) and its type name.

Function print

By declaring printArray as a generic function, we eliminated the need for the overloaded functions of Fig. 11.1 and created a reusable function that can output the String repre-

---

1.   As of Xcode 6.1.1, Xcode playgrounds ignore the Printable conformance of a custom-type object that you pass to the print or println functions—the type's fully qualified name is output rather than the object's description. To test a custom type's Printable conformance, use an Xcode project rather than a playground.

sentations of an Array's elements, regardless of what the type of those elements is. We could have simply used the print function with an Array as an argument—type Array conforms to the Printable protocol and its description property produces a String representation of the Array's elements as a comma-separated list in brackets ([]). In the next section, we show how to place constraints on the type parameters.

11.4 Type Parameters with Type Constraints

Let's consider a generic function maximum (Fig. 11.3) that determines and returns the largest of its three arguments of the same type. The function initially assumes that its first argument (x) is the largest and assigns it to local variable max (line 6). Next, the if statement at lines 8–10 determines whether y is greater than max and, if so, assigns y to max. Then, the if statement at lines 12–14 determines whether z is greater than max and, if so, assigns z to max. Finally, line 16 returns max to the caller.

```
 1   // Fig. 11.3: Maximum.playground
 2   // Generic function maximum with a type constraint on its type parameter.
 3
 4   // determines the largest of three Comparable objects
 5   func maximum<T : Comparable>(x: T, y: T, z: T) -> T {
 6       var max = x // assume x is initially the largest
 7
 8       if y > max {
 9           max = y // y is the largest so far
10       }
11
12       if z > max {
13           max = z // z is the largest
14       }
15
16       return max // returns the largest object
17   }
18
19   println("Maximum of 3, 4 and 5 is \(maximum(3, 4, 5))")
20   println("Maximum of 6.6, 8.8 and 7.7 is \(maximum(6.6, 8.8, 7.7))")
21   print("Maximum of \"pear\", \"apple\", \"orange\" is ")
22   println(maximum("pear", "apple", "orange"))
```

```
Maximum of 3, 4 and 5 is 5
Maximum of 6.6, 8.8 and 7.7 is 8.8
Maximum of pear, apple, orange is pear
```

Fig. 11.3 | Generic function maximum with a type constraint on its type parameter.

Specifying a Type Parameter's Type Constraint
The operator > used in lines 8 and 12 *is not supported by all types*. For this reason, if you were to define function maximum with the generic parameter clause

```
<T>
```

the compiler would generate error messages for the conditions in lines 8 and 12. To prevent this error, you must *restrict* maximum's type parameter so that the compiler allows only aguments of types with support for the > operator. Types that conform to the Comparable protocol—such as the numeric and String types—support the > operator and the other comparative operators (<, <=, >=, == and !=).

You restrict a type parameter with a **type constraint**—a colon (:) followed by one protocol, class name or protocol composition—to the right of the type parameter's name. For example, maximum's generic parameter clause (line 5)

```
<T : Comparable>
```

specifies that type parameter T represents only Comparable types, i.e., only objects of types that conform to the Comparable protocol can be passed to maximum—otherwise, you'll get a compilation error. Type constraints are common in generic functions and types. For example, Dictionary's Key type parameter has a Hashable type constraint.

Type Constraint with the *where* Clause

The type constraint T : Comparable is shorthand notation for

```
<T where T : Comparable>
```

which uses the **where clause** to specify the type constraint. The shorthand notation is normally preferred, but the where clause is often used in more complex type constraints.

Calling Function `maximum`

Line 19 calls maximum<T : Comparable> with the Int values 3, 4 and 5. When the compiler encounters this call, it first looks for a maximum function that takes three arguments of type Int. There's no such function, so the compiler looks for a generic function that takes three arguments of the same generic type and finds generic function maximum<T : Comparable>. The type constraint indicates to the compiler that the arguments must be Comparable. Type Int conforms to the Comparable protocol, so the Ints in line 19 are valid arguments to maximum<T : Comparable>. A similar process occurs for the Double arguments passed in line 20 and the String arguments passed in line 22. Types Double and String each conform to the Comparable protocol, so the arguments in lines 20 and 22 are valid.

11.5 Overloading Generic Functions

A generic function may be overloaded like any other function. You can provide two or more generic functions that specify the same name but different parameters, different type requirements or both. A generic function also can be overloaded by nongeneric functions. When the compiler encounters a function call, it searches for the function definition that best matches the function call's argument types. For example, the generic printArray<T> function of Fig. 11.2 could be overloaded with a version that's specific to Strings, which outputs the Strings in neat, tabular format.

11.6 Generic Types

The concept of a data structure, such as a stack, can be understood *independently* of the element type it manipulates. Generic types are ideal for this purpose. One generic Stack type, for example, could be the basis for creating many Stack objects (e.g., a "Stack of Doubles," a "Stack of Ints," a "Stack of Strings," a "Stack of Employees," etc.). As you saw with the types Array (Chapter 6) and Dictionary (Chapter 7), once you have a generic type, you can use a simple, concise notation to specialize it with the type argument(s) that the compiler should use in place of the type parameter(s). The compiler then ensures the type safety of your code.

*Implementing a Generic **Stack** Type*

Figure 11.4[2] (part of the StackTest.xcodeproj project) declares a generic type named Stack. To be consistent with types Array and Dictionary, we've chosen to make Stack a struct, so it's a value type instead of a reference type. A generic type declaration looks like a nongeneric one, but the type name is followed by a *generic parameter clause* (<T> in line 3). In this case, type parameter T represents the element type the Stack will manipulate. As with generic functions, the generic parameter clause may contain one or more type parameters separated by commas, and each type parameter may specify type constraints. Type parameter T is used throughout type Stack's definition to represent the element type. This Stack type can be specialized for elements of any type, because the type parameter T does not have a type constraint.

```swift
1   // Fig. 11.4: Stack.swift
2   // Generic Stack type that uses an Array to store elements.
3   public struct Stack<T> {
4       private var elements: [T] = [] // Array to store the Stack's elements
5
6       // push element onto stack
7       public mutating func push(element: T) {
8           elements.append(element)
9       }
10
11      // pop and return the top element, or nil if the Stack is empty
12      public mutating func pop() -> T? {
13          return !isEmpty ? elements.removeLast() : nil
14      }
15
16      // return the top element, or nil if the Stack is empty
17      public var top: T? {
18          return elements.last
19      }
20
21      // return true if the Stack is empty; otherwise, return false
22      public var isEmpty: Bool {
23          return elements.isEmpty
24      }
25  }
```

Fig. 11.4 | Generic Stack type that uses an Array to store elements.

2. The example presented here is based on a Stack class example that we've used for many years in the generics and templates chapters of our *How to Program* and *Deitel Developer Series* books. Chapter 9, Structures, Enumerations and Nested Types, explains why Swift programmers often prefer structs to classes.

*Using an **Array** to Store the **Stack's** Elements*
We implement the Stack's storage as an Array of the Stack's element type ([T], line 4).
An Array can grow dynamically (by appending elements to it), so objects of this Stack
type also can grow dynamically.

mutating** Method **push
Method push (lines 7–9) uses Array's append method to add an item to the end of the
elements Array. Because new elements are added to the end, the last Array element represents the Stack's *top*.

mutating** Method **pop
Method pop (lines 12–14) first determines whether the Stack is empty. If not, line 13
returns the result of calling Array's removeLast method; otherwise, line 13 returns nil.
The method might not return a value, so we declared its return type as an optional of the
Stack's element type (T?).
   We test whether the Array is empty before calling removeLast to prevent the runtime
error that occurs when you call removeLast on an empty Array. The client of Stack<T>
must check the optional that's returned.

*Computed Property **top***
Lines 17–19 define the computed property top, which returns the value of the Stack's top
element or nil if the Stack is empty. To accomplish this, the property simply returns as
an optional the value of the Array's **last property**—the value of the Array's highest-
numbered element, or nil if the Array is empty.

*Computed Property **isEmpty***
Lines 22–24 define the Bool computed property isEmpty. This property simply returns
the value of the Array's isEmpty property.

*Testing the Generic **Stack** Type*
Now let's consider an application (Fig. 11.5) that demonstrates the Stack generic type.
This application is another part of the StackTest.xcodeproj project.

```
1   // Fig. 11.5: main.swift
2   // Stack test program.
3
4   // test push method with Stack<Double>
5   func testPush<T>(inout stack: Stack<T>, values: [T], name: String) {
6       print("Pushing elements onto \(name): ")
7
8       // push elements
9       for value in values {
10          print("\(value) ")
11          stack.push(value)
12      }
13
14      println()
15  }
```

Fig. 11.5 | Stack test program. (Part 1 of 2.)

```
16
17    // test pop method with Stack<Double>
18    func testPop<T>(inout stack: Stack<T>, name: String) {
19        print("Popping elements from \(name): ")
20
21        // remove all elements from Stack
22        while let value = stack.pop() {
23            print("\(value) ")
24        }
25
26        println()
27    }
28
29    // Create and test a Stack<Double>
30    let doubles = [1.1, 2.2, 3.3]
31    var doubleStack = Stack<Double>()
32    testPush(&doubleStack, doubles, "doubleStack")
33    testPop(&doubleStack, "doubleStack")
34
35    // Create and test a Stack<Int>
36    let integers = [1, 2, 3]
37    var intStack = Stack<Int>()
38    testPush(&intStack, integers, "intStack")
39    testPop(&intStack, "intStack")
40
41    // Create and test a Stack<Int>
42    let strings = ["apple", "banana", "cherry"]
43    var stringStack = Stack<String>()
44    testPush(&stringStack, strings, "stringStack")
45    testPop(&stringStack, "stringStack")
```

```
Pushing elements onto doubleStack: 1.1 2.2 3.3
Popping elements from doubleStack: 3.3 2.2 1.1
Pushing elements onto intStack: 1 2 3
Popping elements from intStack: 3 2 1
Pushing elements onto stringStack: apple banana cherry
Popping elements from stringStack: cherry banana apple
```

Fig. 11.5 | Stack test program. (Part 2 of 2.)

The declarations in lines 31, 37 and 43 of Fig. 11.5 specialize the Stack generic type to create a Stack<Double> (pronounced "Stack of Double"), a Stack<Int> (pronounced "Stack of Int") and a Stack<String> (pronounced "Stack of String"), respectively. The types Double, Int and String are type arguments. The compiler uses them to replace the type parameter T throughout Fig. 11.4. This enables the compiler to perform type checking to ensure that only Ints are used with the Stack<Int>, only Doubles with the Stack<Double> and only Strings with the Stack<String>.

Generic Function testPush
The generic function testPush (lines 5–15) receives three arguments—a Stack object (by reference because of inout), an Array of elements to push onto the Stack and a String

that identifies the Stack being manipulated. Lines 9–12 invoke the Stack's push method repeatedly to place each element of the Array argument onto the given Stack.

Generic Function testPop

The generic function testPop (lines 18–27) receives two arguments—a Stack object (by reference) and a String that identifies the Stack being manipulated. Lines 22–24 invoke the Stack's pop method repeatedly until all the values are removed from the Stack. Line 22 uses optional binding in a while statement to determine whether each call to pop returns an element value—the loop terminates when pop returns nil.

Testing the Stacks

Lines 30–33, 36–39 and 42–45 create and test Stacks of Doubles, Ints and Strings, respectively. Lines 32, 38 and 44 call function testPush to push elements onto each Stack, and lines 33, 39 and 45 call function testPop to pop all of the elements from each Stack. The output shows that the values pop off each Stack in last-in, first-out order—the defining behavior of stacks.

11.7 Note About Associated Types for Protocols

An *associated type* is a generic type that's used in a protocol. Unlike other generic types, protocols do not support generic parameter clauses, so associated types are defined *inside* a protocol with the typealias keyword (e.g., typealias T). The actual type used is determined by the classes, structs or enums that conform to the protocol. Associated types are used to develop library types, methods and functions, such as those in the Swift Standard Library. For an example of associated types, see the Container protocol in *The Swift Programming Language* at:

```
http://bit.ly/SwiftAssociatedTypes
```

11.8 Wrap-Up

In this chapter, we showed how to define generic functions, methods and types. You added generic parameter clauses to functions and types, and specified type parameters in generic parameter clauses. We discussed how Swift determines a generic function's type arguments from the argument values in a function call. We also showed how to use type constraints to restrict a type parameter's type arguments. You defined a generic data structure type and used explicit type arguments to define specialized objects of the generic type.

In the next chapter, we discuss operator overloading, which enables you to define how existing operators work for your own types, add operator support to existing types (via extensions), define subscript operators ([]) for your own types and define entirely new operators.

12

Operator Overloading and Subscripts

12.1 Introduction

You manipulate objects by invoking their methods and accessing their properties. These notations can be cumbersome for certain kinds of operations—for example, arithmetic with mathematical types. For such types, it would be convenient to use Swift's rich set of built-in operators to specify object manipulations. In this chapter, we show how to use **operator overloading** to enable operators to work with class and `struct` objects.

You've actually been using overloaded operators throughout the book—they're built into the Swift Standard Library. For example, Swift overloads the addition operator (+) to perform differently, depending on its context—using + with `Int` operands *adds* the two `Int` values and returns their sum, whereas using + with two `String` operands *concatenates* the `String`s' contents and returns a new `String`.

You can overload any built-in operator except the assignment operator (=) and the ternary conditional operator (?:). The jobs performed by overloaded operators also can be performed by explicit function calls, but operator notation is often more natural and concise. As you'll see, you also can create entirely new operators.

We begin by demonstrating the Swift Standard Library's `String` type (Section 12.2), which has lots of overloaded operators. This enables you to see a variety of overloaded operators in use before implementing your own. In that example, we'll also create a custom `String` operator and demonstrate various additional `String` methods.

In Section 12.3, we'll create a custom type for representing complex numbers and overload several standard arithmetic operators and an arithmetic assignment operator for that type. As you'll see, these operators enable you to perform complex-number arithmetic using simple arithmetic notations.

As you saw in Section 8.10, doing arithmetic with Foundation framework class NSDecimalNumber is verbose due to the lengths of the class's method names. In Section 12.4, we'll overload arithmetic operators for NSDecimalNumbers to simplify those calculations. We'll also show how to overload the prefix and postfix ++ and -- operators for NSDecimalNumbers (Section 12.5).

You've used subscripts ([]) with Array indices and Dictionary keys. You can define *custom subscripts* for any class, struct or enum type. In Section 12.6, we'll define a struct with overloaded custom subscripts—one that receives an Int and one that receives a String.

Finally in Sections 12.7—12.8 we'll discuss the details of creating entirely new operators, then implement a custom exponentiation operator—first for type Int, then with generics for any of Swift's signed integer types.

Good Programming Practice 12.1
For clarity, overloaded operators should mimic the functionality of their built-in counterparts—e.g., the + operator should perform addition-like or concatenation-like operations.

Good Programming Practice 12.2
Avoid excessive or inconsistent use of operator overloading, as this can make programs cryptic to read. Use operator overloading to make your code clearer—avoid obfuscation.

Software Engineering Observation 12.1
Objective-C does not have operator overloading. However, you can define overloaded operators in Swift for Objective-C classes and use those classes and operators in your Swift code. We'll do this in Section 12.4.

12.2 String Operators and Methods

In the preceding chapters, we demonstrated various String capabilities, including String concatenation with +, the String property isEmpty and how to use NSString features with Swift Strings. The playground in Fig. 12.1 demonstrates many of String's overloaded operators, defines and uses a custom String overloaded unary ! operator, and demonstrates several other useful String methods.

```
1   // Fig. 12.1: SwiftStrings.playground
2   // String operators and other String methods
3
4   // custom prefix unary ! operator returns String isEmpty property's value
5   prefix func !(s: String) -> Bool {
6       return s.isEmpty
7   }
8
9   // create Strings for testing String operators and methods
10  var s1 = "happy"
11  let s2 = " birthday"
12  var s3 = ""
```

Fig. 12.1 | String operators and other String methods. (Part 1 of 3.)

```
13
14   // test overloaded String comparative operators
15   println("s1 is \"\(s1)\"; s2 is \"\(s2)\"; s3 is \"\(s3)\"")
16
17   println("\nTHE RESULTS OF COMPARING S1 AND S2")
18   println("s2 == s1 is \(s2 == s1)")
19   println("s2 != s1 is \(s2 != s1)")
20   println("s2 >  s1 is \(s2 > s1)")
21   println("s2 <  s1 is \(s2 < s1)")
22   println("s2 >= s1 is \(s2 >= s1)")
23   println("s2 <= s1 is \(s2 <= s1)")
24
25   // test String overloaded ! operator
26   println("\nTESTING CUSTOM OVERLOADED ! OPERATOR")
27
28   if !s3 { // uses custom ! prefix unary operator
29       println("s3 is empty; assigning s1 to s3")
30       s3 = s1
31       println("s3 is \"\(s3)\"")
32   }
33
34   // test overloaded String concatenation operators
35   println("\nTESTING STRING CONCATENATION")
36   println("The result of s1 + s2 is the new String \"\(s1 + s2)\"")
37   s1 += s2 // no return value, so can't insert in a String via interpolation
38   println("After s1 += s2, s1 is \"\(s1)\"")
39
40   // using String's [] substring operator
41   println("\nTESTING [] FOR SUBSTRINGS")
42   let index = advance(s1.startIndex, 5)
43   let substring1 = s1[s1.startIndex ..< index]
44   println("s1[s1.startIndex ..< index] is \"\(substring1)\"")
45   let substring2 = s1[index ..< s1.endIndex]
46   println("s1[index ..< s1.endIndex] is \"\(substring2)\"")
47
48   // test various other String methods
49   println("\nTESTING OTHER STRING METHODS")
50   var result = s1.hasPrefix("hap") // check whether s1 starts with "hap"
51   println("s1.hasPrefix(\"hap\"): \(result)")
52   result = s1.hasSuffix("day") // check whether s1 ends with "day"
53   println("s1.hasSuffix(\"day\"): \(result)")
54
55   s1.removeAtIndex(index) // removes space at position index
56   println("After s1.removeAtIndex(index), s1 is \"\(s1)\"")
57
58   s1.insert(" ", atIndex: index) // insert a space at position index
59   println("After s1.insert(\" \", atIndex: index), s1 is \"\(s1)\"")
60
61   s1.append(Character("!")) // append ! to the end of s1
62   println("After s1.append(Character(\"!\")), s1 is \"\(s1)\"")
63
64   s1.removeAll() // remove all characters in s1
65   println("After s1.removeAll(), s1 is \"\(s1)\"")
```

Fig. 12.1 | String operators and other String methods. (Part 2 of 3.)

```
66
67   let joinResult = "*".join(["1", "2", "3"]) // concatenate elements
68   println("\"*\".join([\"1\", \"2\", \"3\"]) is \"\(joinResult)\"")
```

```
s1 is "happy"; s2 is " birthday"; s3 is ""

THE RESULTS OF COMPARING S1 AND S2
s2 == s1 is false
s2 != s1 is true
s2 >  s1 is false
s2 <  s1 is true
s2 >= s1 is false
s2 <= s1 is true

TESTING CUSTOM OVERLOADED ! OPERATOR
s3 is empty; assigning s1 to s3
s3 is "happy"

TESTING STRING CONCATENATION
The result of s1 + s2 is the new String "happy birthday"
After s1 += s2, s1 is "happy birthday"

TESTING [] FOR SUBSTRINGS
s1[s1.startIndex ..< index] is "happy"
s1[index ..< s1.endIndex] is " birthday"

TESTING OTHER STRING METHODS
s1.hasPrefix("hap"): true
s1.hasSuffix("day"): true
After s1.removeAtIndex(index), s1 is "happybirthday"
After s1.insert(" ", atIndex: index), s1 is "happy birthday"
After s1.append(Character("!")), s1 is "happy birthday!"
After s1.removeAll(), s1 is ""
"*".join(["1", "2", "3"]) is "1*2*3"
```

Fig. 12.1 | String operators and other String methods. (Part 3 of 3.)

12.2.1 String Variables and Constants

Lines 10–12 create String variables s1 and s3, and a String constant s2 that we use throughout this example. Line 15 displays these Strings so we can confirm that the rest of the program's outputs are correct.

12.2.2 String Comparative Operators

Type String conforms to the Equatable and Comparable protocols, so you can compare objects using the comparative operators ==, !=, >, <, >= and <=. Lines 18–23 show the results of comparing s2 to s1 by using String's overloaded comparative operators.

Because Swift's String type provides full Unicode support, the details of comparing Strings are more complicated than in some other programming languages. Swift performs String comparisons based on so-called *extended graphene clusters* that take into account the underlying character's linguistic meaning and appearance. So, if two Strings *appear* the same (for example, when displayed on the screen), but are composed of different Unicode characters, they still compare as equal. In Apple's *Swift Programming Language*, the Comparing Strings section of the Strings and Characters chapter discusses these comparisons and provides a sample in which Strings with different Unicode values compare as equal:

```
http://bit.ly/SwiftStringComparisons
```

Software Engineering Observation 12.2

Objects of types that conform to the Equatable protocol can be compared with the == and != operators. Such types need define only the == operator. The Swift Standard Library provides a generic overloaded operator function for != that returns the opposite of == for two objects of a given Equatable type.

Software Engineering Observation 12.3

The Comparable protocol inherits from the Equatable protocol, so Comparable objects are also Equatable objects.

Software Engineering Observation 12.4

Objects of types that conform to the Comparable protocol can be compared with the <, <=, >, >=, == and != operators. Such types need define only the < and == operators. The Swift Standard Library provides generic overloaded operator functions for <=, >, >= and != that use the < and == operators to return appropriate results.

12.2.3 Custom String Unary Prefix Operator !

Type String's isEmpty property returns true if a String contains no characters. In some languages the unary prefix operator ! performs the same task. For demonstration purposes, lines 5–7 define an **overloaded operator function** that specifies how the ! operator works for an object of type String. Overloaded operators are defined as *global* functions in which the name of the function is the operator symbol and the parameter list specifies the operands. For a *unary* operator (i.e., an operator with one operand), the operator function's parameter list must contain *one* parameter. When defining an overloaded unary operator, you must also use the **prefix** (as in line 5) or **postfix** declaration modifier to specify whether the operator is a prefix or postfix unary operator, respectively. The ! operator function simply returns the value of its argument String's isEmpty property.

When the compiler encounters the expression !s3 in the condition at line 28, it invokes the function at lines 5–7, passing the operand s3 as the function's argument. Because s3 is empty, the condition evaluates to true, so line 29 indicates that s3 is empty, line 30 assigns s1 to s3 and line 31 shows that the assignment copied the contents of s1 into s3.

Software Engineering Observation 12.5

You can declare operator functions in a protocol. Any type that conforms to the protocol must define the specified operator functions—again, all operator functions are defined at global scope.

12.2.4 String Concatenation with Operators + and +=

Lines 36–38 demonstrate type String's overloaded + and += operators for *string concatenation*. Line 36 appends the contents of s2 to s1 using the + operator, which returns a new String containing the result and does not modify the operands s1 and s2. Line 37 appends the contents of s2 to s1 using String's overloaded += operator, which stores the result in its left operand. Unlike in most C-based programming languages, Swift's assignment operators do *not* return values, so we cannot use String interpolation to place the result of the expression s1 += s2 into a String for output. Instead, line 38 displays s1's new contents after the assignment.

12.2.5 String Subscript ([]) Operator for Creating Substrings

You've seen that you can use subscripts ([]) with Int values to access an Array's elements and subscripts of a Dictionary's key type to access or store a corresponding value in a Dictionary. Lines 41–46 demonstrate using subscripts ([]) with Strings to extract substrings. The value placed in the subscript is a *range* of String.Index values. The first character in the String is at index 0. Each String contains two properties of this type—**startIndex** is the String.Index of the String's *first character* and **endIndex** is the String.Index of the position *one past the String's last character*. You can create a String.Index by using the global function **advance** (line 42), which for a String receives a String.Index as its first argument and an Int as its second argument. The function increments the String.Index by the function's second argument and returns a String.Index representing that character position in the String. In this case, the String.Index represents the position of the space character in s1. Line 43 then uses a subscript with the range

```
s1.startIndex ..< index
```

which returns a substring containing the characters from the beginning of s1 up to, but *not* including, the character at position index. Line 45 uses a subscript with the range

```
index ..< s1.endIndex
```

which returns a substring containing the characters from the position index to the end of the String. A runtime error occurs if you attempt to access a substring that's outside the String's bounds.

12.2.6 Other String Methods

Type String has various other useful methods, which we demonstrate in lines 49–68:

- Line 50 uses method **hasPrefix** to determine whether s1 *begins* with the String argument's value ("hap"). If so, this method returns true; otherwise, it returns false.

- Line 52 uses method **hasSuffix** to determine whether s1 *ends* with the String argument's value ("day"). If so, this method returns true; otherwise, it returns false.

- Line 55 uses method **removeAtIndex** to remove the Character at the specified String.Index—in this case, the space in "happy birthday".

- Line 58 uses method **insert** to insert the Character in its first argument at the String.Index specified in the second argument—this reinserts the space in "happy birthday".

- Line 61 uses method **append** to add its Character argument to the end of s1.

- Line 64 uses method **removeAll** to *empty* the String s1.

- Line 67 demonstrates the **join** method, which *concatenates* the elements of its [String] (i.e., String Array) argument, inserting the String on which it's called ("*") between each pair of elements.

12.3 Custom Complex Numeric Type with Overloaded Arithmetic Operators

As you saw in Fig. 12.1, operators provide a concise notation for manipulating String objects. You can use operators with your own types as well. Swift allows most existing operators to be overloaded so that, when they're used with objects, they have meaning appropriate to those objects. Operator overloading is *not* automatic—you must write operator functions to perform the desired operations.

To demonstrate operators for your own custom types, Fig. 12.2 defines a Complex struct type (lines 5–13) for representing complex numbers—that is, numbers of the form $a + bi$, where a is the real part, b is the imaginary part and i is $\sqrt{-1}$. We also define overloaded addition (+), subtraction (-), multiplication (*) and addition assignment (+=) operators (lines 16–36) so a program can use common mathematical notation with Complex objects. Type Complex contains Double properties for the real and imaginary parts of a complex number (lines 6–7), and a description property (lines 9–12) that returns Complex number's String representation.

```swift
1   // Fig. 12.2: Complex.swift (ComplexNumbers.xcodeproj)
2   // Defining operators for a custom type Complex
3   import Foundation
4
5   public struct Complex: Printable {
6       public var real: Double = 0.0
7       public var imaginary: Double = 0.0
8
9       public var description: String {
10          return String(format: "(%.1f %@ %.1fi)", real,
11              imaginary < 0 ? "-" : "+", abs(imaginary))
12      }
13  }
14
15  // overload the addition operator
16  public func +(x: Complex, y: Complex) -> Complex {
17      return Complex(real: x.real + y.real,
18          imaginary: x.imaginary + y.imaginary)
19  }
20
21  // overload the subtraction operator
22  public func -(x: Complex, y: Complex) -> Complex {
23      return Complex(real: x.real - y.real,
24          imaginary: x.imaginary - y.imaginary)
25  }
26
```

Fig. 12.2 | Defining operators for a custom type Complex. (Part 1 of 2.)

```
27   // overload the multiplication operator
28   public func *(x: Complex, y: Complex) -> Complex {
29       return Complex(real: x.real * y.real - x.imaginary * y.imaginary,
30           imaginary: x.real * y.imaginary + y.real * x.imaginary)
31   }
32
33   // overload the addition assignment operator
34   public func +=(inout left: Complex, right: Complex) {
35       left = left + right // uses overloaded +
36   }
```

Fig. 12.2 | Defining operators for a custom type `Complex`. (Part 2 of 2.)

12.3.1 Overloaded Operator Functions +, − and *

Lines 16–19 define an overloaded + operator function that adds two `Complex` numbers. For a binary *infix* operator (i.e., an operator with two operands), the operator function's parameter list must contain *two* parameters—the *first* parameter is the operator's *left* operand, and the *second* is the operator's *right* operand. In this case, the overloaded + operator receives two `Complex` numbers and returns a `Complex` number containing their sum.

Lines 17–18 add the parameter's values and return the result as a new `Complex`. Notice that we do *not* modify the contents of either of the original operands passed as arguments x and y. This matches our intuitive sense of how this operator should behave—adding two numbers does not modify either of the original numbers. Of course, `Complex` is a value type, so we are manipulating *copies* of this function's arguments. Lines 22–25 and 28–31 provide similar operator functions for subtracting and multiplying `Complex` numbers, respectively.

Software Engineering Observation 12.6

Avoid nonintuitive use of operators. Programmers expect the binary addition operator (+) to perform addition (as with Swift's numeric types) or concatenation (as with `Strings`). When you overload such a commonly used operator, make it perform the same task or a similar task on objects of your type as it performs on objects of other types.

Software Engineering Observation 12.7

Overloading an arithmetic operator (e.g., *) does not automatically overload the corresponding assignment operator (e.g., *=)

12.3.2 Overloading the Arithmetic Assignment Operator +=

Like their counterparts for Swift's numeric types, the overloaded addition (+), subtraction (−) and multiplication (*) operators of Fig. 12.2 do not modify their `Complex` operands. You could write a statement like:

```
x = x + y
```

to add `Complex` numbers x and y, then modify x by assigning it the calculation's result.

You can simplify the preceding statement for clients of type `Complex` by overloading the += addition assignment operator (lines 34–36). An assignment operator's `left` operand *must* be declared as an `inout` parameter, so the function can replace `left`'s value with the calculation result. This implementation of += uses the overloaded + operator from lines 16–19 of Fig. 12.2 to add the left and right values, then assigns the + function's return value to the left operand to replace its value with the result. You can then write x = x + y as:

```
x += y
```

Software Engineering Observation 12.8

Unlike many other C-based programming languages, Swift's assignment operators do not return values, so an overloaded assignment operator function does not specify a return type.

Error-Prevention Tip 12.1

Because assignment operators do not return values, it's not possible to accidentally use = where == is expected in a condition.

Software Engineering Observation 12.9

When overloading an assignment operator, the overloaded operator function's first parameter represents the assignment operator's left operand. This parameter must be declared inout so that the overloaded operator function can modify the left operand.

12.3.3 Performing Arithmetic with Complex Numbers

The program of Fig. 12.3 demonstrates the overloaded Complex operators +, - and *. Lines 5–6 create and initialize the Complex numbers x and y. Then lines 8–9 display their String representations to confirm that they were initialized properly—because type Complex conforms to the Printable protocol, lines 8–9 implicitly use the Complex objects' descriptions to obtain the String representations.

```
1   // Fig. 12.3: main.swift (ComplexNumbers.xcodeproj)
2   // Overloading operators for complex numbers.
3
4   // create two Complex numbers
5   var x = Complex(real: 2.1, imaginary: 4.2)
6   var y = Complex(real: 5.2, imaginary: -1.1)
7
8   println("Complex x: \(x)")
9   println("Complex y: \(y)\n")
10
11  println("CALCULATION RESULTS")
12  println("\(x) + \(y) = \(x + y)")
13  println("\(x) - \(y) = \(x - y)")
14  println("\(x) * \(y) = \(x * y)")
15
16  println("ADDITION ASSIGNMENT OPERATOR")
17  x += y
18  println("After x += y, x = \(x)")
```

Fig. 12.3 | Overloading operators for complex numbers. (Part 1 of 2.)

```
Complex x: (2.1 + 4.2i)
Complex y: (5.2 - 1.1i)

CALCULATION RESULTS
(2.1 + 4.2i) + (5.2 - 1.1i) = (7.3 + 3.1i)
(2.1 + 4.2i) - (5.2 - 1.1i) = (-3.1 + 5.3i)
(2.1 + 4.2i) * (5.2 - 1.1i) = (15.5 + 19.5i)

ADDITION ASSIGNMENT OPERATOR
After x += y, x = (7.3 + 3.1i)
```

Fig. 12.3 | Overloading operators for complex numbers. (Part 2 of 2.)

Lines 12–14 add, subtract and multiply x and y with the overloaded operators, and output the results. In line 12, we perform the addition by using the addition operator with Complex operands x and y. Without operator overloading, the expression x + y wouldn't make sense—the compiler wouldn't know how two objects of class Complex should be added. This expression works here only because we defined the addition operator for two Complex operands in lines 16–19 of Fig. 12.2. When the two Complex numbers are "added" in line 12 of Fig. 12.3, the compiler generates code that invokes the overloaded operator function, passing the left operand as the first argument and the right operand as the second argument. When we use the subtraction and multiplication operators in lines 13–14, their respective overloaded operator functions are invoked similarly.

Each calculation's result is a new Complex object. When this new object is inserted into a String via String interpolation (or simply output with print or println), its description property (Fig. 12.2, lines 9–12) is *implicitly* invoked to obtain the String representation of the Complex number.

Line 17 uses the += operator to add y's value to x and store the result in x. Line 18 then displays x's value to confirm the result.

12.4 Overloading Arithmetic Operators for Class NSDecimalNumber

Not only can you overload operators for Swift types, you can do so for existing Cocoa and Cocoa Touch classes (or types from third-party libraries) that you use in your Swift code. Figure 12.4 presents an updated version of the compound-interest example of Section 8.10. This new version uses overloaded multiplication (*) and addition (+) operators for NSDecimalNumbers to make more natural and concise the statements that perform the compound-interest calculations. Once you know how to create one arithmetic operator for NSDecimalNumbers, it's trivial to overload others—each simply calls the corresponding NSDecimalNumber method to perform the arithmetic.

```
1  // Fig. 12.4: CompoundInterest.playground
2  // Overloading operators for NSDecimalNumber
3  import Foundation
4
```

Fig. 12.4 | Overloading operators for NSDecimalNumber. (Part 1 of 2.)

```
5    // format a String right aligned in a field
6    func rightAlignedString(string: String, fieldWidth: Int) -> String {
7        let spaces: Int = fieldWidth - countElements(string)
8        let padding = String(count: spaces, repeatedValue: Character(" "))
9        return padding + string
10   }
11
12   // overloaded * operator to multiply NSDecimalNumbers
13   func *(left: NSDecimalNumber, right: NSDecimalNumber) -> NSDecimalNumber {
14       return left.decimalNumberByMultiplyingBy(right)
15   }
16
17   // overloaded + operator to add NSDecimalNumbers
18   func +(left: NSDecimalNumber, right: NSDecimalNumber) -> NSDecimalNumber {
19       return left.decimalNumberByAdding(right)
20   }
21
22   var amount = NSDecimalNumber(string: "1000.00") // amount before interest
23   let rate = NSDecimalNumber(string: "0.05") // interest rate
24
25   // display headers
26   println(String(format: "%@%@", "Year",
27       rightAlignedString("Amount on deposit", 20)))
28
29   // calculate amount on deposit for each of ten years
30   for year in 1...5 {
31       // calculate new amount for specified year using overloaded operators
32       amount = amount * (rate + NSDecimalNumber.one())
33
34       let formattedAmount = NSNumberFormatter.localizedStringFromNumber(
35           amount, numberStyle: .CurrencyStyle)
36
37       // display the year and the amount
38       println(String(format: "%4d%@", year,
39           rightAlignedString(formattedAmount, 20)))
40   }
```

```
Year   Amount on deposit
   1          $1,050.00
   2          $1,102.50
   3          $1,157.62
   4          $1,215.51
   5          $1,276.28
```

Fig. 12.4 | Overloading operators for NSDecimalNumber. (Part 2 of 2.)

12.4.1 Overloading the Multiplication Operator (*)

Lines 13–15 define an overloaded * operator function that receives two NSDecimalNumbers representing the operator's left and right operands and returns an NSDecimalNumber result. Line 14 returns the result of multiplying the left operand by the right operand using NSDecimalNumber method decimalNumberByMultiplyingBy. The parameter names left and right are not required—we chose them for clarity.

12.4.2 Overloading the Addition Operator (+)

Lines 18–20 define an overloaded + operator function that receives two NSDecimalNumbers representing the operator's left and right operands and returns an NSDecimalNumber result. Line 19 returns the result of adding the left and right operands using NSDecimalNumber method decimalNumberByAdding.

12.4.3 Using the Overloaded Operators

Line 32

```
    amount = amount * (rate + NSDecimalNumber.one())
```

uses the * and + operators to simplify the following statement from Fig. 8.14:

```
    amount = amount.decimalNumberByMultiplyingBy(
        rate.decimalNumberByAdding(NSDecimalNumber.one()))
```

As you can see, using the overloaded operators makes the statement easier to code and more natural.

12.4.4 Overloading the *= Multiplication Assignment Operator

Of course, you can simplify line 32 further by overloading the *= multiplication assignment operator as follows:

```
    func *=(inout left: NSDecimalNumber, right: NSDecimalNumber) {
        left = left * right
    }
```

Again, an assignment operator's left operand *must* be declared as an inout parameter, so the function can replace left's value with the calculation result. This implementation of *= uses the overloaded * operator to multiply the left and right values, then assigns the * function's return value to the left operand to store the result. Once you define the *= operator, you can replace line 32 with the following even more concise statement:

```
    amount *= rate + NSDecimalNumber.one()
```

12.5 Overloading Unary Operators: ++ and --

In Section 12.2.3, we discussed how to overload a unary operator that used its operand's value but did not modify it. In this section, we overload the unary operators ++ and -- for use with NSDecimalNumbers. When applied to objects of the Swift Standard Library's numeric types, these operators *modify* their operands (as discussed Section 4.6). The overloaded operators are demonstrated in Fig. 12.5, lines 37, 42, 47 and 52.

For output purposes in this example, line 6 defines an empty extension that makes NSDecimalNumber conform to the Printable protocol. As is the case with many Cocoa and Cocoa Touch classes, NSDecimalNumber already has a description property that returns an NSString. When an NSString is returned to Swift code, it's treated by the runtime as a String, exactly as required by Printable's description property. So we do not need to define this property. Of course, you can *explicitly* access description as necessary. However, to enable functions print and println or String interpolation expressions to use description *implicitly* as in this example, NSDecimalNumber must conform to Printable.

```
1   // Fig. 12.5: PrefixAndPostfix.playground
2   // Overloading ++ and -- operators for NSDecimalNumber
3   import Foundation
4
5   // make NSDecimalNumbers Printable for use in string interpolation
6   extension NSDecimalNumber : Printable {}
7
8   // add 1 to an NSDecimalNumber and return the new value
9   prefix func ++(inout number: NSDecimalNumber) -> NSDecimalNumber {
10      number = number.decimalNumberByAdding(NSDecimalNumber.one())
11      return number
12  }
13
14  // add 1 to an NSDecimalNumber and return the old value
15  postfix func ++(inout number: NSDecimalNumber) -> NSDecimalNumber {
16      let temp = number.copy() as NSDecimalNumber
17      number = number.decimalNumberByAdding(NSDecimalNumber.one())
18      return temp
19  }
20
21  // subtract 1 from an NSDecimalNumber and return the new value
22  prefix func --(inout number: NSDecimalNumber) -> NSDecimalNumber {
23      number = number.decimalNumberBySubtracting(NSDecimalNumber.one())
24      return number
25  }
26
27  // subtract 1 from an NSDecimalNumber and return the old value
28  postfix func --(inout number: NSDecimalNumber) -> NSDecimalNumber {
29      let temp = number.copy() as NSDecimalNumber
30      number = number.decimalNumberBySubtracting(NSDecimalNumber.one())
31      return temp
32  }
33
34  // demonstrate postfix increment operator
35  var decimalValue = NSDecimalNumber(string: "5.5")
36  println("decimalValue before postincrement: \(decimalValue)") // 5.5
37  println("postincrementing decimalValue: \(decimalValue++)") // 5.5
38  println("decimalValue after postincrement: \(decimalValue)\n") // 6.5
39
40  // demonstrate prefix increment operator
41  println("decimalValue before preincrement: \(decimalValue)") // 6.5
42  println("preincrementing decimalValue: \(++decimalValue)") // 7.5
43  println("decimalValue after preincrement: \(decimalValue)\n") // 7.5
44
45  // demonstrate postfix decrement operator
46  println("decimalValue before postdecrement: \(decimalValue)") // 7.5
47  println("postdecrementing decimalValue: \(decimalValue--)") // 7.5
48  println("decimalValue after postdecrement: \(decimalValue)\n") // 6.5
49
50  // demonstrate prefix decrement operator
51  println("decimalValue before predecrement: \(decimalValue)") // 6.5
52  println("predecrementing decimalValue: \(--decimalValue)") // 5.5
53  println("decimalValue after predecrement: \(decimalValue)") // 5.5
```

Fig. 12.5 | Overloading ++ and -- operators for NSDecimalNumber. (Part 1 of 2.)

```
decimalValue before postincrement: 5.5
postincrementing decimalValue: 5.5
decimalValue after postincrement: 6.5

decimalValue before preincrement: 6.5
preincrementing decimalValue: 7.5
decimalValue after preincrement: 7.5

decimalValue before postdecrement: 7.5
postdecrementing decimalValue: 7.5
decimalValue after postdecrement: 6.5

decimalValue before predecrement: 6.5
predecrementing decimalValue: 5.5
decimalValue after predecrement: 5.5
```

Fig. 12.5 | Overloading ++ and -- operators for NSDecimalNumber. (Part 2 of 2.)

12.5.1 Overloading Unary Prefix Operators That Modify Their Operands

Lines 9–12 overload the *prefix* unary operator ++. Once again we use the prefix declaration modifier to specify that the operator is a prefix unary operator. Because ++ is a unary operator, the function definition has *one* parameter representing the operand. However, the ++ operator modifies its operand, so the function's parameter is declared inout. Line 10 assigns to the parameter number the result of adding NSDecimalNumber.one() to number, thus modifying the original NSDecimalNumber in the caller. The function also returns the result for use in a larger expression (such as in line 42, which outputs the result). Lines 22–25 similarly overload the prefix unary operator --, except that line 23 assigns to the parameter number the result of subtracting NSDecimalNumber.one() from number.

12.5.2 Overloading Unary Postfix Operators That Modify Their Operands

Lines 15–19 overload the *postfix* unary operator ++. Here, we use the postfix declaration modifier to specify that the operator is a postfix unary operator. Again, because the ++ operator modifies its operand, the function's parameter is declared inout. The postfix ++ operator adds one to its argument and returns the argument's *previous* value. To accomplish this, we must store the argument's *original* value (line 16) *before* modifying it. Line 16 calls NSDecimalNumber's **copy** method to get a copy of the original value. This method is inherited into NSDecimalNumber from the Foundation class NSObject. (We'll discuss the reason for the as cast operation momentarily.) Next, line 17 assigns to the parameter number the result of adding NSDecimalNumber.one() to number, thus modifying the original NSDecimalNumber in the caller. Then, line 18 returns the argument's *original* value (stored in temp). Lines 28–32 similarly overload the postfix unary operator --, except that line 30 assigns to the parameter number the result of subtracting NSDecimalNumber.one() from number.

12.5.3 Swift's AnyObject Type—Bridging Between Objective-C and Swift

You'll often pass Swift objects into methods of classes written in Objective-C, such as those in the Cocoa Touch classes. Swift's numeric types and its String, Array and Dictionary types can all be used in contexts where their Objective-C equivalents are expected. Similarly, the Objective-C equivalents (NSString, NSMutableString, NSArray, NSMutableArray, NSDictionary and NSMutableDictionary), when returned to your Swift code, are automatically treated as their Swift counterparts. This mechanism—known as **bridging**—is transparent to the developer.

The Foundation framework collections are *not* generic types—they can store *any* objects of any class type, including many different types at the same time. For this reason, when the runtime bridges an NSArray or NSMutableArray to a Swift Array, the Array's type is [AnyObject]. The Swift type **AnyObject** represents an object of any Objective-C or Swift class. Similarly, a bridged NSDictionary's or NSMutableDictionary's type in Swift is [NSObject : AnyObject]. The key type NSObject is the superclass of all classes in the Cocoa and Cocoa Touch frameworks. When you know that a Foundation framework collection contains values of a specific type, you can *downcast* the Swift Array or Dictionary accordingly. For example, if you know an Array of type [AnyObject] contains only NSStrings, you can downcast it to type [String], because NSStrings can be bridged to Swift Strings.

Class NSObject's copy method (lines 16 and 29) returns an NSObject because it can be called on an object of any NSObject subclass. When an NSObject is returned from a Foundation class method into a Swift program, the Swift runtime treats the NSObject as an AnyObject. Similarly, if you pass an AnyObject from a Swift program into a Foundation class method with a parameter of type NSObject, the runtime treats the AnyObject as an NSObject. In fact, when you look at the Swift version of the Cocoa and Cocoa Touch framework documentation online or in Xcode, you'll see the Swift types, not the Objective-C types for cases in which this bridging occurs. So for the copy method, the documentation shows:

```
func copy() -> AnyObject
```

To use an AnyObject in your Swift code, you first cast it to the appropriate type. In lines 16 and 29, we use the as cast operator (rather than as?) to cast copy's return value to NSDecimalNumber, because we know the returned value is a copy of an NSDecimalNumber.

For more details on bridging between Swift and Objective-C types, see Apple's *Using Swift with Cocoa and Objective-C* at:

```
http://bit.ly/UsingSwiftWithObjC
```

12.6 Overloading Subscripts

You've now used subscripts ([]) with Array indices, Dictionary keys and substring ranges for Strings. In this section, we define custom subscripts. You can define subscripts for any class, struct or enum type.

12.6.1 Box Type with Custom Subscripts

Figure 12.6 defines a struct type named Box that stores the length, width and height of a box as a private three-element Array of Doubles (line 7). To enable client code to manipulate the Array elements, we define two overloaded subscripts—one that enables accessing an element via an Int index (lines 17–26) and another that enables accessing an element via a String name (lines 29–40).

```swift
1   // Fig. 12.6: Box.swift (Subscripts.xcodeproj)
2   // Box type with dimensions accessed via subscripts
3   import Foundation
4
5   public struct Box {
6       private static let names = ["length", "width", "height"]
7       private var dimensions = [0.0, 0.0, 0.0]
8
9       // initializer
10      public init(length: Double, width: Double, height: Double) {
11          dimensions[0] = length
12          dimensions[1] = width
13          dimensions[2] = height
14      }
15
16      // subscript to access dimensions by their Int indices
17      public subscript(index: Int) -> Double {
18          get {
19              precondition(index >= 0 && index < dimensions.count)
20              return dimensions[index]
21          }
22          set {
23              precondition(index >= 0 && index < dimensions.count)
24              dimensions[index] = newValue
25          }
26      }
27
28      // subscript to access dimensions by their String names
29      public subscript(name: String) -> Double {
30          get {
31              precondition(
32                  Box.names.filter({$0 == name.lowercaseString}).count == 1)
33              return dimensions[nameToIndex(name)]
34          }
35          set {
36              precondition(
37                  Box.names.filter({$0 == name.lowercaseString}).count == 1)
38              dimensions[nameToIndex(name)] = newValue
39          }
40      }
41
42      // utility function to convert a name into a dimensions Array index
43      private func nameToIndex(name: String) -> Int {
44          var i = 0
45
46          while i < Box.names.count {
47              if name.lowercaseString == Box.names[i] {
48                  return i // name is in names at position i
49              }
50
51              ++i
52          }
53
```

Fig. 12.6 | Box type with dimensions accessed via subscripts. (Part 1 of 2.)

```
54                return -1 // preconditions in subscript(name: String) prevent this
55        }
56  }
```

Fig. 12.6 | Box type with dimensions accessed via subscripts. (Part 2 of 2.)

12.6.2 Subscript Syntax

Subscripts may be defined in a type or in an `extension` for a type. Each subscript begins with the **subscript** keyword and has the following syntax:

```
subscript(parameterList) -> Type {
    get {
        // code to return a value
    }
    set {
        // code to set a value
    }
}
```

The *parameterList* is a comma-separated list containing one or more parameters. The *Type* is the type of the value returned by the required `get` accessor or passed to the optional `set` accessor. A subscript without a `set` accessor is read only—can be used to obtain a value from an object. Like a read-only computed property, a read-only subscript's body can be defined without the `get` keyword and braces. The `set` accessor implicitly receives a constant named `newValue`—like a computed property, you can provide a custom name for `newValue` in parentheses following the `set` keyword. If the *parameterList* contains more than one parameter, the subscript is invoked with a comma-separated list of values in the square brackets. The parameters in the *parameterList*:

- are implicitly constant unless they're declared with `var`.
- cannot be declared `inout`.
- can be variadic (introduced in Section 6.13).
- cannot provide default values.

12.6.3 Type Box's Int Subscript and the precondition Function

For the subscript with an `Int` parameter `index` (Fig. 12.6, lines 17–26):

- The `get` accessor returns the element of the Box's `dimensions` Array at that `index`.
- The `set` accessor assigns a new value to the element of the Array at that `index`.

In each case, we first validate the `index` to ensure that it's within the Array's bounds. To do so, we call Swift's global **precondition** function, which terminates program execution if a precondition is `false`. (An alternate approach would be to use optionals instead.) The precondition for the `get` and `set` accessors is that the index value must be greater than or equal to 0 and less than the Array's number of elements. There are two versions of `precondition`:

- The one-argument version used in this example receives a condition as an argument.

- The two-argument version (used in the example of Fig. 12.8) receives a condition and an error message String. If the program terminates, this version of precondition writes the error message String to the console output.

assert *Global Function*

Swift also provides a similar function named **assert** (https://developer.apple.com/swift/blog/?id=4) that also has two versions with the same arguments as precondition. The difference between these functions is that assert executes only in debug mode, whereas precondition works in debug or release mode.

12.6.4 Type Box's `String` Subscript

For the subscript with a String parameter name (lines 29–40):

- The get uses method nameToIndex (lines 43–55) to determine the index of name in Box's names Array—a stored type property—then returns the element of dimensions at that index.

- The set accessor uses method nameToIndex (lines 43–55) to determine the index of name in Box's names Array, then assigns a new value to the element of dimensions that has the same index.

In each case, we first use function precondition to validate the name by ensuring that it's in the Array names. To do so, we filter the names Array and ensure that the result contains one element.

12.6.5 Using Type Box's Subscripts

The program of Fig. 12.7 demonstrates Box's subscripts:

- Lines 8–10 use the subscript with an Int parameter to get the Box's length, width and height.

- Line 14 uses the subscript with an Int parameter to set the Box's length.

- Line 18 uses the subscript with a String parameter to set the Box's dimension named "width".

- Lines 23, 25 and 27 use the subscript with a String parameter to get the Box's dimensions with the names "length", "width" and "height".

As an experiment, try using these subscripts with invalid Int or String parameters to force the subscript's preconditions to fail and terminate the program.

```
1   // Fig. 12.7: main.swift (Subscripts.xcodeproj)
2   // Using subscripts to access Box dimensions
3
4   var box = Box(length: 3.0, width: 4.0, height: 5.0) // create a Box
5
6   // show dimensions with Int subscript
7   println("CREATED A BOX WITH THE FOLLOWING DIMENSIONS")
8   println("box[0] = \(box[0])")
9   println("box[1] = \(box[1])")
```

Fig. 12.7 | Using subscripts to access Box dimensions. (Part 1 of 2.)

```
                                    ubscript
                                 ')

                                 g subscript
                                 o 5.0")

                                 ubscript
                                 SETTING LENGTH AND WIDTH")
```

```
CREATED A BOX WITH THE FOLLOWING DIMENSIONS
box[0] = 3.0
box[1] = 4.0
box[2] = 5.0

Setting box[0] to 10.0
Setting box["width"] to 5.0

BOX DIMENSIONS AFTER SETTING LENGTH AND WIDTH
box["length"] = 10.0
box["width"] = 5.0
box["height"] = 5.0
```

Fig. 12.7 | Using subscripts to access `Box` dimensions. (Part 2 of 2.)

12.7 Custom Operators

Unlike many other programming languages that have operator overloading, Swift allows you to create custom operators. This section shows how to declare a new operator, then defines an operator function that implements the operator. For additional details of Swift's operators and expression types, see

```
http://bit.ly/SwiftExpressions
```

12.7.1 Precedence and Associativity

As you know, each built-in operator has precedence and associativity. As shown in Appendix B, Operator Precedence Chart, some operators associate from left-to-right, some from right-to-left and some do not have associativity.

When you overload an existing operator, it has the same precedence and associativity as the corresponding built-in operator. Each new operator you create also has precedence and associativity:

- New prefix or postfix unary operators work like built-in unary operators—they're always applied *before* any binary operators in an expression and are nonassociative. If both a unary prefix operator and a unary postfix operator are applied to the *same* operand, the *postfix* operator is applied *first*.

- For each new binary infix operator you create, you can specify its precedence and associativity.

Precedence Values

Each binary operator's precedence is an integer value in the range 0 (lowest) through 255 (highest). If you do not specify a new operator's precedence, the default value is 100. All of the built-in operators have precedence values in the range 90–160.

Software Engineering Observation 12.10

When specifying a new operator's precedence, consider how the compiler should apply that operator with respect to other operators. For example, in arithmetic, exponentiation has higher precedence than multiplication. The built-in multiplication operator has the precedence 150, so you should give a custom exponentiation operator a higher precedence.

Associativity Values

Each binary operator's associativity is **left** (left-to-right), **right** (right-to-left) or **none** (non-associative). If you do not specify a new operator's associativity, the default value is **none**.

Common Programming Error 12.1

A compilation error occurs if multiple operators with the associativity none and the same precedence are used in an expression. For example, Swift's comparative operators are non-associative, so you cannot write an expression like 0 > index < 10.

12.7.2 Symbols Used in Custom Operators

Many symbols can be used to define custom operators, including various ASCII characters and many ranges of Unicode characters. The ASCII characters that you can use to begin an operator's name—known as the *operator head*—are:

```
/ = - + ! * % < > & | ^ ~ ? ..
```

The operator head is followed by one or more *operator characters*—these can be any operator head characters listed above or any characters from additional Unicode characters ranges. For a complete list of acceptable operator characters and the rules for combining them, see

```
http://bit.ly/SwiftCustomOperatorSymbols
```

Symbols Reserved by Swift

Several symbols are reserved for use by Swift:

- The symbols =, ->, //, /*, */, and the dot (.) cannot be overloaded or used to define custom operators.
- You cannot define custom unary prefix operators named <, & or ?.
- You cannot define a custom binary infix operator named ?.
- You cannot define custom unary postfix operators named >, ! or ?.

12.7.3 Defining a Custom Exponentiation Operator for Type Int

The playground of Fig. 12.8 shows how to declare a new binary infix exponentiation operator with the symbol ** (line 6), then defines an operator function to implement the new operator's functionality for Int values (lines 9–23). Lines 26–27 demonstrate the new operator.

```
 1   // Fig. 12.8: CustomOperator.playground
 2   // Creating an exponentiation operator for type Int
 3
 4   // declare new infix ** operator for exponentiation; precedence of 160 is
 5   // higher than * and /; associativity is none
 6   infix operator ** {precedence 160 associativity none}
 7
 8   // define operator function that implements the new ** operator for Ints
 9   func **(base: Int, exponent: Int) -> Int {
10       precondition(exponent >= 0, "exponent must be >= 0")
11
12       if exponent == 0 {
13           return 1
14       } else {
15           var result = 1
16
17           for _ in 1...exponent {
18               result *= base
19           }
20
21           return result
22       }
23   }
24
25   // testing the custom infix exponentiation operator **
26   println("2 ** 0 = \(2 ** 0)")
27   println("2 ** 10 = \(2 ** 10)")
```

```
2 ** 0 = 1
2 ** 10 = 1024
```

Fig. 12.8 | Creating an exponentiation operator for type Int.

Declaring a New Operator
Line 6 declares the new infix binary operator **, and specifies its precedence and associativity. Each new operator you declare must begin with the **declaration modifier** infix, prefix or postfix, followed by the keyword operator, the operator's symbol and a set of braces. For unary prefix or postfix operators, the braces are empty, but required. For a binary infix operator, the braces may *optionally* contain the *context-sensitive keyword* **precedence** followed by a precedence level (0–255) and the context-sensitive keyword **associativity** followed by left, right or none. If the precedence is not specified, it defaults to 100. If the associativity is not specified, it defaults to none. The keywords precedence and associativity are known as context-sensitive keywords because outside the braces of a new operator's definition, they do not have special meaning and *can* be used as identifiers.

In line 6, we provided both the precedence and the associativity. Since, the associativity none is the default, we could have written line 6 as:

```
infix operator ** {precedence 160}
```

We used the precedence 160 because it's higher than the precedence of the multiplication (*), division (/) and remainder (%) operators.

Creating an Operator Function for a Custom Operator

To use a custom operator, you must provide an operator function that implements the operator—this function's parameter list specifies the type(s) of the operand(s). Lines 9–23 define the ** operator for two Int operands. This implementation requires a nonnegative exponent, so line 10 uses the two-argument precondition function to ensure that the exponent is greater than or equal to 0. If the exponent is 0, the function returns 1; otherwise, it uses a loop to calculate the result.

Using the Custom ** Operator Function to Perform Exponentiation

Lines 26 and 27 use the ** operator to calculate 2^0 and 2^{10}, respectively. As an exercise, use a negative exponent to see the precondition fail and terminate the program.

12.8 Custom Generic Operators

Figure 12.8 implemented a custom exponentiation operator for type Int. In this section, we show that you can use generics and type constraints to implement the operator to support *multiple* types. The key differences in this program (Fig. 12.9) are in the operator function at lines 9, 13 and 15. The generic parameter clause in line 9 places a type constraint on the generic type T indicating that this function's base parameter can receive arguments of types that conform to the Swift Standard Library's **SignedIntegerType** protocol. Swift types Int, Int8, Int16, Int32 and Int64 all conform to this protocol. Line 13 returns the result of T(1), which uses the initializer of the type that T represents to create the value 1 in that type. We use the same expression on line 15 to initialize result to 1. The rest of the function's logic remains the same. To test this function, line 26 creates an Int constant initialized to 2 and line 27 creates an Int64 constant initialized to 10. Lines 29 and 30 then use each of these constants with the custom ** exponentiation operator.

```
 1   // Fig. 12.9: CustomOperator.playground
 2   // Creating an exponentiation operator for all SignedIntegerTypes
 3
 4   // declare new infix ** operator for exponentiation; precedence of 160 is
 5   // higher than * and /; associativity is none>
 6   infix operator ** {precedence 160 associativity none}
 7
 8   // define operator function that implements ** operator for integer types
 9   func **<T: SignedIntegerType>(base: T, exponent: Int) -> T {
10       precondition(exponent >= 0, "exponent must be >= 0")
11
```

Fig. 12.9 | Creating an exponentiation operator for all SignedIntegerTypes. (Part 1 of 2.)

```
12       if exponent == 0 {
13           return T(1)
14       } else {
15           var result = T(1)
16
17           for _ in 1...exponent {
18               result *= base
19           }
20
21           return result
22       }
23   }
24
25   // testing the custom infix exponentiation operator **
26   let intValue = 2
27   let int64Value = Int64(10)
28
29   println("intValue ** 0 = \(intValue ** 0)")
30   println("int64Value ** 10 = \(int64Value ** 10)")
```

```
intValue ** 0 = 1
int64Value ** 10 = 10000000000
```

Fig. 12.9 | Creating an exponentiation operator for all `SignedIntegerTypes`. (Part 2 of 2.)

12.9 Wrap-Up

In this chapter, we demonstrated how to overload operators to work with classes and structs, making certain operations more natural and concise. You learned that you can overload any built-in operator except the assignment operator (=) and the ternary conditional operator (?:).

We began by demonstrating the String type's overloaded operators, so you could see a variety of overloaded operators in use before implementing your own. We also created a custom String unary prefix operator (!) and demonstrated various additional String methods.

Next, we created a custom Complex type with several overloaded arithmetic operators and an arithmetic assignment operator, then used these operators to perform complex-number arithmetic using simple arithmetic notation. We overloaded for class NSDecimal-Number the +, *, ++ and -- operators.

To demonstrate custom subscripts, we defined a struct with overloaded subscripts—one that receives an Int and one that receives a String. Finally, we discussed the details of creating entirely new operators, then implemented a custom exponentiation operator—first for type Int, then with generics for any of Swift's signed integer types. In the next chapter, we show how to build a simple GUI-only iOS app that displays text and an image. Then in Chapter 14, you'll build a **Tip Calculator** iOS app with logic implemented in Swift.

13

iOS 8 App Development: Welcome App

Dive-Into® Xcode: Introducing Visual User Interface Design with Cocoa Touch, Interface Builder, Storyboarding and Auto Layout, Universal Apps, Accessibility, Internationalization

Objectives

In this chapter you'll:

- Use the Xcode integrated development environment (IDE) to write, test and debug your iOS apps.
- Use the **Single View Application** project template to quickly begin developing a new app.
- Create a universal app that can run on iPhones, iPod touches and iPads.
- Design an app's UI visually (without programming) using Interface Builder, storyboarding and auto layout.
- Display text and an image in a UI.
- Support both portrait and landscape orientations.
- Edit the attributes of Cocoa Touch UI components.
- Build and launch an app in the iOS simulator.
- Make the app more accessible to visually impaired people by specifying string descriptions for use with iOS's VoiceOver.
- Support internationalization so your app can display strings in different languages based on the user's device settings.

13.1 Introduction

This chapter and Chapter 14 are from our sister book *iOS 8 for Programmers: An App-Driven Approach with Swift, Volume 1.* In this chapter, you'll build the Welcome app that displays a welcome message and an image of the Deitel bug corporate icon—and you'll do this *without writing any code.* You'll use Xcode to create a **universal app** that runs on iPhones, iPod touches and iPads.

You'll create a simple iOS app (Fig. 13.1) using Xcode's Interface Builder, which allows you to create UIs using *drag-and-drop* techniques and *no* Swift programming. You'll execute your app in the iOS simulator for both iPhones and iPads. If you're a paid iOS Developer Program member, you'll also run the app on an iOS device.

Next we'll show how to make the app more accessible for people with impaired vision by providing accessibility strings that describe the image to the user. As you'll see, iOS's VoiceOver accessibility feature can speak the accessibility strings to the user.

Finally, we'll demonstrate how to localize your app so that it can display strings in different spoken languages based on the user's device settings. For demonstration purposes, we'll show one localization in which the app's strings (including the accessibility strings) are translated into Spanish, then incorporated into the app. You'll then run the app in Spanish on the iOS Simulator.

In Chapter 14, you'll combine the UI-building techniques you learn in this chapter with the Swift programming you learned in earlier chapters. You'll create a Tip Calculator app in which the app's logic is implemented in Swift.

Fig. 13.1 | **Welcome** app running in the iPhone simulator.

13.2 Technologies Overview

This section introduces the technologies you'll learn in this chapter.

13.2.1 Xcode and Interface Builder

This chapter introduces the *Xcode IDE*. You'll use it to create a new project (Section 13.3). You'll use Xcode's integrated **Interface Builder** to build a simple user interface (UI) consisting of text and an image (Section 13.5). Interface Builder enables you to visually lay out your UI. You can use it to drag and drop Labels, Image Views, Buttons, Text Fields, Sliders and other UI components onto an app's UI. You'll use Interface Builder's **storyboarding** capability (Section 13.5) to design the app's UI.

13.2.2 Labels and Image Views

This app's text is displayed in a **Label** (an object of class **UILabel** from the Cocoa Touch's UIKit framework) and its picture is displayed in an **Image View** (an object of class **UIImageView**). Using Interface Builder, you'll drag and drop a Label and an Image View onto the UI (Section 13.5). Each will occupy half the screen, and iOS's **auto layout** capabilities will maintain this size relationship when the user rotates the device. You'll see how to edit UI component attributes (e.g., the Text attribute of a Label and the Image attribute of an Image View) to customize them for your app.

13.2.3 Asset Catalogs and Image Sets

When your app is installed on a device, its icon and name appear with all other installed apps in the iOS home screen. You'll specify the icon for your app as part of the app's settings (Section 13.5.2). Your app's icon appears in different sizes and resolutions based on the device and context in which it's displayed. For example, the icons on an iPad are larger than those on an iPhone, and the icons on a retina display device have twice the width and height of the icons on nonretina devices. As you'll see, iOS supports **asset catalogs**, which manage image resources that require different resolutions for different devices. An asset catalog contains **image sets** from which iOS automatically chooses the appropriate image based on the device running the app and the context in which the icon is used—such as in the iOS **Settings** app, in **Spotlight** search or as the app's icon on the home screen. You can also create your own image sets to manage your app's other image resources. If you do not provide icons for each size and resolution, iOS will scale the images that you do provide, using the image that's closest in size to what it needs.

13.2.4 Running the App

After building the app, you'll run it in the **iOS simulator**, which can be used to test iPhone and iPad apps. You'll also learn how to run the app on an iOS device (Section 13.6.2).

13.2.5 Accessibility

iOS contains many *accessibility* features to help people with various disabilities use their devices. For example, people with visual disabilities can use iOS's **VoiceOver** to allow a device to speak screen text (such as the text on a **Label** or **Button**) or text that you provide to help them understand the purpose and contents of a UI component. The user can touch the screen to hear VoiceOver speak what's on the screen near the touch. Section 13.7 shows how to enable these features and how to configure your app's UI components for accessibility.

13.2.6 Internationalization

iOS devices are used worldwide. To reach the largest possible audience with your apps, you should consider customizing them for various *locales* and spoken languages—this is known as **internationalization**. Section 13.8 shows how to provide Spanish text for the **Welcome** app's **Label** and for the **Image View**'s accessibility string, then shows how to test the app in a simulator configured for Spanish.

13.3 Creating a Universal App Project with Xcode

This section overviews Xcode and shows you how to create a new universal app project.

13.3.1 Xcode Projects and App Templates

As you know, a project is a group of related files, such as the Swift code files and any media files (e.g., images, video, audio) that compose an app. To begin working on an app, select either **File > New > Project...** to create a new project or **File > Open...** to open an *existing* project. Selecting **File > New > Project...** displays a sheet containing the templates that you can use as your new project's foundation (Fig. 13.2). Templates save you time by providing preconfigured starting points for commonly used app designs. The dialog's left side shows the template categories for both iOS and OS X development. For iOS apps, you'll use the templates listed in the **iOS** category's **Application** subcategory. Figure 13.3 briefly describes each of the iOS app templates shown in Fig. 13.2.

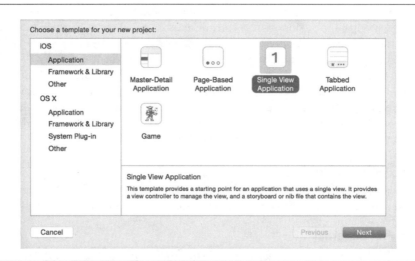

Fig. 13.2 | Choosing a project template.

Template	Template description
Master-Detail Application	Creates an app with a UI that displays a *master list* of items from which a user can choose one item to see its *details* (similar to the built-in **Mail** and **Contacts** apps). For iPad apps, this template also includes a *split view* that can display the master list and the details of one item at the same time.
Page-Based Application	Creates an app in which content is *displayed page by page* (similar to the built-in **iBooks** app).
Single View Application	Creates an app in which everything is *displayed on one screen*—as this chapter's **Welcome** app does.
Tabbed Application	Creates an *app with a tab bar* (similar to the built-in **Clock** app). The user touches a tab to change screens.
Game	Creates an app with features that support game development with one of iOS's gaming APIs—SceneKit, SpriteKit, OpenGL ES or Metal.

Fig. 13.3 | Xcode iOS app templates.

13.3.2 Creating and Configuring a Project

We'll use the **Single View Application** template. Select that app template in the dialog of Fig. 13.2, then click **Next** to display the **Choose options for your new project** sheet (Fig. 13.4).

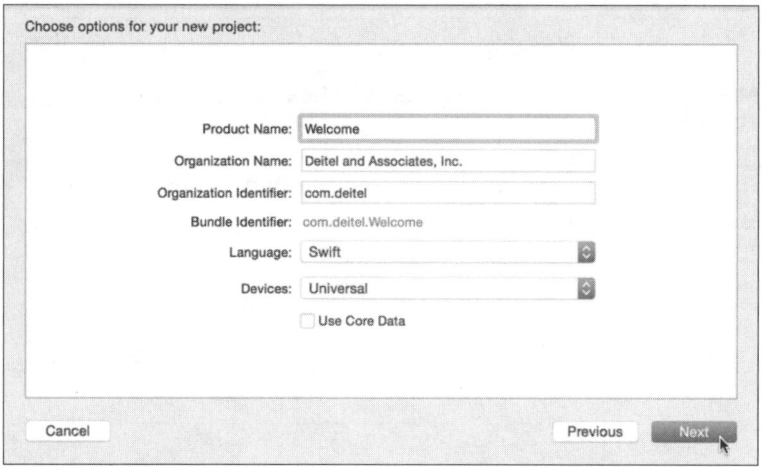

Fig. 13.4 | Configuring the **Welcome** app.

Specify the following options for the app (or use your own values), then click **Next**:

- **Product Name:** Welcome—This specifies *both* your project's name *and* app's name.

- **Organization Name:** Deitel and Associates, Inc.—The developer's company or institution name.

- **Company Identifier:** com.deitel—Typically, this is a *company's domain name in reverse*. It's combined with the app's name to form a *bundle identifier* that uniquely identifies the app in various app settings and in the App Store. Our domain name is deitel.com, so we used com.deitel as the company identifier. *If you're creating apps for learning purposes, some of Apple's tutorials suggest using the company identifier edu.self.*

- **Devices**—Specifies the device types on which your app can run. Select **Universal** to indicate that the app can run on iPhones and iPads. You can also create apps that run only on iPhones or only on iPads.

After clicking **Next**, specify where you'd like to save your project. You can also choose to use *Git* for source-code management. Git is a source-code control system often used to manage projects to which multiple developers contribute, but you can also use it yourself to manage and track the revisions you make to your app. Click **Create** to display the new project's window.

13.4 Xcode Workspace Window

This section discusses Xcode's workspace window in the context of iOS 8 app development. A new project's workspace window (Fig. 13.5) is divided into four main areas below the toolbar: the **Navigator** area, **Editor** area, **Utilities** area and the **Debug** area (which is not initially displayed—we'll explain how to display it shortly).

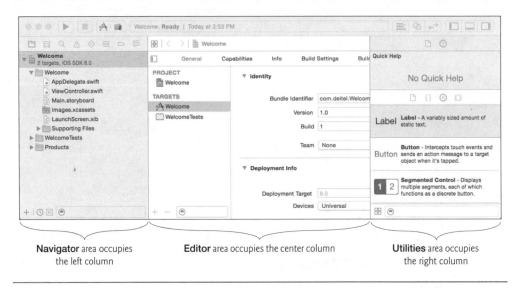

Navigator area occupies   Editor area occupies the center column   Utilities area occupies
      the left column   the right column

Fig. 13.5 | `Welcome.xcodeproj` open in the Xcode workspace window.

13.4.1 Navigator Area

At the top of the **Navigator** area are icons for the **navigators** that can be displayed there:

- **Project** (□)—Shows the files and folders in your project.
- **Symbol** (⌗)—Allows you to browse your project by classes and their contents (methods, properties, etc.).
- **Find** (🔍)—Allows you to search for text throughout your project's files and frameworks.
- **Issue** (⚠)—Shows you warnings and errors in your project by file or by type.
- **Test** (◇)—Enables you to manage your unit tests (for more about unit testing with Xcode, visit `http://bit.ly/TestingWithXcode`).
- **Debug** (▤)—During debugging, allows you to examine your app's threads and method-call stacks.
- **Breakpoint** (▷)—Enables you to manage your debugging breakpoints by file.
- **Report** (◁)—Allows you to browse log files created each time you build and run your app.

You choose which navigator to display by clicking the corresponding button above the **Navigator** area of the window.

13.4.2 Editor Area

To the right of the **Navigator** area is the **Editor** area for editing source code and designing UIs. This area is *always* displayed in your workspace window. When you select a file in the project navigator, its contents are displayed in the **Editor** area. There are three editors:

- The **Standard** editor (☰) shows the selected file's contents.

- The **Assistant** editor (⌾) shows the selected file's contents on the left and related file contents on the right—for example, if you're editing a class that extends another class, the **Assistant** editor will also show the superclass.

- The **Version** editor (⇄) allows you to compare different versions of the same file (e.g., old and new versions).

13.4.3 Utilities Area and Inspectors

At the right side of the workspace window is the **Utilities** area, which displays **inspectors** that allow you to view and edit information about items displayed in the **Editor** area. The set of inspectors you can choose from depends on what you're doing in Xcode. By default, the top half of the **Utilities** area shows either the **File** inspector (⬜) or the **Quick Help** inspector (⑦). The **File inspector** shows information about the currently selected file in the project. The **Quick Help inspector** provides **context-sensitive help**—documentation that's based on the currently selected item in a UI or the cursor position in the source code. For example, clicking on a method name shows a description of the method, its parameters and its return value.

13.4.4 Debug Area

When displayed, the **Debug** area appears at the bottom of the editor area and provides controls for stepping through code, inspecting variable contents and more. We discuss how to hide and show the **Navigator** area, **Utilities** area and **Debug** area momentarily.

13.4.5 Xcode Toolbar

The Xcode toolbar contains options for executing your app (Fig. 13.6(a)), a display area (Fig. 13.6(b)) that shows the progress of tasks executing in Xcode (e.g., project build status) and buttons (Fig. 13.6(c)) for hiding and showing areas in the workspace window. Figure 13.7 overviews the toolbar.

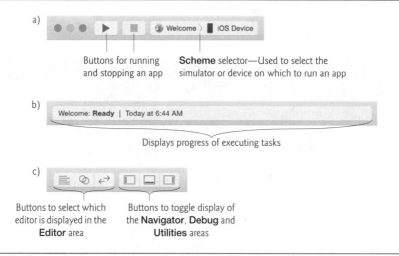

Fig. 13.6 | Xcode 6 toolbar.

Control	Description
Run	Clicking the **Run** button builds then runs the project on the currently selected simulator or device as specified in the **Scheme** selector (Fig. 13.6(a)). Clicking and holding on this button displays **Run, Test, Profile** and **Analyze** options. The **Test** option allows you to run unit tests on your app. The **Profile** option collects information about your running code to help you locate performance issues, memory leaks and more. The **Analyze** option checks your source code for potential logic errors.
Stop	Terminates the running app.
Scheme	Specifies the simulator or device on which the app will run when the **Run** button is clicked.
Editor buttons	Click one of these buttons (Fig. 13.6(c)) to specify which editor is displayed in the **Editor** area.
View buttons	Click these toggle buttons (Fig. 13.6(c)) to specify whether the **Navigator, Debug** and **Utilities** areas of the workspace window are displayed.

Fig. 13.7 | Xcode 6 toolbar elements.

13.4.6 Project Navigator

The **Project** navigator (left side of Fig. 13.5) provides access to all of a project's components. It consists of a series of groups (folders) and files. The most used group is the **project structure group**, which Xcode names the same as the project. This group contains your project's source files, media files and supporting files. The **Products** group contains the .app files for your project. The .app files execute when you test your apps and are also used to distribute your apps via the iOS app store.

13.4.7 Keyboard Shortcuts

Xcode provides many keyboard shortcuts for useful commands. Figure 13.8 shows some of the most useful ones. For the complete list, visit `http://bit.ly/XcodeShortcuts`.

Shortcut	Function	Shortcut	Function
shift + ⌘ + *N*	Create new project.	⌘ + *B*	Build project.
⌘ + *N*	Create new file in current project.	⌘ + *R*	Build and run project.
⌘ + *S*	Save current file.	*shift* + ⌘ + *K*	Clean project.

Fig. 13.8 | Common Xcode keyboard shortcuts.

13.5 Storyboarding the Welcome App's UI

Next, you'll create the **Welcome** app's UI. Recall that you configured the project as a *universal app* that runs on iPhones and iPads. The screen sizes differ on these devices. When you create a new app, Xcode creates a `.storyboard` file that you use to design UIs that are appropriate for the user-interface idiom of each type of device. The **Welcome** app you'll build here simply displays text and an image. In Chapter 14, you'll build an iOS app that contains Swift code. At that point we'll introduce other features of Interface Builder and storyboards that enable you to interact with your UIs programmatically.

13.5.1 Configuring the App for Portrait and Landscape Orientations

As you know, users can hold their devices in *portrait* (long edge vertical) or *landscape* (long edge horizontal) orientation. Many apps support *both* orientations by rearranging their UIs, depending on the current device orientation. You'll support *both* orientations in this app, which is the default.

To view the orientation settings, select the **Welcome** project in the **Project** navigator. This displays the project's settings in the **Editor** area (Fig. 13.9). In the **Deployment Info** section under **Device Orientation**, ensure that **Portrait, Landscape Left** and **Landscape Right** are selected as shown in Fig. 13.9—these are the default settings for supported orientations. Notice that **Upside Down** is *not* selected. If the phone is upside down when the user receives a call, it's more difficult to answer the phone. For this reason, Apple recommends that you *do not* support the **Upside Down** orientation in iPhone apps. With the exception of the **Upside Down** orientation for iPhones, Apple recommends supporting all possible device orientations.

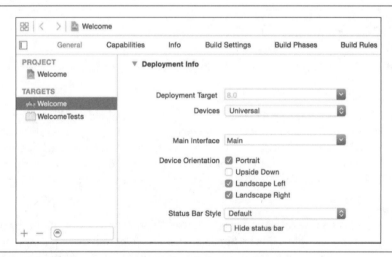

Fig. 13.9 | **Welcome** project's **Deployment Info** settings.

13.5.2 Providing an App Icon

When your app is installed on a device, its icon and name appear with all other installed apps in the iOS home screen. In this step, you'll add an app icon to the project. Due to the variety of iPhones and iPads on which iOS 8 can execute, you'll provide icons of various sizes to support the different screen sizes and resolutions. If you do not provide an icon for a particular size or if the icon you provide is not the correct size, Xcode will provide warnings.

Asset Catalog

Scroll down to the **App Icons and Launch Images** section in the settings, then click the ⊕ icon to the right of **App Icons Source** (or click the project's Images.xcassets group) to display the **asset catalog** (Fig. 13.10), which manages image resources that require different resolutions for different devices. iOS automatically chooses the appropriate image from an image set based on the device running the app and the context in which the icon is used— that is, in the iOS **Settings** app, in **Spotlight** search or as the app's icon on the home screen.

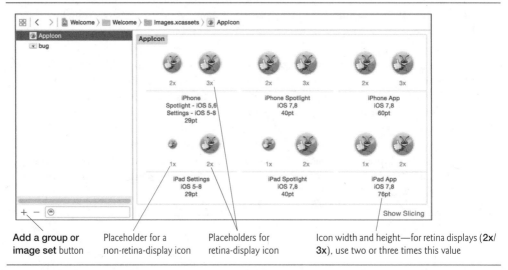

Fig. 13.10 | Asset catalog with **AppIcon** image set selected and the app icons specified.

Icon Placeholders

By default, the **AppIcon** image set is selected and empty placeholders are displayed for the various iPhone and iPad app icons. Each is labeled **1x**, **2x** or **3x**. These represent non-retina-display (**1x**) and retina-display (**2x** or **3x**) devices with difference pixel densities. The measurements are in points. For **1x** icons the relationship is one point = one pixel, for **2x** it's one point = two pixels and for **3x** (the iPhone 6 Plus) it's one point = three pixels.

Icon Sizes

Below the **1x**, **2x** or **3x** the asset catalog provides additional information about the purpose of a given icon. For example, **iPhone Spotlight, iOS 7, 8, 40pt** indicates an icon that would appear in the Spotlight search results on iPhones running iOS 7 or iOS 8. Such an icon must be 40 points (**40pt**) wide and tall. For a placeholder that's labeled **1x**, you provide an icon of the specified size. If that icon is labeled **2x** or **3x**, you provide an image that's two or three times the specified size—80 or 120 points wide and tall, respectively.

Adding the Icons to the Asset Catalog

Open a Finder window and locate the images folder provided with the book's examples, then drag the various Deitelorange icons onto each the asset catalog's placeholders so that the image set appears as shown in Fig. 13.10. Each image file we provided is square (e.g., 29-by-29, 40-by-40, etc.). Place the images as follows:

- For each placeholder labeled **1x** use the image that's named with the listed resolution—for example, use `DeitelOrange_29x29.png` for a placeholder that indicates **29pt** and use `DeitelOrange_76x76.png` for a placeholder that indicates **76pt**.

- For each placeholder labeled **2x** or **3x** use the image that's named with *two* or *three* times the required resolution—for example, use `DeitelOrange_80x80.png` and `DeitelOrange_120x120.png`, respectively, for a placeholder that indicates **40pt**.

When you save your app, these images are all placed into the `Images.xcassets` group in the project's `Welcome` group.

Launch Screen
To improve the user's experience in an app that take several seconds to load, you can also specify a launch screen that your app displays while it's loading, so the user does not see a blank screen. In prior iOS versions, the launch screen was an image. As of iOS 8, it can be a resizable UI that adjusts to fit the device on which the app is running. Xcode adds the file `launchscreen.xib` to each new project you create. This file displays your app's name in the center of the screen. Though we do not do so in this app, you can select this file, then use Interface Builder to customize it.

13.5.3 Creating an Image Set for the App's Image
As with app icons, you'll typically provide multiple versions of each image your app displays to accommodate various device sizes and pixel densities. Placing such images into the asset catalog as image sets allows iOS to choose the correct image for you based on the device resolution. To add a new image set, you can drag an image from a Finder window onto the list of image sets at the left of the asset catalog—Xcode names the image set as the image name without its filename extension and uses that image for devices with **1x** resolution. You can then provide additional images for devices with **2x** and **3x** resolution.

Open a Finder window and locate the `images` folder provided with the book's examples, then from the subfolder `Welcome` drag the `bug.png` icon onto the asset catalog's list of image sets to create the **bug** image set. The new image set appears as shown in Fig. 13.11.

Fig. 13.11 | Asset catalog with **bug** image set selected.

We provided one image for all iOS devices. Images do not always scale well, so it's generally better to provide customized images.

13.5.4 Overview of the Storyboard and the Xcode Utilities Area

You design an app's UI in its storyboard. In the **Project** navigator, select the file `Main.storyboard` in the **Project** navigator to open the storyboard in the **Editor** area (Fig. 13.12). In a storyboard, each *screen* of information is represented as a **scene**—designated by a white rectangular area. For this app, we'll focus on manipulating UI components in the scene. In Chapter 3, we'll begin discussing other Interface Builder features that help you implement your app's logic for responding to user interactions.

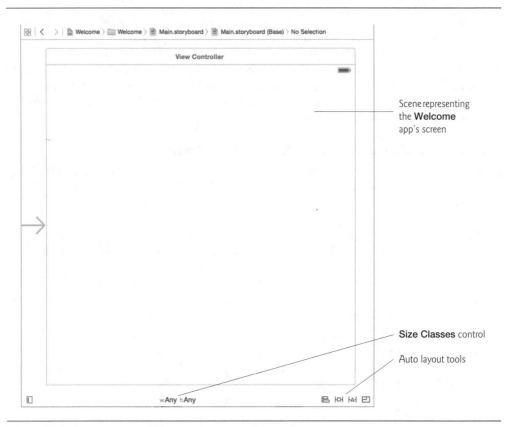

Fig. 13.12 | `Main.storyboard` displayed in the **Editor** area.

Size Classes and Auto Layout Tools
iOS apps can currently execute on iPhones and iPads, and there will be other devices in the future, such as the Apple Watch. On current iOS devices, users can view your apps in either portrait or landscape orientation. At the bottom of Interface Builder are tools for specifying the scene's size classes and the auto layout properties for the scene's UI. **Size classes** help you design scenes for these different screen sizes and orientations. By default, the scene is configured for **Any** width and **Any** height, meaning that the scene is designed for any iOS device

and any device orientation. The **Any/Any** scene is 600-by-600 pixels. Our book *iOS 8 for Programmers* shows how to use size classes to customize scenes so that they display differently based on the device size and orientation. The auto layout tools enable you to specify how UI components adjust their sizes and positions based on a device's size and orientation.

Library *Window*

Once the storyboard is displayed, the bottom part of the **Utilities** area shows the **Library** window (Fig. 13.13), which contains four library tabs:

- **File Template** (📄)—Common file types for quickly adding files to a project.

- **Code Snippet** ({})—Code snippets for quickly inserting and customizing commonly used code, such as control statements, exception handling and more. You can also create your own code snippets.

- **Object** (⊙)—Standard Cocoa Touch UI components for designing iOS apps. A key component of Cocoa Touch is the **UIKit framework**, which contains the UI components we use here and in Chapter 14. You can also learn more at

```
http://bit.ly/CocoaTouch
```

- **Media** (🖼)—The project's media resources (images, audios and videos).

You drag and drop UI components from the **Object** library tab to add them to your scene.

Fig. 13.13 | **Utilities** area showing **Quick Help** and the **Library** window with the **Object** library selected.

13.5.5 Adding an Image View to the UI

You'll now begin customizing the app's UI. First, you'll add the **Image View** that will display the bug.png image. In Cocoa Touch, images are usually displayed by an object of class UIImageView.

1. In the **Library** window, ensure that the **Object** library tab (⊚) is selected, then locate **Image View** by scrolling or by typing Image View into the search field at the bottom of the window (Fig. 13.13).

2. Drag and drop an **Image View** from the **Library** onto the scene as shown in Fig. 13.14. By default, Interface Builder sizes the **Image View** to fill the scene.

Notice the dashed blue guide lines that appear as you drag the **Image View** around the scene. The guide lines suggest component spacing and alignments that help you conform to Apple's *Human Interface Guidelines (HIG)*, which include conventions for *spacing between components*, *component positioning* and *alignment*, *gestures used to interact with apps* and much more. You can learn more about the *HIG* at:

```
http://bit.ly/iOSMobileHIG
```

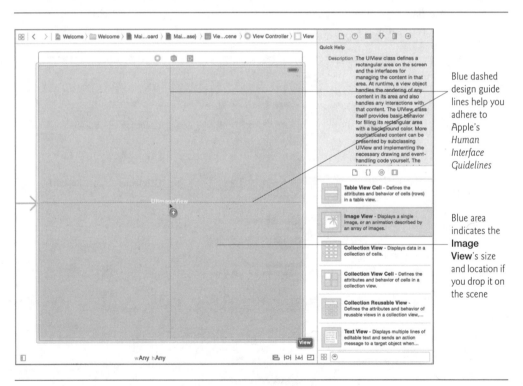

Fig. 13.14 | Dragging an **Image View** from the **Object** library onto the scene.

13.5.6 Using Inspectors to Configure the Image View

Now you'll customize the **Image View** to display bug.png. When you're designing a UI, the top of the **Utilities** area will have additional tabs for the following inspectors:

- **Identity inspector** (⊞)—Used to specify an object's class and accessibility information and to provide a name for the object that appears in the list of objects to the left of the scene design area.

- **Attributes inspector** (⬇)—Used to customize the selected object's attributes, such as the image to display in an **Image View**.

- **Size inspector** (▤)—Used to configure an object's size and position.

- **Connections inspector** (➔)—Used to create connections between code and UI components (e.g., to respond to user interactions with particular components).

In the scene, click the **Image View** you just added to select it, then perform the following steps:

1. Select the **Attributes** inspector tab (⬇) in the **Utilities** area (Fig. 13.15).

Fig. 13.15 | **Image View** attributes in the **Attributes** inspector tab of the **Utilities** area.

2. In the **Image View** section, click the drop-down arrow to the right of the **Image** field and select the bug image set that you added to the asset catalog in Section 13.5.3 as the image to display. By default, the image stretches to fill the **Image View**.

3. In the **Mode** field, select Aspect Fit to force your image to fit in the **Image View** and maintain its aspect ratio—its original width-to-height ratio.

4. Select the **Size inspector** (▤) in the **Utilities** area.

5. Change the **Height** attribute to 300 so the **Image View** occupies half the scene.

6. Change the **Y** attribute to 300 (half the scene's height), so that the **Image View**'s upper-left corner is positioned halfway down the scene. You could also drag the **Image View** to the bottom half of the scene.

The **Image View** should now appear as shown in Fig. 13.16. Interface Builder can also create the **Image View** for you and configure it to display the proper image—simply drag the image from the **Media** library onto the scene, then configure the **Image View**'s attributes. If you do this, you'll also need to resize the **Image View** by using the *sizing handles* that are displayed when the image is selected (also shown in Fig. 13.16).

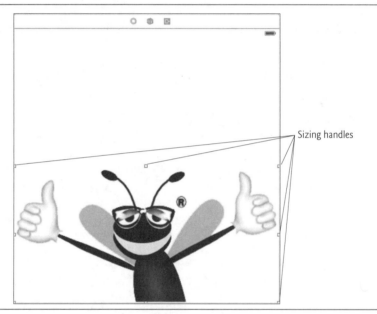

Fig. 13.16 | **Image View** configured to display bug.png.

13.5.7 Adding and Configuring the Label

To complete the scene's design, you'll now add a **Label** containing the text "Welcome to iOS App Development!". Drag and drop a **Label** from the **Object** library into the upper-left corner of the scene above the image (Fig. 13.17). Notice that a blue guide line appears to help you position the **Label**. Next, use the **Size** inspector (▤) to change the **Label**'s **Width** attribute to 600 and **Height** attribute to 300 so that the **Label** occupies the scene's top half (Fig. 13.18).

Fig. 13.17 | Adding a **Label** to the scene.

Fig. 13.18 | Resizing the **Label**.

With the **Label** selected, modify the following attributes in the **Attributes** inspector:

- **Text** attribute—replace "Label" with "Welcome to iOS App Development!". You can also set the text by double clicking the **Label**.

- **Alignment** attribute—select the middle option for *centered* alignment.

- **Lines** attribute—enter 2 for two lines of text.

- **Font** attribute—hold the up arrow to the right of this attribute until the font size is 55. This is the default maximum font size we'd like to use.

- **Autoshrink** attribute—select **Minimum Font Scale**. If the text is too large to fit in the **Label** based on the device size or orientation, iOS by default scales the text by up to half the specified font size, as indicated by the value 0.5 below **Minimum Font Scale**.

The **Label** should now appear as shown in Fig. 13.19.

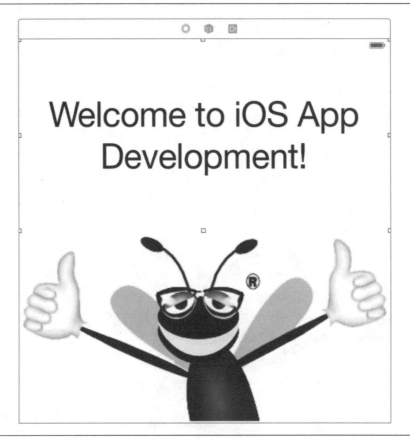

Fig. 13.19 | Welcome app scene before setting auto layout constraints.

13.5.8 Using Auto Layout to Support Different Screen Sizes and Orientations

Though the design appears to be complete, if you were to run the app now using the iOS simulator, you'd see various problems (if you'd like to run it now, see Section 13.6):

- The **Label** and **Image View** will not resize based on the device and orientation.

- On an iPhone in portrait orientation the **Label** and **Image View** will be too wide for the screen, and in landscape orientation the screen will not be tall enough to display both components.

- On an iPad, the **Label** and **Image View** will be too small to fill the screen and will be positioned at the screen's left edge.

You use *auto layout constraints* to specify how UI components are positioned relative to other components and how components should resize and reposition based on the device and device orientation. You'll use auto layout constraints in this app to ensure that the **Label** and **Image View**:

- Fill the screen horizontally regardless of the screen orientation.

- Fill the screen vertically and scale appropriately regardless of the screen orientation.

- Resize based on the device running the app and the current device orientation.

When the user rotates the device, auto layout will use these constraints as it repositions and resizes the **Label** and **Image View** based on the new orientation. To configure this app's auto layout constraints:

1. In the bottom-left corner of the storyboard, click the **Show Document Outline** (▣) button to display the document outline window (Fig. 13.20), which appears to the left of the design area. The **document outline window** shows you all of the UI components that make up your scene(s) and other features that we present in our book *iOS 8 for Programmers: An App-Driven Approach with Swift, Volume 1.*

Fig. 13.20 | Document outline window.

2. In the document outline, hold the *control* key, drag from the **Label** node (**Welcome to iOS App Development!**) to the **Top Layout Guide** node, which represents the top of the scene, then release the mouse to complete the drag—we'll refer to this operation as "*control* drag" going forward. From the popup menu that appears, select **Vertical Spacing** (Fig. 13.21)—this attaches the **Label**'s top edge to the top edge of the scene so the **Label** *always* appears at the top. Because the **Label** is already positioned at the top, this creates an auto layout constraint requiring 0 points of space between the **Label**'s top edge and the **Top Layout Guide**.

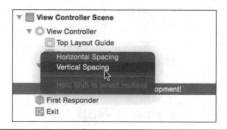

Fig. 13.21 | Document outline.

3. *Control* drag from the **Image View** (bug) node to the **Bottom Layout Guide** node. From the popup menu, select **Vertical Spacing**—this attaches the **Image View**'s bottom edge to the bottom edge of the scene so the **Image View** *always* appears at the bottom. Because the **Image View** is already positioned at the bottom, this cre-

ates an auto layout constraint requiring 0 points of space between the **Image View**'s bottom edge and the **Bottom Layout Guide**.

4. In a **Single View Application**, the scene has a root **View** that contains the scene's other UI components—in this case the **Label** and **Image View** (nested below the **View** node in the document outline). In this app, the **Label** and **Image View** should each have the **View**'s width, which changes depending on the device and orientation. To accomplish this, you'll attach these components to the **View**'s leading and trailing edges. In left-to-right languages, the leading edge is at the left and the trailing edge is at the right. In right-to-left languages, this is reversed. This is an iOS *internationalization* feature that enables iOS to adapt your UIs based on the user's spoken language.

    Next, *control* drag from the **Label** node to the **View** node, and select **Leading Space to Container Margin**, then *control* drag from the **Label** node to the **View** node and select **Trailing Space to Container Margin**. The **Label** is already the same width as the **View** (based on the settings in Section 13.5.7), so this creates auto layout constraints that require the **Label**'s left and right edges to be 0 points from the **View**'s left and right edges, respectively. Repeat this step for the **Image View**.

5. We'd like the **Label** and **Image View** to each occupy half the screen's height and to scale based on the screen size and orientation. To accomplish this, we'll indicate that they should have equal heights and that there should be a fixed amount of space between them vertically. *Control* drag from the **Label** to the **Image View** and select **Equal Heights**. Next, *control* drag from the **Label** to the **Image View** and select **Vertical Spacing**. Because there is no space between the components based on the prior design steps, this creates an auto layout constraint that requires the **Label**'s bottom edge to be 0 points from the **Image View**'s top edge.

The constraints set in *Step 5* above—combined with the **Label**'s vertical spacing constraint to the **Top Layout Guide** and the **Image Views**'s vertical spacing constraint to the **Bottom Layout Guide**—ensure that these components each occupy 50% of the screen's height and scale based on the device and orientation.

Optional: Viewing the Constraints
You can view the complete list of constraints Xcode created by expanding the **Constraints** node in the document outline's **View** node. If you select a constraint, you can view and manipulate its attributes with the inspectors in the **Utilities** area. Also, if you select a UI component, you can view all of the constraints applied to it in the **Size** inspector, and you can click each constraint's **Edit** link to modify the constraint.

13.6 Running the Welcome App

In this section, we discuss running the app on the iOS simulator and on an iOS device. To test on a device, you must be a member of the fee-based iOS Developer Program—see the Before You Begin section of this book for more information.

13.6.1 Testing on the iOS Simulator
You'll now execute the app using the iOS simulator.

1. Click the **Scheme** selector (Fig. 13.6(a)) on the Xcode toolbar to display the list of iOS simulators and devices on which you can test the app (Fig. 13.22). As you can see, there are various simulators that you can use including resizable simulators in which you can specify different widths and heights so you can see how your app's UI dynamically adjusts.

Fig. 13.22 | List of iOS simulators and devices in the Scheme selector.

2. Select **iPhone 6** to indicate that you'd like to test the app on a simulator configured based on the size and features of an iPhone 6 device.

3. Click the **Run** (▶) button on the Xcode toolbar, select **Run** from the **Product** menu or type ⌘ + *R*. This builds the project, installs the **Welcome** app in the **iPhone 6** simulator and runs the app. Initially, the app is displayed in portrait orientation (Fig. 13.23(a)). Depending on your computer's screen size, the simulator window

a) App running in portrait orientation

b) App running in landscape orientation

Fig. 13.23 | **Welcome** app running on the iPhone simulator in portrait and landscape modes.

might be too tall to show the entire app. In this case, use the simulator's **Window > Scale** menu to scale the simulator window to a smaller size.

4. To change the device orientation, select **Hardware > Rotate Left** or **Hardware > Rotate Right**. Figure 13.23(b) shows the app running in landscape orientation. While your app is running, the **Stop** (■) button in Xcode is enabled. Clicking **Stop** terminates the app, but leaves the simulator running. You can click the app's icon on the simulator's home screen to re-run the app in the Simulator.

5. To run the app on the iPad simulator, choose **iPad Air** from the **Scheme** selector, then run the app. Figure 13.24 shows the app executing in the iPad simulator.

a) Running on the iPad simulator in portrait orientation

b) Running on the iPad simulator in landscape orientation

Fig. 13.24 | **Welcome** app running on the iPad simulator in portrait and landscape modes.

13.6.2 Testing on a Device (for Paid Apple iOS Developer Program Members Only)

To test your app on an iOS device, you must first set up your paid developer account in Xcode.

1. Select **Xcode > Preferences...**.

2. Click the **Accounts** tab.

3. Click the **+** button and select **Add Apple ID...**.

4. Enter your Apple ID and password, then click **Add**.

Next, connect the iOS device to your computer. Once connected, the device will show up in Xcode's **Scheme** selector. Choose your device, then run the app. If the device has not yet been added to your developer account, Xcode will assume you want to use the device for testing and will handle the details of adding the device to your developer account for you. Then Xcode will build the app, install it onto your device and run it. Try rotating the device to see how the app adjusts to portrait and landscape orientations.

13.7 Making Your App Accessible

iOS contains various *accessibility* features to help people with various disabilities use their devices. For people with visual and physical disabilities, iOS's VoiceOver can speak the screen text (such as the text on a **Label** or **Button**) or text that you provide to help the user understand the purpose of a UI component. When VoiceOver is enabled and the user touches an accessible UI component, VoiceOver speaks the accessibility text associated with the component. All UIKit framework components support accessibility and many have it enabled by default. For example, when the user touches a **Label**, VoiceOver speaks the **Label**'s text. VoiceOver can be enabled in the **Settings** app under **General > Accessibility**. From there, you can also set the **Accessibility Shortcut** to **VoiceOver** so that you can triple click the device's *Home* button to toggle VoiceOver on and off. VoiceOver is *not* currently supported in the iOS simulator, so you must run this app on a device to hear VoiceOver speak the text. However, in the simulator you can use the **Accessibility Inspector** to view the text that VoiceOver will speak, as you'll see in Section 13.7.2.

13.7.1 Enabling Accessibility for the Image View

The Xcode **Identity** (▣) inspector's **Accessibility** section enables you to provide descriptive text that VoiceOver can speak when the user selects a given component. In the **Welcome** app, we don't need more descriptive text for the **Label**, because VoiceOver will read the **Label**'s content. Accessibility is *not* enabled by default for **Image Views**, so we'll show how to enable it and provide descriptive text for the **Image View** in the storyboard. Perform the following steps:

1. In Xcode, select `Main.storyboard` in the **Project** navigator.

2. Select the **Image View** in the scene.

3. Click the **Identity** inspector's icon (▣) in the **Utilities** area, then scroll to the **Accessibility** section (Fig. 13.25). The **Image** and **User Interaction Enabled** checkboxes are selected by default, but are used only if accessibility is enabled.

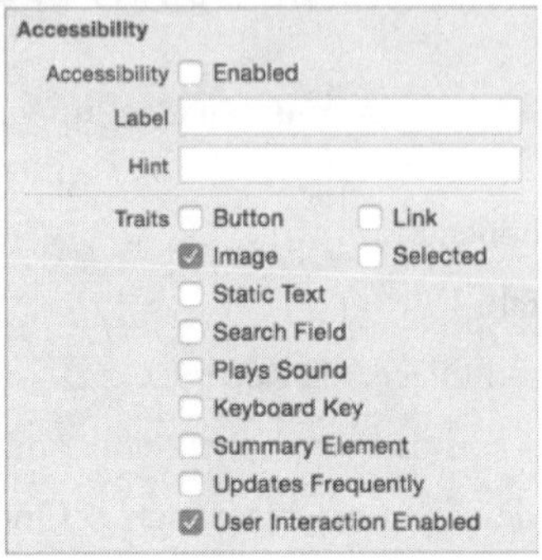

Fig. 13.25 | Accessibility section of the **Identity** inspector.

4. Select the **Enabled** checkbox to enable accessibility for the **Image View**.

5. The **Label** provides a brief description of the UI component. In the **Label** field, enter "Deitel logo".

6. If a more detailed description is required to help the user understand the UI component's purpose, you can enter a string in the **Hint** field. Enter "Deitel double-thumbs-up bug logo" there now.

7. Save the storyboard.

Run this app on a device with VoiceOver enabled, then touch the **Label** or the **Image View** to hear VoiceOver speak the corresponding text.

Some apps dynamically generate UI components in response to user interactions. For such UI components, you can programmatically set the accessibility text using properties from the **UIAccessibility** protocol.

13.7.2 Confirming Accessibility Text with the Simulator's Accessibility Inspector a

If you're not a paid member of the iOS Developer Program, you can use the simulator's **Accessibility Inspector** to ensure that your accessibility text is set correctly. To do so:

1. With the app running in a simulator, select **Hardware > Home** from the simulator's menus to return to the simulator's home screen. If there are multiple pages of apps, you can "swipe" left or right by dragging the mouse in the appropriate direction.

2. Locate and open the **Settings** app, then navigate to **General > Accessibility**.

3. Enable the **Accessibility Inspector**. This opens an **Accessibility Inspector** window that hovers over what's currently displayed on the simulator's screen (Fig. 13.26(a)).

4. Next, select **Hardware > Home** to return to the home screen. You'll notice that you cannot swipe left or right with the mouse. To allow normal navigation in the simulator, click the **x** button in the upper-left corner of the **Accessibility Inspector** to minimize it. Then locate and run the **Welcome** app, and click the **x** button again to expand the **Accessibility Inspector**.

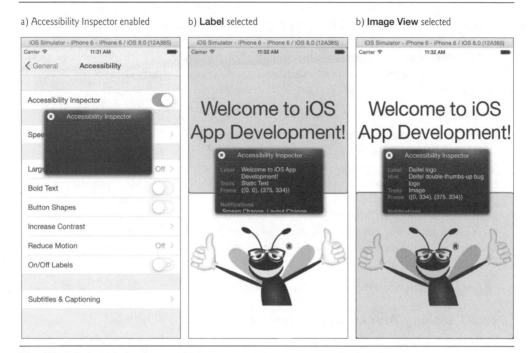

a) Accessibility Inspector enabled   b) **Label** selected   b) **Image View** selected

Fig. 13.26 | iOS simulator with the **Accessibility Inspector** displayed.

5. Click the **Label** to view its accessibility text. The simulator highlights the entire **Label** and displays its accessibility information (Fig. 13.26(b))—the text in the **Accessibility Inspector**'s **Label** line is what VoiceOver will speak on a device.

6. Click the **Image View** to view its accessibility text. The simulator highlights the **Image View** and displays its accessibility information, including both the **Label** and the **Hint** that you added earlier in this section (Fig. 13.26(c))—VoiceOver will first speak the text in the **Accessibility Inspector**'s **Label** line, followed by the **Hint** text (if any).

13.8 Internationalizing Your App

To reach the largest possible audience with your apps, consider customizing them for various locales and spoken languages. Preparing your app to do this is known as **internationalization**, and creating the resources for each locale (such as text in different languages) is know as **localization**.

Using auto layout to design your UI is a key part of internationalization—when used correctly, auto layout enables iOS to present your UI in a manner appropriate for each locale. For example, a UI arranged left-to-right for some languages (e.g., English, French, Spanish, etc.) would typically be arranged right-to-left for others (e.g., Arabic, Hebrew, etc.).

Another important aspect of internationalization is preparing your string resources so that iOS can replace them with appropriate translated strings for the user's locale. Xcode now supports XLIFF (XML Localization Interchange File Format) files for managing localized string resources. XLIFF is a standard XML representation for localizable data. As you'll see, Xcode can export an XLIFF file containing all of your app's localizable text. You provide this file to a translator and then import the translated XLIFF file. When your app executes on devices with different locale settings, iOS automatically chooses the correct string resources for that locale. You can learn more about XLIFF at

```
http://en.wikipedia.org/wiki/XLIFF
```

By default, each app you create uses **base internationalization**—the string resources in your app are separated from your storyboard and used as a template for providing localized strings for other languages. The language you use during development (in our case, English) is known as your app's **base language**. If you don't provide strings in the appropriate language for a given locale, iOS uses the *base language* strings by default.

In this section, we'll demonstrate how to provide Spanish strings for the **Welcome** app's **Label** and for its **Image View**'s accessibility strings. Then, we'll demonstrate how to test the app for a Spanish locale. See Apple's *Internationalization and Localization Guide* for more information:

```
http://bit.ly/iOSInternationalization
```

13.8.1 Locking Your UI During Translation

Localization is best performed once you've completed your app's UI or when it's nearly complete. Each UI component has a unique ID that's used as part of the internationalization and localization process—if these IDs change (e.g., when you add/remove UI components), then Xcode will not be able to apply the localized string resources properly and some of your UI components might not have localized string resources.

If you're still developing your app and want to have your string resources translated in parallel, you can *lock* your UI components for an entire storyboard or individually so they cannot be modified accidentally. There are four locking options:

- **Nothing**—You can modify all of a UI component's properties.

- **All Properties**—You can't modify any of a UI component's properties.

- **Localizable Properties**—You can't modify a UI component's localizable properties (e.g., the text of a **Label** or the accessibility **Label** and **Hint** for a given UI component). You'd use this option to continue working on your UI while you wait for translated resources that you can import into your app project.

- **Non-localizable Properties**—You can modify only a UI component's localizable properties. You'd use this option when importing translated resources to ensure that you don't modify non-localizable properties accidentally.

If you wish to lock storyboard components:

1. Select the storyboard in the **Project** navigator.

2. Select **Editor > Localization Locking**, then select one of the locking options.

If you wish to lock a specific UI component:

1. Select the UI component in your storyboard.

2. In the **Identity** inspector's **Document** category, change the value of the **Lock** attribute. (For your reference, the UI component's unique ID is also shown in the **Identity** inspector's **Document** category.)

13.8.2 Exporting Your UI's String Resources

You'll now create an XLIFF file containing the app's string resources. You'll provide a copy of this file—renamed to indicate the locale it represents—to the person responsible for translating the strings. Perform the following steps:

1. Select your app in the Xcode **Project** navigator.

2. Select **Editor > Export for Localization…**, specify where to save the XLIFF file (outside your project's folders) and click **Save**. By default, Xcode creates a folder with your app's name and places the file en.xliff in that folder.

The filename depends on your app's base language—for our apps this is English, so the language ID en is used. You can see the complete list of language and locale IDs at:

```
http://bit.ly/iOSLanguageLocaleIDs
```

Xcode extracts the localizable strings from all the files in your project (not just the ones in the storyboard) and places them in the XLIFF file. For this demonstration, we'll discuss only the strings in the storyboard. Figure 13.27 shows the portion of the generated XLIFF file that corresponds to Main.storyboard (reformatted for readability). Lines 8–12 represent the **Label**'s string, lines 13–17 represent the **Image View**'s accessibility **Hint** string and lines 18–22 represent the **Image View**'s accessibility **Label** string. The unique IDs that Xcode assigned to the **Label** and **Image View** are highlighted—these must not be modified in the translated XLIFF file; otherwise, Xcode will not know what the corresponding strings apply to. The original source strings are specified in lines 9, 14 and 19.

```
1   <file original="Welcome/Base.lproj/Main.storyboard" source-language="en"
2      datatype="plaintext">
3      <header>
4         <tool tool-id="com.apple.dt.xcode" tool-name="Xcode"
5            tool-version="6.0" build-num="6A280e"/>
6      </header>
7      <body>
8         <trans-unit id="GCg-Ah-7Id.text">
9            <source>Welcome to iOS App Development!</source>
10           <note>Class = "IBUILabel"; text = "Welcome to iOS App
11              Development!"; ObjectID = "GCg-Ah-7Id";</note>
12        </trans-unit>
13        <trans-unit id="waJ-nz-oow.accessibilityHint">
14           <source>Deitel double-thumbs-up bug logo</source>
15           <note>Class = "IBUIImageView"; accessibilityHint = "Deitel
16              double-thumbs-up bug logo"; ObjectID = "waJ-nz-oow";</note>
17        </trans-unit>
```

Fig. 13.27 | Portion of the XLIFF file that corresponds to Main.storyboard. (Part 1 of 2.)

```
18          <trans-unit id="waJ-nz-oow.accessibilityLabel">
19             <source>Deitel logo</source>
20             <note>Class = "IBUIImageView"; accessibilityLabel =
21                "Deitel logo"; ObjectID = "waJ-nz-oow";</note>
22          </trans-unit>
23        </body>
24    </file>
```

Fig. 13.27 | Portion of the XLIFF file that corresponds to `Main.storyboard`. (Part 2 of 2.)

13.8.3 Translating the String Resources

Next, you'll make a copy of the `en.xliff` and add the Spanish language strings:

1. In Finder, locate the `en.xliff` file you created in Section 13.8.2, make a copy of it and rename it `es.xliff` (es is the language ID for Spanish).

2. Double click the `es.xliff` file to open it in Xcode.

3. In the XML, locate line 1 from Fig. 13.27 and modify it to include the XLIFF's `target-language` attribute. This tells Xcode which locale's strings the file represents. The line should now appear as follows.

    ```
    <file original="Welcome/Base.lproj/Main.storyboard"
       source-language="en" target-language="es" datatype="plaintext">
    ```

4. Locate line 9 from Fig. 13.27, insert a blank line after it and enter the translated string resource:

    ```
    <target>¡Bienvenido al Desarrollo de App iOS!</target>
    ```

5. Locate line 14 from Fig. 13.27, insert a blank line after it and enter the translated string resource:

    ```
    <target>El logo de Deitel que tiene el insecto con dedos pulgares
       hacia arriba</target>
    ```

6. Finally, locate line 19 from Fig. 13.27, insert a blank line after it and enter the translated string resource:

    ```
    <target>Logo de Deitel</target>
    ```

7. Save and close the file.

13.8.4 Importing the Translated String Resources

Next, you'll import the XLIFF file containing the app's Spanish string resources.

1. Select your app in the Xcode **Project** navigator.

2. Select **Editor > Import Localizations…**, locate the `es.xliff` file and click **Open**.

3. Xcode displays a sheet in which you can compare the source strings and the translated strings. In this case, it also shows several warnings, because we did not provide translated strings for various string resources (such as the app's product name that appears with the app icon on a device's home screen). Click **Import** to import the Spanish strings into the project.

Xcode extracts the storyboard's translated Spanish strings from the XLIFF file and places them into a file named `Main.strings`. This file is nested in the `Main.storyboard` node in the **Project** navigator.

13.8.5 Testing the App in Spanish

To test the app in Spanish, you must change the language settings in the iOS simulator (or your device). To do so, open the simulator by selecting **Xcode > Open Developer Tool > iOS Simulator**, then perform the following steps:

1. If the home screen is not displayed, select **Hardware > Home** from the iOS simulator menu or press the *home* button on your device.

2. Locate and select the **Settings** app.

3. Select **General** then **Language & Region**.

4. Select **iPhone Language**, then select **Español** from the list of languages and press **Done**, then confirm that you'd like to change the language.

The simulator or device will change its language setting to Spanish and return to the home screen. Use Xcode to run the **Welcome** app again. Figure 13.28 shows the app running in Spanish. VoiceOver supports many spoken languages. If you run the app on a device with VoiceOver enabled, VoiceOver will speak the Spanish versions of the accessibility strings. You can also confirm your Spanish accessibility strings using the simulator's **Accessibility Inspector**, as we showed in Section 13.7.2.

Fig. 13.28 | **Welcome** app running in Spanish in the iOS simulator.

Returning the Simulator (or Your Device) to Its Original Language Settings
To return the simulator or your device back to its original language, you can perform the same steps you used in Section 13.8.5, but select **English** (or your own language). You can also return the simulator to its *default* settings. With the simulator running, select **iOS Simulator > Reset Content and Settings…**. This displays a dialog asking you to confirm the operation. If you press **Reset**, any apps you've installed on that specific simulator for testing will be removed and all of its settings will return to their original values.

13.9 Wrap-Up

In this chapter, you used Xcode to create a universal app that can run on iPhones and iPads. You used Xcode's **Single View Application** template as the foundation for your new app and learned how to configure a new project. We discussed Xcode's workspace window, its toolbar and the various items that can be displayed in its **Navigator**, **Editor**, **Utilities** and **Debug** areas. We discussed an app's supported user-interface orientations, which can consist of portrait, upside down, landscape left and landscape right orientations.

You used Xcode's Interface Builder to drag an **Image View** (an object of the Cocoa Touch class `UIImageView`) and a **Label** (an object of class `UILabel`) from the Xcode **Object** library onto a storyboard scene.

We showed how to add an app's icon images to your project's `Images.xcassets` file and how to create a new image set containing an image that could be displayed in an **Image View**. You used inspectors in the Xcode **Utilities** area to edit UI component attributes, such as the **Text** attribute of the **Label** and the **Image** attribute of the **Image View**, to customize them for your app. You also used auto layout capabilities to support various iOS devices, to ensure that the **Image View** and **Label** had the same width and height and to maintain that size relationship when the user rotates a given device.

You executed the app using the iOS simulator for the iPhone and for the iPad, and you learned how to simulate device orientation changes with the iOS Simulator's **Hardware** menu. We also showed how to run an app on an iOS device if you're a member of Apple's paid iOS Developer Program. You learned how to make the app more accessible and how to internationalize the **Welcome** app so that it could display a different welcome message based on the language settings of the user's device.

In the next chapter, you'll use Swift programming to develop the **Tip Calculator** app. iOS development is a combination of UI design and Swift coding. You use Interface Builder to develop UIs visually—avoiding tedious UI programming—and Swift programming to specify the behavior of your apps.

The **Tip Calculator** app calculates a range of tip possibilities when given a restaurant bill amount. You'll once again build a **Single View Application** and design its UI using Interface Builder and a storyboard, as you did in this chapter. You'll also add Swift code to specify how the app should respond to user interactions and display the tip calculation results.

iOS 8 App Development: Tip Calculator App

Introducing Swift, Text Fields, Sliders, Outlets, Actions, View Controllers, Event Handling, NSDecimalNumber, NSNumberFormatter and Automatic Reference Counting

Objectives

In this chapter you'll:

- Use Swift to develop an app.

- Use NSDecimalNumbers to perform precise monetary calculations.

- Create locale-specific currency and percentage Strings with NSNumberFormatter.

- Use Text Fields and Sliders to receive user input.

- Programmatically manipulate UI components via outlets.

- Respond to user-interface events with actions.

- Understand the basics of automatic reference counting (ARC).

- Execute an interactive iOS app.

14.1 Introduction

The **Tip Calculator** app (Fig. 14.1(a)) calculates and displays possible tips and bill totals for a restaurant bill amount. As you enter each digit of an amount by touching the *numeric keypad*, the app calculates and displays the tip amount and total bill amount for a 15% tip and a custom tip (Fig. 14.1(b)). You specify the custom tip percentage by moving a **Slider**'s *thumb*—this updates the custom tip percentage **Label**s and displays the custom tip and bill total in the righthand column of yellow **Label**s below the **Slider** (Fig. 14.1(b). We chose 18% as the default custom percentage, because many restaurants in the U.S. add this tip percentage for parties of six people or more, but you can easily change this.

First, you'll test-drive the app in the iOS simulator to see it in action. Then, we'll overview the technologies used to build the app. Next, you'll build the app's UI using Interface Builder. As you'll see, Interface Builder's visual tools can be used to connect UI components to the app's code so that you can manipulate the corresponding UI components programmatically and respond to user interactions with them.

For this app, you'll write Swift code that responds to user interactions and programmatically updates the UI. You'll use Swift object-oriented programming capabilities, including objects, classes, inheritance, methods and properties, as well as various data types, operators, control statements and keywords. We'll present the app's complete source code and do a detailed code walkthrough, reviewing the Swift language features that we use as we encounter them.

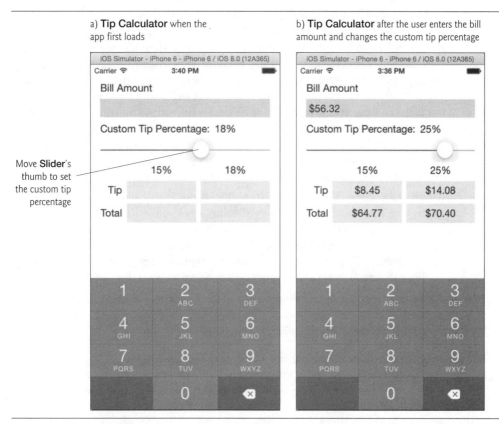

a) **Tip Calculator** when the app first loads

b) **Tip Calculator** after the user enters the bill amount and changes the custom tip percentage

Move **Slider**'s thumb to set the custom tip percentage

Fig. 14.1 | **Tip Calculator** when the app first loads, then after the user enters the bill amount and changes the custom tip percentage.

14.2 Test-Driving the Tip Calculator App in the iPhone and iPad Simulators

In this section, you'll run and interact with the **Tip Calculator** app.

Test-Driving the Completed Application Using the iOS Simulator

The following steps show you how to test-drive the app:

1. *Locating the app folder.* Open a **Finder** window and navigate to the folder containing the book's examples.

2. *Opening the TipCalculator project.* Open the TipCalculator folder, then double click the file name TipCalculator.xcodeproj to open the project in Xcode.

3. *Launching the Tip Calculator app.* In Xcode, click the **Scheme** selector to the right of the **Run** and **Stop** buttons in the upper-left corner of the Xcode IDE, then select the **iPhone 6** simulator. Next, click the **Run** button (or type ⌘ + R) to run the app in the simulator.

4. *Entering a Bill Total.* Enter the bill total 56.32 by touching numbers on the displayed numeric keypad. If you make a mistake, press the delete button (⊗) in the bottom-right corner of the keypad to erase the last digit you entered. The keypad does *not* contain a decimal point. Each time you touch a digit or delete one, the app reads what you've entered so far and converts it to a number, divides the value by 100 and displays the result in the blue **Label** with two digits to the right of the decimal point, and calculates and updates the various tip and total amounts that are displayed. This app uses iOS's *locale-specific currency formatting* capabilities to display monetary values formatted for the user's current locale. For the U.S. locale, as you enter the four digits, the bill total is displayed successively as $0.05, $0.56, $5.63 and $56.32, respectively.

5. *Selecting a Custom Tipping Percentage.* The **Slider** allows you to select a custom percentage, and the **Labels** in the right column below the **Slider** display the corresponding tip and the total bill. Drag the **Slider**'s thumb to the right until the custom percentage reads **25%**. As you drag the thumb, the **Slider**'s value continuously changes. The app updates the custom tip percentage, amount and total accordingly for each **Slider** value until you release the thumb (Fig. 14.1(b)).

6. *Closing the app.* Close your running app by clicking the *Home* button on the simulator, or by clicking the **Stop** button in Xcode or by selecting **iOS Simulator > Quit iOS Simulator** from the menu bar.

Test-Driving the Completed Application Using the iPad Simulator
To test-drive the app using the iPad simulator, click the **Scheme** selector, then select the **iPad Air** simulator. Next, click the **Run** button to run the app in the simulator.

14.3 Technologies Overview

This section reviews the Xcode, Interface Builder and Swift features you'll use to build the **Tip Calculator** app.

14.3.1 Swift Programming

The app's code uses Swift data types, operators, control statements and keywords, and other language features, including functions, overloaded operators, type inference, variables, constants and more. We'll use Swift object-oriented programming features, including objects, classes, inheritance, methods and properties.

14.3.2 Swift Apps and the Cocoa Touch® Frameworks

A great strength of iOS 8 is its rich set of prebuilt components that you can *reuse* rather than "reinventing the wheel." These capabilities are grouped into iOS's **Cocoa Touch frameworks**. These powerful libraries help you create apps that meet Apple's requirements for the look-and-feel of iOS apps. The frameworks are written mainly in Objective-C (some are written in C). Apple has indicated that new frameworks will be developed in Swift.

Foundation Framework
The Foundation framework includes classes for basic types, storing data, working with text and strings, file-system access, calculating differences in dates and times, inter-app notifica-

tions and much more. In this app, you'll use Foundation's `NSDecimalNumber` and `NSNumberFormatter` classes. Foundation's class names begin with the prefix `NS`, because this framework originated in the NextStep operating system.

UIKit Framework

Cocoa Touch's **UIKit** framework includes multi-touch UI components appropriate for mobile apps, event handling (that is, responding to user interactions with the UI) and more.

Other Cocoa Touch Frameworks

Figure 14.2 lists the Cocoa Touch frameworks. We present features from many of these frameworks in *iOS 8 for Programmers: An App-Driven Approach with Swift*. For more information on these frameworks, see the *iOS Developer Library Reference*.

```
http://developer.apple.com/ios
```

List of Cocoa Touch frameworks				
Cocoa Touch	AssetsLibrary	OpenAL	CoreLocation	Social
Layer	AudioToolbox	OpenGLES	CoreMedia	StoreKit
AddressBookUI	AudioUnit	Photos	CoreMotion	SystemConfig-
EventKitUI	CoreAudio	QuartzCore	CoreTelephony	uration
GameKit	CoreGraphics	SceneKit	EventKit	UIAutomation
MapKit	CoreImage	SpriteKit	Foundation	WebKit
MessageUI	CoreMIDI		HealthKit	
Notification-	CoreText	***Core Services***	HomeKit	***Core OS Layer***
Center	CoreVideo	***Layer***	JavaScriptCore	Accelerate
PhotosUI	GLKit	Accounts	MobileCore-	CoreBluetooth
Twitter	GameController	AdSupport	Services	ExternalAccessory
UIKit	ImageIO	AddressBook	Multipeer-	LocalAuthen-
iAd	MediaAccess-	CFNetwork	Connectivity	tication
	ibility	CloudKit	NewsstandKit	Security
Media Layer	MediaPlayer	CoreData	PassKit	System
AVFoundation	Metal	CoreFoundation	QuickLook	

Fig. 14.2 | List of Cocoa Touch frameworks.

14.3.3 Using the UIKit and Foundation Frameworks in Swift Code

To use UIKit framework classes (or classes from any other existing framework), you must **import** the framework into each source-code file that uses it (as we do in Section 14.7.1). This exposes the framework's capabilities so that you can access them in Swift code. In addition to UIKit framework UI components, this app also uses various classes from the Foundation framework, such as `NSDecimalNumber` and `NSNumberFormatter`. We do not `import` the Foundation framework—its features are available to your code because the UIKit framework indirectly imports the Foundation framework.

14.3.4 Creating Labels, a Text Field and a Slider with Interface Builder

You'll again use Interface Builder and auto layout to design this app's UI, which consists of Labels for displaying information, a Slider for selecting a custom tip percentage and a Text Field for receiving the user input. Several Labels are configured identically—we'll show how to duplicate components in Interface Builder, so you can build UIs faster. Labels, the Slider and the Text Field are objects of classes `UILabel`, `UISlider` and `UITextField`, respectively, and are part the UIKit framework that's included with each app project you create.

14.3.5 View Controllers

Each *scene* you define is managed by a **view controller** object that determines what information is displayed. iPad apps sometimes use multiple view controllers in one scene to make better use of the larger screen size. Each scene represents a *view* that contains the UI components displayed on the screen. The view controller also specifies how user interactions with the scene are processed. Class `UIViewController` defines the basic view controller capabilities. Each view controller you create (or that's created when you base a new app on one of Xcode's app templates) inherits from `UIViewController` or one of its subclasses. In this app, Xcode creates the class `ViewController` to manage the app's scene, and you'll place additional code into that class to implement the **Tip Calculator**'s logic.

14.3.6 Linking UI Components to Your Swift Code

Properties

You'll use Interface Builder to generate *properties* in your view controller for programmatically interacting with the app's UI components. Swift classes may contain variable properties and constant properties. Variable properties are read/write and are declared with the **var** keyword. Constant properties, which cannot be modified after they're initialized, are read-only and are declared with **let**. These keywords can also be used to declare local and global variables and constants. A variable property defines a *getter* and a *setter* that allow you to obtain and modify a property's value, respectively. A constant property defines only a *getter* for obtaining its value.

@IBOutlet Properties

Each property for programmatically interacting with a UI component is prefixed with `@IBOutlet`. This tells Interface Builder that the property is an **outlet**. You'll use Interface Builder to *connect* a UI control to its corresponding outlet in the view controller using *drag-and-drop* techniques. Once connected, the view controller can manipulate the corresponding UI component programmatically. `@IBOutlet` properties are *variable* properties so they can be modified to refer to the UI controls when the storyboard creates them.

Action Methods

When you interact with a UI component (e.g., touching a **Slider** or entering text in a **Text Field**), a user-interface *event* occurs. The view controller handles the event with an **action**—an *event-handling method* that specifies what to do when the event occurs. Each action is annotated with `@IBAction` in your view controller's class. `@IBAction` indicates to Interface Builder that a method can respond to user interactions with UI components. You'll use Interface Builder to visually *connect* an action to a specific user-interface event using *drag-and-drop* techniques.

14.3.7 Performing Tasks After a View Loads

When a user launches the **Tip Calculator:**

- Its main storyboard is loaded.
- The UI components are created.
- An object of the app's initial view controller class is instantiated.
- Using information stored in the storyboard, the view controller's @IBOutlets and @IBActions are connected to the appropriate UI components.

In this app, we have only one view-controller, because the app has only one scene. After the storyboard's objects are created, iOS calls the view controller's **viewDidLoad** method—here you perform view-specific tasks that can execute only *after* the scene's UI components exits. For example, in this app, you'll call the method **becomeFirstResponder** on the UITextField to make it the active component—as if the user touched it. You'll configure the UITextField such that when it's the *active* component, the numeric keypad is displayed in the screen's lower half. Calling becomeFirstResponder from viewDidLoad causes iOS to display the keypad immediately after the view loads. (Keypads are *not* displayed if a Bluetooth keyboard is connected to the device.) Calling this method also indicates that the UITextField is the **first responder**—the first component that will receive notification when an event occurs. iOS's **responder chain** defines the order in which components are notified that an event occurred. For the complete responder chain details, visit:

```
http://bit.ly/iOSResponderChain
```

14.3.8 Bridging Between Swift and Objective-C Types

You'll often pass Swift objects into methods of classes written in Objective-C, such as those in the Cocoa Touch classes. As we've mentioned, Swift's numeric types and its String, Array and Dictionary types can all be used in contexts where their Objective-C equivalents are expected. Similarly, the Objective-C equivalents (NSString, NSArray, NSMutableArray, NSDictionary and NSMutableDictionary), when returned to your Swift code, are automatically treated as their Swift counterparts. In this app, for example, you'll use class NSNumberFormatter to create locale-specific currency and percentage strings. These are returned from NSNumberFormatter's methods as NSString objects, but are automatically treated by Swift as objects of Swift's type String. This mechanism—known as bridging—is transparent to you.

14.4 Building the App's UI

In this section, you'll build the **Tip Calculator** UI using the techniques you learned in Chapter 13.

14.4.1 Creating the Project

As you did in Section 13.3, begin by creating a new **Single View Application** iOS project. Specify the following settings in the **Choose options for your new project** sheet:

- **Product Name:** TipCalculator.

- **Organization Name:** `Deitel and Associates, Inc.`—or you can use your own organization name.

- **Company Identifier:** `com.deitel`—or you can use your own company identifier or use `edu.self`.

- **Language**—Swift.

- **Devices: iPhone**—This app is designed for iPhones and iPod touches. The app will run on iPads, but it will fill most of the screen and be centered, as in Fig. 14.3.

After specifying the settings, click **Next**, indicate where you'd like to save your project and click **Create** to create the project.

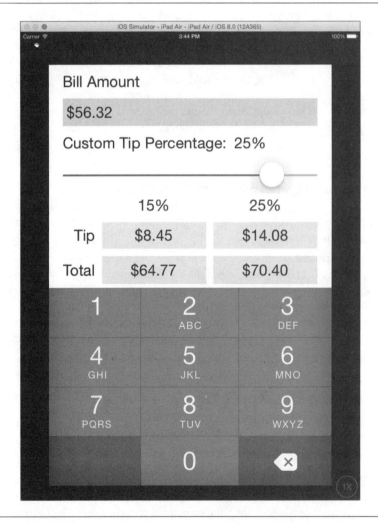

Fig. 14.3 | **Tip Calculator** running in the iPad Air simulator.

Configuring the App to Support Only Portrait Orientation
In landscape orientation, the numeric keypad would obscure parts of the **Tip Calculator**'s UI. For this reason, this app will support only portrait orientation. In the project settings' **General** tab that's displayed in the Xcode **Editor** area, scroll to the **Deployment Info** section, then for **Device Orientation** ensure that only **Portrait** is selected. Recall from Section 13.5.1 that most iPhone apps should support *portrait, landscape-left* and *landscape-right* orientations, and most iPad apps should also support *upside down* orientation. You can learn more about Apple's *Human Interface Guidelines* at:

```
http://bit.ly/HumanInterfaceGuidelines
```

14.4.2 Configuring the Size Classes for Designing a Portrait Orientation iPhone App

In Chapter 13, we designed a UI that supported both portrait and landscape orientations for any iOS device. For that purpose, we used the default size class **Any** for the design area's width and height. In this section, you'll configure the *design area* (also called the *canvas*) for a tall narrow device, such as an iPhone or iPod touch in portrait orientation. Select Main.storyboard to display the design area—also known as the canvas. At the bottom of the canvas, click the **Size Classes** control to display the size classes tool, then click in the lower-left corner to specify the size classes **Compact Width** and **Regular Height** (Fig. 14.4).

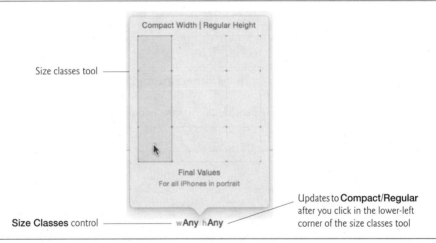

Fig. 14.4 | Size classes tool with **Compact Width** and **Regular Height** selected.

14.4.3 Adding the UI Components

In this section, you'll add and arrange the UI components to create the basic design. In Section 14.4.4, you'll add auto layout constraints to complete the design.

Step 1: Adding the "Bill Amount" Label
First, you'll add the "Bill Amount" **Label** to the UI:

1. Drag a **Label** from the **Object** library to the scene's upper-left corner, using the blue guide lines to position the **Label** at the recommended distance from the

scene's top and left (Fig. 14.5). The ⊕ symbol indicates that you're adding a new component to the UI.

Label with
placement guides
for positioning

Fig. 14.5 │ Adding the "**Bill Amount**" **Label** to the scene.

2. Double click the **Label**, type `Bill Amount`, then press *Enter* to change its **Text** attribute.

Step 2: Adding the Label That Displays the Formatted User Input

Next, you'll add the blue **Label** that displays the formatted user input:

1. Drag another **Label** below the "**Bill Amount**" **Label**, such that the placement guides appear as shown in Fig. 14.6. This is where the user input will be displayed.

Label with
placement guides
for positioning

Placement guides help you
position components so
they're separated by the
recommended amount of
space as described in
Apple's *Human Interface
Guidelines*

Fig. 14.6 │ Adding the **Label** in which the formatted user input will be displayed.

2. Drag the middle sizing handle at the new **Label**'s right side until the blue guide line at the scene's right side appears (Fig. 14.7).

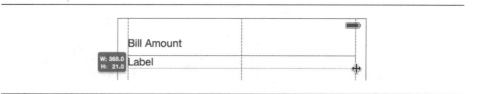

Fig. 14.7 │ Resizing the **Label** where the formatted user input will be displayed.

3. In the **Attributes** inspector, scroll to the **View** section and locate the **Label**'s **Background** attribute. Click the attribute's value, then select **Other...** to display the **Colors** dialog. This dialog has five tabs at the top that allow you to select colors different ways. For this app, we used the **Crayons** tab. On the bottom row, select the **Sky** (blue) crayon as the color (Fig. 14.8), then set the **Opacity** to 50%—this allows the scene's white background to blend with the **Label**'s color, resulting in a lighter blue color. The **Label** should now appear as shown in Fig. 14.9.

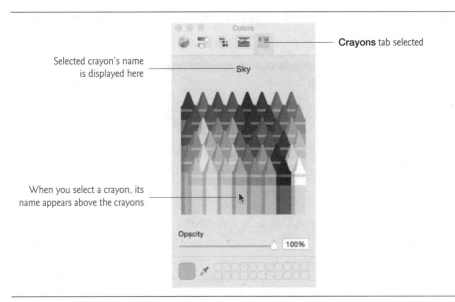

Fig. 14.8 | Selecting the **Sky** crayon for the **Label**'s background color.

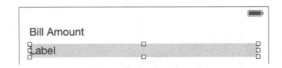

Fig. 14.9 | **Label** with **Sky** blue background and 50% opacity.

4. A **Label**'s default height is 21 points. We increased this **Label**'s height to add space above and below its text to make it more readable against the colored background. To do so, drag the bottom-center sizing handle down until the **Label**'s height is 30 (Fig. 14.10).

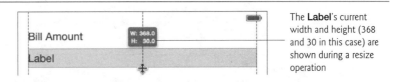

Fig. 14.10 | **Label** with **Sky** blue background and 50% opacity.

5. With the **Label** selected, delete the value for its **Text** property in the **Attributes** inspector. The **Label** should now be empty.

Step 3: Adding the "**Custom Tip Percentage:**" Label and a Label to Display the Current Custom Tip Percentage
Next, you'll add the **Label**s in the UI's third row:

1. Drag another **Label** onto the scene and position it below the blue **Label** as shown in Fig. 14.11.

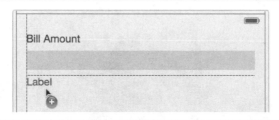

Fig. 14.11 | Adding the "**Custom Tip Percentage:**" **Label** to the scene.

2. Double click the **Label** and set its text to Custom Tip Percentage:.

3. Drag another **Label** onto the scene and position it to the right of the "**Custom Tip Percentage:**" **Label** (Fig. 14.12), then set its text to 18%—the initial custom tip percentage we chose in this app, which the app will update when the user moves the **Slider**'s thumb. The UI should now appear as shown in Fig. 14.13.

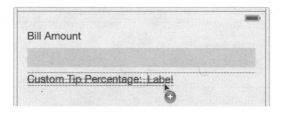

Fig. 14.12 | Adding the **Label** that displays the current custom tip percentage.

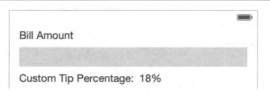

Fig. 14.13 | UI design so far.

Step 4: Creating the Custom Tip Percentage Slider

You'll now create the **Slider** for selecting the custom tip percentage:

1. Drag a **Slider** from the **Object** library onto the scene so that it's the recommended distance from the "**Custom Tip Percentage:**" **Label**, then size and position it as shown in Fig. 14.14.

2. Use the **Attributes** inspector to set the **Slider**'s **Minimum** value to 0 (the default), **Maximum** value to 30 and **Current** value to 18.

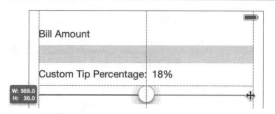

Fig. 14.14 | Creating and sizing the **Slider**.

Step 5: Adding the "15%" and "18%" Labels

Next, you'll add two more **Labels** containing the text **15%** and **18%** to serve as column headings for the calculation results. The app will update the "**18%**" **Label** when the user moves the **Slider**'s thumb. Initially, you'll position these **Labels** approximately—later you'll position them more precisely. Perform the following steps:

1. Drag another **Label** onto the scene and use the blue guides to position it the recommended distance below the **Slider** (Fig. 14.15), then set its **Text** to 15% and its **Alignment** to centered.

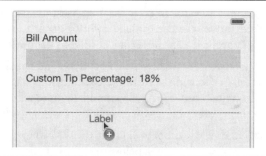

Fig. 14.15 | Adding the **Label** and right aligning it with the blue **Label**.

2. Next you'll duplicate the "**15%**" **Label**, which copies all of its settings. Hold the *option* key and drag the "**15%**" **Label** to the right (Fig. 14.16). You can also duplicate a UI component by selecting it and typing ⌘ + *D*, then moving the copy. Change the new **Label**'s text to 18%.

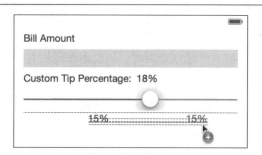

Fig. 14.16 | Duplicating the "**15%**" **Label** so that you can create the "**18%**" **Label**.

Step 6: Creating the Labels That Display the Tips and Totals
Next, you'll add four **Label**s in which the app will display the calculation results:

1. Drag a **Label** onto the UI until the blue guides appear as in Fig. 14.17.

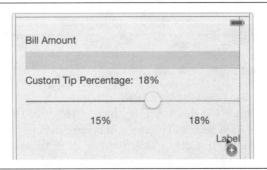

Fig. 14.17 | Creating the first yellow **Label**.

2. Drag the **Label**'s bottom-center sizing handle until the **Label**'s **Height** is 30, and drag its left-center sizing handle until the **Label**'s **Width** is 156.

3. Use the **Attributes** inspector to clear the **Text** attribute, set the **Alignment** so the text is centered and set the **Background** color to **Banana**, which is located in the **Color** dialog's **Crayons** tab in the second row from the bottom.

4. Set the **Autoshrink** property to **Minimum Font Scale** and change the value to .75— if the text becomes too wide to fit in the **Label**, this will allow the text to shrink to 75% of its original font size to accommodate more text. If you'd like the text to be able to shrink even more, you can choose a smaller value.

5. Next duplicate the yellow **Label** by holding the *option* key and dragging the **Label** to the left to create another **Label** below the "**15%**" **Label**.

6. Select both yellow **Label**s by holding the *Shift* key and clicking each **Label**. Hold the *option* key and drag any one of the selected **Label**s down until the blue guides appear as shown in Fig. 14.18.

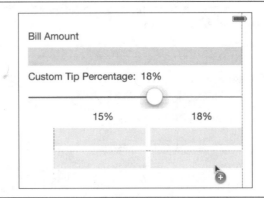

Fig. 14.18 | Creating the second row of yellow **Label**s.

7. Now you can center the "**15%**" and "**18%**" Labels over their columns. Drag the "**Tip**" Label so that the blue guide lines appear as shown in Fig. 14.19. Repeat this for the "**18%**" Label to center it over the right column of yellow Labels.

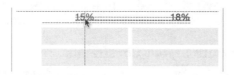

Fig. 14.19 | Repositioning the "15%" Label.

Step 7: Creating the "Tip" and "Total" Labels to the Left of the Yellow Labels
Next you'll create the "**Tip**" and "**Total**" Labels:

1. Drag a **Label** onto the scene, change its **Text** to Total, set its **Alignment** to right aligned and position it to the left of the second row of yellow Labels as in Fig. 14.20.

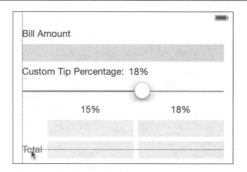

Fig. 14.20 | Positioning the "Total" Label.

2. Hold the *option* key and drag the "**Total**" Label up until the blue guides appear as shown in Fig. 14.21. Change the new Label's text to Tip, then drag it to the right so that the right edges of the "**Tip**" and "**Total**" Labels align.

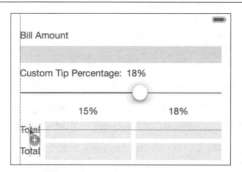

Fig. 14.21 | Duplicating the "Total" Label so that you can create the "Tip" Label.

Step 8: Creating the Text Field for Receiving User Input
You'll now create the **Text Field** that will receive the user input. Drag a **Text Field** from the **Object** library to the bottom edge of the scene, then use the **Attributes** inspector to set its **Keyboard Type** attribute to **Number Pad** and its **Appearance** to **Dark**. This **Text Field** will be *hidden* behind the numeric keypad when the app first loads. You'll receive the user's input through this **Text Field**, then format and display it in the blue **Label** at the top of the scene.

14.4.4 Adding the Auto Layout Constraints

You've now completed the **Tip Calculator** app's UI design, but have not yet added any auto layout constraints. If you run the app in the simulator or on a device, however, you'll notice that—depending on which simulator you use—some of the UI components extend beyond the trailing edge (Fig. 14.22). In this section, you'll add auto layout constraints so that the UI components can adjust to display properly on devices of various sizes and resolutions.

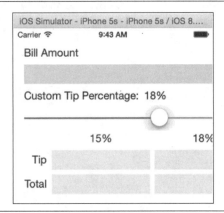

Fig. 14.22 | App in the iPhone 5s simulator without auto layout constraints added to the UI— some components flow off the trailing edge (the right side in this screen capture).

In Chapter 13, you manually added the required auto layout constraints. In this section, you'll use Interface Builder to add missing constraints automatically, then run the app again to see the results. You'll then create some additional constraints so that the app displays correctly in the simulator or on a device.

Step 1: Adding the Missing Auto Layout Constraints
To add the missing auto layout constraints:

1. Click the white background in the design area or select **View** in the document outline window.

2. At the bottom of the canvas, click the **Resolve Auto Layout Issues** (⊬⊣) button and under **All Views in View Controller** select **Add Missing Constraints**.

Interface Builder analyzes the UI components in the design and uses their sizes, locations and alignment to create a set of auto layout constraints for you. In some cases, these constraints will be enough for your design, but you'll often need to tweak the results. Figure 14.23 shows the UI in the iPhone 5s simulator after Interface Builder adds the missing constraints. Now, all of the UI components are completely visible, but some of them are not sized and positioned correctly. In particular, the yellow **Label**s should all be the same width.

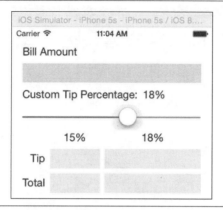

Fig. 14.23 | App in the simulator after Interface Builder adds the missing auto layout constraints—some components are not sized and positioned correctly.

Step 2: Setting the Yellow **Label**s to Have Equal Widths

To set the yellow **Label**s to have equal widths:

1. Select all four yellow **Label**s by holding the *shift* key and clicking each one.

2. In the auto layout tools at the bottom of the canvas, click the **Pin** tools icon (⊡). Ensure that **Equal Widths** is checked and click the **Add 3 Constraints** button, as shown in Fig. 14.24. Only three constraints are added, because three of the **Label**s will be set to have the same width as the fourth.

Fig. 14.24 | Setting **Equal Widths** for the yellow **Label**s.

Figure 14.25 shows the UI in the simulator. Setting the yellow **Labels** to **Equal Widths** caused the 18% **Label** over the right column to disappear and the "**Tip**" and "**Total**" **Labels** to become too narrow to display.

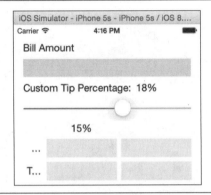

Fig. 14.25 | App in the simulator after setting the yellow **Labels** to equal widths.

Step 3: Debugging the Missing "18%" Label

Based on the initial design, the missing "**18%**" **Label** should be centered over the right column of yellow **Labels**. If you select that **Label** in the canvas and select the **Size** inspector in the **Utilities** area, you can see the missing **Label**'s complete set of constraints (Fig. 14.26).

Fig. 14.26 | "**18%**" **Label**'s constraints.

There are two constraints on the "**18%**" **Label**'s horizontal positioning:

- The **Trailing Space to: Superview** constraint specifies that this **Label** should be 60 points from the scene's trailing edge.

- The **Align Center X to: Label** constraint specifies that this **Label** should be centered horizontally over the specified **Label**.

These two constraints *conflict* with one another—depending on the yellow **Label**'s width, the "**18%**" **Label** could appear different distances from the scene's trailing edge. By removing the **Trailing Space to: Superview** constraint, we can eliminate the conflict. To do so, simply click that constraint in the **Size** inspector and press the *delete* key. Figure 14.27

shows the final UI in the iPhone 5s simulator, but you can test the UI in other simulators to confirm that it works correctly in each.

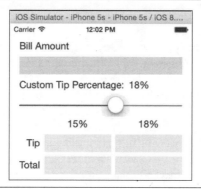

Fig. 14.27 | App with its final UI running in the simulator.

14.5 Creating Outlets with Interface Builder

You'll now use Interface Builder to create the *outlets* for the UI components that the app interacts with programmatically. Figure 14.28 shows the outlet names that we specified when creating this app. A common naming convention is to use the UI component's class name without the UI class prefix at the end of an outlet property's name—for example,

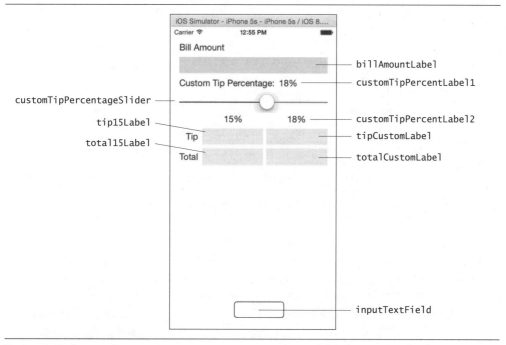

Fig. 14.28 | **Tip Calculator**'s UI components labeled with their outlet names.

`billAmountLabel` rather than `billAmountUILabel`. Interface Builder makes it easy for you to create outlets for UI components by *control* dragging from the component into your source code. To do this, you'll take advantage of the Xcode **Assistant** editor.

Opening the Assistant Editor

To create outlets, ensure that your scene's storyboard is displayed by selecting it in the **Project** navigator. Next, select the **Assistant** editor button (⊘) on the Xcode toolbar (or select **View > Assistant Editor > Show Assistant Editor**). Xcode's **Editor** area splits and the file `View-Controller.swift` (Fig. 14.29) is displayed to the right of the storyboard. By default, when viewing a storyboard, the **Assistant** editor shows the corresponding view controller's source code. However, by clicking **Automatic** in the jump bar at the top of the **Assistant** editor, you can select from options for previewing the UI for different device sizes and orientations, previewing localized versions of the UI or viewing other files that you'd like to view side-by-side with the content currently displayed in the editor. The comments in lines 1–7 are autogenerated by Xcode—later, we delete these comments and replace them with our own. Delete the method `didReceiveMemoryWarning` in lines 18–21 as we will not use it in this app. We'll discuss the details of `ViewController.swift` and add code to it in Section 14.7.

Jump bar
```
1   //
2   //  ViewController.swift
3   //  TipCalculator
4   //
5   //  Created by Paul Deitel on 9/3/14.
6   //  Copyright (c) 2014 Deitel & Associates, Inc. All rights reserved.
7   //
8
9   import UIKit
10
11  class ViewController: UIViewController {
12
13      override func viewDidLoad() {
14          super.viewDidLoad()
15          // Do any additional setup after loading the view, typically
16      }
17
18      override func didReceiveMemoryWarning() {
19          super.didReceiveMemoryWarning()
20          // Dispose of any resources that can be recreated.
21      }
22
```

Fig. 14.29 | `ViewController.swift` displayed in the **Assistant** editor.

Creating an Outlet

You'll now create an outlet for the blue **Label** that displays the user's input. You need this outlet to programmatically change the **Label**'s text to display the input in currency format. Outlets are declared as properties of a view controller class. To create the outlet:

1. *Control* drag from the blue **Label** to below line 11 in `ViewController.swift` (Fig. 14.30) and release. This displays a popover for configuring the outlet (Fig. 14.31).

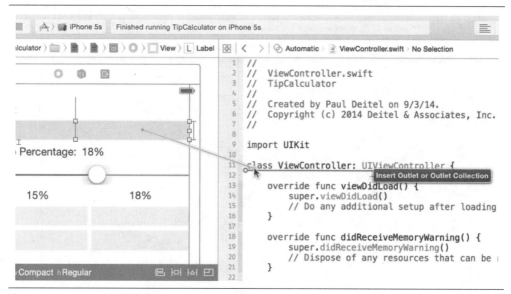

Fig. 14.30 | *Control* dragging from the scene to the **Assistant** editor to create an outlet.

Fig. 14.31 | Popover for configuring an outlet.

2. In the popover, ensure that **Outlet** is selected for the **Connection** type, specify the name billAmountLabel for the outlet's **Name** and click **Connect**.

Xcode inserts the following property declaration in class ViewController:

```
@IBOutlet weak var billAmountLabel: UILabel!
```

We'll explain this code in Section 14.7.3. You can now use this property to programmatically modify the **Label**'s text.

Creating the Other Outlets

Repeat the steps above to create outlets for the other labeled UI components in Fig. 14.28. Your code should now appear as shown in Fig. 14.32. In the gray margin to the left of each outlet property is a small bullseye (◉) symbol indicating that the outlet is connected to a UI component. Hovering the mouse over that symbol highlights the connected UI component in the scene. You can use this to confirm that each outlet is connected properly.

```
    88  <  >  Automatic >  ViewController.swift > No Selection                    + ×
1   //
2   //  ViewController.swift
3   //  TipCalculator
4   //
5   //  Created by Paul Deitel on 9/3/14.
6   //  Copyright (c) 2014 Deitel & Associates, Inc. All rights reserved.
7   //\
8
9   import UIKit
10
11  class ViewController: UIViewController {
12      @IBOutlet weak var billAmountLabel: UILabel!
13      @IBOutlet weak var customTipPercentLabel1: UILabel!
14      @IBOutlet weak var customTipPercentageSlider: UISlider!
15      @IBOutlet weak var customTipPercentLabel2: UILabel!
16      @IBOutlet weak var tip15Label: UILabel!
17      @IBOutlet weak var total15Label: UILabel!
18      @IBOutlet weak var tipCustomLabel: UILabel!
19      @IBOutlet weak var totalCustomLabel: UILabel!
20      @IBOutlet weak var inputTextField: UITextField!
21
22      override func viewDidLoad() {
23          super.viewDidLoad()
24          // Do any additional setup after loading the view, typically from a nib.
25      }
26  }
```

Fig. 14.32 | Code after adding outlets for the programmatically manipulated UI components.

14.6 Creating Actions with Interface Builder

Now that you've created the outlets, you need to create actions (i.e., event handlers) that can respond to the user-interface events. A **Text Field**'s **Editing Changed** event occurs every time the user changes the **Text Field**'s contents. If you connect an action to the **Text Field** for this event, the **Text Field** will send a message to the view-controller object to execute the action each time the event occurs. Similarly, the **Value Changed** event repeatedly occurs for a **Slider** as the user moves the thumb. If you connect an action method to the **Slider** for this event, the **Slider** will send a message to the view controller to execute the action each time the event occurs.

In this app, you'll create one action method that's called for each of these events. You'll connect the **Text Field** and the **Slider** to this action using the **Assistant** editor. To do so, perform the following steps:

1. *Control* drag from the **Text Field** in the scene to ViewController.swift between the right braces (}) at lines 25 and 26 (Fig. 14.33), then release. This displays a popover for configuring an outlet. From the **Connection** list in the popover, select **Action** to display the options for configuring an action (Fig. 14.34).

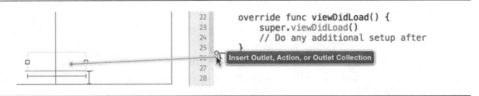

Fig. 14.33 | *Control* dragging to create an action for the **Text Field**.

Fig. 14.34 | Popover for configuring an action.

2. In the popover, specify calculateTip for the action's **Name**, select **Editing Changed** for the **Event** and click **Connect**.

Xcode inserts the following empty method definition in the code:

```
@IBAction func calculateTip(sender: AnyObject) {
    }
```

and displays a small bullseye (◉) symbol (Fig. 14.35) in the gray margin to the left of the method indicating that the action is connected to a UI component. Now, when the user edits the **Text Field**, a message will be sent to the ViewController object to execute calculateTip. You'll define the logic for this method in Section 14.7.6.

Connecting the Slider to Method calculateTip
Recall that calculateTip should also be called as the user changes the custom tip percentage. You can simply connect the **Slider** to this existing action to handle the **Slider**'s **Value Changed** event. To do so, select the **Slider** in the scene, then hold the *control* key and drag from the **Slider** to the calculateTip: method (Fig. 14.35) and release. This connects the **Slider**'s **Value Changed** event to the action. You're now ready to implement the app's logic.

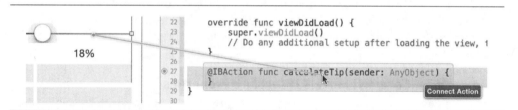

Fig. 14.35 | *Control* dragging to connect an existing @IBAction to the **Slider**.

14.7 Class ViewController

Sections 14.7.1—14.7.7 present ViewController.swift, which contains class ViewController and several global utility functions that are used throughout the class to format NSDecimalNumbers as currency and to perform calculations using NSDecimalNumber objects. We modified the autogenerated comments that Xcode inserted at the beginning of the source code file.

14.7.1 import Declarations

Recall that to use features from the iOS 8 frameworks, you must *import* them into your Swift code. Throughout this app, we use the UIKit framework's UI component classes. In Fig. 14.42, line 3 is an import declaration indicating that the program uses features from the UIKit framework. All import declarations must appear *before* any other Swift code (except comments) in your source-code files.

```
1   // ViewController.swift
2   // Implements the tip calculator's logic
3   import UIKit
4
```

Fig. 14.36 | import declaration in ViewController.swift.

14.7.2 ViewController Class Definition

In Fig. 14.37, line 5—which was generated by the IDE when you created the project— begins a **class definition** for class ViewController.

```
5   class ViewController: UIViewController {
```

Fig. 14.37 | ViewController class definition and properties.

*Inheriting from Class **UIViewController***
The notation : UIViewController in line 5 indicates that class ViewController inherits from class UIViewController—the UIKit framework superclass of all view controllers. This relationship indicates that a ViewController *is a* UIViewController. It also ensures that ViewController has the basic capabilities that iOS expects in all view controllers, including methods like viewDidLoad (Section 14.7.5) that help iOS manage a view controller's lifecycle. The class on the left of the : in line 5 is the *subclass* (derived class) and one on the right is the *superclass* (base class). Every scene has its own UIViewController subclass that defines the scene's event handlers and other logic. Unlike some object-oriented programming languages, Swift classes are not required to directly or indirectly inherit from a common superclass.

14.7.3 ViewController's @IBOutlet Properties

Figure 14.38 shows class ViewController's nine @IBOutlet property declarations that were created by Interface Builder when you created the outlets in Section 14.5. Typically, you'll define a class's *properties* first followed by the class's *methods*, but this is not required.

```
6       // properties for programmatically interacting with UI components
7       @IBOutlet weak var billAmountLabel: UILabel!
8       @IBOutlet weak var customTipPercentLabel1: UILabel!
9       @IBOutlet weak var customTipPercentageSlider: UISlider!
10      @IBOutlet weak var customTipPercentLabel2: UILabel!
```

Fig. 14.38 | ViewController's @IBOutlet properties. (Part I of 2.)

```
11    @IBOutlet weak var tip15Label: UILabel!
12    @IBOutlet weak var total15Label: UILabel!
13    @IBOutlet weak var tipCustomLabel: UILabel!
14    @IBOutlet weak var totalCustomLabel: UILabel!
15    @IBOutlet weak var inputTextField: UITextField!
16
```

Fig. 14.38 | ViewController's @IBOutlet properties. (Part 2 of 2.)

@IBOutlet *Property Declarations*

The notation @IBOutlet indicates to Xcode that the property references a UI component in the app's storyboard. When a scene loads, the UI component objects are created, an object of the corresponding view-controller class is created and the connections between the view controller's outlet properties and the UI components are established. The connection information is stored in the storyboard. @IBOutlet properties are declared as *variables* using the var keyword, so that the storyboard can assign each UI component object's reference to the appropriate outlet once the UI components and view controller object are created.

Automatic Reference Counting (ARC) and Property Attributes

As we've mentioned, Swift manages the memory for your app's reference-type objects using automatic reference counting (ARC), which keeps track of how many references there are to a given object. The runtime can remove an object from memory only when its *reference count* becomes 0.

Property attributes can specify whether a class maintains an ownership or nonownership relationship with the referenced object. By default, properties in Swift create **strong references** to objects, indicating an ownership relationship. Every strong reference increments an object's reference count by 1. When a strong reference no longer refers to an object, its reference count decrements by 1. The code that manages incrementing and decrementing the reference counts is inserted by the Swift compiler.

The @IBOutlet properties are declared as weak references, because the view controller *does not own* the UI components—the view defined by the storyboard that created them does. A weak reference does *not* affect the object's reference count. A view controller does, however, have a strong reference to its view.

Type Annotations and Implicitly Unwrapped Optional Types

The type annotation in line 7 (Fig. 14.38) indicates that billAmountLabel is a UILabel!. Recall that the exclamation point indicates an implicitly unwrapped optional type and that variables of such types are initialized to nil by default. This allows the class to compile, because these @IBOutlet properties are initialized—they'll be assigned actual UI component objects once the UI is created at runtime.

14.7.4 Other ViewController Properties

Figure 14.39 shows class ViewController's other properties, which you should add below the @IBOutlet properties. Line 18 defines the constant decimal100 that's initialized with an NSDecimalNumber object. Identifiers for Swift constants follow the same camel-case naming conventions as variables. Class NSDecimalNumber provides many initializers—this one receives a String parameter containing the initial value ("100.0"), then returns an NS-DecimalNumber representing the corresponding numeric value. We'll use decimal100 to calculate the custom tip percentage by dividing the slider's value by 100.0. We'll also use it to divide the user's input by 100.0 for placing a decimal point in the bill amount that's displayed at the top of the app. Initializers are commonly called constructors in many other object-oriented programming languages. Line 19 defines the constant decimal15Percent that's initialized with an NSDecimalNumber object representing the value 0.15. We'll use this to calculate the 15% tip.

```
17      // NSDecimalNumber constants used in the calculateTip method
18      let decimal100 = NSDecimalNumber(string: "100.0")
19      let decimal15Percent = NSDecimalNumber(string: "0.15")
20
```

Fig. 14.39 | ViewController class definition and properties.

14.7.5 Overridden UIViewController method viewDidLoad

Method viewDidLoad (Fig. 14.40)—which Xcode generated when it created class View-Controller—is inherited from superclass UIViewController. You typically *override* it to define tasks that can be performed only *after* the view has been initialized. You should add lines 25–26 to the method.

```
21      // called when the view loads
22      override func viewDidLoad() {
23          super.viewDidLoad()
24
25          // select inputTextField so keypad displays when the view loads
26          inputTextField.becomeFirstResponder()
27      }
28
```

Fig. 14.40 | Overridden UIViewController method viewDidLoad.

Recall that when overriding a superclass method, you declare it with keyword override preceding the keyword func, and the first statement in the method's body typically uses the super keyword to invoke the superclass's version of the method (line 23). The keyword super references the object of the class in which the method appears, but is used to access members inherited from the superclass.

Displaying the Numeric Keypad When the App Begins Executing
In this app, we want inputTextField to be the selected object when the app begins executing so that the numeric keypad is displayed immediately. To do this, we use property inputTextField to invoke the UITextField method becomeFirstResponder, which programmatically makes inputTextField the *active component* on the screen—as if the user touched it. You configured inputTextField such that when it's selected, the numeric keypad is displayed, so line 26 displays this keypad when the view loads.

14.7.6 ViewController Action Method calculateTip

Method calculateTip (Fig. 14.41) is the *action* (as specified by @IBAction on line 31) that responds to the **Text Field**'s **Editing Changed** event and the **Slider**'s **Value Changed** event. Add the code in lines 32–81 to the body of calculateTip. (If you're entering the Swift code as you read this section, you'll get errors on several statements that perform NS-DecimalNumber calculations using overloaded operators that you'll define in Section 14.7.7.) The method takes one parameter. Each parameter's name must be declared with a type annotation specifying the *parameter's type*. When a view-controller object receives a message from a UI component, it also receives as an argument a reference to that component—the event's **sender**. Parameter sender's type—the Swift type AnyObject—represents *any* type of object and does not provide any information about the object. For this reason, the object's type must be determined at runtime. This **dynamic typing** is used for actions (i.e., event handlers), because many different types of objects can generate events. In action methods that respond to events from multiple UI components, the sender is often used to determine which UI component the user interacted with (as we do in lines 42 and 57).

```
29    // called when the user edits the text in the inputTextField
30    // or moves the customTipPercentageSlider's thumb
31    @IBAction func calculateTip(sender: AnyObject) {
32        let inputString = inputTextField.text // get user input
33
34        // convert slider value to an NSDecimalNumber
35        let sliderValue =
36            NSDecimalNumber(integer: Int(customTipPercentageSlider.value))
37
38        // divide sliderValue by decimal100 (100.0) to get tip %
39        let customPercent = sliderValue / decimal100
40
41        // did customTipPercentageSlider generate the event?
42        if sender is UISlider {
43            // thumb moved so update the Labels with new custom percent
44            customTipPercentLabel1.text =
45                NSNumberFormatter.localizedStringFromNumber(customPercent,
46                    numberStyle: NSNumberFormatterStyle.PercentStyle)
47            customTipPercentLabel2.text = customTipPercentLabel1.text
48        }
49
50        // if there is a bill amount, calculate tips and totals
51        if !inputString.isEmpty {
52            // convert to NSDecimalNumber and insert decimal point
53            let billAmount =
54                NSDecimalNumber(string: inputString) / decimal100
55
56            // did inputTextField generate the event?
57            if sender is UITextField {
58                // update billAmountLabel with currency-formatted total
59                billAmountLabel.text = " " + formatAsCurrency(billAmount)
60
```

Fig. 14.41 | ViewController action method calculateTip. (Part 1 of 2.)

```
61                    // calculate and display the 15% tip and total
62                    let fifteenTip = billAmount * decimal15Percent
63                    tip15Label.text = formatAsCurrency(fifteenTip)
64                    total15Label.text =
65                        formatAsCurrency(billAmount + fifteenTip)
66                }
67
68                    // calculate custom tip and display custom tip and total
69                    let customTip = billAmount * customPercent
70                    tipCustomLabel.text = formatAsCurrency(customTip)
71                    totalCustomLabel.text =
72                        formatAsCurrency(billAmount + customTip)
73                }
74            else { // clear all Labels
75                billAmountLabel.text = ""
76                tip15Label.text = ""
77                total15Label.text = ""
78                tipCustomLabel.text = ""
79                totalCustomLabel.text = ""
80            }
81        }
82    }
83
```

Fig. 14.41 | `ViewController` action method `calculateTip`. (Part 2 of 2.)

Getting the Current Values of `inputTextField` and `customTipPercentageSlider`
Line 32 stores the value of `inputTextField`'s **text** property—which contains the user's input—in the local `String` variable `inputString`—Swift infers type `String` because UI-TextField's text property is a `String`.

Lines 35–36 get the `customTipPercentageSlider`'s **value** property, which contains a `Float` value representing the **Slider**'s *thumb position* (a value from 0 to 30, as specified in Section 14.4.3). The value is a `Float`, so we could get tip percentages like, 3.1, 15.245, etc. This app uses only whole-number tip percentages, so we convert the value to an `Int` before using it to initialize the `NSDecimalNumber` object that's assigned to local variable `sliderValue`. In this case, we use the `NSDecimalNumber` initializer that takes an `Int` value named `integer`.

Line 39 uses the overloaded division operator function that we define in Section 14.7.7 to divide `sliderValue` by 100 (`decimal100`). This creates an `NSDecimal-Number` representing the custom tip percentage that we'll use in later calculations and that will be displayed as a *locale-specific* percentage `String` showing the current custom tip percentage.

Updating the Custom Tip Percentage Labels When the Slider Value Changes
Lines 42–48 update `customTipPercentLabel1` and `customTipPercentLabel2` when the **Slider** value changes. Line 42 determines whether the `sender` *is a* `UISlider` object, meaning that the user interacted with the `customTipPercentageSlider`. The **is** operator returns `true` if an object's class is the same as, or has an *is a* (inheritance) relationship with, the class in the right operand.

We perform a similar test at line 57 to determine whether the user interacted with the inputTextField. Testing the sender argument like this enables you to perform *different* tasks, based on the component that caused the event.

Lines 44–46 set the customTipPercentLabel1's text property to a locale-specific percentage String based on the device's current locale. NSNumberFormatter class method localizedStringFromNumber returns a String representation of a formatted number. The method receives two arguments:

- The first is the NSNumber to format. Class NSDecimalNumber is a subclass of NSNumber, so you can use an NSDecimalNumber anywhere that an NSNumber is expected.

- The second argument (which has the external parameter name numberStyle) is a constant from the enumeration **NSNumberFormatterStyle** that represents the formatting to apply to the number—the PercentStyle constant indicates that the number should be formatted as a percentage. Because the second argument must be of type NSNumberFormatterStyle, Swift can infer information about the method's argument. As such, it's possible to write the expression NSNumberFormatterStyle.PercentStyle with the shorthand notation:

```
.PercentStyle
```

Line 47 assigns the same String to customTipPercentLabel2's text property.

Updating the Tip and Total Labels
Lines 51–80 update the tip and total Labels that display the calculation results. Line 51 uses the Swift String type's **isEmpty** property to ensure that inputString is not empty— that is, the user entered a bill amount. If so, lines 53–72 perform the tip and total calculations and update the corresponding Labels; otherwise, the inputTextField is empty and lines 75–79 clear all the tip and total Labels and the billAmountLabel by assigning the empty String literal ("") to their text properties.

Lines 53–54 use inputString to initialize an NSDecimalNumber, then divide it by 100 to place the decimal point in the bill amount—for example, if the user enters 5632, the amount used for calculating tips and totals is 56.32.

Lines 57–66 execute only if the event's sender was a UITextField—that is, the user tapped keypad buttons to enter or remove a digit in this app's inputTextField. Line 59 displays the currency-formatted bill amount in billAmountLabel by calling the formatAsCurrency method (defined in Section 14.7.7). Line 62 calculates the 15% tip amount by using an overloaded multiplication operator function for NSDecimalNumbers (defined in Section 14.7.7). Then line 63 displays the currency-formatted value in the tip15Label. Next, lines 64–65 calculates and displays the total amount for a 15% tip by using an overloaded addition operator function for NSDecimalNumbers (defined in Section 14.7.7) to perform the calculation, then passing the result to the formatAsCurrency function. Lines 69–72 calculate and display the custom tip and total amounts based on the custom tip percentage.

14.7.7 Global Utility Functions Defined in ViewController.swift
Figure 14.42 contains several global utility functions used throughout class ViewController. Add lines 84–103 after the closing right brace of class ViewController.

```
84   // convert a numeric value to localized currency string
85   func formatAsCurrency(number: NSNumber) -> String {
86       return NSNumberFormatter.localizedStringFromNumber(
87           number, numberStyle: NSNumberFormatterStyle.CurrencyStyle)
88   }
89
90   // overloaded + operator to add NSDecimalNumbers
91   func +(left: NSDecimalNumber, right: NSDecimalNumber) -> NSDecimalNumber {
92       return left.decimalNumberByAdding(right)
93   }
94
95   // overloaded * operator to multiply NSDecimalNumbers
96   func *(left: NSDecimalNumber, right: NSDecimalNumber) -> NSDecimalNumber {
97       return left.decimalNumberByMultiplyingBy(right)
98   }
99
100  // overloaded / operator to divide NSDecimalNumbers
101  func /(left: NSDecimalNumber, right: NSDecimalNumber) -> NSDecimalNumber {
102      return left.decimalNumberByDividingBy(right)
103  }
```

Fig. 14.42 | ViewController.swift global utility and overloaded operator functions.

Function *formatAsCurrency*

Lines 85–88 define the function formatAsCurrency, which receives one parameter (number) of type NSNumber (from the Foundation framework). We use formatAsCurrency throughout class ViewController to format NSDecimalNumbers as locale-specific currency Strings. NSDecimalNumber is a subclass of NSNumber, so any NSDecimalNumber can be passed as an argument to this function. An NSNumber parameter can also receive as an argument any Swift numeric type value—such types are automatically *bridged* by the runtime to type NSNumber.

Lines 86–87 invoke NSNumberFormatter class method localizedStringFromNumber, which returns a locale-specific String representation of a number. This method receives as arguments the NSNumber to format—formatAsCurrency's number parameter—and a constant from the NSNumberFormatterStyle enum that specifies the formatting style—the constant CurrencyStyle specifies that a *locale-specific currency format* should be used. Once again, we could have specified the second argument as .CurrencyStyle, because Swift knows that the numberStyle parameter must be a constant from the NSNumberFormatterStyle enumeration and thus can infer the constant's type.

Defining Overloaded Operator Functions for Adding, Subtracting and Multiplying *NSDecimalNumbers*

Lines 91–93, 96–98 and 101–103 create global functions that overload the addition (+), multiplication (*) and division (/) operators, respectively. These functions enable us to:

- add two NSDecimalNumbers with the + operator (lines 65 and 72 of Fig. 14.41)
- multiply two NSDecimalNumbers with the * operator (lines 62 and 69 of Fig. 14.41)
- divide two NSDecimalNumbers with the / operator (lines 39 and 54 of Fig. 14.41)

Each of these functions receives two NSDecimalNumbers representing the operator's left and right operands.

The addition (+) operator function (lines 91–93) returns the result of invoking NSDecimalNumber instance method decimalNumberByAdding on the left operand with the right operand as the method's argument—this adds the operands. The multiplication (*) operator function (lines 96–98) returns the result of invoking NSDecimalNumber instance method decimalNumberByMultiplyingBy on the left operand with the right operand as the method's argument—this multiplies the operands. The division (/) operator function (lines 101–103) returns the result of invoking NSDecimalNumber instance method decimalNumberByDividingBy on the left operand with the right operand as the method's argument—this divides the left operand by the right operand.

14.8 Wrap-Up

This chapter presented the **Tip Calculator** app that calculates and displays 15% and custom tip percentage tips and totals for a restaurant bill. The app uses **Text Field** and **Slider** UI components to receive user input and update suggested tips and bill totals in response to each user interaction.

We used several of Swift's object-oriented programming capabilities, including objects, classes, inheritance, methods and properties. As you saw, the app's code required various Swift data types, operators, control statements and keywords.

You used Interface Builder to design the app's UI visually. We showed how to build your UI faster by duplicating UI components that had similar attribute settings. You learned that **Labels** (UILabel), **Sliders** (UISlider) and **Text Fields** (UITextField) are part of iOS's UIKit framework that's automatically included with each app you create.

You learned that a scene is managed by a view-controller object that determines what information is displayed and how user interactions with the scene's UI are processed. Our view-controller class inherited from class UIViewController, which defines the base capabilities required by view controllers in iOS.

You used Interface Builder to generate @IBOutlet properties (outlets) in your view controller for programmatically interacting with the app's UI components. You used visual tools in Interface Builder to connect a UI control to a corresponding outlet in the view controller. Once a connection was made, the view controller was able to manipulate the corresponding UI component programmatically.

You saw that interacting with a UI component caused a user-interface event and sent a message from the UI component to an action (event-handling method) in the view controller. You learned that an action is declared in Swift code as an @IBAction. You used visual tools in Interface Builder to connect the action to specific user-interface events.

Next, you learned that after all the objects in a storyboard are created, iOS sends a viewDidLoad message to the corresponding view controller so that it can perform view-specific tasks that can be executed only after the UI components in the view exist. You also called the UITextField's becomeFirstResponder method in viewDidLoad so that iOS would display this keypad immediately after the view loaded.

You used NSDecimalNumbers for precise financial calculations. You also used class NSNumberFormatter to create locale-specific currency and percentage string representations of `NSDecimalNumber`s. You used Swift's operator overloading capabilities to simplify `NSDecimalNumber` calculations.

We provide an online Other Topics chapter (`www.deitel.com/books/SwiftFP`) which covers miscellaneous additional Swift topics. Swift is new and evolving rapidly, so we'll keep this chapter up-to-date with changes to the language.

We hope you've enjoyed reading *Swift for Programmers*. We'd appreciate your comments, criticisms and suggestions for improving the book. You can reach us at:

```
deitel@deitel.com
```

and we'll always respond promptly.

Keywords

Figure A.1 lists Swift's keywords. Apple organizes the keywords into several categories. Keywords are reserved for use by the language and may not be used as identifiers, with the exception of the keywords that are reserved for use in particular contexts—these may be used as identifiers outside those contexts, but doing so is not recommended.

Swift Keywords

Keywords used in declarations

class	deinit	enum	extension	func
import	init	internal	let	operator
private	protocol	public	static	struct
subscript	typealias	var		

Keywords used in statements

break	case	continue	default	do
else	fallthrough	for	if	in
return	switch	where	while	

Keywords used in expressions and types

as	dynamicType	false	is	nil
self	Self	super	true	__COLUMN__
__FILE__	__FUNCTION__	__LINE__		

Keywords reserved in particular contexts

associativity	convenience	dynamic	didSet	final
get	infix	inout	lazy	left
mutating	none	nonmutating	optional	override
postfix	precedence	prefix	Protocol	required
right	set	Type	unowned	weak
willSet				

Fig. A.1 | Swift keywords. `http://bit.ly/SwiftKeywords`

Operator Precedence Chart

Operators are shown in decreasing order of precedence from top to bottom (Fig. B.1).[1]

Operator	Description	Associativity	Precedence Level
++	unary increment	none	
--	unary decrement		
+	unary plus		
-	unary minus		
!	unary logical NOT		
~	unary bitwise NOT		
<<	left shift	none	160
>>	signed right shift		
*	multiplication	left to right	150
/	division		
%	remainder		
&*	multiplication (ignores overflow)		
&/	division (ignores overflow)		
&%	remainder (ignores overflow)		
&	bitwise AND		

Fig. B.1 | Operator precedence chart. (Part 1 of 2.) `http://bit.ly/SwiftOperators`

---

1. The unary operators at the top of the diagram are always applied before any other operators in an expression and are nonassociative. If the prefix and postfix versions of ++ and -- are applied to the same operand, the postfix operator is applied first. The documentation says that the assignment operators have right-to-left associativity, even though they do not return values. According to Apple's Swift team, this is because the assignment operators actually return Swift type `Void`.

Operator	Description	Associativity	Precedence Level
+	addition or string concatenation	left to right	140
-	subtraction		
&+	addition (ignores overflow)		
&-	subtraction (ignores overflow)		
|	bitwise OR		
^	bitwise XOR		
...	closed range	none	135
..<	half-open range		
is	type check	none	132
as	type cast		
<	less than	none	130
<=	less than or equal		
>	greater than		
>=	greater than or equal		
==	equal		
!=	not equal		
===	identical		
!==	not identical		
~=	pattern match		
&&	logical AND	left to right	120
||	logical OR	left to right	110
??	nil coalescing	right to left	110
?:	ternary conditional	right to left	100
=	assignment	right to left	90
*=	multiplication assignment		
/=	division assignment		
%=	remainder assignment		
+=	addition assignment		
-=	subtraction assignment		
<<=	bitwise left-shift assignment		
>>=	bitwise signed-right-shift assignment		
&=	bitwise AND assignment		
^=	bitwise XOR assignment		
|=	bitwise OR assignment		
&&=	logical AND assignment		
||=	logical OR assignment		

Fig. B.1 | Operator precedence chart. (Part 2 of 2.) http://bit.ly/SwiftOperators

Labeled **break** and **continue** Statements

C.1 Introduction

In Chapter 4, we discussed the break and continue statements, which enable programmers to alter the flow of control in control statements. Swift also provides the labeled break and continue statements for cases in which a programmer needs to conveniently alter the flow of control in nested control statements. This appendix demonstrates the labeled break and continue statements with examples using nested for...in statements.

C.2 Labeled **break** Statement

The break statement presented in Sections 4.7 and 4.12 enables a program to break out of the loop or switch in which the break statement appears. Sometimes these control statements are nested in other loop or switch statements. A program might need to exit the entire nested statement in one operation, rather than wait for it to complete execution normally. To break out of such nested statements, you can use the **labeled break statement**. This statement, when executed in a loop or switch, causes immediate exit from that control statement and any number of enclosing statements. Program execution resumes with the first statement after the enclosing **labeled statement**. The statement that follows the label can be either a loop statement or a switch.

Figure C.1 demonstrates the labeled break statement in a nested for...in statement. The loop in lines 2–12 begins with a **label** (an identifier followed by a colon) at line 2; here we use stop:. When the if at line 4 detects that row is equal to 5, the break statement at line 5 executes. This statement terminates both the loop at lines 3–9 and its enclosing loop at lines 2–12. Then the program proceeds immediately to the first statement after the labeled statement—in this case, the end of the program is reached and the program terminates. The outer loop fully executes its body only four times.

```
 1  // figC-01: Demonstrating a labeled break statement
 2  stop: for row in 1...10 { // should iterate 10 times
 3      for column in 1...5 {
 4          if (row == 5) {
 5              break stop // terminate loop labeled "stop:"
 6          }
 7
 8          print("* ")
 9      }
10
11      println()
12  }
```

```
* * * * *
* * * * *
* * * * *
* * * * *
```

Fig. C.1 | Labeled break statement exiting a nested for statement.

C.3 Labeled continue Statement

The continue in Section 4.12 proceeds with the next iteration of the immediately enclosing loop. The **labeled continue statement** skips the remaining statements in a loop's body and any number of enclosing loop statements, then proceeds with the next iteration of the enclosing labeled loop. Labeled while and do...while statements evaluate the loop-continuation test. Labeled for...in statements continue with the next value. Labeled for statements execute the increment expression then evaluate the loop-continuation test.

Figure C.2 uses a labeled continue statement in a nested for...in to enable execution to continue with the next iteration of the outer loop. The labeled loop (lines 2–12) actually starts at the nextRow label. When the if at line 6 in the inner loop (lines 5–11) detects that column is greater than row, the continue statement at line 7 executes, and program control continues with the next iteration of the outer loop. Even though the inner loop counts from 1 to 5, the number of * characters output on a row never exceeds the value of row, creating a triangle pattern.

```
 1  // figC-02: Demonstrating a labeled continue statement
 2  nextRow: for row in 1...5 {
 3      println()
 4
 5      for column in 1...5 {
 6          if (column > row) { // should iterate 5 times
 7              continue nextRow // jump to next iteration of nextRow loop
 8          }
 9
10          print("* ")
11      }
12  }
```

Fig. C.2 | Labeled continue statement moving to the next iteration of an outer loop. (Part 1 of 2.)

```
13
14   println()
```

```
*
*  *
*  *  *
*  *  *  *
*  *  *  *  *
```

Fig. C.2 | Labeled continue statement moving to the next iteration of an outer loop. (Part 2 of 2.)

Index

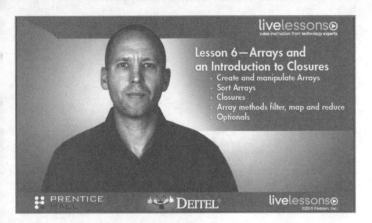